COMMANDER X PRESENTS

FIGHTING THE FEDERAL RESERVE

The Controversial Life and Works of Congressman Louis Thomas McFadden

Comments And Statements by Ron Paul

Global Communications

Fighting the Federal Reserve
by Congressmen Louis T. McFadden
Congressman Ron Paul
& Commander X

Timothy Green Beckley: Editorial Director
Carol Rodriguez: Publishers Assistant
Sean Casteel: Associate Editor
Cover Art: Tim R. Swartz

Printed in the United States of America

For free catalog write:
Global Communications
P.O. Box 753
New Brunswick, NJ 08903

Free Subscription to Conspiracy Journal E-Mail Newsletter
www.conspiracyjournal.com

Table of Contents

Fighting the Federal Reserve

Everything Old Is New Again -
The Conspiracy of Greed and Power

By Commander X

The economy is in a shambles. Millions of people are unemployed. The once popular President is blamed for problems he inherited from previous administrations. And in turn, partisanship in Washington has completely crippled the political process to the point that nothing is being done to fix the country's growing woes.

You are right if this scenario sounds familiar. However, if you think that this is only a description of the current situation in the United States, you are somewhat mistaken. This is what was going on in the United States in the early 1930's.

The Stock Market Crash in October 1929 devastated the economy and was a key factor in beginning the Great Depression. Much like the Great Recession that started in 2008, after Wall Street tumbled in 1929 there was a lot of finger pointing and accusations of illegal activity within the banking industry and other large corporations. Unfortunately, most Washington politicians were unwilling to dig deep into the probable financial conspiracies that devastated the economies of almost every country on the planet. Instead, politicians saw the economic turmoil as an opportunity to gain political power. So instead of working together to help fix the country's problems, everything was done to make sure that things got worse in order to bring down rival politicians on voting day.

Much of this partisan backstabbing was being financed under the table by those who had gotten extremely rich off the stock market crash; these wealthy elites wanted to make sure that nothing was going to stop their gravy train of gold. They saw to it that their well-paid political lackeys in Washington either did nothing, or passed laws to ensure nothing would hinder the continued plundering of the nation's assets, all of this to the detriment of the rest of the population, many who were left flat broke and homeless.

As we can see, nothing has really changed in the last 80 years.

~ v ~

Fighting the Federal Reserve

Enter into this fray a Congressman from Pennsylvania by the name of Louis Thomas McFadden. McFadden was the President of the First National Bank in Canton, Pennsylvania, and was elected in 1914 as a Republican Representative to the Sixty-fourth Congress. Because of his financial background, McFadden had a clear view on what caused the Great Depression, as well as how and why it was being sustained.

To Congressman McFadden, the chief instigator of the world's economic problems was the Federal Reserve.

The Creation of the Federal Reserve

Essentially, the Federal Reserve is a central bank. The U.S. experimented with three central banks over the course of its history. Two of them met with political opposition and failure in 1811 and 1836. The current central bank, the Federal Reserve System, was created in 1913.

Before the Federal Reserve, the nation had a system of federally regulated national banks. Unfortunately, this system was unstable and prone to banking panics, leading to uncertainty in the financial system. A crisis spawned by financial manipulation from the existing banking establishment in 1907 nearly brought down the entire financial system. Because of this, it was decided that a nationally chartered bank must be created to step in and provide lending support to banks.

Signed into law by Woodrow Wilson, the Federal Reserve was thrust into its first major test with the outbreak of World War I. The Federal Reserve helped to make sure trade goods continued to flow into Europe until the United States entered the war in 1917. After the war ended, the Fed discovered open market operations, a major part of Fed policy.

In order to decentralize power regionally, in the Federal sense, the Fed is organized into 12 regional banks, currently with 25 branches, with the country partitioned geographically, so that local interests will share power in the same sense that the US Congress is composed of regional interest that share power. There are around 2,800 member commercial banks, and these banks must deposit a certain proportion of their bank reserves, called the required reserve ratio, with a Federal Reserve branch bank. Each of the 12 regional banks is managed by nine directors, with six of the nine directors in each region selected by the 2,800 member banks, and the other 3 directors in each region being appointments by the Board of Governors. The Board of Governors is comprised of seven individuals who control and coordinate Fed activities. A new Fed Governor is appointed every other year by the U.S. President, and must be confirmed by the US Senate, to serve out a 14-year term, without the possibility of reappointment. This gives the Fed Governors a degree of political autonomy, which is needed in order to prevent monetary policy from being driven by populist sentiment.

A common strategy for the Fed's monetary policies is to lean against the wind. Former Fed Chairman William McChesney Martin, a man who served under five presidents from 1951 until 1970, said his job was to "take the punch bowl away as soon as the party gets started." The Fed's worst historical failures have come when they did not follow this edict. In the late 1920s, Chairman Roy A. Young's easy money policies, lax regulation, and weak leadership contributed greatly to the Great Crash of 1929, just as a similar philosophy championed by Chairman Alan Greenspan contributed to the housing bubble and panic of 2008.

Controversy and Conspiracy

Right from the very beginning, controversy has surrounded the Federal Reserve. Bankers clearly understood that government action and stronger central bank subsidies allowed for the creation of increased corruption, monopoly, and central planning of mundane activity and commerce. Rather than reigning in corrupt banking policies, the Federal Reserve granted new powers to the National Banks by permitting overseas branches and new types of banking services. The greatest gift to the bankers was a virtually unlimited supply of loans when they experience liquidity problems.

Fighting the Federal Reserve

From the early 1920s to 1929, the monetary supply expanded at a rapid pace and the U.S. experienced wild economic growth. Curiously, however, the number of banks started to decline for the first time in American history.

Toward the end of the period, speculation and loose money had propelled asset and equity prices to unreal levels. The stock market crashed, and as the banks struggled with liquidity problems, the Federal Reserve actually cut the money supply. Without a doubt, this is the greatest financial panic and economic collapse in American history - and it never could have happened on this scale without the Fed's intervention. All together, 9,000 banks failed during the 1930s and a few of the old robber barons' banks managed to swoop in and grab up thousands of competitors for pennies on the dollar.

Was it just a coincidence that all the Wall Street giants, J.P. Morgan, Joe F. Kennedy, J.D. Rockefeller, Bernard Baruch, got out of the stock market and put their assets in gold just before the 1929 crash? Was it a coincidence that these Wall Street giants all received a secret directive on March 8, 1929 by Paul Warburg, a member of the advisory council of the Federal Reserve Board, and president of the advisory council, warning of the upcoming stock market disaster?

According to Milton Friedman, Nobel Prize winning economist, it was no coincidence, "The Federal Reserve definitely caused the Great Depression by contracting the amount of currency in circulation by one-third from 1929 to 1933."

On June 10, 1932, Congressman Louis T. McFadden, who had been the Chairman of the House Committee on Banking and Currency from 1920 to 1931, addressed the House of Representatives and documented crimes of the private banks which had been consolidated under the Federal Reserve Act. This act gave these non-assented private banks the power to draw unlimited, unearned profit from a currency costing practically nothing to private banking institutions that are neither federal, nor a reserve. McFadden testified that the excesses of non-assented profit not only manifested in mightily arming foes of the world's wars, and even instigating wars; they further comprise not only all the "interest" and multiplication of cost we have endured since 1914, but the sum of our crippling private and public debt as well.

McFadden Takes on the Fed

McFadden argued, "The Federal Reserve Board has cheated the Government of the United States and the people of the United States out of enough money to pay the national debt. The depredations and iniquities of the Federal Reserve Board and the Federal Reserve Banks acting together have cost this country enough money to pay the national debt several times over."

He pointed out that the private banks comprising the so-called Federal Reserve are of foreign origin, and that the Federal Reserve banks financed, with U.S. money, Trotsky's mass meetings of discontent and rebellion in New York, paid Trotsky's passage from New York to Russia, instigated the Russian revolution and the rise of Communism.

McFadden also provided staggering statistics documenting the consequences of the Great Depression, such as a single state auctioning 60,000 dispossessed homes in a single day. He furthermore describes the purposely crooked machinery of the so-called Federal Reserve; the deceit leading to its creation; the roles of principal players; and prophetic projections that our monetary gold will disappear.

Congressman McFadden believed that a return to the gold standard would establish a vital economy, saying, "What is needed here is a return to the Constitution of the United States. The old struggle that was fought out here in Jackson's day must be fought over again."

Before concluding his speech, McFadden asked for an audit of the Federal Reserve, which to this day has never been done. He asked that faithless government officers who have violated their oaths of office be impeached and brought to trial. Finally, he declared that the Federal Reserve Board has usurped the government of the United States and that it controls both our national and international affairs.

On January 13, 1932, McFadden introduced a resolution indicting the Federal Reserve Board of Governors for "Criminal Conspiracy": "Whereas I charge them, jointly and severally, with the crime of having treasonably conspired and acted against the peace and security of the United States and having treasonably conspired to destroy constitutional government in the United States. Resolved, that the Committee on the Judiciary is authorized and directed as a whole or by subcommittee to investigate the official conduct of the Federal Reserve Board and agents to determine whether, in the opinion of the said committee, they have been guilty of any high crime or misdemeanor which in the contemplation of the Constitution requires the interposition of the Constitutional powers of the House."

No action was taken on this Resolution. McFadden came back on December 13, 1932 with a motion to impeach President Herbert Hoover. Only five Congressmen stood with him on this, and the resolution failed. The Republican majority leader of the House remarked, "Louis T. McFadden is now politically dead."

On May 23, 1933, McFadden introduced House Resolution No. 158, Articles of Impeachment against the Secretary of the Treasury, two Assistant Secretaries of the Treasury, the Federal Reserve Board of Governors, and officers and directors of the Federal Reserve Banks for their guilt and collusion in causing the Great Depression.

"I charge them with having unlawfully taken over 80 billion dollars from the United States Government in the year 1928, the said unlawful taking consisting of the unlawful recreation of claims against the United States Treasury to the extent of over 80 billion dollars in the year 1928, and in each year subsequent, and by having robbed the United States Government and the people of the United States by their theft and sale of the gold reserve of the United States."

The resolution never reached the floor. A whispering campaign that McFadden was insane swept Washington, and in the 1934 Congressional elections, McFadden lost his reelection bid to a Democrat by 561 votes.

~ X ~

Fighting the Federal Reserve

After losing his congressional seat, McFadden remained in the public eye as a vigorous opponent of the financial system. However, McFadden may have made enemies in high places as there were several attempts on his life. The first attack came when someone tried to shoot McFadden as he was leaving a cab in front of a Washington hotel. The next attempt came in the form of poison in his food at a political banquet in Washington. McFadden's life was saved by a fast thinking doctor who had his stomach pumped.

Unfortunately, for McFadden, the third time was the charm. He died suddenly at the age of 60 on October 3, 1936 of a "dose" of "intestinal flue" after attending a banquet in New York City.

Disinformation

Since his death, Louis T. McFadden has not been treated very kindly by history. His detractors state that he hated Jews and believed an international cabal of Jews ran the Federal Reserve. In fact, many Anti-Semitic websites have bought into this smear campaign and have applauded McFadden for his alleged position against the Jews.

History is written by the winners, and the true facts about Louis T. McFadden have been effectively obscured to the point that little remains of the details of his life and motivations. It is obvious that McFadden did not play the political game that has ruled politics in the United States for many, many years. Because of his maverick ways, McFadden was swiftly taken out of the picture, both contemporarily and historically.

Very little has changed since that time. Politicians still ignore the burdens of 99% of the population while catering almost exclusively to the wealthy elite. In fact, today, most who hold political power in the U.S. now belong to the wealthy elite. It is almost impossible to run for any position in Washington unless you are a multi-millionaire.

Voter ignorance on what their elected officials are doing is at an all time high. No one seems to notice that the same politicians, who declare their hatred for Washington, are fighting tooth and nail to gain access to the very same government they claim to loathe so much.

Doesn't it ever occur to anyone why these politicians are so eager to join a government they claim to hate so much? Hasn't anyone noticed that once these elected officials get to Washington they quickly forget their promises to help curtail big government and instead become part of it?

Perhaps the greedy lure of money and power has something to do with it. Maybe this is why political parties do everything they can to deny any success for a president of the opposing party, even to the point that the very financial infrastructure of the U.S. has been brought to the point of collapse. This could also be the reason why it has been so easy for billionaire fat cats like David and Charles Koch to secretly bankroll the Tea Party Movement and push their radical political agenda.

The Tea Party would like to think that they are a grassroots movement, when actually they are the puppets of corporate interests that want to completely abolish not only Social Security, federal regulatory agencies and welfare but also the F.B.I., the C.I.A., and public schools — in other words, any government enterprise that would inhibit business profits.

Both the GOP and the Tea Party oppose a federal deficit, but have no objection to running up trillions in red ink in tax cuts to corporations and the super rich. They oppose the extension of unemployment benefits and demand a freeze on federal regulations in an era when abuses in the oil, financial, mining, pharmaceutical and even egg industries (among others) have been outrageous.

The wealthy elite must be laughing all the way to the bank knowing that working Americans are aiding and abetting their selfish interests. It is a shame that we no longer have someone as brave as Louis T. McFadden to speak out against such abuses against American citizens. Maybe it is time for someone to step up, take the torch once carried by those such as McFadden, reveal the dark underbelly of this country, and finally wrest control from the slimy denizens that have secretly been in charge for way too long.

Exposés by Congressman Ron Paul

Fighting the Federal Reserve

Ronald Reagan & Ron Paul

Abolish the Fed

by Rep. Ron Paul, MD

In the House of Representatives, September 10, 2002

Mr. Speaker, I rise to introduce legislation to restore financial stability to America's economy by abolishing the Federal Reserve.

Since the creation of the Federal Reserve, middle and working-class Americans have been victimized by a boom-and-bust monetary policy. In addition, most Americans have suffered a steadily eroding purchasing power because of the Federal Reserve's inflationary policies. This represents a real, if hidden, tax imposed on the American people.

From the Great Depression, to the stagflation of the seventies, to the burst of the dotcom bubble last year, every economic downturn suffered by the country over the last 80 years can be traced to Federal Reserve policy. The Fed has followed a consistent policy of flooding the economy with easy money, leading to a misallocation of resources and an artificial "boom" followed by a recession or depression when the Fed-created bubble bursts.

With a stable currency, American exporters will no longer be held hostage to an erratic monetary policy. Stabilizing the currency will also give Americans new incentives to save as they will no longer have to fear inflation eroding their savings. Those members concerned about increasing America's exports or the low rate of savings should be enthusiastic supporters of this legislation.

Though the Federal Reserve policy harms the average American, it benefits those in a position to take advantage of the cycles in monetary policy. The main beneficiaries are those who receive access to artificially inflated money and/or credit before the inflationary effects of the policy impact the entire economy. Federal Reserve policies also benefit big spending politicians who use the inflated currency created by the Fed to hide the true costs of the welfare-warfare state. It is time for Congress to put the interests of the American people ahead of the special interests and their own appetite for big government.

Abolishing the Federal Reserve will allow Congress to reassert its constitutional authority over monetary policy. The United States Constitution grants to Congress the authority to coin money and regulate the value of the currency. The Constitution does not give Congress the authority to delegate control over monetary policy to a central bank. Furthermore, the Constitution certainly does not empower the federal government to erode the American standard of living via an inflationary monetary policy.

In fact, Congress' constitutional mandate regarding monetary policy should only permit currency backed by stable commodities such as silver and gold to be used as legal tender. Therefore, abolishing the Federal Reserve and returning to a constitutional system will enable America to return to the type of monetary system envisioned by our nation's founders: one where the value of money is consistent because it is tied to a commodity such as gold. Such a monetary system is the basis of a true free-market economy.

In conclusion, Mr. Speaker, I urge my colleagues to stand up for working Americans by putting an end to the manipulation of the money supply which erodes Americans' standard of living, enlarges big government, and enriches well-connected elites, by cosponsoring my legislation to abolish the Federal Reserve.

Dr. Ron Paul is a Republican member of Congress from Texas.

The Fed's Funny Money

by Ron Paul

Before the US House of Represenatives Subcommittee on Domestic Monetary Policy, Hearing on the Impact of Monetary Policy on the Economy, July 26, 2011

Today's hearing is the second in a series examining the relationship between Federal Reserve policy and the performance of the United States economy. Today we are receiving testimony from the Federal Reserve banks. Of the half-dozen Reserve banks we contacted, only President Hoenig was willing to testify in front of this subcommittee, and we welcome him here today.

Like many critics of the Fed's monetary policy, I fear that quantitative easing will soon return. Despite what we hear from the cheerleaders in government and in the media, the economy remains in a complete shambles. Unemployment remains high and seven million jobs lost during the recession have yet to be regained. The Federal Reserve has kept interest rates at or near zero for over two and a half years and pumped trillions of dollars into the banking system in a vain attempt to revive the economy. Yet even now after the failure of the zero interest rate policy (ZIRP) and quantitative easing have become readily apparent, we still hear calls for more stimulus, more easing, more loose money. Like any other government program, the solution for failure is to throw more money at the problem, never mind the fact that throwing more bad money after good in such instances has never succeeded.

Reading the press releases from the Federal Open Market Committee (FOMC) we see that the FOMC intends to keep interest rates at a low level for an extended period. Chairman Bernanke has hinted at a further round of quantitative easing, the effects of which will undoubtedly be calamitous. Moneyholders seek a return on their holdings, and in an era of near-zero interest courtesy of the Fed, saving makes no sense. Combined with the still-shaky condition of the banking and financial sector, it is not surprising that much of the recently-created easy money has flowed into tangibles such as agricultural commodities, metals, and land. Rather than allowing the housing bubble to burst, overall prices to return to normal and overleveraged banks to break up, the Fed has thrown more fuel onto the fire and created the conditions for an even larger bubble that will eventually burst.

The Fed's easy money policy has also enabled the federal government to increase its total debt by 56% since 2008, an increase of over $5 trillion. Thanks to the Fed driving down interest rates and purchasing debt as fast as the Treasury has issued it, the federal government faces a crunch not only in terms of running up against the debt ceiling, but also in the structure of the debt. Large amounts of short-term debt are coming due in a short period of time. ZIRP and quantitative easing cannot hold down interest rates forever, as at some point investors will rebel and insist on higher interest rates for US debt. At this point this maturing debt will either have to be paid off or rolled over at higher interest rates, both of which will be very costly for taxpayers.

While I disagree with Pres. Hoenig on many matters of monetary policy and especially on key policy issues such as the existence of the Federal Reserve System, we both have been critical of the Fed's policy of quantitative easing and its maintenance of zero interest rates. Pres. Hoenig has been the most outspoken member of the Federal Reserve System against Chairman Bernanke's policies, consistently voting against the Chairman during meetings of the Federal Open Market Committee last year. Due to Pres. Hoenig's impending retirement, the Fed will lose a much-needed counterbalance to the inflationists who dominate at the Fed.

Both Pres. Hoenig and I realize that printing money out of thin air as the Fed has done and threatens to continue to do is not a panacea. If zero interest rates and quantitative easing could really solve unemployment, there would be no reason not to maintain such policies in perpetuity. Such policies, however, lead to the formation of asset bubbles, as both Pres. Hoenig and I know. Chairman Bernanke's predecessor Alan Greenspan fueled the dot-com bubble and attempted to stave off its collapse by resorting to one percent interest rates. That created the housing bubble whose collapse Chairman Bernanke is attempting to stymie through zero percent interest and massive quantitative easing. The next bubble is already forming, although which sector will be hit hardest remains to be seen. Pres. Hoenig has alluded to some possible bubble sectors in his district, so I look forward to his testimony and his answers to our questions.

July 28, 2011

The Fed Undermines Foreign Policy

by Ron Paul

Last week I was both surprised and pleased when the Supreme Court upheld lower court decisions requiring the Federal Reserve Bank to comply with requests for information made by Bloomberg under the Freedom of Information Act ("FOIA"). Bloomberg simply wanted to know who received loans from the Fed's discount window in the aftermath of the 2008 financial market crisis, and how much each entity received. Surely this is basic information that should be available to every American taxpayer. But the Fed fought tooth and nail all the way to the Supreme Court to preserve their privileged secrecy. However, transparency and openness won the day. There are some 29,000 pages to decipher, but a few points stand out initially.

The Fed lent huge sums of our money to foreign banks. This in itself was not surprising, but the actual amount is staggering! In one week at the height of the crisis, about 70% of the money doled out went to foreign banks. We were told that bailing out banks was going to stave off a massive depression. Depression for whom? We now know that the Fed's bailout had nothing to do with helping the American people, who have gotten their depression anyway with continued job losses and foreclosures. But now we learn that a good deal of the money did not even help American banks!

In light of recent world events, perhaps the most staggering revelation is that quite a bit of money went to the Arab Banking Corp., in which the Libyan Central Bank owned about a third of its stock. This occurred while Libya, a declared state sponsor of terrorism, was under strict economic sanctions! How erratic the US must appear when we shower a dictator alternately with dollars and bombs! Also, we must consider the possibility that those loans are inadvertently financing

~ xix ~

weapons Gaddaffi is using against his own people and western militaries. This would not be the first time the covert activities of the Fed have undermined not only our economy and the value of the dollar, but our foreign policy as well.

Of course I can't say I'm surprised by the poor quality of the data provided by the Fed. The category of each loan made, whether from the "Primary Discount Window", the "Secondary Discount Window," or "Other Extensions of Credit," is redacted. Thus, we don't know with certainty how much discount window lending was provided to foreign banks and how much was merely "other extensions of credit". Also, some of the numbers simply do not seem to add up. We are of course still wading through the massive document dump, but it does seem as though several billions of dollars are unaccounted for.

As the world economy continues to falter in spite of – or rather because of – cheap money doled out by the Federal Reserve, its ability to deceive financial markets and American taxpayers is coming to an end. People are beginning to realize that when the Fed in effect doubles the worldwide supply of US dollars in a relatively short time, it has the effect of stealing half your money through reduced purchasing power. Rapid inflation will continue as trillions in new money and credit recently created by the Fed flood into the commodity markets.

It is becoming more and more obvious that the Fed operates for the benefit of a few privileged banks, banks that never suffer for bad decisions they make. Quite the opposite – as we have seen since October 2008, under our current monetary system politically-connected banks are paid to make bad decisions.

April 8, 2011

Dr. Ron Paul is a Republican member of Congress from Texas.

Deception at the Fed

by Ron Paul

For the past three decades, the Federal Reserve has been given a dual mandate: keeping prices stable and maximizing employment. This policy relies not only on the fatal conceit of believing in the wisdom of supposed experts, but also on numerical chicanery.

Rather than understanding inflation in the classical sense as a monetary phenomenon – an increase in the money supply – it has been redefined as an increase in the Consumer Price Index (CPI). The CPI is calculated based on a weighted basket of goods which is constantly fluctuating, allowing for manipulation of the index to keep inflation expectations low. Employment figures are much the same, relying on survey data, seasonal adjustments, and birth/death models, while the major focus remains on the unemployment rate. Of course, the unemployment rate can fall as discouraged workers drop out of the labor market altogether, leading to the phenomenon of a falling unemployment rate with no job growth.

In terms of keeping stable prices, the Fed has failed miserably. According to the government's own CPI calculators, it takes $2.65 today to purchase what cost one dollar in 1980. And since its creation in 1913, the Federal Reserve has presided over a 98% decline in the dollar's purchasing power. The average American family sees the price of milk, eggs, and meat increasing, while packaged household goods decrease in size rather than price.

Loose fiscal policy has failed to create jobs also. Consider that we had a $700 billion TARP program, nearly $1 trillion in stimulus spending, a government takeover of General Motors, and hundreds of billions of dollars of guarantees to Fannie Mae, Freddie Mac, HUD, FDIC, etc. On top of those programs the Federal Reserve has provided over $4 trillion worth of assistance over the past few years through its credit facilities, purchases of mortgage-backed securities, and now its second round of quantitative easing. Yet even after all these trillions of dollars of spending and bailouts, total nonfarm payroll employment is still seven million jobs lower than it was before this crisis began.

In this same period of time, the total U.S. population has increased by nine million people. We would expect that roughly four million of these people should have been employed, so we are really dealing with eleven million fewer employed people than would otherwise be expected.

It should not be surprising that monetary policy is ineffective at creating actual jobs. It is the effects of monetary policy itself that cause the boom and bust of the business cycle that leads to swings in the unemployment rate. By lowering interest rates through its loose monetary policy, the Fed spurs investment in long-term projects that would not be profitable at market-determined interest rates. Everything seems to go well for awhile until businesses realize that they cannot sell their newly-built houses, their inventories of iron ore, or their new cars. Until these resources are redirected, often with great economic pain for all involved, true economic recovery cannot begin.

Over $4 trillion in bailout facilities and outright debt monetization, combined with interest rates near zero for over two years, have not and will not contribute to increased employment. What is needed is liquidation of debt and malinvested resources. Pumping money into the same sectors that have just crashed merely prolongs the crisis. Until we learn the lesson that jobs are produced through real savings and investment and not through the creation of new money, we are doomed to repeat this boom and bust cycle.

February 17, 2011

The Real Reasons Behind Fed Secrecy

by Ron Paul

Last week I was very pleased that the Financial Services Committee held a hearing on the Federal Reserve Transparency Act, HR 1207. The bill has 295 cosponsors and there is also strong support for the companion bill in the Senate. This hearing was a major step forward in getting the bill passed.

Fighting the Federal Reserve

I was pleased that the hearing was well-attended, especially considering that it was held on a Friday at nine o'clock in the morning! I have been talking about the immense, unchecked power of the Federal Reserve for many years, while the attention of Congress was always on other things. It was gratifying to see my colleagues asking probing questions and demonstrating genuine concern about this important issue as well.

The witness testifying in favor of HR 1207 made some very strong points, which was no surprise considering the bill is simply common sense. It was also no surprise that the witness testifying against the bill had no good arguments as to why a full audit should not be conducted promptly. He attempted to make the case that the Fed is already sufficiently accountable to Congress and that the current auditing policy is adequate. The fact is that the Fed comes to Congress and talks about only what it wants to talk about, and the GAO audits only what the current laws allow to be audited. The really important things however, are off limits. There are no convincing arguments that it is in the best interests of the American people for anything the Fed does to be off limits.

It has been argued that full disclosure of details of funding facilities like TALF and PDCF that enabled massive bailouts of Wall Street would damage the financial position of those firms and destabilize the economy. In other words, if the American people knew how rotten the books were at those banks and how terribly they messed up, they would never willingly invest in them, and they would fail. Failure is not an option for friends of the Fed. Therefore, the funds must be stolen from the people in the dark of night. This is not how a free country works. This is not how free markets work. That is crony corporatism and instead of being a force for economic stabilization, it totally undermines it.

If the Fed gave its actual arguments against a full audit, they would not have mentioned anything about political independence or economic stability. Instead they would admit they don't want to be audited because they enjoy their current situation too much. Under the guise of currency control, they are able to help out powerful allies on Wall Street, in exchange for lucrative jobs or who-knows-what favors later on. An audit would expose the Fed as a massive fraud perpetrated on this country, enriching a privileged few bankers at the top of our economic food chain, and leaving the rest of us with massively devalued dollars which we are forced to use by law. An audit would make people realize that, while Bernie Madoff defrauded a lot of investors for a lot of money, the Fed has defrauded every one of us by destroying the value of our money. An honest and full accounting of how the money system really works in this country would mean there is not much of a chance the American people would stand for it anymore.

September 30, 2009

Fed and Inflation

by Ron Paul

Last week, the subcommittee which I chair held a hearing on monetary policy and rising prices. Whether we consider food, gasoline, or clothing, the cost of living is increasing significantly. True inflation is defined as an increase in the money supply. All other things being equal, an increase in the money supply leads to a rise in prices. Inflation's destructive effects have ruined societies from the Roman Empire to Weimar Germany to modern-day Zimbabwe.

Blame for the most recent round of price increases has been laid at the feet of the Federal Reserve's program of credit expansion for the past three years. The current program, known as QE2, sought to purchase a total of $900 billion in US Treasury debt over a period of 8 months. Roughly $110 billion of newly created money is flooding into commodity markets each month.

The price of cotton is up more than 170% over the past year, oil is up over 40%, and many categories of food staples are seeing double-digit price growth. This means that food, clothing, and gasoline will become increasingly expensive over the coming year. American families, many of whom already live paycheck to paycheck, increasingly will be forced by these rising prices into unwilling tradeoffs: purchasing ground beef rather than steak, drinking water rather than milk, and choosing canned vegetables over fresh in order to keep food on the table and pay the heating bill. Frugality can be a good thing, but only when it is by choice and not forced upon the citizenry by the Fed's ruinous monetary policy.

While the Fed takes credit for the increase in the stock markets, it claims no responsibility for the increases in food and commodity prices. Most economists fail to understand that inflation is at its root a monetary phenomenon. There may be other factors that contribute to price increases, such as famine, flooding, or global unrest, but those effects are transient. Consistently citing only these factors, while never acknowledging the effects of monetary policy, is a cop-out.

The unelected policymakers at the Fed are also the last to feel the effects of inflation. In fact, they benefit from it, as does the government as a whole. Those who receive this new money first, such as government employees, contractors, and bankers are able to use it before price increases occur, while those further down the totem pole suffer price increases before they see any wage increases. By continually reducing the purchasing power of the dollar, the Fed's monetary policy also punishes savings and thrift. After all, why save rapidly depreciating dollars?

Unfortunately, those policymakers who exercise the most power over the economy are also the least likely to understand the effects of their policies. Chairman Bernanke and other members of the Federal Open Market Committee were convinced in mid-2008 that the economy would rebound and continue to grow through 2009, even though it was clear to many observers that we were in the midst of a severe economic crisis. Even Greenspan was known for downplaying the importance of the growing housing bubble just as it was reaching its zenith. It remains impossible for even the brilliant minds at the Fed to achieve both the depth and breadth of knowledge necessary to enact central economic planning without eventually bringing the country to economic ruin. Our witnesses delved deeply into these issues and explained this phenomenon in very logical, simple terms. The American people increasingly understand what is going on with our money. I only hope the Fed is listening.

March 24, 2011

~ **xxv** ~

Our Enemy, the Fed

by Ron Paul

Before the US House of Representatives Committee on Financial Services
Monetary Policy and Rising Prices, March 17, 2011

There is perhaps no topic as important to the average American today as rising prices. Whether we consider food, gasoline, or clothing, the cost of living is increasing significantly. At a time of high unemployment, rising prices trap American families between a rock and a hard place. While rising prices colloquially are referred to as "inflation," true inflation is defined as an increase in the money supply, and all other things being equal, an increase in the money supply leads to a rise in prices. Inflation is and always has been throughout history a monetary phenomenon, and its destructive effects have ruined societies from the Roman Empire to Weimar Germany to modern-day Zimbabwe.

Blame for the most recent round of price increases has been laid at the feet of the Federal Reserve's program of quantitative easing, and rightly so in my opinion. This program, known as QE2, sought to purchase a total of $900 billion in US Treasury debt over a period of 8 months. Roughly $110 billion of newly created money is flooding into markets each month, markets which still have not fully recovered from the financial crisis of the last few years. Banks still hold billions of dollars in underperforming mortgage-backed securities on their books, securities which would render numerous major banks insolvent if they were "marked to market." These nervous banks are hesitant to loan out further money, instead holding well over a trillion dollars on reserve with the Fed. Is it any wonder, then, that the Fed's new hot money is flowing into commodity markets?

The price of cotton is up more than 170% over the past year, oil is up over 40%, and many categories of food staples are seeing double-digit price growth. This means that food, clothing, and gasoline will become increasingly expensive over the coming year. American families, many of whom already live paycheck to paycheck, increasingly will be forced by these rising prices into unwilling tradeoffs. Rising prices lead to consumers purchasing ground beef rather than steak, drinking water rather than milk, and choosing canned vegetables over fresh. Clothes are worn until they are threadbare, in order to conserve money that keeps food on the table and pays the heating bill. While some might argue that this new frugality is a good thing, frugality is virtuous only when it results from free choice, not when it is forced upon the citizenry by the Fed's ruinous monetary policy.

While the Fed takes credit for the increase in the stock markets, it claims no responsibility for the increases in food and commodity prices. Even most economists fail to understand that inflation is at root a monetary phenomenon. As the supply of money increases, more money chases the same amount of goods, and prices rise. There may be other factors that contribute to price rises, such as famine, flooding, or global unrest, but these effects on prices are always short-term, not long-term. Consistently citing rising demand, bad weather, or energy supply uncertainty while never acknowledging the effects of monetary policy is a cop-out. Governments throughout history have sought to blame price increases on bad weather, speculators, and a whole host of other factors, rather than acknowledging the effects of their inflationary monetary policies. Indeed, tyrants of many stripes have debased their nations' currencies while denying responsibility for the suffering that results.

The unelected policymakers at the Fed are also the last to feel the effects of inflation, in fact, they benefit from it, as does the government as a whole. Inflation results in a rise in prices, but those who receive this new money first, such as government employees, contractors, and bankers are able to use it before prices begin to increase, while those further down the totem pole suffer price increases before they see any of this new money. By reducing the purchasing power of the dollar, the Fed's monetary policy also harms savers, encouraging reckless indebtedness and a more present-oriented pattern of consumption. Hard work and thrift are punished, so economic actors naturally respond by spending more, borrowing more, and saving less. After all, why save rapidly depreciating dollars?

Fighting the Federal Reserve

We must also remember that those policymakers who exercise the most power over the economy are also the least likely to understand the effects of their policies. Chairman Bernanke and other members of the Federal Open Market Committee were convinced in mid-2008 that the economy would rebound and continue to grow through 2009, even though it was clear to many observers that we were in the midst of a severe economic crisis. Chairman Greenspan before him was known for downplaying the importance of the growing housing bubble, even while it was reaching its zenith. It remains impossible for even the brilliant minds at the Fed to achieve both the depth and breadth of knowledge necessary to enable centralized economic planning. As Friedrich von Hayek stated in his Nobel Prize address:

"The recognition of the insuperable limits to his knowledge ought indeed to teach the student of society a lesson of humility which should guard him against becoming an accomplice in men's fatal striving to control society – a striving which makes him not only a tyrant over his fellows, but which may well make him the destroyer of a civilization which no brain has designed but which has grown from the free efforts of millions of individuals."

March 18, 2011

End the Fed

by Ron Paul

Before the US House of Representatives, February 4, 2009, introducing the The Federal Reserve Board Abolition Act, H.R. 833.

Madame Speaker, I rise to introduce legislation to restore financial stability to America's economy by abolishing the Federal Reserve. Since the creation of the Federal Reserve, middle and working-class Americans have been victimized by a boom-and-bust monetary policy. In addition, most Americans have suffered a steadily eroding purchasing power because of the Federal Reserve's inflationary policies. This represents a real, if hidden, tax imposed on the American people.

Fighting the Federal Reserve

From the Great Depression, to the stagflation of the seventies, to the current economic crisis caused by the housing bubble, every economic downturn suffered by this country over the past century can be traced to Federal Reserve policy. The Fed has followed a consistent policy of flooding the economy with easy money, leading to a misallocation of resources and an artificial "boom" followed by a recession or depression when the Fed-created bubble bursts.

With a stable currency, American exporters will no longer be held hostage to an erratic monetary policy. Stabilizing the currency will also give Americans new incentives to save as they will no longer have to fear inflation eroding their savings. Those members concerned about increasing America's exports or the low rate of savings should be enthusiastic supporters of this legislation.

Though the Federal Reserve policy harms the average American, it benefits those in a position to take advantage of the cycles in monetary policy. The main beneficiaries are those who receive access to artificially inflated money and/or credit before the inflationary effects of the policy impact the entire economy. Federal Reserve policies also benefit big spending politicians who use the inflated currency created by the Fed to hide the true costs of the welfare-warfare state. It is time for Congress to put the interests of the American people ahead of special interests and their own appetite for big government.

Abolishing the Federal Reserve will allow Congress to reassert its constitutional authority over monetary policy. The United States Constitution grants to Congress the authority to coin money and regulate the value of the currency. The Constitution does not give Congress the authority to delegate control over monetary policy to a central bank. Furthermore, the Constitution certainly does not empower the federal government to erode the American standard of living via an inflationary monetary policy.

In fact, Congress' constitutional mandate regarding monetary policy should only permit currency backed by stable commodities such as silver and gold to be used as legal tender. Therefore, abolishing the Federal Reserve and returning to a constitutional system will enable America to return to the type of monetary system envisioned by our nation's founders: one where the value of money is consistent because it is tied to a commodity such as gold. Such a monetary system is the basis of a true free-market economy.

In conclusion, Mr. Speaker, I urge my colleagues to stand up for working Americans by putting an end to the manipulation of the money supply which erodes Americans' standard of living, enlarges big government, and enriches well-connected elites, by cosponsoring my legislation to abolish the Federal Reserve.

Crimes of the Fed - Bailing Out Banks

by Ron Paul

There has been a lot of talk in the news recently about the Federal Reserve and the actions it has taken over the past few months. Many media pundits have been bending over backwards to praise the Fed for supposedly restoring stability to the market. This interpretation of the Fed's actions couldn't be further from the truth.

The current market crisis began because of Federal Reserve monetary policy during the early 2000s in which the Fed lowered the interest rate to a below-market rate. The artificially low rates led to overinvestment in housing and other malinvestments. When the first indications of market trouble began back in August of 2007, instead of holding back and allowing bad decision-makers to suffer the consequences of their actions, the Federal Reserve took aggressive, inflationary action to ensure that large Wall Street firms would not lose money. It began by lowering the discount rates, the rates of interest charged to banks who borrow directly from the Fed, and lengthening the terms of such loans. This eliminated much of the stigma from discount window borrowing and enabled troubled banks to come to the Fed directly for funding, pay only a slightly higher interest rate but also secure these loans for a period longer than just overnight.

After the massive increase in discount window lending proved to be ineffective, the Fed became more and more creative with its funding arrangements. It has since created the Term Auction Facility (TAF), the Primary Dealer Credit Facility (PDCF), and the Term

Securities Lending Facility (TSLF). The upshot of all of these new programs is that through auctions of securities or through deposits of collateral, the Fed is pushing hundreds of billions of dollars of funding into the financial system in a misguided attempt to shore up the stability of the system.

The PDCF in particular is a departure from the established pattern of Fed intervention because it targets the primary dealers, the largest investment banks who purchase government securities directly from the New York Fed. These banks have never before been allowed to borrow from the Fed, but thanks to the Fed Board of Governors, these investment banks can now receive loans from the Fed in exchange for securities which will in all likelihood soon lose much of their value.

The net effect of all this new funding has been to pump hundreds of billions of dollars into the financial system and bail out banks whose poor decision making should have caused them to go out of business. Instead of being forced to learn their lesson, these poor-performing banks are being rewarded for their financial mismanagement, and the ultimate cost of this bailout will fall on the American taxpayers. Already this new money flowing into the system is spurring talk of the next speculative bubble, possibly this time in commodities.

Worst of all, the Treasury Department has recently proposed that the Federal Reserve, which was responsible for the housing bubble and subprime crisis in the first place, be rewarded for all its intervention by being turned into a super-regulator. The Treasury foresees the Fed as the guarantor of market stability, with oversight over any financial institution that could pose a threat to the financial system. Rewarding poor-performing financial institutions is bad enough, but rewarding the institution that enabled the current economic crisis is unconscionable.

April 16, 2008

The Guilty Fed and Feds

by Rep. Ron Paul, MD

Last week the US Treasury department issued a warning to the Chinese government with regard to its policy of pegging the value of the Chinese yuan to the US dollar. In essence, the Treasury department accuses China of artificially suppressing the value of its currency by tying it to the dollar, thus making Chinese imports very cheap and worsening our trade imbalance.

This kind of bluster may serve political interests, but in reality we have nobody to blame but ourselves for the sharp decline in the US dollar. Congress and the Federal Reserve, not China, are the real culprits in the erosion of your personal savings and buying power. Congress relentlessly spends more than the Treasury collects in taxes each year, which means the US government must either borrow or print money to operate — both of which cause the value of the dollar to drop. When we borrow a billion dollars every day simply to run the government, and when the Federal Reserve increases the money supply by trillions of dollars in just 15 years, we hardly can expect our dollars to increase in value.

If anything, the US government should be embarrassed that another nation has depressed its currency by tying it to the US dollar. An economically sound nation would take pride in its currency, one that maintains a stable value and provides incentive for savers. Yet here we are, mad at China for our own sin of flooding the world with cheap dollars.

The root of the problem is the Federal Reserve and our fiat monetary system itself. Since US dollars and other major currencies are not backed by gold, they have no inherent value. Their relative values are subject to political events, and fluctuate constantly in highly volatile currency markets. A fiat system means every dollar you have can be eroded into nothing by the actions of politicians and central bankers. In essence, paper currencies like the US dollar operate as articles of faith — faith in the policies of the governments and central banks that issue them. When it comes to a government as deeply indebted as our own, that faith is sorely lacking among investors worldwide. Politicians often manage to fool voters and the media, but they rarely fool financial markets over time. The precipitous drop in the US dollar over the past few years is proof that investors around the globe are very concerned about American deficits and debt. When investors lack faith in the U.S. dollar, they really lack faith in the economic policies of the U.S. government.

Unlike wealthy currency traders, most Americans are stuck with their U.S. dollars. Average people, particularly those who depend on savings or fixed incomes to fund their retirement years, cannot abide the continued devaluation of our currency. A true strong-dollar policy would not depend on the actions of China or any other nation. It would, however, require a constriction of the money supply and higher interest rates, both of which would cause some short-term pain for the American economy. In the long run, however, such a correction is the only alternative to the continued erosion of our dollars.

May 24, 2005

Paper Money and Tyranny

by Rep. Ron Paul, MD

US House of Representatives, September 5, 2003

All great republics throughout history cherished sound money. This meant that the monetary unit was a commodity of honest weight and purity. When money was sound, civilizations were found to be more prosperous and freedom thrived. The less free a society becomes, the greater the likelihood its money is being debased and the economic well-being of its citizens diminished.

Alan Greenspan, years before he became Federal Reserve Board Chairman in charge of flagrantly debasing the U.S. dollar, wrote about this connection between sound money, prosperity, and freedom. In his article "Gold and Economic Freedom" (*The Objectivist*, July 1966), Greenspan starts by saying: "An almost hysterical antagonism toward the gold standard is an issue that unites statists of all persuasions. They seem to sense...that gold and economic freedom are inseparable." Further he states that: "Under the gold standard, a free banking system stands as the protector of an economy's stability and balanced growth." Astoundingly, Mr. Greenspan's analysis of the 1929 market crash, and how the Fed precipitated the crisis, directly parallels current conditions we are experiencing under his management of the Fed. Greenspan explains: "The excess credit which the Fed pumped into the economy spilled over into the stock market — triggering a fantastic speculative boom." And, "...By 1929 the speculative imbalances had become overwhelming and unmanageable by the Fed." Greenspan concluded his article by stating: "In the absence of the gold standard, there is no way to protect savings from confiscation through inflation." He explains that the "shabby secret" of the proponents of big government and paper money is that deficit spending is simply nothing more than a "scheme for the hidden confiscation of wealth." Yet here we are today with a purely fiat monetary system, managed almost exclusively by Alan Greenspan, who once so correctly denounced the Fed's role in the Depression while recognizing the need for sound money.

The Founders of this country, and a large majority of the American people up until the 1930s, disdained paper money, respected commodity money, and disapproved of a central bank's monopoly control of money creation and interest rates. Ironically, it was the abuse of the gold standard, the Fed's credit-creating habits of the 1920s, and its subsequent mischief in the 1930s, that not only gave us the Great Depression, but also prolonged it. Yet sound money was blamed for all the suffering. That's why people hardly objected when Roosevelt and his statist friends confiscated gold and radically debased the currency, ushering in the age of worldwide fiat currencies with which the international economy struggles today.

If honest money and freedom are inseparable, as Mr. Greenspan argued, and paper money leads to tyranny, one must wonder why it's so popular with economists, the business community, bankers, and our government officials. The simplest explanation is that it's a human trait to always seek the comforts of wealth with the least amount of effort. This desire is quite positive when it inspires hard work and innovation in a capitalist society. Productivity is improved and the standard of living goes up for everyone. This process has permitted the poorest in today's capitalist countries to enjoy luxuries never available to the royalty of old.

But this human trait of seeking wealth and comfort with the least amount of effort is often abused. It leads some to believe that by certain monetary manipulations, wealth can be made more available to everyone. Those who believe in fiat money often believe wealth can be increased without a commensurate amount of hard work and innovation. They also come to believe that savings and market control of interest rates are not only unnecessary, but actually hinder a productive growing economy. Concern for liberty is replaced by the illusion that material benefits can be more easily obtained with fiat money than through hard work and ingenuity. The perceived benefits soon become of greater concern for society than the preservation of liberty. This does not mean proponents of fiat money embark on a crusade to promote tyranny, though that is what it leads to, but rather they hope they have found the philosopher's stone and a modern alternative to the challenge of turning lead into gold.

Our Founders thoroughly understood this issue, and warned us against the temptation to seek wealth and fortune without the work and savings that real prosperity requires. James Madison warned of "The pestilent effects of paper money," as the Founders had vivid memories of the destructiveness of the Continental dollar. George Mason of Virginia said that he had a "Mortal hatred to paper money." Constitutional Convention delegate Oliver Ellsworth from Connecticut thought the convention "A favorable moment to shut and bar the door against paper money." This view of the evils of paper money was shared by almost all the delegates to the convention, and was the reason the Constitution limited congressional authority to deal with the issue and mandated that only gold and silver could be legal tender. Paper money was prohibited and no central bank was authorized. Over and above the economic reasons for honest money, however, Madison argued the moral case for such. Paper money, he explained, destroyed "The necessary confidence between man and man, on necessary confidence in public councils, on the industry and morals of people and on the character of republican government."

Fighting the Federal Reserve

The Founders were well aware of the biblical admonitions against dishonest weights and measures, debased silver, and watered-down wine. The issue of sound money throughout history has been as much a moral issue as an economic or political issue.

Even with this history and great concern expressed by the Founders, the barriers to paper money have been torn asunder. The Constitution has not been changed, but is no longer applied to the issue of money. It was once explained to me, during the debate over going to war in Iraq, that a declaration of war was not needed because to ask for such a declaration was "frivolous" and that the portion of the Constitution dealing with congressional war power was "anachronistic." So too, it seems that the power over money given to Congress alone and limited to coinage and honest weights, is now also "anachronistic."

If indeed our generation can make the case for paper money, issued by an unauthorized central bank, it behooves us to at least have enough respect for the Constitution to amend it in a proper fashion. Ignoring the Constitution in order to perform a pernicious act is detrimental in two ways. First, debasing the currency as a deliberate policy is economically destructive beyond measure. Second, doing it without consideration for the rule of law undermines the entire fabric of our Constitutional republic.

Though the need for sound money is currently not a pressing issue for Congress, it's something that cannot be ignored because serious economic problems resulting from our paper money system are being forced upon us. As a matter of fact, we deal with the consequences on a daily basis, yet fail to see the connection between our economic problems and the mischief orchestrated by the Federal Reserve.

All the great religions teach honesty in money, and the economic shortcomings of paper money were well known when the Constitution was written, so we must try to understand why an entire generation of Americans have come to accept paper money without hesitation, without question. Most Americans are oblivious to the entire issue of the nature and importance of money. Many in authority, however, have either been misled by false notions or see that the power to create money is indeed a power they enjoy, as they promote their agenda of welfarism at home and empire abroad.

Money is a moral, economic, and political issue. Since the monetary unit measures every economic transaction, from wages to prices, taxes, and interest rates, it is vitally important that its value is honestly established in the marketplace without bankers, government, politicians, or the Federal Reserve manipulating its value to serve special interests.

Money As a Moral Issue

The moral issue regarding money should be the easiest to understand, but almost no one in Washington thinks of money in these terms. Although there is a growing and deserved distrust in government per se, trust in money and the Federal Reserve's ability to manage it remains strong. No one would welcome a counterfeiter to town, yet this same authority is blindly given to our central bank without any serious oversight by the Congress.

When the government can replicate the monetary unit at will without regard to cost, whether it's paper currency or a computer entry, it's morally identical to the counterfeiter who illegally prints currency. Both ways, it's fraud.

A fiat monetary system allows power and influence to fall into the hands of those who control the creation of new money, and to those who get to use the money or credit early in its circulation. The insidious and eventual cost falls on unidentified victims who are usually oblivious to the cause of their plight. This system of legalized plunder (though not constitutional) allows one group to benefit at the expense of another. An actual transfer of wealth goes from the poor and the middle class to those in privileged financial positions.

In many societies the middle class has actually been wiped out by monetary inflation, which always accompanies fiat money. The high cost of living and loss of jobs hits one segment of society, while in the early stages of inflation, the business class actually benefits from the easy credit. An astute stock investor or home builder can make millions in the boom phase of the business cycle, while the poor and those dependent on fixed incomes can't keep up with the rising cost of living.

Fiat money is also immoral because it allows government to finance special interest legislation that otherwise would have to be paid for by direct taxation or by productive enterprise. This transfer of wealth occurs without directly taking the money out of someone's pocket. Every dollar created dilutes the value of existing dollars in circulation. Those individuals who worked hard, paid their taxes, and saved some money for a rainy day are hit the hardest, with their dollars being depreciated in value while earning interest that is kept artificially low by the Federal Reserve easy-credit policy. The easy credit helps investors and consumers who have no qualms about going into debt and even declaring bankruptcy.

If one sees the welfare state and foreign militarism as improper and immoral, one understands how the license to print money permits these policies to go forward far more easily than if they had to be paid for immediately by direct taxation.

Printing money, which is literally inflation, is nothing more than a sinister and evil form of hidden taxation. It's unfair and deceptive, and accordingly strongly opposed by the authors of the Constitution. That is why there is no authority for Congress, the Federal Reserve, or the executive branch to operate the current system of money we have today.

Money As a Political Issue

Although the money issue today is of little political interest to the parties and politicians, it should not be ignored. Policy makers must contend with the consequences of the business cycle, which result from the fiat monetary system under which we operate. They may not understand the connection now, but eventually they must.

In the past, money and gold have been dominant issues in several major political campaigns. We find that when the people have had a voice in the matter, they inevitably chose gold over paper. To the common man, it just makes sense. As a matter of fact, a large number of Americans, perhaps a majority, still believe our dollar is backed by huge hoards of gold in Fort Knox.

Fighting the Federal Reserve

The monetary issue, along with the desire to have free trade among the states, prompted those at the Constitutional Convention to seek solutions to problems that plagued the post-revolutionary war economy. This post-war recession was greatly aggravated by the collapse of the unsound fiat Continental dollar. The people, through their representatives, spoke loudly and clearly for gold and silver over paper.

Andrew Jackson, a strong proponent of gold and opponent of central banking (the Second Bank of the United States,) was a hero to the working class and was twice elected president. This issue was fully debated in his presidential campaigns. The people voted for gold over paper.

In the 1870s, the people once again spoke out clearly against the greenback inflation of Lincoln. Notoriously, governments go to paper money while rejecting gold to promote unpopular and unaffordable wars. The return to gold in 1879 went smoothly and was welcomed by the people, putting behind them the disastrous Civil War inflationary period.

Grover Cleveland, elected twice to the presidency, was also a strong advocate of the gold standard.

Again, in the presidential race of 1896, William McKinley argued the case for gold. In spite of the great orations by William Jennings Bryant, who supported monetary inflation and made a mocking "Cross of Gold" speech, the people rallied behind McKinley's bland but correct arguments for sound money.

The 20th Century was much less sympathetic to gold. Since 1913 central banking has been accepted in the United States without much debate, despite the many economic and political horrors caused or worsened by the Federal Reserve since its establishment. The ups and downs of the economy have all come as a consequence of Fed policies, from the Great Depression to the horrendous stagflation of the '70s, as well as the current ongoing economic crisis.

A central bank and fiat money enable government to maintain an easy war policy that under strict monetary rules would not be achievable. In other words, countries with sound monetary policies would rarely go to war because they could not afford to, especially if they were not attacked. The people could not be taxed enough to support wars without destroying the economy. But by printing money, the cost can be delayed and hidden, sometimes for years if not decades. To be truly opposed to preemptive and unnecessary wars one must advocate sound money to prevent the promoters of war from financing their imperialism.

Look at how the military budget is exploding, deficits are exploding, and tax revenues are going down. No problem; the Fed is there and will print whatever is needed to meet our military commitments, whether it's wise to do so or not.

The money issue should indeed be a gigantic political issue. Fiat money hurts the economy, finances wars, and allows for excessive welfarism. When these connections are realized and understood, it will once again become a major political issue, since paper money never lasts. Ultimately politicians will not have a choice of whether to address or take a position on the money issue. The people and circumstances will demand it.

We do hear some talk about monetary policy and criticism directed toward the Federal Reserve, but it falls far short of what I'm talking about. Big-spending welfarists constantly complain about Fed policy, usually demanding lower interest rates even when rates are at historic lows. Big-government conservatives promoting grand worldwide military operations, while arguing that "deficits don't matter" as long as marginal tax rates are lowered, also constantly criticize the Fed for high interest rates and lack of liquidity. Coming from both the left and the right, these demands would not occur if money could not be created out of thin air at will. Both sides are asking for the same thing from the Fed for different reasons. They want the printing presses to run faster and create more credit, so that the economy will be healed like magic — or so they believe.

This is not the kind of interest in the Fed that we need. I'm anticipating that we should and one day will be forced to deal with the definition of the dollar and what money should consist of. The current superficial discussion about money merely shows a desire to tinker with the current system in hopes of improving the deteriorating economy. There will be a point, though, when the tinkering will no longer be of any benefit and even the best advice will be of no value. We have just gone through two-and-a-half years of tinkering with 13 rate cuts, and recovery has not yet been achieved. It's just possible that we're much closer than anyone realizes to that day when it will become absolutely necessary to deal with the monetary issue — both philosophically and strategically — and forget about the band-aid approach to the current system.

Money As an Economic Issue

For a time, the economic consequences of paper money may seem benign and even helpful, but are always disruptive to economic growth and prosperity.

Economic planners of the Keynesian-socialist type have always relished control over money creation in their efforts to regulate and plan the economy. They have no qualms with using this power to pursue their egalitarian dreams of wealth redistribution. That force and fraud are used to make the economic system supposedly fairer is of little concern to them.

There are also many conservatives who do not endorse central economic planning as those on the left do, but nevertheless concede this authority to the Federal Reserve to manipulate the economy through monetary policy. Only a small group of constitutionalists, libertarians, and Austrian free-market economists reject the notion that central planning, through interest-rate and money-supply manipulation, is a productive endeavor.

Many sincere politicians, bureaucrats, and bankers endorse the current system, not out of malice or greed, but because it's the only system they have known. The principles of sound money and free market banking are not taught in our universities. The overwhelming consensus in Washington, as well as around the world, is that commodity money without a central bank is no longer practical or necessary. Be assured, though, that certain individuals who greatly benefit from a paper money system know exactly why the restraints that a commodities standard would have are unacceptable.

Fighting the Federal Reserve

Though the economic consequences of paper money in the early stage affect lower-income and middle-class citizens, history shows that when the destruction of monetary value becomes rampant, nearly everyone suffers and the economic and political structure becomes unstable. There's good reason for all of us to be concerned about our monetary system and the future of the dollar.

Nations that live beyond their means must always pay for their extravagance. It's easy to understand why future generations inherit a burden when the national debt piles up. This requires others to pay the interest and debts when they come due. The victims are never the recipients of the borrowed funds. But this is not exactly what happens when a country pays off its debt. The debt, in nominal terms, always goes up, and since it is still accepted by mainstream economists that just borrowing endlessly is not the road to permanent prosperity, real debt must be reduced. Depreciating the value of the dollar does that. If the dollar loses 10% of its value, the national debt of $6.5 trillion is reduced in real terms by $650 billion. That's a pretty neat trick and quite helpful — to the government.

That's why the Fed screams about a coming deflation, so it can continue the devaluation of the dollar unabated. The politicians don't mind, the bankers welcome the business activity, and the recipients of the funds passed out by Congress never complain. The greater the debt, the greater the need to inflate the currency, since debt cannot be the source of long-term wealth. Individuals and corporations who borrow too much eventually must cut back and pay off debt and start anew, but governments rarely do.

But where's the hitch? This process, which seems to be a creative way of paying off debt, eventually undermines the capitalist structure of the economy, thus making it difficult to produce wealth, and that's when the whole process comes to an end. This system causes many economic problems, but most of them stem from the Fed's interference with the market rate of interest that it achieves through credit creation and printing money.

Nearly 100 years ago, Austrian economist Ludwig von Mises explained and predicted the failure of socialism. Without a pricing mechanism, the delicate balance between consumers and producers would be destroyed. Freely fluctuating prices provide vital information to the entrepreneur who is making key decisions on production. Without this information, major mistakes are made. A central planning bureaucrat cannot be a substitute for the law of supply and demand.

Though generally accepted by most modern economists and politicians, there is little hesitancy in accepting the omnipotent wisdom of the Federal Reserve to know the "price" of money — the interest rate — and its proper supply. For decades, and especially during the 1990s — when Chairman Greenspan was held in such high esteem, and no one dared question his judgment or the wisdom of the system — this process was allowed to run unimpeded by political or market restraints. Just as we must eventually pay for our perpetual deficits, continuous manipulation of interest and credit will also extract a payment.

Artificially low interest rates deceive investors into believing that rates are low because savings are high and represent funds not spent on consumption. When the Fed creates bank deposits out of thin air making loans available at below-market rates, mal-investment and overcapacity results, setting the stage for the next recession or depression. The easy credit policy is welcomed by many: stock-market investors, home builders, home buyers, congressional spendthrifts, bankers, and many other consumers who enjoy borrowing at low rates and not worrying about repayment. However, perpetual good times cannot come from a printing press or easy credit created by a Federal Reserve computer. The piper will demand payment, and the downturn in the business cycle will see to it. The downturn is locked into place by the artificial boom that everyone enjoys, despite the dreams that we have ushered in a "new economic era." Let there be no doubt: the business cycle, the stagflation, the recessions, the depressions, and the inflations are not a result of capitalism and sound money, but rather are a direct result of paper money and a central bank that is incapable of managing it.

Our current monetary system makes it tempting for all parties, individuals, corporations, and government to go into debt. It encourages consumption over investment and production. Incentives to save are diminished by the Fed's making new credit available to everyone and keeping interest rates on saving so low that few find it advisable to save for a rainy day. This is made worse by taxing interest earned on savings. It plays havoc with those who do save and want to live off their interest. The artificial rates may be 4, 5, or even 6% below the market rate, and the savers — many who are elderly and on fixed incomes — suffer unfairly at the hands of Alan Greenspan, who believes that resorting to money creation will solve our problems and give us perpetual prosperity.

Lowering interest rates at times, especially early in the stages of monetary debasement, will produce the desired effects and stimulate another boom-bust cycle. But eventually the distortions and imbalances between consumption and production, and the excessive debt, prevent the monetary stimulus from doing very much to boost the economy. Just look at what's been happening in Japan for the last 12 years. When conditions get bad enough the only recourse will be to have major monetary reform to restore confidence in the system.

The two conditions that result from fiat money that are more likely to concern the people are inflation of prices and unemployment. Unfortunately, few realize these problems are directly related to our monetary system. Instead of demanding reforms, the chorus from both the right and left is for the Fed to do more of the same — only faster. If our problem stems from easy credit and interest-rate manipulation by the Fed, demanding more will not do much to help. Sadly, it will only make our problems worse.

Ironically, the more successful the money managers are at restoring growth or prolonging the boom with their monetary machinations, the greater are the distortions and imbalances in the economy. This means that when corrections are eventually forced upon us, they are much more painful and more people suffer with the correction lasting longer.

Today's Conditions

Today's economic conditions reflect a fiat monetary system held together by many tricks and luck over the past 30 years. The world has been awash in paper money since removal of the last vestige of the gold standard by Richard Nixon when he buried the Bretton Woods agreement — the gold exchange standard — on August 15, 1971. Since then we've been on a worldwide paper dollar standard. Quite possibly we are seeing the beginning of the end of that system. If so, tough times are ahead for the United States and the world economy.

A paper monetary standard means there are no restraints on the printing press or on federal deficits. In 1971, M3 was $776 billion; today it stands at $8.9 trillion, an 1100% increase. Our national debt in 1971 was $408 billion; today it stands at $6.8 trillion, a 1600% increase. Since that time, our dollar has lost almost 80% of its purchasing power. Common sense tells us that this process is not sustainable and something has to give. So far, no one in Washington seems interested.

Although dollar creation is ultimately the key to its value, many other factors play a part in its perceived value, such as: the strength of our economy, our political stability, our military power, the benefit of the dollar being the key reserve currency of the world, and the relative weakness of other nation's economies and their currencies. For these reasons, the dollar has enjoyed a special place in the world economy. Increases in productivity have also helped to bestow undeserved trust in our economy with consumer prices, to some degree, being held in check and fooling the people, at the urging of the Fed, that "inflation" is not a problem. Trust is an important factor in how the dollar is perceived. Sound money encourages trust, but trust can come from these other sources as well. But when this trust is lost, which always occurs with paper money, the delayed adjustments can hit with a vengeance.

Following the breakdown of the Bretton Woods agreement, the world essentially accepted the dollar as a replacement for gold, to be held in reserve upon which even more monetary expansion could occur. It was a great arrangement that up until now seemed to make everyone happy.

We own the printing press and create as many dollars as we please. These dollars are used to buy federal debt. This allows our debt to be monetized and the spendthrift Congress, of course, finds this a delightful convenience and never complains. As the dollars circulate through our fractional reserve banking system, they expand many times over. With our excess dollars at home, our trading partners are only too happy to accept these dollars in order to sell us their products. Because our dollar is relatively strong compared to other currencies, we can buy foreign products at a discounted price. In other words, we get to create the world's reserve currency at no cost, spend it overseas, and receive manufactured goods in return. Our excess dollars go abroad and other countries — especially Japan and China — are only too happy to loan them right back to us by buying our government and GSE debt. Up until now both sides have been happy with this arrangement.

But all good things must come to an end and this arrangement is ending. The process put us into a position of being a huge debtor nation, with our current account deficit of more than $600 billion per year now exceeding 5% of our GDP. We now owe foreigners more than any other nation ever owed in all of history, over $3 trillion.

A debt of this sort always ends by the currency of the debtor nation decreasing in value. And that's what has started to happen with the dollar, although it still has a long way to go. Our free lunch cannot last. Printing money, buying foreign products, and selling foreign holders of dollars our debt ends when the foreign holders of this debt become concerned with the dollar's future value.

Once this process starts, interest rates will rise. And in recent weeks, despite the frenetic effort of the Fed to keep interest rates low, they are actually rising instead. The official explanation is that this is due to an economic rebound with an increase in demand for loans. Yet a decrease in demand for our debt and reluctance to hold our dollars is a more likely cause. Only time will tell whether the economy rebounds to any significant degree, but one must be aware that rising interest rates and serious price inflation can also reflect a weak dollar and a weak economy. The stagflation of the 1970s baffled many conventional economists, but not the Austrian economists. Many other countries have in the past suffered from the extremes of inflation in an inflationary depression, and we are not immune from that happening here. Our monetary and fiscal policies are actually conducive to such a scenario.

In the short run, the current system gives us a free ride, our paper buys cheap goods from overseas, and foreigners risk all by financing our extravagance. But in the long run, we will surely pay for living beyond our means. Debt will be paid for one way or another. An inflated currency always comes back to haunt those who enjoyed the "benefits" of inflation. Although this process is extremely dangerous, many economists and politicians do not see it as a currency problem and are only too willing to find a villain to attack. Surprisingly the villain is often the foreigner who foolishly takes our paper for useful goods and accommodates us by loaning the proceeds back to us. It's true that the system encourages exportation of jobs as we buy more and more foreign goods. But nobody understands the Fed role in this, so the cries go out to punish the competition with tariffs. Protectionism is a predictable consequence of paper-money inflation, just as is the impoverishment of an entire middle class. It should surprise no one that even in the boom phase of the 1990s, there were still many people who became poorer. Yet all we hear are calls for more government mischief to correct the problems with tariffs, increased welfare for the poor, increased unemployment benefits, deficit spending, and special interest tax reduction, none of which can solve the problems ingrained in a system that operates with paper money and a central bank.

If inflation were equitable and treated all classes the same, it would be less socially divisive. But while some see their incomes going up above the rate of inflation (movie stars, CEOs, stock brokers, speculators, professional athletes), others see their incomes stagnate like lower-middle-income workers, retired people, and farmers. Likewise, the rise in the cost of living hurts the poor and middle class more than the wealthy. Because inflation treats certain groups unfairly, anger and envy are directed toward those who have benefited.

The long-term philosophic problem with this is that the central bank and the fiat monetary system are not blamed; instead free market capitalism is. This is what happened in the 1930s. The Keynesians, who grew to dominate economic thinking at the time, erroneously blamed the gold standard, balanced budgets, and capitalism instead of tax increases, tariffs, and Fed policy. This country cannot afford another attack on economic liberty similar to what followed the 1929 crash that ushered in the economic interventionism and inflationism which we have been saddled with ever since. These policies have brought us to the brink of another colossal economic downturn and we need to be prepared.

Fighting the Federal Reserve

Big business and banking deserve our harsh criticism, but not because they are big or because they make a lot of money. Our criticism should come because of the special benefits they receive from a monetary system designed to assist the business class at the expense of the working class. Labor leader Samuel Gompers understood this and feared paper money and a central bank while arguing the case for gold. Since the monetary system is used to finance deficits that come from war expenditures, the military industrial complex is a strong supporter of the current monetary system.

Liberals foolishly believe that they can control the process and curtail the benefits going to corporations and banks by increasing the spending for welfare for the poor. But this never happens. Powerful financial special interests control the government spending process and throw only crumbs to the poor. The fallacy with this approach is that the advocates fail to see the harm done to the poor, with cost of living increases and job losses that are a natural consequence of monetary debasement. Therefore, even more liberal control over the spending process can never compensate for the great harm done to the economy and the poor by the Federal Reserve's effort to manage an unmanageable fiat monetary system.

Economic intervention, financed by inflation, is high-stakes government. It provides the incentive for the big money to "invest" in gaining government control. The big money comes from those who have it — corporations and banking interests. That's why literally billions of dollars are spent on elections and lobbying. The only way to restore equity is to change the primary function of government from economic planning and militarism to protecting liberty. Without money, the poor and middle class are disenfranchised since access for the most part requires money. Obviously, this is not a partisan issue since both major parties are controlled by wealthy special interests. Only the rhetoric is different.

Our current economic problems are directly related to the monetary excesses of three decades and the more recent efforts by the Federal Reserve to thwart the correction that the market is forcing upon us. Since 1998, there has been a sustained attack on corporate profits. Before that, profits and earnings were inflated and fictitious, with WorldCom and Enron being prime examples. In spite of the 13 rate cuts since 2001, economic growth has not been restored.

Paper money encourages speculation, excessive debt, and misdirected investments. The market, however, always moves in the direction of eliminating bad investments, liquidating debt, and reducing speculative excesses. What we have seen, especially since the stock market peak of early 2000, is a knock-down, drag-out battle between the Fed's effort to avoid a recession, limit the recession, and stimulate growth with its only tool, money creation, while the market demands the elimination of bad investments and excess debt. The Fed was also motivated to save the stock market from collapsing, which in some ways they have been able to do. The market, in contrast, will insist on liquidation of unsustainable debt, removal of investment mistakes made over several decades, and a dramatic revaluation of the stock market. In this go-around, the Fed has pulled out all the stops and is more determined than ever, yet the market is saying that new and healthy growth cannot occur until a major cleansing of the system occurs. Does anyone think that tariffs and interest rates of 1% will encourage the rebuilding of our steel and textile industries anytime soon? Obviously, something more is needed.

The world central bankers are concerned with the lack of response to low interest rates and they have joined in a concerted effort to rescue the world economy through a policy of protecting the dollar's role in the world economy, denying that inflation exists, and justifying unlimited expansion of the dollar money supply. To maintain confidence in the dollar, gold prices must be held in check. In the 1960s our government didn't want a vote of no confidence in the dollar, and for a couple of decades, the price of gold was artificially held at $35 per ounce. That, of course, did not last.

In recent years, there has been a coordinated effort by the world central bankers to keep the gold price in check by dumping part of their large horde of gold into the market. This has worked to a degree, but just as it could not be sustained in the 1960s, until Nixon declared the Bretton Woods agreement dead in 1971, this effort will fail as well.

The market price of gold is important because it reflects the ultimate confidence in the dollar. An artificially low price for gold contributes to false confidence and when this is lost, more chaos ensues as the market adjusts for the delay.

Monetary policy today is designed to demonetize gold and guarantee for the first time that paper can serve as an adequate substitute in the hands of wise central bankers. Trust, then, has to be transferred from gold to the politicians and bureaucrats who are in charge of our monetary system. This fails to recognize the obvious reason that market participants throughout history have always preferred to deal with real assets, real money, rather than government paper. This contest between paper and honest money is of much greater significance than many realize. We should know the outcome of this struggle within the next decade.

Alan Greenspan, although once a strong advocate for the gold standard, now believes he knows what the outcome of this battle will be. Is it just wishful thinking on his part? In an answer to a question I asked before the Financial Services Committee in February 2003, Chairman Greenspan made an effort to convince me that paper money now works as well as gold: "I have been quite surprised, and I must say pleased, by the fact that central banks have been able to effectively simulate many of the characteristics of the gold standard by constraining the degree of finance in a manner which effectively brought down the general price levels." Earlier, in December 2002, Mr. Greenspan spoke before the Economic Club of New York and addressed the same subject: "The record of the past 20 years appears to underscore the observation that, although pressures for excess issuance of fiat money are chronic, a prudent monetary policy maintained over a protracted period of time can contain the forces of inflation."

There are several problems with this optimistic assessment. First, efficient central bankers will never replace the *invisible hand* of a commodity monetary standard. Second, using government price indexes to measure the success of a managed fiat currency should not be reassuring. These indexes can be arbitrarily altered to imply a successful monetary policy. Also, price increases of consumer goods are not a litmus test for measuring the harm done by the money managers at the Fed. The development of overcapacity, excessive debt, and speculation still occur, even when prices happen to remain reasonably stable due to increases in productivity and technology. Chairman Greenspan makes his argument because he hopes he's right that sound money is no longer necessary, and also because it's an excuse to keep the inflation of the money supply going for as long as possible, hoping a miracle will restore sound growth to the economy. But that's only a dream.

We are now faced with an economy that is far from robust and may get a lot worse before rebounding. If not now, the time will soon come when the conventional wisdom of the last 90 years, since the Fed was created, will have to be challenged. If the conditions have changed and the routine of fiscal and monetary stimulation don't work, we better prepare ourselves for the aftermath of a failed dollar system, which will not be limited to the United States.

An interesting headline appeared in the *New York Times* on July 31, 2003, "Commodity Costs Soar, But Factories Don't Bustle." What is observed here is a sea change in attitude by investors shifting their investment funds and speculation into things of real value and out of financial areas, such as stocks and bonds. This shift shows that in spite of the most aggressive Fed policy in history in the past three years, the economy remains sluggish and interest rates are actually rising. What can the Fed do? If this trend continues, there's little they can do. Not only do I believe this trend will continue, I believe it's likely to accelerate. This policy plays havoc with our economy; it reduces revenues, prompts increases in federal spending, increases in deficits and debt occur, and interest costs rise, compounding our budgetary woes.

The set of circumstances we face today are unique and quite different from all the other recessions the Federal Reserve has had to deal with. Generally, interest rates are raised to slow the economy and dampen price inflation. At the bottom of the cycle interest rates are lowered to stimulate the economy. But this time around, the recession came in spite of huge and significant interest rate reductions by the Fed. This aggressive policy did not prevent the recession as was hoped; so far it has not produced the desired recovery. Now we're at the bottom of the cycle and interest rates not only can't be lowered, they are rising. This is a unique and dangerous combination of events. This set of circumstances can only occur with fiat money and indicates that further manipulation of the money supply and interest rates by the Fed will have little if any effect.

The odds aren't very good that the Fed will adopt a policy of not inflating the money supply because of some very painful consequences that would result. Also there would be a need to remove the pressure on the Fed to accommodate the big spenders in Congress. Since there are essentially only two groups that have any influence on spending levels, big-government liberals and big-government conservatives, that's not about to happen. Poverty is going to worsen due to our monetary and fiscal policies, so spending on the war on poverty will accelerate. Our obsession with policing the world, nation building, and pre-emptive war are not likely to soon go away, since both Republican and Democratic leaders endorse them. Instead, the cost of defending the American empire is going to accelerate. A country that is getting poorer cannot pay these bills with higher taxation nor can they find enough excess funds for the people to loan to the government. The only recourse is for the Federal Reserve to accommodate and monetize the federal debt, and that, of course, is inflation.

It's now admitted that the deficit is out of control, with next year's deficit reaching over one-half trillion dollars, not counting the billions borrowed from "trust funds" like Social Security. I'm sticking to my prediction that within a few years the national debt will increase over $1 trillion in one fiscal year. So far, so good, no big market reactions, the dollar is holding its own and the administration and congressional leaders are not alarmed. But they ought to be.

I agree, it would be politically tough to bite the bullet and deal with our extravagance, both fiscal and monetary, but the repercussions here at home from a loss of confidence in the dollar throughout the world will not be a pretty sight to behold. I don't see any way we are going to avoid the crisis.

We do have some options to minimize the suffering. If we decided to, we could permit some alternatives to the current system of money and banking we have today.

* Already, we took a big step in this direction. Gold was illegal to own between 1933 and 1976. Today millions of Americans do own some gold.

* Gold contracts are legal, but a settlement of any dispute is always in Federal Reserve notes. This makes gold contracts of limited value.

* For gold to be an alternative to Federal Reserve notes, taxes on any transactions in gold must be removed, both sales and capital gains.

* Holding gold should be permitted in any pension fund, just as dollars are permitted in a checking account of these funds.

* Repeal of all legal tender laws is a must. Sound money never requires the force of legal tender laws. Only paper money requires such laws.

These proposals, even if put in place tomorrow, would not solve all the problems we face. It would though, legalize freedom of choice in money, and many who worry about having their savings wiped out by a depreciating dollar would at least have another option. This option would ease some of the difficulties that are surely to come from runaway deficits in a weakening economy with skyrocketing inflation.

Curbing the scope of government and limiting its size to that prescribed in the Constitution is the goal that we should seek. But political reality makes this option available to us only after a national bankruptcy has occurred. We need not face that catastrophe. What we need to do is to strictly limit the power of government to meddle in our economy and our personal affairs, and stay out of the internal affairs of other nations.

Conclusion

It's no coincidence that during the period following the establishment of the Federal Reserve and the elimination of the gold standard, a huge growth in the size of the federal government and its debt occurred. Believers in big government, whether on the left or right, vociferously reject the constraints on government growth that gold demands. Liberty is virtually impossible to protect when the people allow their government to print money at will. Inevitably, the left will demand more economic interventionism, the right more militarism and empire building. Both sides, either inadvertently or deliberately, will foster corporatism. Those whose greatest interest is in liberty and self-reliance are lost in the shuffle. Though left and right have different goals and serve different special-interest groups, they are only too willing to compromise and support each other's programs.

If unchecked, the economic and political chaos that comes from currency destruction inevitably leads to tyranny — a consequence of which the Founders were well aware. For 90 years we have lived with a central bank, with the last 32 years absent of any restraint on money creation. The longer the process lasts, the faster the printing presses have to run in an effort to maintain stability. They are currently running at record rate. It was predictable and is understandable that our national debt is now expanding at a record rate.

The panicky effort of the Fed to stimulate economic growth does produce what it considers favorable economic reports, recently citing second quarter growth this year at 3.1%. But in the footnotes, we find that military spending — almost all of which is overseas — was up an astounding 46%. This, of course, represents deficit spending financed by the Federal Reserve's printing press. In the same quarter, after-tax corporate profits fell 3.4%. This is hardly a reassuring report on the health of our economy and merely reflects the bankruptcy of current economic policy.

Real economic growth won't return until confidence in the entire system is restored. And that is impossible as long as it depends on the politicians not spending too much money and the Federal Reserve limiting its propensity to inflate our way to prosperity. Only sound money and limited government can do that.

Dr. Ron Paul is a Republican member of Congress from Texas.

Collective Speeches of Congressman Louis T. McFadden

As Compiled from the Congressional Record

Congressmen Louis T. McFadden
August 18, 1934 - Newsweek

The cover photo appeared in the August 18, 1934 issue of News-Week with the following article.

G. O. P.: Representative McFadden In Role of a Modern Lazarus

In Pennsylvania last week, a man arose biblical-fashion from the land of the dead. The person to achieve this feat was Louis T. McFadden, United States Republican Representative from the G. O. P.'s strongest State.

Mr. McFadden spectacularly sank into oblivion at the tail-end of the Hoover administration. Dec. 13, 1932, the House of Representatives was up to its neck in work. Representative McFadden, arch-harrier of vested interests, strode the length of the gray-carpeted chamber to obtain the floor on a point of constitutional privilege.

As a rule, House orators have to yell to make themselves heard above the clatter of conversation. But as the quiet-mannered Mr. McFadden got under way, the audience snapped to attention, straining to catch every word.

Mr. McFadden had proposed nothing less than impeachment of President Hoover on charges of "high crimes and misdemeanors." To make matters worse, the Representative referred to the President simply as Hoover. When it was announced that the vote to table the resolution was carried by 361-8, cheers and wild applause echoed from the House's glass ceiling. Senator David A. Reed, ranking Republican wheelhorse, declared thenceforth the party would consider apostate McFadden as "dead."

Last week Mr. McFadden came to life under the wing of the National Republican Committee. In a radio address he railed against the New Deal's "pulmotored" prosperity. The ostracized politician seemed once again pulled to the official bosom.

Meanwhile, the "national nuisance," as he was called, was pleased with his return to favor. Glibly he belittled recovery measures. "Don't spend your time worrying over the alleged tyrannies of Hitler," he said. "Look first to your own case."

Louis Thomas McFadden

LOUIS THOMAS MCFADDEN was born in Troy, Bradford County, Pennsylvania on October 1, 1876. He attended public schools and a commercial college. At sixteen he took a job as office boy in the First National Bank in Canton, Pa., a small town near his birthplace. Seven years later he was a cashier, and in 1916 he became the president of the bank. Meanwhile, in 1898, he had married Helen Westgate of Canton, by whom he had three children: two sons and one daughter.

McFadden's political career began in 1914 when he was elected to Congress as Republican representative from the 15th district of Pennsylvania. In 1920, he was appointed chairman of the influential House Committee on Banking and Currency, a position which he held until 1931.

McFadden's later career was marked by violent criticism of his party's financial policies. Opposition to the Hoover moratorium on war debts led him to propose in the House (December 13, 1932) that the President be impeached. He bitterly attacked the governors of the Federal Reserve Board for "having caused the greatest depression we have ever known." Both the President and the Board, he was convinced, were conspiring with the "international bankers" to ruin the country.

McFadden lost his seat to a Democrat in 1934, although two years previously he had had the support of the Republican, Democratic, and Prohibition parties. He died in 1936 while on a visit in New York City.

INTRODUCTION

Few Americans today recognize the names of men like Congressman Charles Augustus Lindbergh, Sr., father of the famed aviator, who fought against the passage of the Federal Reserve Act in 1913 and conducted one of the first investigations of the Banking and Money Trust in Congress; and of Congressman Louis Thomas McFadden. These men spent their lives in heroic combat, as grim and as hopeless as the winter at Valley Forge, but they never admitted the possibility of defeat. And they never lost the courage to go on. But America lost, because America did not support them in their struggle, and America is the loser today.

The province of this volume is to pay homage to but one of these great Americans, Congressman Louis T. McFadden. Congressman Charles A. Lindbergh, Sr. has fortunately already left us a rich legacy of three books published some fifty years ago in which he gives a full account of his inspiring efforts in Congress. (See Bibliography. Ed.)

Congressman Louis T. McFadden was born in the heartland of America, a true product of its original and unadulterated self, and because of that heritage, he could do no else but battle for the land which he loved. And battle he did. Armed with the courage of his convictions and the certitude of his cause he hurled his thundering charges against those who were plundering America and drenching the world in blood with their insane greed. Congressman McFadden refused obeisance to the high priests of Mammon, the International Bankers, for whom he reserved the full force of his attacks. The enormity of his revealments against the Federal Reserve Board and the Federal Reserve Banks will stagger the credibility of the reader.

The din of the battle being waged by Congressman McFadden against his opponents reverberated not only in the halls of Congress but throughout the Capitol. The dean of Washing newspapermen at that time and founder of the National Press Club, Mr. George Stimpson, when asked in later years to comment on the seriousness and magnitude of the charges being made by McFadden he replied, "It was incredible. This town went into a state of shock, we couldn't believe what we were hearing. Of course they said right away that he had lost his mind." "Do you think he had?" Stimpson was asked. "Oh no," came the reply. "But it was too much, too much for one man to do."

It was too much for one man to do, and this proved his heroism. It speaks volumes for the courage and character of Louis T. McFadden that he made these speeches knowing that there was no support, that there would be no support. Was it too quixotic of him? Should he have waited, quietly gathering his information until it could have been put to more practical use?

But why was there no support? We must remember that when McFadden made these speeches we were in the darkest days of the Great Depression, when the nation was prostrate, and in the dark night of the soul of the American people. A sad and defeated nation, destroyed from within, brought to its knees, could offer no help when McFadden opened every door, named every name, exposing every secret of the underground government.

How could any American youth fail to be moved by the spectacle of a small town banker rising to the leadership of our Congressional Committee on Banking and Currency, and, in that capacity, refusing to be bought by those who buy and sell men like cattle? Instead, he nearly brought to a halt the vast and intricate machinations of international bankers and their sinister schemes to attain perpetual and limitless wealth at the expense of an enslaved, drugged and brainwashed population of drone workers. For twenty years, he fought our fight, while we knew little or nothing of his efforts, and when he died, seemingly the record of that struggle was buried with him.

Now we bring it to light, every word faithfully reproduced from the Congressional Record, not only to enshrine his memory in our hearts, but also to give us a standard to which we can rally. We can no longer endure the pitiful half-men, half-women, posturing on the slave block in their efforts to present their best side to the sneering slave-dealers, and we do not refer here to some mythical beings, but rather to the so-called public representatives, the men who have inherited Louis Mc-Fadden's mantle in the Congress of the United States. These men are a poor bargain even for their masters, and even less a bargain are they for us. Let us demand from them the heroism, the self-sacrifice, the patriotism which Louis T. McFadden gave us without our asking for it. And if they do not have it to give, then sweep them out.

Do we dare to admit that everything which has happened to America since the Whiskey Rebellion has been the result of foreign influences, of alien conspiracies carried out through fetid and subterranean corridors of power, the work of the government that dares not speak its name. The Civil War, World War I, the Great Depression, World War II, these were events which were not desired by the American people, they were not planned by the American people, they were not voluntarily entered into by the American people. But all of these events were the result of the planning of men who have no addresses, no fixed homes, no substantial loyalties save only to their own criminal interests. These are men who in healthier times were sent to the gibbet, but today we make them presidents of our banks and universities, and we watch appalled at the chaos and destruction which ensues from their every act.

Let us remember that for ten years, Congressman McFadden had been Chairman of the House Banking and Currency Committee. While exercising the duties of this position he exposed some of the greatest crimes of the century, including his stinging indictment of the Board of Governors of the Federal Reserve System in which he charged them "with having treasonably conspired to destroy constitutional government in the United States."

Because of these exposures, Louis T. McFadden had unleashed the full power of the international criminals against him. When he made these speechs, he was alone. He had nothing to look forward to save his own political demise. The power and pelf of his enemies was brought to bear and the political life of this great servant of the people was terminated in the November 1934 elections held in the 15th Congressional District of Pennsylvania.

Thus these speeches are the personal signature of a great man, a hero fighting to the death, surrounded but never thinking of surrender, the final gesture of a man we should all honor and emulate, an American worthy of the name.

"As a result of the war, corporations have been enthroned and an era of corruption in high places will follow and the MONEY POWER of the country will endeavor to prolong its reign by working on the prejudices of the people until wealth is aggregated in the hands of a few and the Republic is destroyed. I feel at this moment more anxiety for the safety of my country than ever before, even in the midst of war."

—ABRAHAM LINCOLN

Congressman Louis McFadden and Martin B. Madden

I

THE FEDERAL RESERVE SYSTEM AND THE BANK FOR INTERNATIONAL SETTLEMENTS

February 26, 1930

Mr. McFADDEN. Mr. Speaker, I want to refer briefly to one or two things. The month of February is the month in which this country and this House usually celebrates the memory of Washington and Lincoln. Two years from now we are going to celebrate the two hundredth anniversary of the birth of George Washington; and as a text of what I am about to say I want to quote from Washington's Farewell Address, because I think it is a proper text for me to have as an introduction to the remarks which are to follow.

The SPEAKER. The Chair assumes that the gentleman is speaking in his time of one hour?

Mr. McFADDEN. No, Mr. Speaker; I asked for 30 minutes to address the House out of order not to be taken out of the hour.

The SPEAKER. The Chair understood that that was objected to. The gentleman from Pennsylvania asks unanimous consent to proceed for 30 minutes out of order. Is there objection?

There was no objection.

Mr. McFADDEN. I read from Washington's Farewell Address:

Against the insidious wiles of foreign influence (I conjure you to believe me fellow citizens), the jealousy of a free people ought to be constantly awake; since history and experience prove that foreign influence is one of the most baneful foes of republican government. But that jealousy, to be useful, must be impartial, else it becomes the instrument of the very influence to be avoided, instead of a defense against it. Excessive partiality for one foreign nation and excessive dislike for another, cause those whom they actuate to see danger only on one side, and serve to veil and even second the arts of influence on the other. Real patriots, who may resist the intrigues of the favorite, are liable to become suspected and odious; while its tools and dupes usurp the applause and confidence of the people, to surrender their interests.

The great rule of conduct for us, in regard to foreign nations, is, in extending our commercial relations, to have with them as little political connection as possible. So far as we have already formed engagements, let them be fulfilled with perfect good faith. Here let us stop.

Mr. Speaker, reports emanating from Frankfort, Germany, the latter part of January stated that Gates W. McGarrah, chairman of the board and Federal reserve agent of the Federal Reserve Bank of New York, was to become chairman of the board of directors of the Bank for International Settlements. Confirmation of this assumption has appeared in the New York papers during the past week, and on February 22, Washington's Birthday, the New York Times said in its headlines:

G. L. Harrison sails for bank policy. Local Federal reserve's head will confer abroad on gold and other problems. Wide interest aroused. America's part in operation of international bank expected to be discussed.

2

The article states that Mr. Harrison, who is governor of the Federal Reserve Bank of New York, sailed for Europe on last Friday evening on the *Majestic;* that during his stay abroad he will visit the principal European correspondents of the reserve bank; that this trip is particularly opportune, coming at a time when the central banks of Europe and this country are faced with a number of perplexing problems, and stresses particularly the foreign-exchange markets and the international gold situation. The article says that he will have discussions with the governors of the Bank of England and the Bank of France, and incidentally mentions that another subject to come up for discussion, when the governors of the central banks meet, is the part which the Federal reserve is expected to play in the operation of the Bank for International Settlements, which is soon to be established at Basel, Switzerland. It adds that the governors of the banks of issue are expected to meet in Rome to elect a board of directors of the international bank and at that time they will choose the American directors of the institution and extend invitations to them. The article states further that it has become a regular practice in recent years for the governors of the European central banks and the governor of the Federal Reserve Bank of New York to visit each other for the purpose of considering central banking problems and refers to the two visits to America last year of Montague Norman, governor of the Bank of England.

It will be recalled that on the first visit of Governor Norman a definite change of Federal reserve policy took place—a policy of inflation to a policy of deflation. On his second visit, further restrictive measures were agreed upon and put into operation both by the Federal reserve system and the Bank of England, and shortly thereafter the financial debacle of last October occurred.

There is no question about the importance of these conferences between the governor of the Federal Reserve Bank of New York and these foreign bankers. The article quoted further states that it is the policy of the Bank of England and of the Federal Reserve Bank of New York to describe these interchange of visits of their governors as "vacations," and that no significance is ever attached to them in official circles, and the social aspects of the trips are stressed.

However, the news item mentioned must be based on some official statement issued by the Federal Reserve Bank of New York; and I am now inquiring as to whether it is true that the Federal Reserve Bank of New York is proceeding contrary to the administration's policy as described by Secretary Stimson, of the Department of State, on May 19, 1929. I believe that the State Department should immediately call upon the Federal Reserve Board for full information regarding any activities of the officers and directors of the Federal reserve banks, and the board itself may have engaged in, in connection with the organization or proposed operations of the Bank for International Settlements. If the State Department does not do this, we can feel justified in assuming that the department's statement of last May meant nothing, and was issued for some other purpose than the impression that it created at that time. The statement was apparently intended to be definite and complete in expressing administration opposition to our being involved officially in any way with the machinery or affairs of the international bank. Does this mean that the Federal reserve management has been acting contrary to a mandate of the State Department? If the Federal reserve management is participating in any manner in the discussions attending the organization of the Bank for International Settlements, so as to insure the control and management of all international financial transactions between this country and other countries through the use of the assets of the Federal reserve system, it apparently means that the participation of the country in the Bank for International Settlements is to be by and through the banking house of J. P. Morgan & Co. I insist that Congress should be fully advised and that legislative authority for such relationship with J. P. Morgan & Co. to represent the Federal reserve system in all international financial operations should be considered, or the right of the Federal reserve system to participate indirectly by and through the private banking house of J. P.

Morgan & Co. in their contact on international matters should be forbidden.

Let me analyze for a moment the position of the State Department as regards the vexing question of German reparations. The position of the Government is clearly stated that it does not desire to have any American official directly or indirectly participate in the collection of German reparations through the agency of the Bank for International Settlements, and in this its position is perfectly consistent. Our Government has never accepted membership on the Reparation Commission. It has declined to join the allied powers in the confiscation of the sequestered German property and the application of that property to its war claims. It does not now wish to take any step which would indicate a reversal of that attitude, and therefore it issued the statement of May 19, 1929, that it would not permit any officials of the Federal reserve system either to themselves serve or to select American representatives as members of the proposed international bank.

To make clear the position that the United States does not propose to tie up German reparations with the payment of loans owed to this Government by foreign countries, I desire to quote from the *Yale Review*, winter of 1930, issue an article on the war debts by Gerrard Winston, former Undersecretary of the Treasury and secretary of the Debt Refunding Commission, as follows:

> The American policy of making each loan on the sole credit of the particular borrower and refusing to accept any substitution of debtors began when the first dollar was loaned. It runs through each Liberty bond issue and every document and governmental action. The statement in the Balfour note that we loaned other nations on England's credit was sharply contradicted and its incorrectness admitted. The plan to have the United States accept Germany as debtor on the Belgian prearmistice loans was declined. The law authorizing the debt settlements specifically prohibited any substitution of debtors. In each settle-

5

ment the ability to pay of the particular debtor was alone considered. If anything could establish an American policy it has been done; step after step consistently the United States has insisted that the war debts to it were not to be conditioned upon German reparation payments. This was sound policy. We wanted to stay clear of European entanglements and to treat with those to whom we loaned money, not with strangers. In this there was also logic because our debts represented war costs, and under the armistice terms and the treaty of Versailles, Germany was not required to pay any war costs of the Allies. So much for the American policy. Europe to-day boasts, and boasts loudly, that it has finally outmaneuvered the United States. In the Young plan Europe thinks that it has tied together reparations and war debts. It has already been suggested that France, for example, by directing the new international bank to collect from Germany the reparations representing its debt to the United States, and to pay these sums over to the United States, relieves itself of all obligations to America. Mr. Winston Churchill an energetic protagonist of British debt views, has indicated that England has no further interest in war debts so long as Germany pays. This, of course, does not represent the view of the administration at Washington.

The concurrent memorandum, attached to the Young plan, and not signed by the American experts, is an interesting example of the game which must have gone on during those months of negotiation in Paris. The German reparation installments are fixed for the first 37 years to cover reparations and war debts, and for the last 22 years to cover only war debts. The concurrent memorandum provides that in the first period the benefit of any reduction of war debts goes two-thirds to Germany and one-third to the war debtor, and in the last period all benefit accrues to Germany. If the Allies want to collect from Germany only enough to pay their war debts, why should they retain a one-third interest in any cancellation, or why should

6

this be for a part and not all? It is amusing to note the way hoped-for charity from America has been used for chips in the international poker game.

None can avoid the proposition that reparations and war debts have a connection. Receipts from Germany give a nation funds in addition to what it raises from taxation, with which to pay its debts, to the benefit of both debtor and creditor. But to step beyond this and argue that the war debtor may force his creditor to release him and to accept a new debtor, is an attempt to make a new contract for the creditor against his consent. To take a simple example, I may loan a sum of money to a young man having a small salary and allowance from his father. If the allowance stops, perhaps my loan is endangered, but if in the meantime the young man has materially increased his salary my loan is still good. Certainly I would object to being told I must look to the allowance alone for repayment. If German reparations fail, a nation could, if it saw fit, refuse to fulfill its solemn undertaking represented by its debt settlement. If it had any other means of payment, this refusal could not be justified by any Young plan or any bank for international settlements. It would be simply repudiation—a privilege accorded alone to sovereignty.

I have referred previously to the fact that the Bank for International Settlements comes from the creative mind of the vice chairman of the board of the Federal Reserve Bank of New York, and have pointed out that the assistant Federal reserve agent of the Federal Reserve Bank of New York was in close consultation with its sponsors at Paris at the launching of the bank during the formulation of the Young plan. I have shown how the present chairman of the board of the Federal reserve bank became a director of the Reichsbank of Germany under the Dawes plan, and I have referred to the fact that the first chairman of the board of the Federal Reserve Bank of New York resigned his position and accepted a position under the reparations agent in Germany, who was charged with the responsibility of collecting German reparations funds. I have shown how the chairman of the board and the present Federal reserve agent of the Federal Reserve Bank of New York is to become president and a director of the Bank for International Settlements, and I have quoted from last Saturday's *New York Times* from a statement showing that the governor of the Federal Reserve Bank of New York sailed last Friday to confer with the heads of the foreign banks of issue who are to become directors and officers of the Bank for International Settlements, and that while he is abroad an important meeting is to be held in Rome, Italy, when the final consummation of the board of directors and all details looking toward the opening of the bank is to be held.

At this point I wish to make a statement in regard to the meetings of the heads of the central banks so that we may understand exactly how this close-working arrangement started and has continued.

Mr. WINGO. Before the gentleman leaves that subject will he yield?

Mr. McFADDEN. I yield to the gentleman.

Mr. WINGO. Is it not a fair assumption that the State Department has the same information before it as the gentleman has?

Mr. McFADDEN. I do not know.

Mr. WINGO. They can read as well as the gentleman. Does not the gentleman know that everything that has been done has been done with the full knowledge of the State Department and the Federal Reserve Board?

Mr. McFADDEN. The statement issued by the Secretary of State last May would not indicate that such was the case.

Mr. WINGO. That was an academic statement intended—from the gentleman's standpoint—as camouflage. The fact is that the Federal Reserve Bank of New York goes contrary to the policy of the Federal Reserve Board after consultation with the board, and they have not condemned it. Has the gentleman got any inside information as to why the Secretary of

State and the board are being overruled?

Mr. McFADDEN. I am taking the statement as shown on the face of it, and that no other information is apparently being given out.

Mr. WINGO. The gentleman is not so unsophisticated as to know that the intention is to slip us into the League of Nations by the back door.

Mr. McFADDEN. I think that is exactly what is taking place.

Mr. WINGO. Why not call on them to give you the information directly? Why not introduce a resolution asking the President to give you the information?

Mr. McFADDEN. Before I finish my remarks the gentleman will be satisfied with the course that I propose taking.

Mr. WINGO. No; I will be frank with the gentleman. I think it is the duty of the gentleman to say to his own State Department and his own Federal Reserve Board—if I were to do it they would say, "Oh, the Democrats are playing politics." The gentleman knows that they are doing the things of which he complains with the consent of the State Department and the Federal Reserve Board, and if it is wrong why does not the gentleman take the necessary steps to prevent these things?

Mr. McFADDEN. I will say to the gentleman that I have prepared and am about to introduce a resolution calling upon the Secretary of State and the Secretary of the Treasury to furnish this Congress with full detailed information with regard to this matter.

Mr. WINGO. And in the meantime the devilment is going on, a meeting is being held in Rome, and we are being committed to these things. Why wait until the horse is stolen before we lock the door? Why not take some action instead of talking about it, assuming the gentleman's charges are true?

Mr. McFADDEN. I began to discuss this matter a year ago, and I discussed it in this House 10 days ago. However, there was no apparent notice of it either by the State Department or the Federal Reserve Board. I have concluded, and part of my remarks here to-day is an indication of a definite action by the introduction of two resolutions which have a preferred

9

status in this case, and if they are not acted on immediately the House can act on the matter itself.

Mr. WINGO. Is it not true that the administration assumes that since the Senator from Missouri, Mr. Reed, has gone that they can safely get away with this, and that the only person who criticizes it is the gentleman from Pennsylvania. [Mr. McFADDEN], who talks about it but does nothing?

Mr. McFADDEN. The gentleman is talking about the Senate, and a mere Member of the House would not want to discuss the procedure in the Senate.

Mr. WINGO. I am talking about an ex-Member of the Senate. The gentleman is apparently the only defender of the Washingtonian theory against entangling alliances, so the administration feels safe. Uncle Andy is not scared by what the gentleman is saying is he? If they are doing wrong, why does not the gentleman by proper resolution say they shall not do it, that they shall not turn the Federal reserve system into a partnership with these European banks and unload on us the German reparations bonds and make us pay Germany's debts to the Allies?

Mr. McFADDEN. Let us get the information first correctly from the departments.

The year 1923 witnessed the culmination of the postwar crisis in European finance. Monetary conditions were in a state of chaos. Exchanges were completely demoralized. The League of Nations, realizing this critical situation, elaborated and put into operation a reconstruction scheme, and, in cooperation with the governments which were relinquishing their priority claims and guaranteeing a portion of the reconstruction loans, enabled Austria to obtain the funds required for the stabilization of the kron. The Bank of England made an advance to the Austrian national banks for stabilization purposes between the period of the conclusion of the agreements and the actual issue of the loan. This support was the first public act of cooperation between central banks after the war.

Prior to that the only knowledge we have of central-bank cooperation was in the case of the Bank of France with the

Bank of England during the Baring crisis.

During the war there was, of course, some cooperation between the allied central banks, and also between the Reichsbank and other banks of issue among the German allies. It was not, however, until after the war that a systematic movement was attempted and, it was largely, if not exclusively, due to the initiative of Mr. Montague Norman, governor of the Bank of England, through his personal friendship and with the late Benjamin Strong, governor of the Federal Reserve Bank of New York, that the United States was induced to cooperate financially, if not politically, in European affairs. Most of Mr. Norman's work for reconstruction was done behind the scenes. The alliance began with a select group of leading institutions, but later included almost all of European central banks. Nor was it confined to Europe and the Federal reserve system—or more particularly the Federal Reserve Bank of New York—which played the leading part from the outset. The Japanese and the Egyptian banks of issue were also aided. There were some indications that eventually all central banks within and outside of Europe would cooperate. Two purposes were to be served—monetary stabilization and the prevention of a scramble for gold by central banks. There was also a secondary objective, which was a means to an end rather than an end itself; that is, the establishment of closer business relations between central banks, which would at the same time help solve the problem of reparations transfers.

The promise of an advance made at the instance of the League of Nations by the cooperating banks, principally the Bank of England, to the Austrian National Bank enabled Austria to benefit by the loan months before it was actually issued. Similar services were rendered to the Hungarian National Bank.

When it came to Germany's turn to be assisted, a group of central banks was formed to support the Reichsbank by means of placing capital at the disposal of the gold discount banks. In this a large number of central banks participated. The stabilization of the franc, the lira, the zloty, the drachma, and the

11

other units of exchange was carried on through the aid of the credits granted by the grouping of central banks, and, as I have already said, this cooperation was, of course, given to the restoration of the gold standard in Great Britain. This, however, was granted exclusively by the Federal reserve system.

Although the efforts of central banks were generally conducted within the League of Nation's scheme, on occasions they acted independently. Take the case of Poland, for instance. There a plan was arranged without any assistance from the League of Nations by a group of central banks. Assistance was also given to Rumania by the central banks, notwithstanding the fact that there was some controversy as between the Franco-American scheme and the League of Nations scheme.

Similar credits were granted for stabilization purposes to Bulgaria and Estonia, under the auspices of the League of Nations. Such assistance was also given, though principally by the Bank of England, to Greece, Asia Minor, and parts of Turkey, and the Bank of England assisted the Bank of Danzig. The Bank of Spain was, during this period, assisted by Anglo-American banking groups, headed by the Midland Bank of London and J. P. Morgan & Co. It was indicated, and probably not without reason, that this loan was made on the principles of the finance committee of the league, which were largely inspired from Threadneedle Street. It is perfectly plain that the assistance given by these central banks to those countries desirous of stabilizing their currency was not prompted exclusively by philanthropic considerations. There were many self-benefits to be derived.

The second principal aim of this movement of cooperation between central banks was the regulation of the demand for gold for central banks. Although the principal holders of gold are willing to assist these central banks in their endeavor to build up their gold stocks, they have a natural desire to prevent any sudden demand upon their own resources. Take the case of New York. Heavy withdrawals by a number of foreign central banks could be very embarrassing. This applies equally to London. Inasmuch as the gold stock is greater in New York than in London, a lesser withdrawal from London would be more embarrassing. Because of this fact, these central banks, which includes the Federal Reserve Bank of New York, have reached an understanding by which central banks try not to withdraw any gold from one without the others consent, and the same principle governs the earmarking and release of gold held by the Bank of England and by the Federal Reserve Bank of New York on account of foreign central banks. This is a splendid working arrangement for these foreign banks of issue who are hard put to maintain sufficient gold to back their legal reserve requirements.

Another auxiliary, beside the cooperation of central banks, which has been used to facilitate their task of the transfer of funds, is the agent general for reparation payments. These arrangements have been largely made and carried out behind the scenes and the agent general for reparation payments has frequently participated in the conferences of the central banks.

That Montague Norman, Governor of the Bank of England, is the moving spirit in all of these international economic, financial, and political relationships involving the Federal reserve system there can be no doubt, nor can there be any doubt that it was his influence over the late Governor Strong that brought about the active cooperation of the Federal Reserve Bank of New York, thus involving the Federal reserve system. His frequent visits here—some of them very secretive—particularly his visit in 1926 when the conference took place in the Treasury Department between the head of the Reichsbank, the head of the Bank of France, and the reparations agent in regard to a plan involving the pledging of the railways of Germany back of a note issue which was to be underwritten in France, Germany, and the United States, and which, I understand, was agreed to by our Treasury authorities, but was headed off by President Coolidge, further indicates the tie-up of reparations international bank conferences and the Federal reserve system with international affairs. If this plan had not been blocked by President Coolidge, we would have witnessed a commercialization of the German war debt and a transference

13

from the allied countries, to whom Germany owed these debts, to the private investors of these countries and the United States. It was proposed in the treaty of Versailles that the German war debt should be commercialized and unloaded upon the United States. So the framers of the Dawes and Young plans and the reparations agents and the international bankers have not changed—they never do; they still intend to do this in some way. They know not defeat.

Mr. RAMSEYER. Mr. Speaker, will the gentleman yield?

Mr. McFADDEN. Yes.

Mr. RAMSEYER. The gentleman speaks of an agreement made in the treaty of Versailles about unloading this on the United States. That was not incorporated in the treaty.

Mr. McFADDEN. Oh, no.

Mr. RAMSEYER. It is probably an understanding on the outside with the international bankers?

Mr. McFADDEN. Oh, yes; it is clearly read in between the lines.

It will be plainly seen how closely these conferences have to do with the financial department of the League of Nations, reparations, and international financial transactions. These conferences, originating with the governor of the Bank of England, have become so important a part of European economic, financial, and political affairs that they are to be given a legal status by centering their future activities in the Bank for International Settlements. Because of this fact we are about to witness another one of these important conferences between central banks, at which conference the finishing touches will be put upon the organization of this International Bank for Settlements.

The plan of the organizers of this bank indicates that its board of directors is to be composed of the governors of the Banks of England, Belgium, France, Italy, and one other director of each of these banks, and that Gates W. McGarrah, now chairman of the board of the Federal Reserve Bank of New York, and Leon Fraser are to represent J. P. Morgan & Co., the managers; and I quote an article from the *New York Herald-*

14

Tribune, "World's Bank Directorate Nearly Filled," bearing a Washington headline, as follows:

WORLD'S BANK DIRECTORATE NEARLY FILLED—MOREAU AND BRINCARD TO SERVE FOR FRANCE; ADDIS FOR BRITAIN; McGARRAH AND FRASER FOR AMERICA

WASHINGTON, February 18.—The make-up of the board of directors of the Bank for International Settlements has been virtually completed, it was learned in authoritative circles here to-day, and an announcement of the names of the directors chosen by the governors of the several central banks is expected to be made from Rome next week.

The French directors, it is learned definitely, will be Emile Moreau, governor of the Bank of France; Baron Brincard, president of the Credit Lyonnaise, one of the largest commercial banks in Paris; and Baron der Vogue, president of the Suez Canal Co.

One of the two English directors will be Sir Charles Addis, vice president of the Hong Kong and Shanghai Bank, who was a delegate, following the death of Lord Revelstoke, to the experts' conference which drew up the Young plan in Paris a year ago. Whether Montague Norman, governor of the Bank of England, will exercise his prerogative, as Governor Moreau is exercising his, to name himself to the international bank's board is not yet known, but it is considered quite likely.

BELGIUM'S TWO DIRECTORS

Belgium's two directors will be Emile Franqui, vice governor of the Societe Generale de Belgique, Brussels, who was a member of both the Young and Dawes plan committees, and Paul van Zeeland, of the Bank of Belgium, who is now a member of the subcommittee which is completing plans for the setting up of the new bank.

The United States will have Gates W. McGarrah, now chairman of the board and Federal reserve agent of the Federal Reserve Bank of New York, and Leon Fraser,

New York attorney, who for three years was general counsel for the Dawes plan on the board of directors of the international bank.

Indication has not yet come from Germany as to the names of the three directors which the country will be allowed to have on the bank's board. Well-informed persons here have heard rumors of the identity of the German directors, but as the reports are unofficial it is not known how much faith should be placed in them. No information is yet available regarding Italy's directors, although it is held quite probable that Governor Stringher, of the Bank of Italy, will himself serve as one of the directors.

MEETING IN ROME FEBRUARY TWENTY-SIXTH

Governor Norman, of the Bank of England; Governor Moreau, of the Bank of France; Governor Franck, of the Bank of Belgium; Governor Schacht, of the Reichsbank; and Governor Stringher, of the Bank of Italy, are scheduled to meet in Rome on February 26 to compile finally the list of directors of the new bank. Inasmuch as it is already agreed—except, perhaps, in the case of Germany— just who the bank's directors will be, it is thought that the governors will announce the names of the international bank's directors on the first day of their meeting in Rome.

Another matter for the governors to decide at their Rome meeting is whether Pierre Quesnay, of the Bank of France, will receive the appointment as managing director of the new bank. He is favored by most of the nations which will be directly interested in the international, but opposition to his appointment has developed in Germany.

It was originally planned that the central bank governors would meet in Rome on February 15, but at the last moment a postponement until next week was asked by one of the governors.

The information here is that Mr. McGarrah and Mr. Fraser most likely will sail for Europe within the next two weeks, probably around March 1, and will proceed to Basel, Switzerland, where the new bank will be located, for the first meeting of directors probably on March 10. At that meeting the directors are scheduled to proceed formally with the election of Mr. McGarrah as chairman of the board and president of the bank of international settlements. It is expected that from among the directors several vice presidents will be chosen. The information reaching Washington is that Mr. Fraser will be selected deputy president of the bank and charged with the responsibility of presiding at meetings of the board of directors when Mr. McGarrah is absent.

MOREAU HELPED STABILIZE FRANC

Emile Moreau has been governor of the Bank of France, one of the most important banks of issue in the world, since 1926, having been appointed by Premier Cailleaux to succeed Governor Robineau. Governor Moreau played a prominent role in the stabilization of the French franc, and his work in defending the franc and insuring its stability was recognized by his promotion in February, 1927, to the rank of grand officer of the Legion of Honor.

M. Moreau began his banking career in 1906 when he was appointed a director of the Bank of Algeria. Five years later he was made its director general. As governor of the Bank of France, M. Moreau occupies an unusually important role in the world finance because of the large gold reserve now at the institution's command.

Baron Brincard is one of France's commercial bankers by virtue of the position he holds as president of the administrative council of Credit Lyonnaise. Baron Brincard also is an administrator of the Society Fonciere Lyonnaise, of the Credit Union of National Industry, and of the Compagnie des Forges de Chatillon. He is an officer of the Legion of Honor.

Sir Charles Stewart Addis is a British financial authority of international reputation. Born in November, 1861, he received an appointment in 1880 to the London office of

17

the Hong Kong and Shanghai Bank. In 1886 he was sent to China as manager of the bank's Peking branch, where he remained until 1905, when he was recalled to become joint manager in London. In 1911 he was appointed London manager of the Hong Kong and Shanghai Bank, and in 1913 was knighted.

ADDIS CONFERRED AT PARIS

After the Dawes plan was adopted he was made British representative on the general council of the Reichsbank, a position which Mr. McGarrah has held for the United States. He was appointed alternate to the experts conference in Paris early last year, and upon the death of Lord Revelstoke he was named head of the British delegation to the conference.

The board of directors of the international bank will have no more colorful member than Emile Francqui, of Belgium, former Minister of Finance, veteran of the Congo and China, who, because of his efforts to stabilize the Belgian franc, was to Belgium what Poincare was to France. He was described at the Paris conference, where he was the chief Belgian delegate, as "a physically magnified Poincare, sharp and unreserved where the French Premier is cold and impersonal. M. Francqui has been described as burly of figure, burly of voice." He is rated as the richest man in Belgium and among the 12 richest men in Europe. When M. Franck sees fit to retire as the governor of the Bank of Belgium M. Francqui is slated to succeed him.

HELPED FRAME DAWES PLAN

In 1924 M. Francqui was a member of the committee which drew up the Dawes plan. Two years later, when the Belgian currency began its rapid descent, he was appointed Minister of Finance, and in a few weeks succeeded in stabilizing the currency and floating the funded debt. After having completed this task he resigned his portfolio and resumed his business career. He is now vice governor

18

of the Societe Generale de Belgique.

Paul Van Zeeland was associate delegate to the Baden-Baden conference last fall, at which the statutes of the Bank for International Settlements were drawn-up. He attended the later meetings of the bank's organization committee at The Hague last month and was appointed a member of the subcommittee to perfect the final plans for the opening of the bank in April.

Mr. Siepman, of the Bank of England, who also has been serving on the bank's subcommittee, is slated to become associated with the new institution in some capacity, although it is felt unlikely that he will be named a director. Mr. Siepman has had charge of the Bank of England's relations with other central banks and in this work has gained a wide acquaintance in European banking circles. It is believed that he will be engaged by the international bank in a similar capacity.   [END OF ARTICLE.]

As soon as the organization is perfected and the bank opened under the Young plan, almost the first business will be to supervise the issuance of $300,000,000 worth of reparations bonds. Of this issue the plan contemplates the sale in this country of $100,000,000 or more of these reparations bonds or as much more as the American market will absorb, to be immediately followed by a further bond issue of many hundreds of millions of dollars. Accredited authorities estimate that the United States is to absorb within the next five or six years between five and six billion dollars' worth of these German reparation bonds. I respectfully invite the attention of our State Department to this announced plan and ask them whether or not they are going to give their approval publicly or by silence to an exploitation of the American public in this manner. The State Department has heretofore assumed to pass upon or disapprove issues of securities by foreign countries to be sold in the American market, which precedent should establish a definite responsibility in this particular instance.

In view of the fact that the Morgan firm is very shortly

19

going to offer these securities to the American investing public, I desire now to raise the question definitely as to the legality of these reparation bonds, proposed to be issued and sold in part to the American people through the house of J. P. Morgan & Co. and the Bank for International Settlements.

Mr. Briggs. Mr. Speaker, will the gentleman yield?

Mr. McFadden. Yes.

Mr. Briggs. The effect of that would be to transfer from European nations to the United States the relationship of creditor to Germany with respect to reparations.

Mr. McFadden. I think the gentleman is correct. My attention has just been directed to a stipulation in the convention of April 1, 1920, articles 5 and 8, which has to do with the pledge of the property and income of the Federal States in Germany under the Dawes plan as continued under the Young plan. This act provided, and has been so interpreted by the councilor of the Reichsgericht, that the Government must have the consent beforehand of the interested State. And the Reichstag in August, 1924, was advised by the representatives of several of the States when they voted against the railway law, then under consideration, that they were compelled to abstain because they were not authorized to consent to the pledging of the States' property for the funding of the Government debts contracted before the 1st of April, 1920, which, of course, means the war debts, the payment for which these reparation bonds are to be issued.

From the German legal point of view, this matter is of far-reaching importance and can not be brushed aside by any well-meaning or plausible arguments which do not alter the basic fact of legality. It is important for us to understand in this connection that the Reichsgericht is the supreme court of justice, the Reichstag is the parliament, the Reichsrath is the empire council, and the Landtag is the States' legislature. Let us bear in mind that the Young plan, of which the Bank for International Settlements is a part, was submitted for ratification to the German Reichsrath, the empire council, and not a parliamentary institution. The members of this council are not elected; they are the direct delegates of the various governments of the Federal States. They are consequently State officials and absolutely independent of the German Government. The German Government concluded a convention with the German States, dated April 1, 1920, wherein the German Government was declared to be a trustee for the railways. Therefore, this convention was in fact a charter fixing and limiting body of the German Government to manage the railways. Incidentally, the railways own the properties of the Federal States. In this connection, I wish to refer to part 3 (a) of the Young plan dealing with the composition of the annuities. The "railway company" as mentioned in this plan is an administrative body appointed by the German Government and consequently has no connection with the Federal States. Therefore, the railway company is under the direction and exclusive control of the German Government and the power granted by the latter to it is limited by the convention of April 1, 1920. By article 8 of that convention the German Government can not pledge the revenues of the railways except with the express consent of the various States. This consent, I understand, the German Government has never received, either under the Dawes plan or the Young plan, although the Reichstag, the parliament, has ratified the Dawes plan. This ratification, however, does not bind the independent legislatures of the Federal States who alone can decide such matters; consequently the German Government has pledged the revenues of the railways to the foreign countries. It would appear that it expects, by this method, to confiscate the properties belonging to the Federal States. This decision is most important, as article 5 of the convention of April, 1920, expressly stipulates that the revenues of the railways can not be applied for war-debt payments. Therefore, I insist that the Reichsgericht, the supreme court of Germany, can cancel such confiscation authority which, if done, will release the German Government of any guaranty to her former allies on account of war debts, as a fundamental illegal act can not have a legal responsibility.

Mr. BRIGGS. Mr. Speaker, will the gentleman yield?

21

Mr. McFadden. Yes.

Mr. Briggs. Assuming that what the gentleman predicts is correct, that the ultimate intention is to float about five or six billion dollars worth of bonds, largely to be absorbed in the United States, what recourse would the bondholders have within the United States for the payment of the bonds in the event of default thereon?

Mr. McFadden. I think they would have all kinds of difficulties and would probably be appealing to their Government for relief?

Mr. Briggs. In other words, the United States would have to come to the rescue, as far as it could, and meet those obligations, and its only recourse would be upon Germany in that case?

Mr. McFadden. Yes.

Mr. Briggs. With the resulting pressure to be relieved of these responsibilities as part of the war debts, as time goes on?

Mr. McFadden. Yes.

Mr. Briggs. In other words, leaving the United States to bear and absorb the reparations which Germany undertakes to pay to the European allies?

Mr. McFadden. The gentleman is correct. I am dealing more fully with that situation a little later on.

Part 8 of the Young plan provides that the basis of payment under the Dawes plan shall cease as of August 31, 1929, and that from the effective date of the Young plan, Germany's previous obligation shall be entirely replaced by the obligation laid down in the later plan, and that the payment in full of the proposed annuities in accordance with this plan shall be accepted by the creditor powers as a final discharge of all the liabilities of Germany still remaining undischarged, referred to in section 11, part 1, of the Dawes plan as subsequently interpreted under the London agreement of August 30, 1924. This means that the Bank for International Settlements is to collect the reparation payments and distribute them to the former allies.

Now, I desire to point out that if the railway contributions under the Dawes plan were illegal, it stands to reason that, in accordance with the convention of April, 1920, as interpreted by the Supreme Court of Germany, it is also illegal for the contribution to be effected under the Young plan. The amount of annual contributions under the Dawes as well as under the Young plan are 660,000,000 gold marks. One difference is that the bonds which were delivered by the railway, according to the Dawes plan, will be destroyed, and in lieu thereof the railway must deliver a certificate acknowledging that the debt will be paid. A further difference is that in the Dawes plan annual payments were called contributions but under the Young plan they will be called taxes. This is flagrantly an instance of doing in an indirect way what can not be legally done in a direct way and is absolutely illegal.

If competent legal German authority is to be believed—and I am relying on the opinion of Doctor Hüfner, who is councilor of the Reichsgericht, a position similar to a member of the Supreme Court of the United States—the promoters of the Dawes plan have completely disregarded the German laws. This must necessarily continue to create a chain of irregularities with disastrous consequences.

For your further information, I desire to call your attention to paragraphs on pages 773-774 of the Reichsgesetzblatt No. 95, 1920, as follows:

SECTION FIVE—SECURITY

1. The Reich is pledged to pay the amounts of interest and amortization for the consolidated debts which it has assumed, and for that part of the settlement which was not covered by taking over the debts of the states in the first place, from the gross surplus of the Reich Railway Administration (surplus of the ordinary revenues over continuous expenses). The items of income and expenditure which are contained in chapters 3 and 87 of the budget of the Reich Railroad for the financial year 1918 are considered ordinary income and continuous expenditure. The responsibility of the Reich is not altered in case a gross surplus is not attained or in case the gross surplus

does not suffice to cover the amounts of interest and amortization.

2. The capital and revenues of the Reich Railroad Administration are not responsible for debts incurred by the Reich prior to April 1, 1920.

3. Upon the demand of a state, the Reich, in order to safeguard for the states that part of the settlement allowing time for payment, will grant a lien to the land and other property belonging to the railroad enterprises of the Reich.

SECTION EIGHT—SALE, MORTGAGE

The Reich must have the sanction of the state governments to any sale or mortgage of the railroads which have been acquired under this contract.

If contrary views are held by the creditors of Germany in regard to this matter, they can not alter the facts. If they are accepting, as they apparently are, the decision of the Reichstag, they must also accept the higher German authority of the Reichsgericht. Because of these facts, the bonds, when issued, will be subject to repudiation. I consider this matter of the highest importance and point to the fact that the colossal war debt in Europe is not considered to be a commercial debt, and in authoritative German quarters it is no secret that they propose to take advantage of this irregularity. Also I would point to the fact that the late Minister Stresemann disclosed categorically that Germany means to pay only for a period of 10 years, while the Young plan contemplates payment over a period of 58 years. So just suppose that we are to believe the statement of that most distinguished statesman in regard to this matter; that in 10 years there will be billions of dollars worth of German reparation bonds in the United States, owned by our citizens, purchased through the Bank for International Settlements and the house of J. P. Morgan & Co., indirectly assisted by the Federal reserve system. What will the situation be in this country if repudiation takes place? And I call your attention specifically to Article IV of the Constitution of the United States, by which financial obligations of the various States are restricted to the United States. A number of the States of this Union have taken advantage of this restriction to repudiate the debts contracted to foreign countries, and I point to the fact that this repudiation by the States is still a matter of serious controversy between England and the United States.

Mr. Ramseyer. Mr. Speaker, will the gentleman yield?

Mr. McFadden. Yes.

Mr. Ramseyer. With regard to the statement of Herr Stresemann, was that made in a public address before the Reichstag? I never hear of it before.

Mr. McFadden. I hold in my hands at this time a copy of the *London Times* dated June 25, 1929, and refer to an article headed Reparations—Germany and the Young Plan. It is dated Berlin, June 24, and is from the *London Times* correspondent, reporting the proceedings of that day, in which the language of Stresemann was quoted.

Mr. Ramseyer. Was that speech made in the Reichstag?

Mr. McFadden. In the Reichstag. I read:

> "Do you think," Herr Stresemann asked the Nationalists, "that any member of the Government regards the Young plan as ideal? Do you believe that any individual can give a guaranty for its fulfillment? Do you believe that anybody in the world expects such a guaranty from us? The plan would only represent in the first place a settlement for the coming decade. The point is whether it loosens the shackles which fetter us and lightens the burdens which we have yet to fulfill."

I am citing this to show that here is apparently a precedent which is of very great moment affecting the validity of these reparation bonds.

In connection with the possible repudiation, I desire to quote from the February 15, 1930, issue of the *London Economist*, page 351, an article headed "The Reichstag and the Young

25

COLLECTIVE SPEECHES OF HON. LOUIS T. MCFADDEN

Plan," which refers to the bill then pending before the Reichsrath as the "Bill for the Enslavement of the German People," saying that this is as the German Nationalists have dubbed the bill to ratify the Young plan, and on the question of possible repudiation, I quote from this article following:

> The most interesting contribution to the debate was the description by the Minister of Finance, Doctor Moldenhaur, of what would happen if Germany demanded a moratorium. The creditor powers would forthwith declare a moratorium for their payments to America, and the whole matter would then have to be fundamentally reconsidered. * * * The most doubtful point in this forecast is the suggested ability and willingness of the creditor powers to suspend payment to America. Whether such a moratorium were declared or not, it is perfectly plain that any fundamental revision of the Young plan settlement must depend on the attitude toward the war debts adopted by the United States, and it is well that Germany should realize that fact.

Press reports under date of February 24 indicate that—

> The ratification by the Reichstag of the Young plan and Germany's various liquidation pacts may now be deferred until the middle of March owing to the Cabinet's inability to complete its program of financial reforms. Dr. Paul Moldenhauer, Minister of Finance, has not been able to find a solution to the vexed problem of meeting the old and new deficits with which he is confronted by the change in the present method of including unemployment doles in the regular budget. * * * The secret debate on the Young plan and the liquidation of the pacts which has been going on for the past 10 days in the joint sessions of the Reichstag's budget and foreign relations committees will be concluded this week, but no plan of agreement has yet been reached with respect to the proposal of having the liquidation pact with Poland linked up with the Young plan.

Competent legal authorities, among them Dr. Walter Simons, former president of the Reich supreme bench, allege that the terms of the German-Polish treaty involve a constitutional amendment. Such a procedure, Doctor Simons asserts, demands the sanction of the German people. As Doctor Curtius, the foreign minister, insists that the understanding with Poland should be ratified with the Young plan, there is the further prospect that the Government will not be able to clear its slate of the various complications in time to permit the second and third readings of its reparation laws before next week, and there is a strong possibility that the Reichstag may not reach a final vote before the middle of March.

This indicates that Germany is still struggling with the ratification of the Young plan.

So much for the Bank for International Settlements.

Now, in regard to the indicated change of Federal reserve policy referred to in the same article that noted the sailing of Governor Harrison, of the Federal Reserve Bank of New York, which indicated that the recent course of the foreign exchange market here has carried the price of a number of European currencies, notably the franc and the sterling, to levels little above those at which gold might be expected to flow here from abroad, and that banking authorities in this country are understood to be opposed to a movement of gold from Europe to the United States, and means to avert such a development will, it is thought, be discussed when Governor Harrison confers with the governors of the bank of England and the bank of France.

I insist that it would be more to the point and more to the best interests of the American people if this contemplated change in policy were inaugurated in the United States at this time rather than in London, Paris, or Rome where the central bank management are about to meet in connection with the organization of the Bank for International Settlements.

In speaking of the gold situation, the article further states that the recent period of high money rates and world-wide stock speculation, although it has been succeeded by a collapse of security prices and a general reduction of money rates, has left in its wake a number of difficult situations with respect to international credit conditions which also will come up for discussion during Governor Harrison's visit abroad; and in addition it states that the central banking authorities in this country desire to avoid an influx of gold to this market, and points, as the best way to avert such a gold flow, to the possible purchase of bills in the London market by the Federal Reserve Bank of New York.

In extenso, bankers are quoted as saying that they regard it as a possibility that a still further cut in the reserve rate may be ordered after while, not merely as a measure of cooperation with Europe but also to stimulate American business; and they point to the fact that there is some dispute, however, as to whether a lower discount rate will be either justified or efficacious, saying that a number of important bankers felt that present money rates give a false impression of the true condition of credit. All of which tends to indicate that we are on the eve of an important change in Federal reserve policy, which changes of late have come about as a result of conferences like the one that is now scheduled to take place in Europe.

And as further indicated in the article, to which I have just referred, to avoid the possible shipment of gold from England and Europe to the United States, we are about to purchase millions of dollars' worth of English bills. It seems to me that it is about time that we had a clarification of our views regarding the purpose and significance of our banking policy and its effect on the money market and upon general business. The crash of last October has taken stock prices and brokers' loans out of the field of Federal reserve activity, I hope, for all time; and the experience of the Federal reserve management in this respect has undoubtedly changed their inclination to govern its future banking policy by reference to the condition of the stock market. This situation does, however, tend to bring out the fact that the Federal reserve system should now adopt some definite working rule upon which to base and regulate, so far as possible, its discount and open-market policies.

A careful perusal of the financial statements of all member banks will show that the total loans and investments are about as high as they were prior to the deflation and that the total volume of Federal reserve credit at present outstanding has scarcely been diminished; and, of course, in this the direct question of future policy is involved. Therefore the management should look the situation squarely in the face and determine whether it is advisable to attempt a forcible restriction of Federal reserve credit, or whether it should, taking into consideration the business situation over the next few years, permit a further expansion of credit.

We may as well make up our minds that unless there is a great influx of gold into this country there will remain permanently outstanding for some time to come at least a minimum of $500,000,000 of Federal reserve credit. Whether this credit shall be in the form of rediscounts or investments is purely a matter of policy and not especially important. It is important, however, to know whether or not the Federal reserve system believes that it is advisable, and the thought has been running in the minds of some in the determination of policy, whether within the next few years we should not entirely curtail the use of Federal reserve credit. In this connection we should recognize the fact that if we should reduce the present outstanding Federal reserve credit, amounting to from a billion two hundred fifty million to a billion five hundred million, it would mean a contraction in the loans and investment of member banks of approximately $15,000,000,000. This pre-supposes, however, that there is not in the meantime imported or produced in this country a billion and a quarter to a billion and a half worth of gold.

In view of this situation, is it not important that some definite statement of the purpose of the open market and rediscount policies of the Federal reserve system be announced? An examination of recent Federal reserve operations would indicate that there is no present desire of the reserve banks to bring about a total elimination of reserve-bank credit.

During the late stock-market fiasco, the Federal reserve system pursued a policy toward reduction of member bank security loans to eliminate the use of Federal reserve credit in the stock market, and there was much discussion and many exaggerated notions regarding the effect of these outstanding security loans. I am sure that this experience has taught the Federal reserve management that the total volume of brokers' loans is not so important as is the stock price structure and the value of collateral upon which these loans are based. We are not hearing so much about brokers' loans as we did prior to the crash of last October since which crash the administration and the heads of big business have been confering, and quite properly so, to overcome the shock of this financial debacle. For some time past certain important elements have indicated a great economical change, particularly in the constantly declining price levels on commodities in this country tends to mark and confirm a material change in our conditions. There is nothing that will help more to rehabilitate business in this country and give it assurances abroad than an announcement by the Federal reserve management of the factor that will govern its future policy.

It is perfectly patent that the Federal reserve policy can not now be governed entirely by an effort to protect the gold reserve, because the reserve is now beyond our needs and far above the legal-reserve ratio; and from its recent experience I think it can be well said that it will not be their policy to control security loans. The thing the country wants to know is: What, then, will govern Federal reserve policy?

If the system is to pursue a policy which would result in the liquidation entirely of the present outstanding Federal reserve credit, it will mean higher interest rates in general and will tend to have a depressing effect upon prices, business, and industry, and will thus accentuate the further decline of the present lowering price levels. And it would seem, therefore, because of the present economic conditions that the future

30

policy of the system must be to adopt a policy which will permit a gradual increase of credit so as to accommodate business and industry, at least to the existing price levels; and it would also seem that this policy must be based upon the assumption that neither a rising nor a general level of prices due to banking policy is desirable. It would seem clear to me that this is the lesson which the management of Federal reserve has had by a scrutinizing of their experiences during the past two years.

Much has been said regarding the inflation and deflation policy of the Federal reserve system of 1920 and 1921. We must recognize, however, that in this connection during this period the system was not free and was not permitted to work independently of the Treasury, as construed by the then Secretary of the Treasury, who felt that, in order to float the Victory loan, a certain amount of inflation was necessary which was followed immediately thereafter by the inevitable deflation of 1920 and 1921. It was during this period and shortly thereafter that the Federal reserve began to operate under new policies and newly discovered powers and new determinations governing Federal reserve policy.

We should remember, however, that the maintenance of the gold reserve ratio has never been the basis for the establishment of Federal reserve policy, and during the past two years the two factors to which I have already referred were paramount in the formation and carrying out of policy: First, the attempt to restore the gold standard in Europe in the summer of 1927 when the discount rate was lowered to 3½ per cent, which resulted in the shipment of $500,000,000 worth of gold to Europe and the release of an excessive amount of credit here; and, second, the attempt to prevent the diversion of the Federal reserve credit into the market, which culminated in the statement of the Federal Reserve Board on February 6, 1929, and was further carried out during the past summer.

I desire to read into the RECORD at this point a letter which I have just received from a professor of finance of the University of Pennsylvania, referring to a recent article of mine in the February 15 issue of the *Saturday Evening Post*, as follows:

UNIVERSITY OF PENNSYLVANIA,
PHILADELPHIA, FEBRUARY 21, 1930.

HON. LOUIS T. McFADDEN,
    CHAIRMAN COMMITTEE ON BANKING AND CURRENCY,
        HOUSE OF REPRESENTATIVES, WASHINGTON, D.C.

Dear Mr. McFadden: I am very much interested in your article Convalescent Finance *appearing in the February 15 issue of the Saturday Evening Post. I was particularly impressed by your statement concerning the meddling of the Federal Reserve Board in the condition of the stock market, and also the influence of the foreign central banking officials on the decision reached by the Federal reserve authorities in determining their policies. I agree with you whole-heartedly on these two points. It seems to me that the Federal reserve authorities in their attempts to bring about a decrease in public participation in the securities market have brought about a business situation which is a great deal worse than was the speculation in the securities market. The evil effects of a depression, even though it be slight, are such that certainly a central banking system ought at all times to utilize its facilities in an effort to avert such a situation. The reserve authorities applied such violent methods to cure the disease speculation that the patient (business activity) was practically killed. In other words, the cure was worse than the disease.*

I am of the opinion that the heads of our banking system are perhaps not quite as astute bankers as some of the managers of the central banks of Europe, and therefore extreme care should be used in entangling alliances or engagements with European central banks.

Articles such as yours will, I am sure, be helpful in bringing this important matter to the attention of the public. Incidentally you may be interested in learning that the reading of the article has been given as an assignment to the group taking the course in banking offered by this institution.

Very truly yours,

LUTHER HARR,
ASSISTANT PROFESSOR OF FINANCE.

32

This *Saturday Evening Post* article was on the financial crash of last October and also dealt with the international financial situation. Because of its bearing on this particular discussion, I am going to ask unanimous consent to insert it in the Appendix of the Record, as well as two additional articles pertaining to this same subject published on July 20 and October 19, 1929.

I also desire to insert in the Record at this point extracts of an editorial in the *Financial Chronicle* of February 22, 1930, commenting on my discussion of February 10 on this same subject:

After Mr. McFadden's address, the Journal of Commerce again referred to the subject, in its issue of February 14. This article we also reproduced, as follows:

"Chairman McFadden, of the House Committee on Banking and Currency, has furnished, in an address on the floor of the House, a review of the objects and methods of those who are organizing the new International Bank, which ought to have the attention of everyone who is interested in the future welfare of our foreign trade, and of our domestic finance as well.

"We do not need to go into the specific details stated by Mr. McFadden, or to consider the individual and firm names which he uses, to reach a conclusion that the general state of things which Mr. McFadden complains of—viz, the surreptitious participation of the reserve banking system in an enterprise (the International Bank), for which it has no legal power of affiliation, and in which the President has already directed that no Federal reserve bank shall share—is unquestionably as described, and unquestionably serious. Mr. McFadden gives a detailed story of events that have received practically no public attention whatever, but are of the greatest national significance. We may differ as we will about the League of Nations and the international debts, and a variety of other questions to which this matter is allied, but we can not doubt the absolute necessity of maintaining control of our own international relationships and of having them dealt with by qualified and authorized representatives of the public. That condition is not now being fulfilled, but quite the contrary.

"Mr. McFADDEN quotes the statement of one of the officers of the local reserve bank (since denied by the latter, but amply confirmed by those who heard it as well as borne out by events), to the effect that the reserve banking system will act as correspondent to the new establishment, and will make 'important deposits of gold' in it. He further calls special attention to the fact that the statutes of the new establishment have been prepared in such a way as to avoid the necessity of getting any legislative sanction or support. Precisely the same statement is being made in England at this same time. Thus there is no reason to doubt the actual facts as set forth by Mr. McFADDEN, and amply confirmed by many who are cognizant with them.

"In these circumstances it seems a shortsighted policy for the press to minimize Mr. McFADDEN's efforts or to sneer at the state of things to which he has called attention. It is, in fact, a real state of affairs which he sets forth, and the problem it presents is one that comes close to the very root of our whole present system of international, economic, and financial arrangements. Why should it not be fully discussed? Mr. McFADDEN has done valuable work in directing attention to it.

"It remains only to add, as emphasizing the need of getting implicit assurances that the gold holdings of the reserve banks are not, in large part or in small part, in the shape of deposits or otherwise, to be put at the command of the Bank for International Settlements; that Gates W. McGarrah, Federal reserve agent at New York, is to be the head of the International Settlements Bank; that W. Randolph Burgess, assistant reserve agent at New York, spent weeks in Europe last year to lend a helping hand in the organization of the new institution; and that last night George L. Harrison, at present governor of the Federal Reserve Bank of New York, sailed for Europe aboard the White Star liner *Majestic* for some unannounced purpose, yet one not unlikely to be associated with the setting up of the new institution. All this tends to establish such close and intimate relations with the International Bank that inasmuch as the reserve banks carry the entire gold reserves of the country, and it is a matter of such vital importance that these reserves shall not be trenched upon, it behooves every thoughtful person to see to it that the reserve banks maintain a position of absolute independence free from any alliance with the new institution in conformance with the order of the President and the Secretary of State."

I desire also to insert an editorial from the February 12 issue of the *Baltimore Sun*, as follows:

ABOVE THE BOARD

It is pleasing to hear Chairman McFADDEN, of the House Banking and Currency Committee, voicing on the floor of Congress his conviction that the United States is being hooked up with the International Bank, called for by the Young plan. It is not that this is necessarily a dangerous departure or that there is anything to sit up nights about in Mr. McFADDEN's charge that "we are being led by a group of clever internationalists" and the house of Morgan. There is, indeed, a great deal that the International Bank can do in the field in international finance that can be most definitely helpful to the United States, and a good case can be made for direct and straightforward American participation in the effort.

The strength of Mr. McFADDEN's remarks lies in the fact that they call to attention what is clearly recognized in most financial circles, namely, that the United States and its Federal reserve system is going to be involved in the International Bank's operations for all practical purposes, but that it is pussy footing in by the back door. If Mr. McFADDEN can use his place in the House to clarify the true nature of this transaction, and thus strengthen the case for "open covenants openly arrived at," he can make a valuable contribution to the good cause of straightforward dealing.

The Federal reserve system should discontinue their attempt to control the flow of credit for speculative purposes and they should learn the lesson by a careful scrutiny of the results of such a policy during the past two years. I know that they disclaim the power to control speculation, and I have repeatedly said that it is beyond their control, and it is beyond their province, and not a proper action for them to attempt to control stock speculation.

On February 7, 1929, the day following the announcement by the Federal Reserve Board of their second warning in regard to the credit situation which marked a complete change of Federal reserve policy and established the policy of deflation, I said in a speech in the House, among other things that—

I do not understand at this time that the gold reserve is in danger, nor do I see any indication of a general rise in the commodity price level, and because of these facts, I do not think that the Federal reserve system should concern itself about the condition of the stock market or of the security loan market.

I desire to quote from a speech I delivered before the American Bankers' Association in Philadelphia on October 1, 1928, as follows:

"The Federal reserve system is charged with a grave responsibility in dealing with this situation because it would be easy for them to produce a business slump without intending to do so. In this connection, it is interesting to note the views of a leading British authority on the subject of finance, who is a student and close observer of our Federal reserve operations: 'I am now more concerned lest the Federal reserve authorities should accidentally bring about a general business depression by attempting to take action toward the stock markets which, however well meant, is not really compatible with the system's duty toward business. I think the Federal reserve system may have been quite right to try to frighten the speculators a few months ago, but this having failed, I think they would be much better advised to leave Wall Street alone and let it boil over of itself, rather than do things which, if continued, will certainly put at risk the general prosperity of the country * * *.

"There is a tendency to pay too much attention to the spectacular action of the stock market. But we should remember that the business man, the worker, and the farmer are not greatly concerned as such about stock speculation. Their chief interest is in the continuity of business and of the stability of general prices, which serve as guide to industrial activity and help to maintain employment, wages, and profits.

"I do not think that the Federal Reserve System should at the present time concern itself about security loans unless there is a tendency to speculations in commodities, which means a disturbance in the industrial mechanism. To disturb industry merely to prevent stock speculation seems to me to be unwarranted and would work a gross injustice upon the business man and the working man. This I suggest might be the result of an abortive attempt to restrict speculation investment activities by banking policy."

I do not think, after what happened last October and the subsequent business depression, which began to show in certain important lines last June, that I need make any further comment at this time, as the very thing that I suggested might occur, has occurred. The system should profit by the experiences of the past two years.

I believe that there is a way to control the unwarranted diversion of credit for speculative purposes and that it can

37

be done by restricting the limit upon the amount which banks may loan on particular stocks. This is a matter entirely in the hands and under the discretion of the banks of the country and not a Federal reserve matter, and this restriction can be regulated by the banks to cover speculative loans and not loans for legitimate business purposes. Such a regulation would tend to protect the solvency of individual banks throughout the country who, during times of stock boom prices, take stocks as collateral for loans at prices far exceeding their values. Such a policy of limiting local value on stocks would also have a tendency to reduce the great amount of fixed liquidation which takes place during every crash and tends to so upset the confidence of the country.

I insist that if the Federal reserve system is to properly pursue its policy of accommodating commerce and business by its control of member banks' reserves, and indirectly the volume of member-bank loans, it must get rid of the responsibility to adapt this policy to the control of stock speculation.

On several occasions during the past year I have invited the attention of the country to the possible danger of mixing our Federal reserve system and its policies with international policies and the international bank. Matters now are proceeding at such a rapid pace in regard to such involvement that I do not think I should temporize any longer with this possibility, and I am, therefore, introducing two resolutions in the House to-day calling on the State Department and the Secretary of the Treasury, respectively, for full information in regard to this matter. I believe that this House and the country at large need to know the facts. [Applause.]

In further confirmation of what I have said I append here an article in today's *New York Journal of Commerce* headed "Broad Powers for Reparations Bank," being extracts from a speech delivered yesterday in New York City before the Bond Club by Jackson E. Reynolds, president of the First National Bank of New York, who was one of the two American experts to work out the details of organization of the Bank for International Settlements.

Broad Powers for Reparations Bank Seen by Reynolds—
First National Chairman Outlines Scheme for War
Payments—May Become Depository of World's Gold—
Visions Coordination of Central Institutions Through
International Bank

The coordination of the central banks of the world
will be one of the major by-products of the formation of
the Bank for International Settlements, declared Jackson
E. Reynolds, chairman of the First National Bank, yesterday in an address before the luncheon meeting of the
Bond Club. Mr. Reynolds was the chairman of the committee which drafted the charter of the international bank.

He pointed out the possibility that the bank may
gradually become the depository of the gold of the world
or some part of it. Indicating that the bank will have the
authority to borrow from and lend to central banks, he
said that it is possible that such functions may be developed and come in time to resemble the inter-district
borrowings of the Federal reserve system. Furthermore,
he continued, the bank will undoubtedly buy and sell long-
term securities.

BANK'S LIMITATIONS

Although the bank will enjoy these broad powers, Mr.
Reynolds pointed out, its operations nevertheless will be
subject to various limitations indicated in the charter.
Among these he included the provision that it may not
undertake any operation in any country against the objection of the central bank of that country and the absence of
acceptance powers to the bank. The bank will have no
powers of note issue.

In the first part of his address Mr. Reynolds outlined
the scheme under which the bank will be trustee for the
transfer of reparations payments. This latter part of the
address was given to the consideration of its additional
powers. Respecting these, he declared in part:

39

"In the first place, one by-product of the institution will be to coordinate the central banks of the world. You can see it is a natural evolution, that the board of directors that will probably have on it most of the heads of the central banks of Europe, and some others from other parts of the world, who will be meeting ten times a year; for men that are engaged in central banking who have international problems and heretofore have not met very often, there will be a kind of a forum, from which a great deal of good will follow through coordination of the central banks' operations among themselves, in addition to what they accomplish through the bank itself.

"The bank has authority to buy and sell gold, and it is an interesting field of speculation to the extent in which its work in that domain will grow. The possibility of the bank gradually getting the confidence of the world, and having the gold of the world, or some part of it, deposited by the owners, and transferred by book credits and earmarks, indicates a very cnsiderable potentiality for the saving of money in the loss of interest on gold in transit, the freight while it is moving insurance, and other expenses which we have avoided in comparable ways in the Federal reserve system in America.

"The bank has authority to borrow from central banks and lend to central banks. Its operations in that respect will very possibly grow, as they have here in the borrowing and lending between the various districts of the Federal reserve system. They will inevitably deal with exchange in large volume, and in the lowering of the transfer rate of these reichsmarks into the currency of the various creditor powers who are to receive them.

"It will have a considerable power to attract permanent deposits which will find their place in long-term investments and will undoubtedly buy and sell securities of long maturity. It is supposed it will naturally deposit with a good many of the central banks, and receive deposits from a good many of the central banks. It will have agency relationships with the central banks of the world, in some cases acting as agent for them and in some cases their acting as agent for it. All of these are broad powers which time alone can tell the extent to which they will be extended."

II

BANK FOR INTERNATIONAL
SETTLEMENTS

Tuesday, April 1, 1930

Mr. McFadden. Mr. Speaker, under leave to extend my remarks in the RECORD, I present an address delivered by me as
the fifth of a series of patriotic broadcasts under the auspices
of the national society of Daughters of the American Revolution, Thursday night, March 27, 1930, as follows:

The Daughters of the American Revolution is a national
women's organization with an ever-growing influence for nationalism and patriotism as against socialism, internationalism,
paternalism, and pacifism; and I am delighted to speak to you
under their auspices this evening.

The full force of European propaganda influences, now apparent in our country, is intended to mislead the American
people into believing that there is no harm, nor anything to
be sacrificed, in the doctrine of internationalism. The Daughters of the American Revolution, who are firm believers in national independence, constantly advocate adequate national
preparedness against war and invasion, and are unalterably opposed to disruptive international influences. They are truly in
accord with the admonitions enunciated in George Washington's Farewell Address wherein he warned against "the insidious wiles of foreign influence" and proclaimed that "as a free
people, we ought to be constantly awake, since history and ex-

42

perience prove that foreign influence is one of the most baneful foes of republican government." Washington particularly cautioned Americans against any involvement of this country in the political system of Europe as a certain menace to American peace and welfare.

The outbreak of the World War in 1914 foreshadowed necessary cooperation between the United States and the allied countries to win against Germany. This cooperation was greatly accelerated in 1917 when it became necessary for us to enter actively into the war. Serious entanglement was, however, avoided at the outset—thanks to Gen. John J. Pershing—when he demanded that the American troops on the battle fronts should be maintained independently as fighting American units under American generalship, instead of intermingling or losing their idenity with the armies of the allied countries as was sought by the European allied leadership. The wisdom of General Pershing's course has subsequently been fully demonstrated.

Later on we were confronted with what might have been an even more sinister and dangerous entanglement with Europe. I refer to the participation of President Wilson in the negotiations leading up to the armistice and the appointment of American delegates to the peace conference which wrote the treaty of Versailles, itself a culmination of the insidious wiles of European politics. But, fortunately for America, the treaty of Versailles was rejected by us, although the organization of the League of Nations was effected by our former allies. Since that time there has been no discontinuance of insidious efforts to persuade the United States to join the league. Many proposals have been made repeatedly toward that end. Fortunately all have thus far been refused.

More recently we entered into the Kellogg-Briand pact, intended to render war obsolete. The folly of this step has been manifested in the deliberations of the present so-called disarmament conference in London. We shall do well if before this conference ends we are not running grave risks of fresh involvement in European affairs.

43

Two opposing principles since the World War have been contending for control of our national policy, namely, nationalism and internationalism, with the result of the struggle still in the balance. In this controversy the internationalists have the offensive; the nationalists the defensive, for theirs is the traditional policy of the United States, and they are therefore holding the citadel erected by Washington. The present form of internationalism has no precedent in history.

It contemplates the abandonment of national sovereign power to international sovereign power. The struggle is being waged in the fields of politics, economics, and finance. It is in the financial field that the attacks of the internationalists are more dangerous, in that they are more subtle and their purpose, therefore, less obvious.

The insidious arguments for adhesion to the League of Nations and the World Court all assert that such a union of the United States with Europe and the rest of the world will banish war, that the decisions of the league and the court will have such authority that the world thereafter will be kept in order by peaceful means. In my judgment, the independence and safety of the American people will, however, be best subserved by remaining outside of the League of Nations and the World Court. Only thus may questions arising between Europe and the United States be clearly defined and settled.

Even more dangerous, I believe, than proleague propaganda is that which, under the guise of private banking transactions, would tie up the United States with Europe economically and financially.

The international bankers of New York City are the most powerful in our domestic banking system. Their influence largely determines the character of the investments in which the American people put their savings. New York City is the great security and investment market of the country. Vast issues of stocks and bonds are put out there and the sponsors of these securities have the confidence of the general investing public.

The enormous investment in European securities since the

war has been made in this way. The investors have little direct knowledge as to the safety of their investment. The high interest yield attracts them and their bankers assure them security is good. Thus having confidence in the advice of the international bankers, they do not hesitate to buy these securities.

In the particular international situation at present confronting us, the leading international banking house is J. P. Morgan & Co., the most dominant banking influence to-day in the world. They are not only a potential influence in Federal reserve operations in this country, but are the fiscal agents of Great Britain, France, Belgium, and Italy; and now that the State Department has forbidden any participation on the part of the Federal reserve banking system in the organization or operation of the Bank for International Settlements, J. P. Morgan & Co. have assumed that representation in so far as this country is to participate therein. To thoroughly understand just what this means, we must go back to the year 1916 when these relationships were enlarged so as to include the Federal Reserve Bank of New York and the Bank of England in conferences which have subsequently continued up to the present time.

The beginning of these conferences attracted no particular attention and assumed no proportions of importance other than the carrying out of the necessary arrangements as were incident to the financing of the gigantic operations necessary to win the war. It has, however, furnished a basis for a continuance of meetings between the heads not only of the Bank of England and the Federal Reserve Bank of New York but of the principal central banks of Europe, which since the close of the war has included the Reichsbank of Germany.

The first definite knowledge had by the Congress that our Federal reserve banking system was becoming involved in European financial affairs was when the governor of a Federal reserve bank appeared before the House Banking and Currency Committee and stated that the 12 Federal reserve banks had granted a gold loan or credit of $200,000,000 to the

45

Bank of England, which loan was guaranteed by a special act of Parliament by the British Government.

The consummation of this particular loan had given definite assurance to European central banks that our Federal reserve system had been made readily available for their assistance. Thus, was established a dangerous precedent to mark further cooperation between the Federal Reserve Bank of New York and European banks. Since then it has been made known that our Federal reserve banks are participating in the granting of other loans to other foreign banks. It has also been ascertained that these negotiations are usually carried on by the governor of the Federal Reserve Bank of New York jointly with the private banking house of J. P. Morgan & Co. acting in the capacity of fiscal agents.

The 12 banks comprising the Federal reserve system are the custodians of the legal cash reserves of the over 8,000 member banks comprising the system. The loanable funds of the Federal reserve system are made up of its capital stock, surplus, and profits, and the deposits, representing the legal reserve. This system was created to serve the people of the United States and there was no intention on the part of the creators of this system that it would be permitted to loan its reserves to a foreign bank or government.

The climax of these international bank relationships was reached in the summer of 1927 when the heads of the central banks of the major countries of Europe came to the United States and held one of their confidential meetings with the officers of the Federal Reserve Bank of New York. This conference lasted for a period of two weeks. The results of this conference were made known to the Federal Reserve Board in Washington. At this conference a definite change of policy on the part of the Federal reserve system was declared. Immediately the discount rate was lowered to 3½ per cent and large amounts of money were released into the money market through active operations in the open market causing the release of a large volume of credit which resulted in the export of over $500,000,000 worth of gold to Europe. Thus was carried out the scheme of the foreign bankers to get a further grip on our banking resources. In order to make sure the carrying out of this plan for the financial relief of Europe, an excess amount of credit was released which resulted in the beginning of the orgy of speculation that continued unrestricted through the year 1928 up until the disastrous panic of last October (1929).

It will be remembered that it was decided at Geneva, Switzerland, in January, 1929, that a committee of experts should be appointed and report a plan for the final settlement of the reparations question. This was the committee which assembled at Paris on February 1, 1929, and became known as the Young committee. Strenuous diplomatic efforts were made to induce President Coolidge to appoint American experts to this committee. This he refused to do, whereupon the interested European governments appointed Mr. J. P. Morgan, Mr. Thomas W. Lamont, Mr. Owen D. Young, and Mr. Thomas N. Perkins. They did not represent the United States. The result of their efforts brought forth the Young plan which had embodied therein the suggestion for the bank for international settlements and authorized the appointment of a committee to work out the plans for the organization of the bank and designated Mr. Jackson E. Reynolds, president of the First National Bank of New York, and Mr. Melvin A. Traylor, president of the First National Bank of Chicago, with other European delegates who met at The Hague and have just recently completed the organization set-up of the Bank for International Settlements. This meeting was presided over by Mr. Jackson E. Reynolds as chairman. The Young plan was fully adopted and has been ratified by the German Reichstag and is now being debated in the House of Deputies in Paris.

Upon the completion of the organization of the bank, the board of directors, representing the several participating countries, were agreed upon, and Gates W. McGarrah resigned his position as chairman of the board of the Federal Reserve Bank of New York and accepted the presidency of the Bank for International Settlements. The other director in the United States who was invited and accepted is Leon Fraser, a New

York attorney, formerly counsel for the Dawes commission.

Lord Melchett, one of the leading financial authorities in England, asserts that the Bank for International Settlements can not succeed without the full force of American participation. Nearly 50 per cent of the world's gold now belongs to the people of the United States. These internationally minded men who are attempting to direct our participation in international political, economic, and financial affairs know the importance of the mobilization of our financial resources with the financial resources of Europe through the Bank of International Settlements and through the sale of billions of dollars' worth of German reparation bonds to our people here in exchange for our gold. They know that these entangling alliances will eventually drag us into the World Court, the Bank for International Settlements, and eventually into the League of Nations.

Apparently Federal reserves' participation in the Bank for International Settlements is, through an edict of the State Department, to be by and through the firm of J. P. Morgan & Co. This action of the State Department in forbidding any further participation by the Federal reserve banking system in the Bank for International Settlements turns over to the Morgan firm one of the most valuable franchises which any private banking house in the world has ever possessed. It is of more than passing interest when you consider the fact that they are the fiscal agents for the leading countries whose central-bank officers are the directors of the Bank for International Settlements.

It is apparent to close observers in this country that it is the policy of those who are promoting the organization of this bank to minimize its functions and purposes as was recently done in an address by Owen D. Young, delivered this week in California, which is quite in contrast to a statement made in England on March 6 by Sir Charles Addis, a director of the Bank of England, chairman of the Hong Kong and Shanghai Bank, and a director of the Bank of International Settlements. When speaking at Cardiff, England, to the Cardiff Business

Club, he said that one of the primary but not one of the most important functions of the bank would be to collect and distribute German annuities. He further declared that we would have to wait until we saw what the bank did before describing what it was; that until then they would have to describe it as a cooperative undertaking by the central banks of the reparation countries. He further stated that great importance was attached to the task of the bank in promoting cooperation between central banks, which he regarded as essential for the preservation of the international financial structure; that it was this task that he conceived the most salutary and beneficial influence of the new bank; and that it was possible to conceive with an institution of this kind some kind of association—a financial league of nations in which the central banks should be leagued together alongside the political institutions as a powerful adjunct for promoting international peace.

I would ask you now to contrast this last statement with the statement in the speech of Owen D. Young to which I have just referred as follows:

"The question has been raised whether the League of Nations and the Bank for International Settlements might not unite their forces. The league represents international political cooperation and the bank international financial cooperation. Well, if that means that the bank will come under the domination of the league and so there will be added to the political forces of the league the financial resources of the bank, I think we may dismiss once and for all our fears if we are opposed to the league, or our hopes if we are its proponents."

When we have such conflicting statements from two such competent authorities, what are we to believe?

I think that we Americans should be very grateful to Sir Charles Addis for his clear definition of the purpose to be served by this bank. He has substantiated what I have charged heretofore was back of this proposal for this bank; that is, that it is a proposal to head up the financial division of the League of Nations.

The bank, as now constituted, is authorized not only to

49

collect and remit the reparation payments but is to continue the cooperation between the central banks of the world. As soon as the organization is perfected and the bank is opened, almost the first business will be to supervise the issuance of $300,000,000 worth of reparation bonds. Out of the proceeds of the sale of this issue, $100,000,000 is to be paid to Germany and $200,000,000 paid to France. It is understood that the major portion of this latter amount is to be used to refund loans which France has made through the house of J. P. Morgan & Co. Accredited authorities estimate that the United States is to absorb within the next five or six years between five and six billion dollars' worth of these German reparation bonds. Why should the people of the United States assume the debt that is now owed by Germany to the European allied countries, particularly when the legality of these bonds is seriously questioned? I have definitely raised the question of the legality of these reparation bonds and am calling upon the State Department to advise the American investors as to whether or not these commercialized German reparation bonds are legal. These bonds will be offered through the Bank for International Settlements and under the direction of J. P. Morgon & Co. in this country.

The agreement signed by Germany under the Dawes and Young committees is held by good authority to be void in law. The records show that in April last, while the committee was sitting, there was an extraordinary flow of gold out of the German Reichsbank to Paris, New York, and London. So great and rapid was this outflow that a currency panic manifested itself in Germany and a flight from the mark like that of 1923 was threatened. Hjalmar Schacht, president of the Reichsbank, who was Germany's representative at the Young conference, informed the industrialists of the Ruhr that there was no alternative but to sign the agreement and it was to prevent catastrophy in Germany that the German delegates signed the Young report.

The late Herr Stresemann, the leading statesman of Germany, pointed out the illegality of this agreement and stressed the point that Germany would only pay for 10 years. Only this week, during the debate in Paris, where the Young plan is up for ratification, the French right chief, Louis Marin, in assailing the Young plan exclaimed: "Without counting the consequences, we are abandoning every guarantee, and in return we not only get nothing but we are left at the mercy of the international commissions in which France will be a minority." He asked, "Who does not view with anxiety the possibility of Germany's suspension of payments and a moratorium being settled by the committee of the international bank in which we have only 3 representatives among the 28?"

He demanded, "Who can accept without indignation that the entire benefit of the reductions made by the United States in the debt settlements shall be passed over to Germany? Who even has confidence that the international bond issues will be continuously successful even if the first one is a success, which is doubtful? Who does not look with misgiving on the installation by the world bank of a formidable financial power free from all governmental control, capable of influencing international affairs of all nations by exerting economic pressure?"

This statement clearly indicates that France understands that the influence of the house of Morgan is going to dominate the future of the Bank for International Settlements. I am told that the signature of France to the Young pact was secured by the promise that they would receive $200,000,000 out of the first flotation of reparation bonds.

Those who have followed the course of the history of German reparations can but conclude that the framers of the treaty of Versailles visualized fully the fact that Europe had lost most of its liquid wealth to America, and that by certain provisions in that treaty they hope to turn world history aside.

Do not forget that the league was designed for three things: First, to disarm the United States and transfer to either the league or the four dominant members of its council the war-making powers of Congress; second, to persuade the United States to obey the decisions of its advisory court, made in advance of the issue in the absence of positive treaty agree-

51

ment, and allow such decisions to fix the status of international practice in dealing with every question involving the policy of the open door and commercial spheres of influence; and, third, to induce the United States to furnish its central banking resources and its gold to create a revolving fund to be used in the organization of a world bank to stabilize the finances of its council members.

I desire to warn the American people of the danger in this newly proposed association in this Bank for International Settlements and against absorbing these illegal reparation bonds, and to warn American bankers who are custodians of trust estates not to trade these sacred estates, which belong to American widows and orphans, for these securities. Should Germany ever repudiate these securities, that would tend to involve us in European political, economic, and financial affairs.

III

INTERNATIONAL FINANCE

April 9, 1930

Mr. McFadden. Mr. Speaker, under leave to extend my remarks in the RECORD, I present an address delivered by me before the Government Club, Hotel Astor, New York City, April 7, 1930, as follows:

Banking in the United States from the time of the adoption of the Constitution up until the time of the Civil War met with a variety of successes and failures. The necessities of financing the public Civil War debt was largely responsible for the organization of the national bank act. Banking proceeded under the authority of this national act and the development of State banking under the various State laws during the period from 1863 until 1913. Several years prior to 1913, a widespread discussion had taken place regarding modernization of our method of carrying on our financial operations which resulted in the creation of a superbanking method called the Federal reserve system.

Banking prior to the enactment of the national bank act had proceeded somewhat along the lines being pursued through Europe. The adoption of the Federal reserve system, while it was supposed to be a decentralized system, has proven to be a centralized group banking system. This system has afforded the necessary nucleus for the development of concerted action by and between our present Federal banking system and the central banks of Europe and the world, the beginning of which was in the year 1916. During the last 10 years these relationships have been growing and have become much closer, until at the present time there is a very close collaboration on all gold movement, international exchange, discount rates, open-market operation, and other powers, making effective changes in policies of operations.

The large necessary financial transactions and borrowings by the allied countries engaged in the war completely upset gold standards throughout the world, resulting in the concentration of nearly 50 per cent of the world's gold in the United States banking system. At the close of the war allied Governments began to readjust their financial structures to synchronize their situations so as to enable normal international trade and financial operations to resume. The question of the establishment of relationships between Germany and the allied countries and the fixing of reparation debts and methods of payment resulted finally in the setting up of the Dawes plan, the working out of which plan was largely the result of the participation in these deliberations unofficially of Americans.

Under the plan provided for the settlements proceeded under the direction of the machinery thus set up, until in 1928 it became apparent that a readjustment was immediately imminent and necessary. When a conference was arranged in Paris, where representatives of Germany and the allied countries, together with unofficial representatives from the United States, met and brought forth the Young plan, the American banking system, principally through the Federal Reserve Bank of New York in its close affiliation and working arrangements with the central banks of the countries involved, had, during this period of time, been rendering financial assistance to enable such of the foreign countries as were able to do so to return to a gold or a modified gold basis, and they also aided in the stabilization of international exchanges. These activities were apparently acquiesced in by our administrations in the Federal Reserve Board and the Treasury and State Departments.

The United States had established and carried out the precedent, so far as the official government policy was concerned, of keeping free from any participation in discussion of war debts or reparations or the mixing of the debts owed to this country by European countries with reparation settlements.

Notwithstanding the very evident intent and plan of the participating European countries to involve the United States systems with their own financial, political, and economic systems, and the debts owed to this country and reparations settlements between Germany and the allied countries, a certain group of international, financially minded men did, however, participate in, and largely directed the organization of the Dawes plan and the subsequent Young plan, and participated in most of the intervening conferences leading up to the adoption of both of these plans.

Both of these plans contemplated the commercialization and sale in the United States of a large part of the reparation payments to the allies.

Prior to the conference in Paris at the time of the creation of the Young plan, the then Premier Poincare, in a speech at Carcassone on April 2, 1928, told his audience in a veiled way that his Government would approve what was being discussed as the bankers' plan, which involved the sale of the German reparation bonds in the United States. In fact, he was returned to power on the basis of his approval of this plan, and thus the French Government was officially committed to the reparations scheme, the basis of which had been previously laid out.

It is interesting for us to note that some days after Premier Poincare's speech he received the foreign correspondents of the press and made a labored effort to qualify what he had said at Carcassone. We should not lose sight of the fact that this expressed attitude of France caused considerable concern to President Coolidge, who found it necessary to again reaffirm our attitude as regards this subject. It will be recalled that it was largely due to President Coolidge's attitude that the commercialization of a large part of the reparation debt secured by a deposit of the railroad securities of Germany and the sale of the same to American investors were forbidden. This was the plan the reparations agent made a special trip to the

United States to conclude. It is interesting in this connection for us to note that, at or about that time, Mr. S. Parker Gilbert, agent general of reparations, who was then in Rome, Italy, made this unexpected and then apparently irrelevant public statement:

"There is no connection between German reparations and allied debts to the United States."

Careful analysis of these two statements would indicate that some communication had passed between Washington and Paris with reference to Premier Poincare's speech at Carcassone. The files of our State Department should throw some light on the nature of the communications which would almost seem to indicate that the foreign governments had not taken seriously President Coolidge's announced policy of not permitting our debts to be intermingled with reparations settlements. It is not unfair to say that this announced group who were working to involve us in every way possible in international tie-ups.

The Young plan is the culmination of the international plan which began with the writing of the reparations provisions of the treaty of Versailles. The amount of the German reparations was determined without regard to Germany's moral and legal obligations under the armistice agreement or her capacity to pay. They were to be fixed at an amount which, if made immediately available in cash, might be sufficient to rehabilitate Europe economically.

The provisions in annex 2 to the financial clauses of the treaty provide that the reparations total shall be issued in gold bonds, payable to bearer, and that the bonds owned by the allied governments might be commercialized by them. With no market in Europe for these bonds, it was the intention to sell them upon the outside market to which Europe's gold had flowed and was still flowing. With the flow of gold thus reversed and upon an enormous scale, Europe might be rehabilitated in a few years in spite of the effects of the war.

It was upon the United States that the eyes of the supreme war council were fixed, and it was to the United States almost exclusively that Europe was relinquishing its gold. It was to the American public then that the bulk of the German reparation bonds were to be sold, and to accomplish this purpose a systematic falsification of historical, financial, and economic fact was necessary in order to create in America a state of mind that would make the sale of the bonds successful.

The Young plan is the culmination of 10 years of European secret diplomacy in which the connivance of the international bankers of New York has been continuously dependent upon and accorded. There have been 10 years of systematic concealment from the American public of the intent and purpose involved in this diplomacy. Great American news agencies have been brought under the control of foreign interests through the hold exercised over them by international financiers, and the influence of these powerful financiers has also permeated the policies of American publishing houses, so that books and weekly and monthly periodicals have been used to mislead the American public and to exclude from their pages authentic information upon the subject of German reparations and the movements of European diplomacy which have centered about the subject of reparations.

This systematic abuse of the confidence of the American public goes back to the armistice period, for vitally important historical events between the day of armistice and the day of the signing of the treaty of Versailles six months later were concealed and falsified at the time. The existing structure of international political and economic relations is founded upon this substructure of falsity of facts and would have to be reconstructed if these false representations were allowed to be swept away. This is why all the powers of the European governments and the international financiers have been sleeplessly exerted to control the sources of information available to the American people. The motive which required suppression of the facts of 1919 has required suppression of the facts throughout the subsequent years, and it is this motive which requires suppression of the facts in connection with the Young plan to-day.

It is the purpose now to put the Young plan reparation bonds on sale in Wall Street along with ordinary industrial securities that brokers sell, disassociated from war animosities or of apprehensions as to their safety because of political relationships in Europe. They are to be given the character of commercial securities concerning which a purchaser need not inquire as to the aspects of their political background. In the words of Mr. Thomas W. Lamont, of J. P. Morgan & Co., the "reparations" will lose even that name "and simply become swallowed up in the general flow of international trade and international exchange."

But this is too sanguine a view to take. The political status quo upon which Mr. Lamont depends is too unstable to justify it. The bonds will be issued with the assurance that they are a safe investment because a stable, political status quo exists in Europe, whereas, in fact, a most unstable status quo exists there, and the real purpose of offering these bonds in America, besides that of financial advantage to Europe, is to make the powerful United States an ally of the weak allied States in guaranteeing the existing, but ramshackle, status quo.

The present juncture offers the first opportunity since the war to reexamine the basis of the present political structure in Europe, for under the Young plan the United States is being asked to guarantee it. If such an examination is not made now the opportunity will not come again for many years, and when it does come the problems will be far more grave than they are now.

At this point I want to call attention to the fact that the Young plan has been adopted by the principal European governments and has been approved by the executive branch of the United States Government. Approval by the Congress of the United States is asked through a bill now under consideration by the Ways and Means Committee of the House proposing to ratify an independent settlement of the debt due by Germany to the United States in connection with occupation of the Ruhr by armed forces of the United States. If and when the Congress approves this proposal, it will but in-

58

directly be giving congressional approval of the Young plan.

The validity of the treaty of Versailles is one of the subjects of discussion which has been suppressed. Suppression of this discussion has been successful for 10 years; it may be successful for 10 years more, but the time will undoubtedly come when the validity of the treaty will be challenged. It is the hope of the allied governments that great quantities of the Young reparation bonds will have been sold in the United States by that time, and that for this reason the Government of the United States will find it necessary to support the validity of the treaty.

In this connection, it is interesting to note an extract from a speech delivered by the late Herr Stresemann in the Reichstag on June 24, 1929, when, in speaking of the proposed Young plan, he said: "Do you think," Herr Stresemann asked the Nationalists, "that any member of the Government regards the Young plan as ideal? Do you believe that any individual can give a guaranty for its fulfillment?

"Do you believe that anybody in the world expects such a guaranty from us? The plan would only represent in the first place a settlement for the coming decade. The point is whether it loosens the shackles which fetter us and lightens the burdens which we have yet to fulfill."

In his California address a few days ago Owen D. Young deplored, by implication, the intrusion at The Hague of politics which succeeded in modifying the economic features of the Young plan by the introduction of sanctions "in a most attenuated form" in case Germany should voluntarily default. Here is a direct intimation of the possibility of default in German reparation settlements by the principal author of the Young plan.

On March 23, in the House of Deputies, Louis Marin, the French right chief, in assailing the Young plan, said: "Without counting the consequences, we are abandoning every guarantee, and in return we not only get nothing but we are left at the mercy of the international commissions in which France will be in a minority." He then asked, "Who does not view with

59

anxiety the possibility of German suspension of payments and a moratorium being settled * * *? Who ever has confidence that the international bond issues will be continually successful even if the first one is a success, which is doubtful? Who does not look with misgiving on the installation by the world bank of a formidable financial power free from all governmental control, capable of influencing international affairs of all nations by exerting economic pressure?"

It is also interesting to note in this connection the expressed attitude of Dr. Hjalmar Schacht, late president of the Reichsbank, who by his recent resignation voiced his opposition to the Young plan as finally adopted; and in this connection also the expressed attitude of Mr. Albert Voegler, president of the Ruhr Steel Trust, certainly can not be ignored in this country.

In the discussion in the Reichsrath of Germany in regard to the Young plan, the Minister of France, Doctor Moldenhaur, spoke of what would happen if Germany should demand a moratorium. He said, "The creditor powers would forthwith declare a moratorium for their payments to America and the whole matter would then have to be fundamentally reconsidered."

Furthermore, if competent legal German authority is to be believed—and I am relying on the opinion of Doctor Hüffner, who is councillor of the Reichsgericht, a position similar to a member of the Supreme Court of the United States—and whom I quote, "the promoters of the Dawes plan and the Young plan have completely disregarded the German laws, that this must necessarily continue to create a chain of irregularities with disastrous consequences."

What will the situation be in this country if repudiation takes place?

These are men of standing and wide influence in Germany and France, and it should be understood that they speak for a considerable section of the intelligent German and French citizenship, and their words and action hardly indicate that the original political character of reparation payments has been eliminated by the so-called commercialization of these payments.

The seeds of a future war, in which a united Europe would be arrayed against the United States, are involved in this contingency. In proportion as the United States increases its holdings of German reparation bonds, the allied Governments decrease their holdings of them, for it is from the allied Governments that the American investors buy the bonds. (Please note that "American investors will not buy these reparation bonds from Germany.") Thus in time the allied Governments might have received payment of reparations in full, while the United States was still demanding payment of annuities by Germany for many years to come. If the treaty of Versailles and the subsequent agreements pursuant to it are in fact invalid and founded upon falsity, all Europe might at some future date join Germany in a demand for their abrogation and for repudiation of the financial obligations to America imposed by them. The United States, to protect its financial interests, would have to stand upon morally indefensible ground.

The gravity of the present juncture lies in the fact that the treaty of Versailles was in reality illegally imposed and that the Germans are aware of this and have no moral doubt of it. There is undoubtedly a deep sense of moral outrage among the informed classes in Germany that the German Government has never been permitted at any conference to discuss the "juridical" questions which they know to be pertinent, and in a more vague way the German masses know that Germany was enslaved through allied bad faith. During the 10 years' time the war psychology in Europe has not been mollified; its expression only has been suppressed. The statements in the report of the Young committee that war hatreds have been dissipated and that a peaceful understanding has been attained are knowingly false and are dangerously misleading.

The reasons why the treaty of Versailles is illegitimate and not binding upon Germany are that under international law the provisions of a definitive treaty of peace are legitimate only if they remain within the scope of the preliminary agreement which brought hostilities to an end. This the treaty of Versailles did not do. In the exercise of bad faith the allied

61

States, after inducing Germany to disarm, varied the terms of the preliminary agreement by force to the prejudice of the German State.

The Germans have all the necessary evidence of this fact, evidence that would be sufficient, and overwhelmingly convincing in any un-prejudiced court. But they are not permitted to bring it forward, for it would make the rehabilitation of Europe through the sale of Young plan reparation bonds in America an impossibility. They are too weak at present to secure a hearing, for to insist would bring upon them a reopening of the war hatred, expressing itself in new acts of Allied aggression. But they know that they are not morally obligated to sustain the burden of paying reparation annuities under the Young plan, and they will assert the illegality of these burdens at the earliest moment that they can make their voice heard.

A close examination of the facts pertaining to the last settlement of German reparations when taken into consideration with the financial, political, and economic conditions prevailing since the armistice right up to date indicate that we are not through with further consideration of reparation settlements. I have referred to the close working arrangements between central European banks and the Federal reserve system.

I now desire to refer to a statement that I made last summer wherein I said that the Federal reserve policy then being put into operation was for the purpose of deflating the American stock and investment market in preparation for the flotation in this country of large issues of foreign bonds, including the sale of these commercialized reparation bonds. I now point to the fact of this accomplishment.

We are in the midst of an ideal cheap money market in the United States which forecasts a most favorable opportunity for the exploitation of the American investing public through the sale of foreign securities in this market, whether they be reparation bonds, other Government, State, or municipal securities, or bonds issued to promote the industrial welfare of European countries; and in addressing myself to this subject I am emphasizing the danger that lies before us in connection with the synchronizing of our own banking operations with those of foreign countries whose main thought is, first, to assure necessary finances to rehabilitate their countries, and, second, if not the foremost reason, to involve the United States through these financial operations in the economic and political affairs of Europe.

The Bank for International Settlements will be opened on or about May 1 at Basel, Switzerland. Shortly thereafter the proposed issue of $300,000,000 worth of reparation bonds will be offered to the investors of the world under the auspices of this bank, which offering in this country, as stated by Thomas W. Lamont, will be from $75,000,000 to $150,000,000, and will undoubtedly be offered by a syndicate of bankers organized by J. P. Morgan & Co. and headed by the First National Bank of New York and the First National Bank of Chicago.

I desire again to warn the American investing public of the danger of investing in these particular bonds at this time because of their questioned legality of issue and the possibility through their purchase of involving the United States in international entanglements. Inquiry as to the legality of these securities should be directed to our State Department, which department I have called upon to advise the American people as to whether or not these bonds are legal. The State Department has on previous occasions assumed to forbid the issuance of foreign securities in this market. If the State Department does not certify as to the legality and bona fide issue of these bonds, I shall cause to be introduced in Congress a resolution forbidding the sale of these reparation bonds in the United States.

IV

BASIS OF CONTROL OF ECONOMIC CONDITIONS

July 3, 1930

Mr. McFadden. Mr. Speaker and gentlemen, time and events have arrived at a point where we should no longer deceive ourselves concerning the business situation. Continued statements of unfounded optimism will have only an unhappy effect upon the minds of the millions of our citizens who are now unemployed and who, in the circumstances, must continue to be unemployed for many months to come. The economic condition in which we find ourselves is too sustained and deeply seated to be met by pronouncements that it does not exist.

Let us face the truth—that we and the world are undergoing a major economic and business adjustment which is and will be both drastic and painful. These consequences will be particularly severe in the United States, because they will force many people to recede from the standards of living and expenditure attained during the past 14 years.

Some part of this condition is the natural consequence of the operation of basic economic laws which function with little regard for human legislation. A large part is due to mismanagement of our national affairs. A still larger part is due to a deliberately contrived and executed program which has as its object the impoverishment of the people of the United States.

64

The end of the World War found us with a greatly expanded industrial and credit structure, too large. by far for the requirements of our national needs as the latter existed before the beginning of the war period of abnormal consumption. It was clearly a time to halt and to analyze fundamental economic facts. We did not do this.

Rather we chose to proceed with our abnormal production and to stretch the limits of credit still further. War production and its profits had made Americans drunk with power, and ambition for more power. Luxuries developed in the disorganization of war became necessities with the reestablishment of peace.

The American people entered upon a decade in which the whole structure of their lives was to be passed upon the principle of discounting the future. A vast system of installment credit sprang into life almost overnight, aided by the optimism of the Federal reserve system. The automobile industry expanded more rapidly and to greater size than any industry had expanded in history. The public was encouraged by advertising and propaganda to buy beyond its immediate means. Further industrial expansion was financed by the same expansion of credit which made installment buying possible. Consumption was expanded and financed upon the consumer's promise to pay and production was expanded by capitalizing the producer's hope that the consumer would keep that promise.

In the period between 1920 and the present time we experienced the full use and purpose of the credit machinery built up within the Federal reserve system. It was but a logical development that anticipated profits should be capitalized as anticipated production and consumption had been capitalized—and that the Federal reserve system should in turn finance this capitalization of anticipated profits.

The entry of millions of Americans of moderate means into stock-market speculation with a natural consequence of the policy of expansion to which we had committed ourselves. It was also a logical development that the Federal reserve should expand brokers loans to make possible a huge inflation of the business of speculating in securities on margins.

All this brought the country to a point where the individual was living beyond his present means, buying more than he could afford on his hope that he could afford to pay for it in the future and then speculating in the hope that he could make enough profit to pay his debts when they came due. In brief, the greater part of the American business structure was built upon the anticipated profits of the next year's pay checks.

This circle of discounted hope could persist only while it was in motion. When the rotation of the system was stopped even for a moment the wheel disintegrated and its component parts answered the call of gravity and crashed to the ground.

The geniuses in the management of credit who presided over this defiance of the laws of economic gravitation were the world's greatest financiers and industrialists. They came to the realization that optimism could not forever serve as the basis of a constantly expanding credit. In 1928 these men convened themselves and decided that a readjustment was imperative; that the world's economic, industrial, and financial procedure should undergo a complete change or evolution. Since the date of that decision the machinery to perfect this accomplishment has been in full force and effect.

We are only beginning to feel the effect of this decision by the economic powers. Commodity price levels are being reduced to practically the 1913 basis; wages are being reduced through the creation of a labor surplus; by the slowing up of production to an extent which has thrown 4,000,000 or more of our people out of employment.

We must realize that we are going to a new price level, much lower than that which has prevailed during the past decade. We must also realize that before this change is fully accomplished to the entire satisfaction of those who are directing it much suffering and hardship will prevail. Unemployment and hardship always bring unsettlement in the public mind, sometimes to a degree which results in anarchy and revolution. It is natural and right that the average citizen should resent having his livelihood made the subject of manipulation.

The war resulted in bringing our industrial and financial leaders into contact with the industrial and financial leaders of the rest of the world. One of the consequences of this contact was the assumption by our industrial and financial leaders of control of such affairs throughout the world.

This control of the world business structure and of human happiness and progress by a small group is a matter of the most intense public interest. In analyzing it, we must begin with the international group which centers itself around J. P. Morgan & Co. Never before in the history of the world has there been such a powerful centralized control over finance, industrial production, credit, and wages as is at this time vested in the Morgan group.

The Morgan interest is able to exercise a high degree of control in international exchange, loans, and commerce through the fact that the parent Morgan company acts as fiscal agent for Great Britain, France, Belgium, and Italy, is the dominating influence in the new Bank for International Settlements, and is the most potential influence in the Federal-reserve system, which last is virtually a pool of our national assets. The Morgan control of the Federal reserve system is exercised through control of the management of the Federal Reserve Bank of New York and the mediocre representation and acquiescence of the Federal Reserve Board in Washington.

This international association of financial organizations under a central control marks a new epoch in world financial history and is the basis of the greatest danger free government has had to face in centuries.

Hand in hand with this financial control marches an equally potent and dangerous organization of international political and industrial control. Politically this control has expressed itself in the United States by a control of the press and the executive departments of the Government with the object of bringing about the adoption of measures calculated to make the people and the resources of this country an acquiescent part in the international plan.

67

The primary object of these measures is to persuade our people to assume the cost of the World War and to pay Germany's much-disputed reparations to the Allies, we to assume the responsibility of collecting these reparations from Germany over a long term of years, if, as, and when Germany is willing or able to pay them. Through the sale of bonds to American investors the allied Governments are to receive cash for their claims against Germany. The burden of establishing the validity of these bonds and of collecting principal and interest would thus be shifted to the United States and a large part of the liquid capital of the United States would be shifted to Europe.

The current effort to sell German bonds in the United States under the seeming approval of the State Department and the Treasury is only another phase of the program which has persisted since our entry into the war. The endeavor to involve us in the complex settlements of the Versailles peace treaty was a part of this program, as was the effort to persuade us into membership in the League of Nations. The failure of these efforts was succeeded by the debt-cancellations campaign and that, in turn, was followed by the vigorous propaganda which had as its avowed object the purpose of securing our adherence to the Permanent Court of International Justice of the League of Nations, sometimes euphemistically styled the World Court.

Another phase of this program has been the continuing effort to induce us to take the right of determining the size and character of our national naval defense out of the hands of the Congress, in which it was placed by the Constitution, and to place it in the hands of some foreign tribunal such as the Washington conference of 1922 or the recent London naval conference. Once having left the hands of the Congress, it is almost a certainty that this control of our national defenses would be placed in the hands of the League of Nations by those in whose hands we first delivered it.

V

INTERNATIONAL POLITICS AND FINANCE AS THEY AFFECT THE FEDERAL RESERVE SYSTEM

December 16, 1930

Mr. McFadden. Mr. Chairman and ladies and gentlemen of the committee, this country is in the midst of a serious business, economic, and financial depression. Several times during the last session of Congress I took occasion to direct the attention of the House and of the country to the possible serious involvement of our Federal reserve system in not only international finance but in international politics.

I am now taking the time of the House to further direct the attention of this House to international finance, and I hope that the few remarks that I may make will be heard somewhat in the other end of the Capitol, because of the fact that before the Senate at this time are matters which tend to further involve the Federal reserve system in internationalism, particularly as regards such financial activities.

The seriousness of this situation is perfectly apparent. You Members heard several of the things that I said during the closing days of the last session of Congress about the involvement of the Federal reserve system, or possible involvement of it, in the organization of the Bank for International Settlement. Those people who attempted to answer my remarks in regard to this attempted to minimize the importance of the operation of the Bank for International Settlement. Subsequent events, however, have confirmed everything that I said last spring as regards the magnitude of this important financial institution. We are now beginning to get the facts pertaining to the important part which this institution is to play with regard to international financial and political operations. I need only cite in this connection the recent visit to the Capitol and to the White House, to the Treasury, the Federal Reserve Board, and to the Department of State of the head of the Bank for International Settlement, Mr. Gates W. McGarrah.

I also call attention to a speech which that gentleman made in the city of New York only 10 days ago, in which he pointed out the important part which this institution is to play in the future in regard to world finances. He said it was the purpose to mobilize, and the reports indicate that mobilization of the world's gold is beginning. They propose to deal with international operations. He also told us in this New York speech of the important part which the Bank for International Settlements played in upholding the plan of the Finance Minister in Germany, Mr. Bruening, in the last session of the Reich. I want to point out to you just prior to that an important step that was taken by the same international banking group; that is, they financed and sold in this country $300,000,000, or a part of it, of the commercial reparation loan. You gentlemen, I am sure, will remember my criticism of that and my attack upon the legality and the unwisdom of the sale of these securities in this market as a possible involvement of our people in international affairs to an extent that they did not realize.

This morning I simply want to point out the facts that those bonds have declined from a value of 91¾ to a low of 68. The market on Saturday was 70, representing a loss to American investors in these particular securities of over $20,000,000. The particular reference which I make to this financing is that it was a private undertaking. The syndicate was headed by Lee Higginson & Co., which is really the back door of J. P. Morgan & Co., who financed an additional loan of $125,000,000.

70

This is a new loan that was given Germany subsequently to the sale of the $100,000,000 commercialized reparations loan—that was not even advertised locally in this country, but taken by nearly the same group of banks that handled the first loan—but this time instead of the J. P. Morgan firm heading the syndicate it was headed by Lee Higginson & Co. This makes a total of apparently $225,000,000 given to Germany since the Young plan was adopted, and we do not now know how much more was granted by the Bank for International Settlements.

That last loan of $125,000,000 was made for the purpose of aiding Mr. Bruening in organizing the Reich, in order to put through his financial plan for the stabilization of Germany. Imagine, if you please, any financial house in Europe coming into this body and granting loans and bringing pressure to bear on the organization of the House of Representatives. Yet that is almost exactly what the Bank for International Settlements has done, and our banking houses here have been placing this tremendous financial power in the hands of the Bruening financial leader of the Reichstag.

In connection with what I have further to say here this morning, I want to point out to you the serious additional step that is about to be taken.

Mr. STAFFORD. Will the gentleman yield?

Mr. McFADDEN. I yield.

Mr. STAFFORD. Do I understand the gentleman is criticizing American banking institutions for loaning money to the accredited representative of the German Government?

Mr. McFADDEN. No; I am not suggesting that. I am suggesting that American financiers, who are international financiers——

Mr. STAFFORD. And properly so.

Mr. McFADDEN. Are using American money to help organize the Reichstag's financial operations.

Mr. STAFFORD. That was a governmental function—loaning money to the recognized representatives of the German Government. What is wrong with that?

Mr. McFADDEN. I am speaking of the possible involvement of our Federal reserve system in internationalism. I would like to point out further to the gentleman, and to the Members of the House, that that which I am referring to here is a possible further involvement in this situation. There is pending before the Senate at this time, having been reported favorably by the Senate Banking and Currency Committee, the nomination to be a member of the Federal Reserve Board, and its governor, the name of Mr. Eugene Meyer, Jr. This appointment should not be confirmed by the United States Senate, and I want to make that just as positive as it is possible for me to make it. If you want to turn the Federal reserve system over to international financiers, place Mr. Meyer in that particular post at this time.

A careful analysis discloses the fact that Mr. Meyer has been very closely connected, during his whole financial career, with banking houses of international reputation. He has a very close connection with J. P. Morgan & Co., and as the head of the War Finance Corporation, and in carrying on its activities, those close relationships were actively disclosed. He is a Wall Street man. I want to point out just what has happened in order to make that nomination and appointment possible. Gov. Roy Young, from Minnesota, was the governor of the Federal Reserve Board. His resignation was secured by appointing him as governor of the Federal reserve bank in Boston, and, because of that clause in the Federal reserve act which prohibits two members serving on the Federal Reserve Board from one Federal reserve district, Mr. Edmund Platt, the vice governor of the Federal Reserve Board, with eight years yet to go, was likewise removed by giving him a position with the Marine Midland Bank in New York. I understand that a new position of vice president was created, and two operations had to be performed in order to create a vacancy which would permit of the appointment of Mr. Meyer.

The Senate of the United States should not confirm his appointment without going into the details as to why these changes were made and why the appointment of Mr. Meyer was made necessary.

The Chairman. The time of the gentleman from Pennsylvania has expired.

Mr. Dickinson. Mr. Chairman, I yield the gentleman five additional minutes.

Mr. McFadden. He is recognized as an international financier; he is a Wall Street banker and closely affiliated with these international banking groups.

I want to point out in connection with that that at the present time we have a particularly pertinent and interesting situation as regards the mobilization of the world's gold. Over 60 per cent of the world's gold is now in France and in the United States, controlled by the Bank of France and the Federal reserve system. I want you to understand that situation because of what I am going to say to you next. I want to point out the close relationship which exists between this proposed member of the Federal reserve system and the French at this time.

Mr. O'Connor of New York. Will the gentleman yield?

Mr. McFadden. Yes.

Mr. O'Connor of New York. I have seen many contradictory statements as to where the gold reserve is throughout the world. The last figures I saw were that there was about $4,000,000,000 here and about $2,000,000,000 in France, but that there was about $4,000,000,000 or $5,000,000,000 distributed throughout the rest of the world. What are the gentleman's figures with respect to the gold reserve?

Mr. McFadden. Between 60 and 62 per cent is deposited in the United States and in France.

Mr. O'Connor of New York. What are the figures in dollars?

Mr. McFadden. Well, the total world's gold is something like $10,000,000,000, and 62 per cent would be something over $6,000,000,000.

Mr. O'Connor of New York. In both the United States and France, the gentleman means?

Mr. McFadden. Yes. The gold in the United States is principally under the control of the Federal reserve system and the gold in France is largely under the control of the Bank of France, and that has an important bearing on this whole situation.

I want to point out that Mr. Meyer is a brother-in-law of Mr. George Blumenthal, a member of the firm of J. P. Morgan & Co., who, I understand, represents the Rothschild interests, and that he is liaison officer between the French Government and J. P. Morgan & Co. That has a very important bearing on this particular situation.

I want to make it perfectly plain that in placing Mr. Meyer at the head of the Federal reserve system you are turning it over completely to this international financial group. I do not believe that the people of the United States want this thing to happen. This is an unpleasant duty for me to perform. But, ladies and gentleman of the House, I am interested in our country and its institutions, as is every man, women, and child in the United States.

The Federal reserve system controls the credit system not only of the United States to-day but is the dominating factor in finance throughout the whole world.

I could not let this opportunity pass without at least directing this to the attention of this House, and, I hope, the attention of the Senate, before they take this additional step.

There is no question that the Federal reserve system is playing with international financial operations through the Bank of International Settlements. Otherwise, why would Mr. McGarrah be here reporting to the President of the United States, the Treasury Department, the governor of the Federal Reserve Board, and the State Department? Why would he be making statements with regard to the operations of the Bank for International Settlements?

I am simply throwing out these thoughts to you to show how extensively we are becoming involved and how our financial system is becoming involved in the affairs of international finance.

At the opening of my remarks I pointed to the fact that

we are in the midst of a terrific business and financial depression in the United States, and it is just at such times that deals of this character are put over.

Gentlemen, I do not want to be too pessimistic with regard to our financial situation, but the fact remains that this year practically 1,100 banks will have failed in the United States. It is a serious financial crises, and I am hoping that before this session is over the committee over which I preside as chairman may have an opportunity to look into the causes of the failures of these particular banks.

The CHAIRMAN. The time of the gentleman from Pennsylvania has expired.

Mr. DICKINSON. Mr. Chairman, I yield the gentleman five additional minutes.

Mr. McFADDEN. I may say to you that the analysis I have already made of the causes of the failure of some of these banks indicates clearly that these failures are not due entirely to agricultural depression in the country districts. An examination of the portfolios of these banks will disclose that in many instances the impairment in the capital of these banks is caused by the investments in their portfolios.

You are going to find that these large big-city financial institutions—that in the past few years have been floating and financing these various consolidated enterprises that we have been in a mad rush to put together, where practically every business throughout the country that has gained any standing or any basis of earnings has been merged or mobilized and financed in New York and elsewhere—have been emitting securities, after pulling out the cream of the values in securities, and unloading the remaining worthless securities not only on the banks but on innocent investors throughout the country; and in mentioning this I put at the top of the last the international banks who are financing these domestic operations and the large amount of foreign securities as a whole, many of which have depreciated in this country over 50 per cent. The failed banks are/full of these worthless securities, and they have been sold to the banks and to the innocent investors in this country by banking houses of the type which I have just mentioned.

Mr. O'CONNOR of New York. Will the gentleman yield?

Mr. MCFADDEN. I yield.

Mr. O'CONNOR of New York. Does not the gentleman also think that one of the underlying causes for the condition of some of the banks is that they have left the strictly banking business and have gone into the financing business with their side companies called finance, and so forth, companies?

Mr. MCFADDEN. The gentleman is quite correct. That is one of the serious phases of this question. Banks have not been content to do a legitimate banking business, but they have organized affiliated companies under State laws that have permitted them to do those things which are prohibited directly under the law. There is no doubt but that the matter which the gentleman has referred to is responsible for a lot of things that have been going on and for a large part of the losses that have been sustained; in fact, they are responsible for a lot of the speculation which occurred last year, where affiliates of some of these large houses were the violators.

They have been the sources from which hundreds of millions of dollars' worth of these fancy securities have been unloaded on the innocent public. This resulted in the wide speculation of last year; in fact, the very thing that caused the crash of last October was the fact that early in the summer these reorganization and financing houses that had all of these reorganizations and financial operations in process became aware of the fact that pressure was on from the Federal Reserve to reduce credit lines and that an economic depression was imminent, and they all tried to get rid of their securities at one and the same time. What happened? It was just like the meeting of two locomotives. The excess amount of the issues of these new securities to which I have referred and the tightening of the credit of the financial system brought them together exactly as two locomotives came together, and there was nothing to prevent a crash.

Mr. BLACK. Will the gentleman yield?

Mr. McFadden. Yes.

Mr. Black. Does the gentleman's committee intend to do anything about all this?

Mr. McFadden. So far as the chairman is concerned, I will say the committee is going to take up very actively a study of this particular phase of the financial troubles that confront this country. [Applause.]

VI

WHY NOT AN
AMERICAN POLICY?

December 20, 1930

Mr. McFADDEN. Mr. Speaker, I ask unanimous consent to address the House for 30 minutes.

The SPEAKER. The gentleman from Pennsylvania asks unanimous consent to address the House for 30 minutes. Is there objection?

Mr. DYER. Reserving the right to object, upon what subject?

Mr. McFADDEN. On the international financial situation.

Mr. DYER. On the same line as the gentleman's previous speech?

Mr. McFADDEN. Somewhat; yes.

Mr. BEEDY. Reserving the right to object, is the gentleman going to discuss the Federal Reserve Board policy and the appointment of the chairman to the board?

Mr. McFADDEN. I am not going to discuss the appointment of the governor of the Federal Reserve Board. I covered that question thoroughly last Tuesday. I am not going to discuss the address of the gentleman from Massachusetts [MR. LUCE] last Wednesday, if that is what is in the gentleman's mind.

Mr. BEEDY. The gentleman at this critical time is going to discuss the policy of the Federal reserve system?

Mr. McFadden. I am going to state some facts pertinent to certain matters connected with the Federal reserve system and the international financial situation.

Mr. Beedy. Mr. Speaker, inasmuch as this is a matter vitally affecting the situation at this critical time, and the fact that it has never been taken up before the committee, I shall object. If we are to discuss the Federal reserve's policy now, I think we should first consider it in the committee.

Mr. Garner. Will the gentleman yield for a question?

Mr. Dyer. Mr. Speaker, I ask for the regular order.

The Speaker. The regular order is demanded.

Mr. McFadden. Mr. Speaker, I ask unanimous consent to insert in the Record the address that I was about to deliver.

The Speaker. Is there objection to the request of the gentleman from Pennsylvania?

Mr. Beedy. I shall have to object to that until I have had some opportunity to inform myself as to the subject matter which it is proposed to discuss.

* * * * * * * *

Mr. Kvale. Mr. Speaker, reserving the right to object, a little while ago a Member was denied the privilege of inserting his own remarks in the Record. I do not want to object to the request of the gentleman from Illinois, but I am wondering whether the gentleman from Pennsylvania has conferred with the other Members of the House and is going to renew his request to-day.

Mr. Beedy. Mr. Speaker, the gentleman is just a little previous. The gentleman from Pennsylvania has very courteously submitted his manuscript to me; and, having read it, I am very glad to withdraw my objection.

Mr. Jones of Texas. Is the gentleman on the board of censors of this House?

Mr. Beedy. Not at all, but I am eager that nothing in the contemplated speech convey the impression that the gentleman from Pennsylvania is about to speak for the Committee on Banking and Currency, of which I am a member. The

79

gentleman from Pennsylvania has very graciously offered to say that he represents himself alone, and does not attempt to speak for anybody else.

* * * * * * * *

PERMISSION TO ADDRESS THE HOUSE

Mr. McFADDEN. Mr. Speaker, inasmuch as the objection to my unanimous-consent request has been withdrawn, I renew the request at this time, namely, to address the House for 30 minutes.

The SPEAKER. The gentleman from Pennsylvania asks unanimous consent to address the House for 30 minutes. Is there objection?

There was no objection.

Mr. McFADDEN. Mr. Speaker, ladies and gentlemen of the House, at the outset I want to make it perfectly clear and reiterate what the gentleman from Maine has already said about the remarks I am about to make. I make them on my own responsibility as a Member of the House, as I always do and I am not speaking for the Banking and Currency Committee, nor am I attempting to speak for anyone else who is a member of this body, nor have I in the past in any remarks I have ever uttered in this House attempted to convey that thought.

Mr. JONES of Texas. Will the gentleman yield?

Mr. McFADDEN. Yes.

Mr. JONES of Texas. Has the gentleman agreed to delete anything from his proposed remarks?

Mr. McFADDEN. I have not. They are going to be delivered exactly as I intended to deliver them when the objection was made.

Mr. Speaker, there are times when it is peculiarly necessary for the Congress of the United State to consider from a broad and comprehensive standpoint the situation in which the country finds itself.

At such times patriotic legislators will diligently examine the multiciplicity of forces that are at work and study the effect of their influence upon the general welfare and the state of the Union. It is precisely at such times that the spirit of controversy will be subordinated and partisan prejudice set aside. It is light that is needed, and its beneficient rays may be depended upon to bring satisfactory solutions and point the way to national policies upon which all parties and factions who are actuated by love of country may unite.

Such, Mr. Speaker, are the times in which we are now meeting. Their problems are not bounded by our frontiers, as they frequently were in an older day. On the contrary, the forces which are now making themselves felt in our daily lives come in large measure from without, and these distant though powerful influences are sometimes obscure and baffling because cause and effect are not clearly visible and the motives which set them in motion are not understood.

These world forces are primarily political. They fall within the purview of this body, and it is the Congress of the United States that must cope with them, and legislate intelligently with reference to them, if the United States is to control them consciously and not be drawn unwittingly into the sweep of policies determined for it from without or privately by the Government's executive branch alone.

Since the New Haven address which Secretary Hughes made in 1921, and increasingly with the passage of the years, we have been exhorted to leave the settlement of foreign problems to the economic experts. There is a school of leadership, very vocal and insistent, which points to the failure of political leadership everywhere, and asks that the financiers and economists in private life be permitted to do well what the politicians can only do badly.

So urgent have been their exhortations that they have, in fact, been given carte blanche by successive administrations to represent the United States abroad where they have wielded enormous power because the Europeans thought that they spoke for the American Government, and where they have put their mark upon the Europe of to-day as effectively as any overlord could do.

Where did the idea come from that American financiers

81

and economic experts could properly adjust the political relationships of the European states among themselves or of those
states with the United States? What type of man is there who
has less interest in political principles, and less regard for
political sensibilities, than the international financier?

The particular gentlemen who, in regard to postwar
Europe have represented American financial prestige in the
treaty settlements there, have succeeded in leaving that distracted continent in a worse condition than that in which they
found it.

They proceeded on the assumption that the settlements of
the treaty of Versailles were final and were to be put into
integral execution, notwithstanding the fact that their own
country had refused to become a party to that treaty.

In their financial negotiations the treaty of Versailles became their bible, and in their interpretations of the reparation obligations of Germany they have shown themselves more
English than the English and more French than the French.

It has been their endeavor, through the successive steps of
the London ultimatum, the Dawes plan, and the Young plan,
to commit their own country to settlements which in their
essence are no whit different from the treaty of Versailles itself.
This would have been an enormous service to the allied states
of Europe for without the support of the United States they
are not strong enough to enforce the unjust treaty, and a
radical revision becomes necessary. They have sought by
economic means to guarantee the political settlements made at
Versailles, instead of inquiring whether political readjustments
were not a condition precedent to economic improvement.

For this reason their activities in Europe have been worse
than useless. They have without doubt complicated and entangled the international situation and perpetuated the fatal
errors of the peace settlement to such an extent that no recovery has been possible in Europe.

There is not a single political wrong to whose solution
they have contributed. They have assumed that there were
no political wrongs in the peace treaty that must first be

82

corrected, and they have proceeded to capitalize the blood money of a vast war tribute into billions-of-dollar bonds which they have brought home with them and offered for sale to the American people with the assurance that Europe's political troubles have been healed by their masterly statesmanship and, incidentally, that the bonds are an excellent investment for the American purchaser.

But the bonds are not an excellent investment for the American purchaser, and the American purchaser does not want them. Some other treatment must be found for the invalid than this comprehensive transfusion of American financial blood.

Mr. Speaker, the financiers and economic experts have had their turn. It is time for them to retire and relinquish the responsibility of determining the policy of the United States Government to the representatives in Congress where it belongs. [Applause.] It is time that the control of the Federal Reserve Bank of New York be taken out of their hands and that, by legislation, its activities be brought into line with a national policy which the Congress of the United States will fix.

The war in Europe profoundly altered the relationship of that continent to the rest of the world, and particularly its relationship to our own country. This fact did not become visible until some years after the war. It was consciously concealed by the European negotiators in the peace conference, and the treaty of Versailles recited th obligation of the vanquished in that war to pay $33,000,000,000 to the victors. Were the makers of that peace treaty under the spell of an illusion that Europe's pre-war wealth remained intact? That the financial settlements of that treaty as between the European States had any connection with reality?

Knowing the undoubtedly high intellectual quality of the minds of the European negotiators we can not believe it. They knew that all Europe must begin the new post-war era in dire poverty and burdened with debt; that the power of stored-up capital had passed from it.

Why, then, did they saddle upon the enemy an utterly

impossible war tribute of $33,000,000,000 to be paid in annual installments over a period of 37 years?

It is a strange fact that it is only in recent years that public attention in the United States has been drawn to that provision in the treaty of Versailles which permits the Allied States to offer their respective shares of the $33,000,000,000 indemnity to private purchasers in the form of bonds.

Even if discreet statesmanship did not desire to stress this provision publicly, it bears so directly on the interests of the American people, and it was such a powerful means of new postwar adjustments which concerned them, that it would seem that the American mind would have been alive to its significance.

It has, however, remained the most obscure feature of the treaty of Versailles, although its influence runs like a red thread through all the postwar negotiations.

The financial illusions upon which the treaty of Versailles were based in 1919 were accepted as realities here. Because of the energy and enterprise of the allied statesmen in presenting their case, we accepted their version of the postwar satuation which followed the cessation of hostilities. As a consequence, the information coming to the Congress and to the American public was not sufficient to enable them to understand the situation in Europe.

When, therefore, Secretary Hughes in 1921 accepted the German indemnity of $33,000,000,000 as a reality and approved of the London ultimatum which imposed it upon Germany, there was no realization that a mere war mirage was being written into world law.

The fact that the London ultimatum provided that $12,-000,000,000 in reparation bonds were to be immediately commercialized did not attract the slightest popular attention in the United States.

The suggestion that the settlement in Europe be left to eminent American financiers followed, and the era of the economic expert in politics was ushered in.

They proceeded to bend their efforts to making the United

States a party to settlements which would permit of the reparation bonds in their billions being offered, almost exclusively, to the American investor.

It was not, however, until this year that the economic experts by the Young plan succeeded in getting into the United States with the reparation bonds. With their sale actually imminent in the United States I undertook in this House last spring to examine in the light of reality what had actually transpired in Europe at the end of the war.

It was necessary to examine the events from the preliminary agreement which brought hostilities to a close in November, 1918, to the settlements of the definitive treaty seven months later. It was found that the terms of the preliminary agreement, which in international law were binding on both sides, had afterwards been almost wholly discarded; that their terms did not permit of punitive damages, afterwards called reparations; but that, nevertheless, the most crushing tribute ever imposed after war was incorporated later in the settlements of the treaty of Versailles.

It was also found that in order to effect this the real conquest of Germany was attained in the six months following the armistice by means of a ruthless food blockade which was maintained throughout the period during which the peace conference sat. All this was done in violation of the preliminary peace agreement.

Undoubtedly, under international law, the German State to-day is not morally or legally bound to carry out the provisions of the treaty of Versailles. It is a pity that this was not perceived by our State Department in 1921 at the time of the London ultimatum, when it entangled us in the postwar mirage and implanted deep in the minds of the European statesmen fond hopes that Europe might be reestablished through the commercialization of the German indemnity in the United States.

Even if Germany had in fact been conquered on the field of battle before the armistice, in which case the settlement would have had some elements of honesty, it would not have

85

been a rational act for the United States to have permitted the commercialization of the indemnity among its citizens. But when, as actually happened, an unconquered enemy, giving up his arms in reliance upon the good faith of an armistice agreement, is afterwards tricked into the power of his adversary, who thereupon reduces him to unconditional surrender by the pressure of starvation and compels him to accept the burden of a colossal war tribute for 37 years, the obligation is fraudulently imposed, and the bonds which are afterwards issued are tainted with illegality.

Such are the reparation bonds of the treaty of Versailles, and it is inconceivable when the real facts of the peace settlement are known that the government of the United States could open its doors to the sale of those bonds among the American people.

That it has now done so is wholly due to the influence through the years that a small and powerful group of our international bankers, and through them the allied governments, have been able to exercise continuously upon the policy of our executives.

Cunning, grapevine methods have placed willing agents at the head of great executive departments and in important subordinate governmental positions, and financial control of newspapers and magazines has made it possible to lead public opinion far astray.

The tangled web of deception in the treaty of Versailles was directed against the American people, who were to become the victims of the clever reparations clauses. To carry out the financial settlements it was a necessary condition that this state of deception be not disturbed; that it be made permanent and allowed to dominate the postwar policy of the United States Government. The hypnotic trance in which the paid American publicists and the political college professors have lived for a decade has enabled the international financiers to use their voices and pens to keep the political deception alive.

Because the definite allied postwar policy has been to secure the quick return from America of the gold stock lost by Europe in the war, and to secure it through application of the provisions of annex 2 to the reparation clauses of the treaty of Versailles, the perpetuation in America of the illusions of 1919 has been essential.

Systematic deception, therefore, has characterized this period, and it is because this deception is not being unmasked that the futility of the Versailles settlements are at last becoming apparent.

Before taking up the financial and economic condition that confronts us to-day, which is a part of the direct result of the Versailles settlements, I wish to review briefly the unfolding of allied policy in Europe during the past 10 years.

In 1921, when allied exasperation was wreaking senseless vengeance upon Germany because the latter refused to acquiesce in the financial settlements of the treaty, Gustav Stresemann, not yet in office, conceived of a policy which might at once save Germany and unify Europe.

Lord D'Abernon, who was then British ambassador at Berlin, has with some naivete disclosed the beginning of the "Stresemann policy." He says that Stresemann called on him in 1922 and requested him to put four blunt questions to Lord Curzon, who was then British Foreign Minister.

With some hesitation D'Abernon did so, and, to his surprise, he received frank answers to them, which he transmitted to Stresemann. Thereupon Stresemann set to work with unflagging persistence to found a German policy upon these answers, to attain public office, and as German Minister of Foreign Affairs to put this policy into effect. There is little doubt that these four questions were as follows:

First. If a way could be found for the economic rehabilitation of Europe by means coming from outside Europe, would Britain be willing to see Germany recuperate?

Second. Would Britain restrain France from aggressions against Germany?

Third. If the commercialization of the German reparation bonds outside of Europe could be effected, would Britain accept this as such a means?

Fourth. Would Britain see to it that Germany should receive a substantial share in the proceeds?

Stresemann did not attain office until 1925. The German governments which preceded him fought stubbornly against commercialization of the German reparations. The Dawes plan, effected in 1924, provided for the commercialization of $4,000,000,000 worth of the bonds, but necessary cooperation failed to come from Germany. The international bankers made repeated efforts to obtain the consent of the Coolidge administration to commercialize the bonds here, but relations on the opposite sides of the Rhine were so threatening that their appeals had little force.

The next year, 1925, witnessed the inauguration of the Stresemann policy. Reconciliation in Europe was announced. On board the *Orange Blossom,* floating on the shimmering waters of Locarno, the personal friends, Stresemann and Briand, reached an understanding for their respective countries. The treaty of Locarno was signed in which France and Germany made peace and Britain agreed impartially to support either party in case of military aggression by the other.

The publicity given this treaty in the United States was thorough and complete. There was not a town or village to which the news was not carried that peace had now come in Europe, and that that continent was bathed in the sunshine of Locarno. With stable peace effected in Europe, why should there be any further hesitation about American investments in European securities?

Evidencing the new accord Germany, a few months later, in September, 1926, was duly admitted to good standing as a member of the League of Nations. Only one step more at the European end of the stage was now needed to bring the Stresemann policies to fruition.

This step was taken immediately after Germany was admitted to the League of Nations. The two personal friends, Stresemann and Briand, met, not unostentatiously, at the rustic inn at Thoiry in the Vosges. Here it was agreed—

First. That Germany would agree to the commercialization

of the reparation bonds outside of Europe.

Second. That France would cease the pin-pricking policy, evacuate the Rhine, and agree that Germany should receive a substantial share of the proceeds from commercialization—one-third, as it afterwards became known.

The next year, 1927, Poincaré promised the French people that if he were returned to power the "bankers' plan," which was to put the Thoiry agreement into execution, would be accepted by France. Stresemann continued to mold policy in Germany in accordance with this purpose. The movement had the support of the British Foreign Office.

In September, 1928, the powers met at Geneva and in solemn conclave took measures for the "final and complete settlement of the reparation question" by the method already adopted in the French elections the preceding year. To this end the appointment of a committee of "experts" was provided for in the following December. This was the Young committee, which assembled in February, 1929, and completed its labors the following June, bringing forth the Young plan, which to-day lies at the heart of any discussion of the world-wide depression which is now with us.

So much for the winding course of postwar diplomacy as it disclosed itself on the other side of the Atlantic. It will be seen that this entire conception presupposes the justice, the adequacy, and the permanency of the settlements of the Versailles treaty in their entirety. The part that the United States is to play under the Young plan is to guarantee by its preponderating power the settlements of the Versailles treaty and to dig deeply into its superabundant financial resources to rehabilitate the depleted treasuries of Europe.

But Stresemann has passed away and a new spirit is coming over the German dreams. The sunshine of Locarno was artificially produced and Briand is discredited in France. Last July marked a rapid and profound change in the political scene in Europe. New combinations are forming of which I will speak later. The Stresemann policy, universally discarded, has vanished almost overnight. Its disappearance coincides with the rejection by the American investing public of the German international 5½ per cent bonds.

Mr. Speaker, let us return to the United States and observe, so far as we can, the impact of these forces from abroad upon our domestic economy.

Simultaneously with the collapse of the Stresemann policy in Europe comes the depression in the United States. When the Young plan was drawn up it was intended that it should go into operation by putting the bonds on sale in the United States not later than November 1, 1929. Their successful flotation, followed by new slices of the loan, would, it was hoped, draw billions out of America's plentiful investment capital into Europe. This would at once give Europe a new purchasing power of billions and stave off its threatening industrial collapse. Languishing trans-Atlantic trade and world trade would revive, production for export in the United States would increase, and the threatening industrial recession here would be checked. The waning confidence of the American public in New York financial leadership would be revived and psychological causes, or in plain words, lack of confidence in financial leadership, would not supervene to cause domestic industrial depression.

But the American investing public have declined to absorb the Young-plan bonds and Europe has abandoned the Stresemann policies. Foreign purchasing power came to an end last year because new loans in America, which would have permitted its continuance, could no longer be made. The fall in investment values took place in the autumn of 1929 and the industrial depression, which is still with us, began.

Mr. Speaker, the liquidation of the war in accordance with the principles of the treaty of Versailles has failed. It is time to discard them and make new adjustments.

Simultaneously with the abdication by Washington of its governmental powers in favor of "economic experts" several years ago it practically abandoned control of the Federal Reserve Bank of New York to the private international financiers. Last February I called attention here to the ambitious

90

policies of that bank, to the frequent visits here of Mr. Montague Norman, governor of the Bank of England, for conferences with the head of that bank, to the advance of a credit of $200,000,000 from the Federal reserve system to the Bank of England, made in 1923.

And right here I desire to digress and call attention to the fact that another one of these conferences has just taken place, when the governor of the Federal Reserve Bank of New York was abroad conferring in London, Paris, and Berlin, with J. P. Morgan, Owen D. Young, and the heads of the various central banks of issue of the countries of the world, and upon their return to New York a meeting was held in the Federal Reserve Bank in New York, where a report was made by Mr. Owen D. Young, Mr. George L. Harrison, and Mr. J. P. Morgan as to the results of their conferences abroad. The public, however, know nothing about the changes that have been decided upon in connection with these various conferences. All we know is the fact that after the other conference held in this country in 1927 a change in the discount policy was made and money was made cheap, which resulted in the shipment out of this country of $500,000,000 worth of gold which, at the same time, released a superabundant amount of credit, which resulted in stimulating the beginning of the stock speculation which ended so disastrously last year.

Since that date it has more and more been the practice of the Federal Reserve Bank of New York to make gold loans to the central banks of Europe and to buy foreign bills on a large scale. The extensions of the powers of this bank have appeared to be a matter of indifference to the Federal Reserve Board in Washington who profess to have but little knowledge of what it is doing.

These loans have all been made to the national banks of the allied governments whose policies have been the integral execution of the provisions of the treaty of Versailles, and the proceeds have been used exclusively to that end. The United States Government has never avowed the policy of upholding the treaty of Versailles. There is a discrepancy here

91

between the financial policy of the Federal Reserve Bank of New York and the policy of the United States Government. The policy of the Federal Reserve Bank of New York has been that of upholding and furthering the Stresemann policy in accordance with the wishes of the "economic experts" to whose control that bank has been abandoned.

This is not as it should be. America's foreign financial policy should be fixed for the Federal reserve banks by the Federal Reserve Board at Washington and not by one of the 12 coordinate Federal reserve banks. And the Federal Reserve Board in Washington should mold its policies in accordance with the foreign policy of the United States Government whose creature the Federal Reserve Board is.

What is the foreign policy of the United States Government at this time? Is it a policy primarily directed to the maintenance of the national interests, to the protection of the Nation's wealth, and to the conserving of the Nation's strength, or is it a policy of timidity and drift which follows the line of least resistance? In view of its tolerance of the London ultimatum and the Dawes plan, and of the hospitality which it now gives to the Young plan and the World Bank, with the implication which these acts carry of choosing sides in Europe and throwing the support of the United States Government to the integral execution of the treaty of Versailles, while at the same time assuring the public that it is having nothing to do with political quarrels in Europe and takes no interest in German reparations, it is to be questioned whether its policy has been in the interests of the American people and whether it has shown that ingenuous quality which ought to characterize the government of a republic.

At the end of the last session I introduced a bill which is intended to prohibit traffic in German reparation bonds in this country. The Congress should pass this bill as a first step in the establishment of a definite policy. Its passage will prevent any possible revival of the Stresemann policy in some other guise and bring to an end the dangerous financial heresies of the treaty of Versailles.

We must recognize that a 12-year policy for the financial settlement of the war in Europe has failed and has come to an end. It depended for its success upon the rapid shifting of a large part of the American gold stock into Europe. In spite of the weakness of our executive branch we have succeeded in preventing this. But to protect our gold in future, legislation is needed here to guide the Secretary of the Treasury and the Federal Reserve Board in Washington.

We must admit that it has been the veiled support by successive administrations in Washington of allied policies in Europe that has concentrated power in the hands of the French and is now bringing the entire continent into revolt against her military dominance. We must admit, too, that the primary purpose of the French power, which we were supporting, was to rivet the reparations obligation upon Germany so that the Stresemann policy could be carried out and the reparation bonds disposed of in the United States.

Events in Europe since last July indicate clearly that combinations are forming against Anglo-French dominance. Simultaneously with the failure of the German international 5½'s on the American investment market, Mussolini called for a revision of the treaty of Versailles, and led Italy out of the allied ranks. Italy is making alliances with the countries who were defeated in the war, and an Italian-Russian-German understanding is taking form which might become formidable in certain eventualities.

And only yesterday my attention was called to a speech by Mussolini in Italy in which he dealt with the financial and economic depression in the United States, and to a great extent laid the economic and financial troubles of Italy to the stock crash in the United States, and to the development of the plan of mass production in this country which has resulted in creating such enormous surpluses. I was asked to comment upon this, and in this connection I recall that on July 3 last in this House I had something to say on this same question, and also in my remarks in the House last Tuesday I confirmed my previous statement as regards this speculation and mass pro-

93

duction and its effect in this country and the whole world.

Reports have recently emanated from Washington to the effect that the State Department has refused to have anything to say in regard to any foreign loans. Only yesterday, at the other end of the Capitol, one of the leading Senators introduced a resolution, and is pressing for action upon it, forbidding the State Department from having anything to say concerning the placing of foreign loans in the United States.

Under these circumstances the chronic weakness of our Executive policy is making itself manifest again. It is obviously being led by Anglo-French suggestion.

By what right has Ambassador Hugh Gibson, sitting in a meeting of the disarmament conference, recently signed this agreement on behalf of the United States:

The present convention shall not in any way diminish the obligations of previous treaties under which certain of the high contracting parties agreed to limit their military, naval, and air armaments and thus fixed in relation to one another their respective rights and obligations in this convention.

Is this to become a treaty settlement by which the United States compels Germany to remain disarmed?

And along with this comes press reports that the United States Government has frowned upon a loan to Italy in order to bring pressure upon that country to follow certain policies.

The tendency of these things, Mr. Speaker, is to draw us into alliance with France and Britain to maintain the status quo of the treaty of Versailles. All the indications point to the fact that unless the treaty of Versailles is radically revised there will be war in Europe. Does the administration contemplate with equanimity the fact that what we are doing to-day will inevitably draw us into that war on the side of the allied States?

It is possible and logical for the United States Government to follow a policy which will keep us out of these entangling alliances, but it is quite obvious that the intervention of the Congress is necessary if this is to be done. The intervention

94

of the Congress is necessary to undo the work of our economic experts in blindly acquiescing in the Stresemann policy, going halfway into the World Court, and accepting the Young plan and the World Bank.

All of these devices were measures to strengthen and bolster the treaty of Versailles and insure French domination of th continent of Europe under the provisions of that treaty. They fall and crumble into dust if the moral support of the United States is not believed to be behind them.

The industrial stagnation in this country to-day is largely due to the distrust of the people in the foreign policy of our Government and in the financial policies of the Federal reserve system. They do not want entangling alliances, but they have seen an increasing tendency toward entangling alliances as the years have passed. They do not want to see their financial system weakened by too great extensions in its commitments abroad, but that is exactly what they fear is happening to-day.

As I said a little while ago, the economic experts have had their turn and they have led us upon the search for a will-o'-the-wisp. They have bogged us deep in the slough of German reparations. Let them return now to their true field of strictly private activities. Let them cease to dream of fixing the foreign policies of the United States. Let us set ourselves to the fixing of fundamental principle and to the formulation of legislation which is made in America and will conserve and safeguard the interests of the American people. [Applause.]

Mr. RAMSEYER. Will the gentleman yield?

Mr. MCFADDEN. I yield.

Mr. RAMSEYER. The gentleman discussed the morality and legality of the Versailles treaty, and I think more and more informed people are taking the view that the gentleman has expressed here. I do not know whether the gentleman remembers a speech on the Versailles treaty made by the late Senator from his own State, Senator Knox, soon after that treaty was laid before the Senate, in which he analyzed the treaty very carefully and came to the conclusion that the treaty would not

95

maintain peace, but on the other hand would provoke wars.

Now, as to the worthlessness of these reparation bonds, I have grave doubts myself as to the advisability of Americans investing in those foreign bonds. It is true that since the war we have lent each year a great deal of money to Europe, something around $1,000,000,000 annually, is it not?

Mr. McFADDEN. It is a total of more than they have paid on the war debts.

Mr. RAMSEYER. Yes; at any rate we have lent each year more to Europe than the balance of trade in our favor amounted to; is not that true?

Mr. McFADDEN. The records of that show.

Mr. RAMSEYER. And that has helped stimulate our trade and helped a great deal in keeping up the prosperity in this country and in the world that we enjoyed during that period, and undoubtedly our failure last year to continue making loans in the same volume had something to do with bringing about this world depression. That is the gentleman's view, is it not?

Mr. McFADDEN. And the loss of money by foreigners in the New York stock market.

Mr. RAMSEYER. The two combined. Now, the gentleman stated at some place in his address that the Versailles treaty and the other settlements had to be scrapped and something else substituted for them, and I thought the gentleman was going to discuss what should be substituted. I listened for that very carefully. If the gentleman said anything in that connection to convey the idea that was something he wanted to substitute, I did not get it. Does the gentleman care to elaborate on that phrase?

Mr. McFADDEN. I did not make such a suggestion, because that will only come after conferences between the interested parties, when a plan will be worked out that will more appropriately fit the case than does the carrying out of the now obsolete Stresemann policies, evidenced by the treaty of Versailles and subsequent Dawes and Young plans.

Mr. RAMSEYER. Is it the gentleman's opinion that before we can get peace in the world and restore prosperity in the

96

world, we have to scrap the Versailles treaty and the Young plan and substitute something else in the place of them?

Mr. MCFADDEN. I do not think we will get a proper solution of this whole matter in Europe until we go back to the very foundation.

If the foundation is faulty, you can not build a safe structure on top of it.

Mr. RAMSEYER. What is the foundation, the Versailles treaty?

Mr. MCFADDEN. The Versailles treaty. [Applause.]

VII

AMERICA'S INTEREST IN THE BANK FOR INTERNATIONAL SETTLEMENTS

January 15, 1931

Mr. McFADDEN. Mr. Speaker, under the leave to extend my remarks in the RECORD, I include the following speech delivered by me Tuesday evening, January 13, 1931, before the Economic Club, of Providence, R. I.:

For nearly a year now the Bank for International Settlements, which in its conception was to have a corporate being free from political control by any sovereign power, has been able to enjoy corporate existence and enter upon its unique functions because the sovereign State of Switzerland generously consented to become its creator.

It was created in this normal and prosaic way because, however, portentous its advent upon the human scene may be, miraculous birth did not seem feasible for it to the members of the Young Committee in 1929. Switzerland was selected as its parent because the thought of its birth and growth from youth to maturity taking place at London aroused such ineradicable apprehensions at Paris, and the thought of such growth taking place at Paris aroused such precisely similar apprehensions at London, that some sovereign power which was not suspect had to be chosen.

Every bank exists by virtue of the physical protection which the state which creates it gives to it. Policemen or gendarme patrol its approaches, and if need be the military forces of the state intervene to guard its treasures against the depredations of marauders. The reciprocal obligation follows of loyalty and obedience on the part of the bank to the will of its sovereign creator and to it alone.

The Swiss are a redoubtable people. Surrounded through the centuries by warlike and aggressive powers, they have expelled every incursion of the foreigner into their mountain fastnesses and maintained their independence unimpaired. They would be quick to oppose any aggression from without.

Swiss honor also is unimpeachable, and the bank's directors may therefore rest easy as to the safety of the funds within its vaults, even though those funds would necessarily be at the disposal of the Swiss state.

Should an aggressive European power, or a coalition of powers, threaten a raid upon those vaults, the entire military force of Switzerland may be depended upon to die to the last man in its defense as they did at Morgarten or St. Jaques.

This is a heavy responsibility for the world to ask the state of Switzerland to accept. But the responsibility may be greatly lightened if the bulk of the gold stocks of the bank may, by arrangement, be left on deposit in Paris or London, so that, for the most part, gold transfers may be effected by mere book entries as is the custom of the central bank of a sovereign state in making transfers of gold between private domestic banks. In such case the total amount of the treasure in the vaults of the bank at Basle might be very small, and it would not be necessary for the promising Swiss youth to pour out its blood upon the steps of the bank.

In such case, also, the strength of the bank will rest upon moral prestige and not upon the support of physical force except such as in an exceptional case the League of Nations might marshall for its protection. So highly does our Federal reserve system esteem the moral prestige of the bank that it has already parted with some of its high officials in order that they

99

may become officers of the Bank for International Settlements and contribute their talents to the bank's success.

It is said that the Federal reserve system puts such great confidence in it that it may entrust a large part of its gold to the custody of the bank, thus obviating the frequent shipment of bullion across the Atlantic in either direction and greatly facilitating international transfer of funds.

As to the safety of the gold, besides the redoubtable guardianship of the Swiss Government, the League of Nations could, at need, marshal the collective military force of Europe against any aggressor who, in defiance of a decision of the World Court, might seek to seize it by force Thus, whatever stocks of gold we entrusted to the Bank for International Settlements would be under the protection of the council of the League of Nations.

In case our Federal reserve bank requested a gold credit, or shipment of gold which we had on deposit in the Bank for International Settlements, and this became a matter of dispute, and the latter bank felt that it must refuse to make the transfer, the American interests could file suit in the World Court, and the Council of the League of Nations could be depended on to put any decision of that court into execution.

While it is a legal truism that possession is nine points of the law, and while possession of the disputed gold in such a case would be held in Europe, the moral and judicial majesty of the World Court will be such that it would be unthinkable for the American litigants to question the decision.

Thus, these beneficent institutions of an enlightened age insure the settlement of all financial differences between the United States and the States of Europe by peaceful means.

I do not desire to make an address here, gentlemen, in an ironical vein. My position in regard to the Bank for International Settlements is known. America should have no more interest in this bank than it has in the Bank of England, the Bank of France, the Reichsbank, of the Bank of Turkey. The function of the Federal reserve system is to protect the gold and regulate the currency of the United States, and its foreign contacts should be only incidental to this purpose. Political motives, such as financial aid in establishing or strengthening any political power in Europe, or financial pressure to compel action by some other political organism in Europe, ought not to be within the authority of the Federal reserve system.

I have spoken frequently during the past year, in Congress and elewhere, upon the tendency of the Federal Reserve Bank of New York to blaze an independent trail by establishing and developing extensive contacts abroad for which it has no authorization in law, and of the deleterious effects of its policies upon our domestic conditions. I have covered the ground quite fully and in that connection have warned against its efforts to involve us in the world bank created by the Young plan.

The banking system of a state is such as the state chooses to set up. To coin money and regulate its value is an attribute of sovereign power, and in the exercise of this power the state establishes its banking system. If the state abandons control of its banking system to others it quickly ceases to be sovereign, for those who control the nation's wealth control the nation. Within the banking system of a sovereign state mutual aid and credit extensions among banks may be carried to great lengths for these funds all remain under the control of the state. This is not true as to foreign banks, and the extension of credits to a foreign state or bank ought not to be exercised at the independent will of the banking system. They ought to be matters for decision by sovereign authority.

We established the Federal reserve system a few months before the war broke out in Europe, and thereby created a centralized control of currency and the use of credit. Each of the 12 Federal reserve banks was to regulate credit in its district according to the needs there, and the activities of the reserve banks were to be coordinated under the supervision of the Federal Reserve Board at Washington.

The banks were given the power to buy and sell gold abroad, but it was the intention of the makers of the Federal reserve act that this power should be merely incidental to the primary purpose of affording proper credit facilities to American citizens. The Federal reserve act did not contemplate the needs of the foreigner; it contemplated the needs of the American people solely.

But no sooner was the act passed and the Federal reserve system set in operation than the war in Europe broke out and exerted a profound influence upon our financial structure. The Federal reserve system became the vehicle for the transfer of vast funds from Europe to America, and especially after we entered the war for the transfer of vast sums of American wealth to Europe. These transfers were nearly all made through the Federal Reserve Bank of New York. This expansion of the purposes of the Federal reserve system was made by the authority of the Government in Washington and was necessitated by the exigencies of war.

After we entered the war the successive Liberty and Victory loans raised the necessary billions through subscription by the people. The billions destined for Europe were, as it were, drawn into a vast funnel whose mouth was the Federal Reserve Bank of New York and from there poured across the Atlantic. This raised the international bankers of New York who were representing foreign governments to a dizzy eminence of financial power and created the most intimate contacts between the agents of the respective financial powers in New York, London, and Paris. The sense of unity with our associated nations in the war found its highest expression in the trans-Atlantic contacts established by these New York bankers. A roomy financial conduit had been constructed across the Atlantic through which the entire liquid wealth of either hemisphere might easily be transferred to the other, provided those who controlled the wealth so desired.

That roomy financial conduit still exists as it was created in war time. After performing its war functions it served again from 1921 to 1924 for the great flow of gold metal westward when Europe made a belated settlement of its vast unpaid trade balance.

When that service was completed the function of this trans-Atlantic financial conduit, this feat of financial engineering, should have come to an end. Having served its war purpose, it should have been dismantled. It is too roomy for peace purposes. Its potentialities are as great as would be those of a tunnel from the United States to Europe built of stone and mortar. A reconsideration of the Federal reserve act ought to have been undertaken in 1925 and legislation effected to curb the powers of the Federal Reserve Bank of New York. As it was not done then, it is urgently needed now. Only a subordinate governmental agency in its nature, the Federal reserve system, dominated by a group of New York international bankers, is now claiming the right to exercise its powers independent of governmental control. It resents the suggestion of action by the Congress to regulate its functions and it aspires to assert equality with, or superiority over, the sovereign Government of the United States.

Suppose the Congress of the United States yields to these claims. History, particularly recent history, shows that the great financiers are able to insinuate their agents into high place with each incoming administration and to control both the State and Treasury Departments. They dominate the policies of the executive branch. If the Congress through the influence of the financial power over it becomes unable to regulate the banking system of the country and thus to curb an autocratic financial power, the political Government at Washington will cease to be a sovereign power and will become but the agent of an irresponsible and world-wide financial autocracy.

And to what uses would the roomy, war-time financial conduit across the Atlantic be put? Those superfinanciers who assume to tell us what is best for us, citizens of the United States as they are, are already saying that a redistribution of the great gold stock of the United States is urgently needed. Assume that, fascinated by these masterful voices, the citizenship of this country interposes no obstacle and permits them to have their way. Before any belated voices might rise in alarmed protest, the deed would be done, and the Eastern Hemisphere would again be dominant through the power of gold. The great savings-bank deposits of the American people

103

would shrink, credit, no longer a common utility, would become the rich man's privilege, money would be scarce and poverty common; or if the effort were made to furnish more currency than the attenuated gold base warranted, there would be the eternal vexation of monetary troubles.

Economics is not one thing and politics another. If this great change were brought about by the financiers, it would be the most stupendous political coup that the world ever saw. Nearly all the currency of this country is now in the possession of the great New York banks. Banks elsewhere and the people hold depreciated securities and can not find the funds needed for legitimate business. This currency ought to go back to the banks of the country and to the people in order that the great internal trade of the country may be stimulated and the great domestic market resume its activity. Gathered into the vaults of New York, this collective liquid wealth of the American people lies entirely too conveniently near to the western mouth of the roomy, war-time financial conduit to Europe.

We know what the money loaned to Europe in the war went for. It went to pay for things which were being consumed in the holocaust of war. Steadily the long-accumulated wealth flowed out of Europe to pay for what the war was continuously burning up. First, they spent their ready cash; then they sold their vast holdings abroad to secure new credits; then, after we entered the war, they borrowed $11,000,000,000 from us.

No bullion shipments were made on account of trade balance after we entered the war, and it was because Europe was very slow to make these shipments after the war ended that we suffered the credit stringency which produced our hard times of 1920 and 1921. It was only after the Allied States were forced to settle their trade balance in gold that the credit base of our financial structure was broadened by the acquisition of an adequate gold stock that restored our banking system to a normal condition. It was only after the exportation of this gold from Europe took place also that the poverty to which the war had reduced all the States of Europe became apparent.

104

It was not until then that realization came in the United States that Europe was improverished and that the United States had become by far the wealthiest country in the world.

Why should responsible authority seek, as it has done for years, to conceal from public knowledge the simple explanation of the great accumulation of our postwar wealth? That accumulation of wealth is due essentially to the fact that from 1921 to 1924 there was a steady flow of gold coming into our ports chiefly from Europe or on European account, reaching by the end of the third year the figure of more than $2,000,000,000. This bullion became gold reserves in the banks and furnished an amount of good currency adequate to the needs of the vigorous industrial population of our continent. Yet a few years ago a great commission of economists appointed by political authority to determine the causes of our postwar prosperity wholly ignored this single definite cause and ascribed it vaguely to "acceleration, spread, and tempo."

Why should they not have been honest and courageous about it? If the public understood the specific cause of our post-war wealth, and realizing the magnitude of that wealth, would it not have a better understanding of the question of debts and reparations?

How could such a stupendous paroxysm of warfare, lasting for nearly five years and exhausting every resource of the entire continent of Europe, have failed to bring a profound change in the world? Its economic consequencies were manifested with singular clearness by those steady shipments westward across the Atlantic from 1912 to 1924 of more than 4,000 tons of gold metal. Vast as have been these shipments of gold, they still leave Europe in our debt; she still owes us the $11,000,-000,000 of public debts which we loaned her in the war, and in addition approximately four billions in private debts contracted since the war ended. Why do not our economists, public and private, acknowledge that it is the acquisition of our great postwar gold stock that explains the economic power of the American Republic to-day and that, if we relinquished possession of our gold, our economic power would wane. Whence

105

came the "acceleration, spread, and tempo" which the committee on economic changes found to be the cause of American prosperity?

The war in Europe must be viewed from one of two opposed standpoints, and in accordance with the view from one of these standpoints the great financial and economic decisions of to-day must be made, fixing the course of history for centuries to come.

In the first view, the war in Europe brought an era of history to a close. It transferred the center of civilization's power from the Eastern Hemisphere to the Western. It made a new and different conception of cultural life predominant in the world.

In the second view, the war in Europe changed nothing permanently. It brought greater temporary exhaustion to Europe than any previous war had done, but recuperation will take place with increasing rapidity and Europe will regain its former relative position in the world.

If the view from the first standpoint prevails, the United States will retain and protect its gold stock and utilizing its resulting economic power in the way it judges best, and Europe will acquiesce in this decision.

If the second view prevails, the American people will regard their possession of $4,000,000,000 in gold as incidental and transitory and acquiesce more or less actively in its redistribution among those who held it before the war. They will suffer the consequent lowering of their economic power with equanimity. Europe will quickly regain possession of it, and with it of the economic and political vigor which characterized that continent before the war.

The struggle goes on between the two sides. Its evidences have been plainly visible during the past decade.

I do not see how any administration in Washington could fail to adopt the first view unequivocally. I do not see how any administration could justify itself for adopting the second. Under any circumstances, it would have no right to adopt and act upon the second view until the question had been made a political issue and the will of the people had been expressed. In a democratic republic, great and vital questions of foreign policy are not to be considered and decided in secret by a handful of men in temporary office in Washington. The people of the Republic have the right to determine their own destiny.

The peoples and governments of Europe are impoverished. They wish and insist that we should pool our wealth with them in order that the pre-war balance may be reestablished. It is too much to ask for us, and the issue should be squarely met. It should be made clear once and for all that the gold stock of the United States is to remain here permanently to water the garden of American industrial life. And it should be made clear also that it is in this way that the United States can make its greatest contribution to the world's civilization.

It is because the statesmen of Europe have for 12 years rejected this reality and have tortured their brains with schemes for effecting the quick return to Europe of its lost gold that no progress in reconstruction has been made. I have recently analyzed the Stresemann policy, which for years all Europe has been pressing and have shown how under it Europe was to be made over again in a few years' time through the acquisition of billions of dollars realized by the sale in the United States of German reparation bonds, and I have shown the more than dubious moral and legal quality of those bonds.

That such a scheme could have been openly pressed by our own leading financiers, and surreptitiously aided by successive administrations in Washington, as it has been, until it has actually reached dangerous proportions for us, is sufficient evidence that it is time for the Congress and public opinion to interest themselves in establishing proper control over our foreign relations.

The surreptitious support of this policy by the State and Treasury Departments has continued for years. When the peace conference convened in Paris after the war, the American delegation was accompanied by a hundred eminent scholars with a library of 10,000 books. Attachés of the American delegation sprang, as it were, from the ground to accord their valuable aid in one or another phase of the work to be done. But the men who emerged from this intellectual welter to sit in the inner councils of the conference and guide the steps of the American delegation were a selected group of the international bankers of New York.

Hand and glove they worked with the internationalists of Europe. The Europeans molded the treaty to suit themselves, and the American financiers persuaded the American delegation to sign it.

The treaty provided for reparations afterwards fixed at $33,000,000,000, and Annex II to the reparation clauses provided that this sum might be capitalized by the Allied Governments and sold as bonds to purchasers on the world's investment markets. If the bonds could be successfully marketed, France would receive about $16,000,000,000 in cash, Britain six or seven billions, and the smaller allies lesser sums.

The purpose of this provision, as subsequent events have proved, was to sell the bonds in the United States chiefly, which would thus pay the German indemnity to the Allies in cash, and look to Germany for reimbursement. If the scheme could have been executed in its pristine brightness, Europe would have been over the effects of the war in 10 years time, and the United States would not have retained its postwar wealth. The roomy, wartime financial conduit was there to facilitate this great transaction.

The provision in Annex II, the financial bankers of New York induced the American delegation to the Peace Conference to accept.

This purpose remains to-day the dominant motive of European diplomacy and politics and the preoccupation of the New York bankers. It found a medium of action in the Stresemann policy of 1925 which has culminated in the launching on our markets of the German international 5½ bonds, which I discussed recently in the House of Representatives. Fortunately, we seem to be taking warning against these bonds in time.

Having gotten the provisions of Annex II into the treaty,

the international bankers of New York came home to work on this side to put it into execution. The refusal of the Senate to ratify the treaty was a great setback, but the efforts went on just the same. After 1921 the bankers attained control of the State Department and the Treasury Department and have never relaxed their grip upon the policies of these departments. Putting the Stresemann policy into execution in the United States could not be openly accomplished. Its purposes could not be openly avowed. The State and Treasury Departments were in sympathy with it but did not dare publicly to avow this sympathy. They were reduced to the practice of round-about and rather surreptitious methods to further, gradually, the purposes of the international bankers and the European governments. The State Department has exercised unseen a definite support of the treaty of Versailles in Europe, and the Treasury Department has not made the slightest effort to check the growth of unwarranted practices and powers in the Federal Reserve Bank of New York. In all really important negotiations concerning our European relations the State Department has left action to private bankers instead of to the responsible officials.

It secretly favored what was done by the Young committee in 1929, and in order that the Young plan might go into operation without the necessity of treaty settlements which would involve consideration of the whole matter by Congress, it made a special agreement with Germany concerning the German debt to us without which the Young plan could not have been adopted, and which required only a joint resolution of Congress approving it with reference to which general and open debate on the floors of the Congress on the whole subject did not need to be risked. The Young plan in its far-reaching significance falls within the purview of the Congress. It ought to have been fully considered there. But in order that this might be obviated and publicity avoided, the leaders of the organization in Congress in both Houses were summoned to the White House on May 19, 1929, while the Young committee was sitting in Paris, and there induced to agree to what was

109

being done in Europe and to promise favorable action in both the Senate and House of Representatives. The result was that inquiry by individual Senators and Congressmen was smothered when the matter came up for action last year, and a matter which should have had the closest consideration by the Congress was railroaded through without debate.

Gentlemen, it is this subtle influence in every branch of our Government at Washington that is now a menace to the Nation's welfare. It is undoubtedly present and its results are visible. All its purposes converge upon a control of the Federal reserve system and of the political government at Washington, in order that national policy may be controlled by a few men and in the interests primarily of the foreigner. The only way to bring this condition to an end is by action in the Congress where alone the interests of the people are represented.

Now, in closing, let me say that under no circumstances ought the Congress or the people to allow the United States Government to be drawn slowly and by courses which can not be detected by a scrutiny of the public press into virtual alliance with the allied states for the maintenance of the status quo in Europe as it is to-day. Under no circumstances ought the ground be prepared for another American intervention in Europe's wars.

The Bank for International Settlements and the World Court are destined to be the financial and judicial part of the League of Nations.

VIII

FINANCIAL FOREIGN
ENTANGLEMENTS

Saturday, February 14, 1931

Mr. McFadedn. Mr. Speaker, at various times during the past year I have discussed the question of foreign debts and the distribution and sale of foreign debts in the United States. Under the leave granted me this morning, not desiring to take up the time of the House unduly, I shall insert in the Record a compilation showing the total of the foreign government, municipal, and industrial loans made in the United States since 1919. It amounts to the enormous sum of over seven and three-quarter billions of dollars, and this amount does not include money invested in foreign countries by the United States directly as a government, nor does it include industrial, corporation loans in their own operations, nor does it include acceptances by the Federal reserve banks.

Mr. Sabath. Mr. Speaker, will the gentleman yield?

Mr. McFadden. For a question.

Mr. Sabath. Will not the gentleman also include the names of the firms who negotiated these loans, and also at what price they have made them and the discount that they have received?

Mr. McFadden. I shall include the names of the banking houses that have floated these loans and show the total loans by the countries to which these loans have been made.

111

Mr. SABATH. And the large commissions which these bankers have charged?

Mr. McFADDEN. That is almost an impossible thing to get. I call the attention of the House especially to these matters they indicate the large extent of the domination and control by international bankers of the diplomatic relations with foreign countries and the finances of the country. I shall also include a list of the interlocking directorates of the members of these firms, where they lead into other controlled financial institutions in the United States. I am doing this at this time because a serious situation has arisen in regard to a further exploitation by these people of American investors. I call attention to an article appearing in the newspapers under date of February 10, dated Habana, Cuba, United Press:

The consolidation of the Cuban debt for $300,000,000 by J. P. Morgan & Co., New York financial house, was confirmed to-day. Negotiations were conducted under the guidance of President Machado. The form of the consolidation has not been revealed, and although negotiations have been going on for some time, confirmation was lacking until late to-night.

That means that $300,000,000 of certain of these New York bankers represent debts that we all know amount to something over $600,000,000 in Cuba.

Cuba is on the verge of bankruptcy, and the Government of Cuba is now in a very serious situation. We find these international bankers are preparing to unload their bad obligations which they have made in Cuba on the innocent American investing public in this kind of refunding operations, and I for one am not going to stand for it and remain silent.

I call attention to the fact that the newspapers under date of February 3 indicate that Peru is requesting a moratorium on foreign debts. Peru is also a heavy borrower in this country. Within the past two weeks Mr. Thomas W. Lamont, of J. P. Morgan & Co., announced a moratorium. He was speaking as chairman of the International Debt Committee for Mexico, where Mexico's debts have been juggled by these international financiers for a period of five years or longer, and now they are declaring a moratorium for another two years.

I say it is about time that the Congress and the people of the United States began to recognize what these international banking houses, who claim to be American, are doing and what is taking place. [Applause.] I say to you Members of the House, and I say it with knowledge, that the financial operations being carried on by these international bankers are tying this country absolutely. Not only are they directing the affairs of finance, but I have repeatedly called your attention to the domination of the State Department by these international groups. It is common knowledge that in the countries where they are carrying on their exploitations they are using the representatives of the State Department as cat's paws to carry on thir diplomatic and financial operations. We have a minister in Cuba at this time who is representing these international financial houses and has been engaged in negotiating this present $300,000,000 loan. Ever since he went to Cuba he has had two expert accountants and possibly more; he was analyzing the financial affairs of Cuba. He had G. M. Jones, of the finance division of the Department of Commerce down there. He has now returned, and now we have the announcement of this great financial operation of the flotation by J. P. Morgan & Co. of $300,000,000 of Cuban bonds.

Mr. O'CONNOR of New York. Will the gentleman yield?

Mr. McFADDEN. I yield.

Mr. O'CONNOR of New York. Does the gentleman know what could have happened in Nicaragua in the financial relations which prevailed upon the Secretary of State to agree to take the marines out of there?

Mr. McFADDEN. I do not know about Nicaragua. I have not had a chance to go into it.

Another country that has defaulted, and from which these international bankers have been throwing their securities on the American market is Bolivia, to the extent of over $58,-000,000—ask the holders of these bonds in the United States to-day. They will tell you how they feel. Then next we come

113

to Germany, and we find that since 1919 these same bankers have loaned to Germany and unloaded these bonds on American banks and investors to the extent of $1,171,646,150, and to Austria $109,000,000, and to Brazil $370,000,000, and to Colombia $182,178,000, and so on.

I now place in the RECORD the statement of the total of foreign government, municipal, and industrial loans made in the United States since 1919, amounting to $7,784,717,430. This amount does not include money invested in foreign countries by the United States industrial corporations in their own operations, nor does it include money loaned privately by individuals, corporate or individual investment, or credits done privately, which amounts, at best, can only be guessed.

The total figure is that of loans wherein securities were sold to the public in the United States and that total only covers the amount that was outstanding in December 31, 1930, in every case except that of Canada, which it is impossible to check owing to the fact that in nearly all cases, Canadian banks are the trustees for the bond issues and they do not make public the amounts which have been retired by the operation of sinking funds or through outright purchase in the market.

In setting up the picture of foreign loans there follows a list of the countries with the amount of each country's obligation in the United States opposite its name.

A complete list of the banks and banking houses in the United States through which these loans were negotiated or which assumed sponsorship.

There are 97 in all; of this number 16 are listed as the important ones, having been the negotiators of over $6,000,-000,000 out of the total. These 16 are designated by the numbers 1 to 16 placed before their names on the list. Banks or banking houses outside of New York do not appear on this list unless they sponsored or negotiated loans themselves; this does not mean that they did not participate in the syndicates formed to distribute the securities; a complete list of all members of syndicates would include every large bank in the United States and that is not the purpose of this report.

The Union Trust Co. of Pittsburgh, a Mellon institution, negotiated $98,000,000 in foreign loans, but is not included in the list of 16 major banks, because most of this $98,000,000 was on behalf of the Aluminum Co. in Canada and the Mellons control that company.

There was a time when the leading banks in New York could be definitely separated into two groups on foreign loans; to-day there is an entirely different picture. J. P. Morgan & Co.'s name never appears on a syndicate list unless they head the group. Kuhn, Loeb & Co.'s name appears in several syndicates headed by Morgan & Co.

Generally speaking there are banks known as "Morgan banks" or in the "Morgan group." They are Bankers Trust Co., Guaranty Trust Co., New York Trust Co., First National Bank, Bank of New York & Trust Co., and Lee, Higginson & Co.

The Kuhn, Loeb & Co. following is Bank of Manhattan & Trust Co., Chemical Bank & Trust Co., International Acceptance Bank, Dillon, Read & Co., J. & W. Seligman & Co., Speyer & Co., Lehman Bros., Hallgarten & Co., Ladenburg, Thalmann & Co., Goldman, Sachs & Co., Central, Hanover Bank & Trust Co., First National Old Colony Trust Co. (Boston). The Chase National Bank, the largest institution in the United States, has no Morgan representatives on its board of directors; there are at least two Kuhn, Loeb & Co. men on the board. The Rockefellers are heavily interested in Chase. Winthrop Aldrich, the president, is their representative.

A typical syndicate on a Morgan issue is as follows:

J. P. Morgan & Co., Kuhn, Loeb & Co., First National Bank, National City Bank, Guaranty Trust Co., Bankers' Trust Co., Kidder, Peabody & Co., Lee, Higginson & Co., Harris, Forbes & Co., that was the syndicate which handled the Austrian international loan.

A typical Kuhn, Loeb & Co., syndicate is:

Kuhn, Loeb & Co., National City Bank, Guaranty Trust Co., First National Bank, Brown Bros., Kidder Peabody & Co., Chase National Bank, Lee, Higginson & Co., Continental & Commercial Trust & Savings Bank (Chicago), Union Trust Co.

115

(Pittsburgh), Mellon National Bank (Pittsburgh), First National Bank of St. Paul, Blair & Co.

The syndicate distributed the Swedish $30,000,000 loan of 1924. It will be seen that most of the houses in the two syndicates are identical.

Another important Kuhn, Loeb & Co. connection is that of the old Anglo-French Bank, now the British and French Investing Co. Sir Oscar Warburg (son of Frederic Warburg) and A. E. Meyer and Sir Frank C. Meyer are said to be partners. Warburg & Co., of Amsterdam, and M. M. Warburg & Co., of Hamburg, Germany. Dr. Hans Meyer is closely connected with both of these last-named firms.

It appears from the amounts opposite their names that Kuhn, Loeb & Co. was instrumental in loaning to foreign countries a great deal less than other houses. That is not really a true reflection, for a great many other items are carried by houses under Kuhn, Loeb & Co.'s direction, and the same can be said of Morgan & Co. in so far as its influence is concerned in the operations of Guaranty Trust Co., and Lee, Higginson & Co. in foreign fields.

Several security companies have been formed within the last few years to handle the smaller loans and investments, such as the United States and Foreign Securities Co., the Tri-Continental Corporation, the American and Continental Securities Corporation. However, they do not appear as participating in any of the Government loans.

There is also a separate list of the banks and banking houses with a number appearing before each one with names of their important directors or partners with numbers after their names. These numbers correspond and show in this simplified way the relationship of one banking house to another, through members of one firm being directors of another.

Paul Warburg, formerly of Kuhn, Loeb & Co. and still personally closely related there, is the means through which Kuhn, Loeb & Co. control Bank of Manhattan Trust Co. the International Acceptance Bank, and the First National Old

Colony Trust Co., of Boston. There is no doubt that the same thing can be said of numerous other banks.

It can be said without fear of contradiction that when Morgan & Co. and Kuhn, Loeb & Co. negotiate a foreign loan they dominate the situation and dictate the terms under which other banks participate with them. Whereas other houses, not under control of these two leaders, not only have to carry on the loan negotiations, but have to sell their proposition to the other banks who join them in syndicates for the purpose of selling the securities to the American public.

That part of the list numbered 17 to 53 contains the names of a good many concerns not directly connected with foreign loans; these banks or banking houses or companies are added to show wherein lies a community of interest on the part of the directors of the major 16, for it is at these "outside" directors' meetings that many of the "understandings" are brought about. If one were to include the directorships in American companies held by the directors and partners of the banking houses, it would be easier to show the community of interest.

Loans made in United States since 1919

Argentine	$ 504,578,800
Australia	109,223,800
Austria	269,275,500
Brazil	370,589,800
Bulgaria	17,300,500
Bolivia	58,128,500
Belgium	252,138,600
Colombia	182,178,800
Canada	1,480,506,900
Chile	359,387,500
Cuba	145,771,500
Costa Rica	9,247,500
Czechoslovakia	46,963,700
Dominician Republic	21,652,500
Denmark	180,507,000
Dutch East Indies	159,848,500

Danzig	4,500,000
Estonia	$ 3,903,000
France	327,982,400
Finland	81,048,500
Greece	34,772,500
Great Britain	159,635,590
Germany	1,171,646,150
Guatemala	300,000
Hungary	102,843,000
Haiti	11,404,000
Holland	52,705,000
Italy	306,528,240
Japan	373,913,800
Norway	206,243,000
Panama	23,720,000
Peru	107,722,000
Poland	128,878,150
Rumania	67,909,400
Saar Basin	8,108,000
Sweden	212,992,500
Switzerland	69,627,500
Salvador	29,116,700
Uruguay	69,160,500
Yugoslavia	56,583,500
Venezuela	3,780,000
Mexico	2,384,000
Total	$7,784,717,430

This total is the amount outstanding as of December 31, 1930.

Banking houses and their participation in foreign loans

Aldred & Co. (Ltd.)	$ 55,560,000
Ames, Emerich & Co.	19,127,500
Baker, Kellogg & Co. (Inc.)	25,452,900
8. Bancamerica-Blair Corporation	414,847,800
12. Bankers' Trust Co. of New York	103,836,000
Chas. D. Barney & Co.	3,000,000

G. E. Barrett & Co. (Inc.) ....$	4,000,000
Bauer, Pond & Vivian	3,949,000
A. G. Becker & Co.	25,388,000
Bennett, Converse & Schwab (Inc.)	640,000
Blyth-Witter & Co.	46,867,900
Boenning & Co.	400,000
Bonbright & Co. (Inc.)	27,500,000
Bond & Goodwin & Tucker (Inc.)	2,250,000
Bridgeport (Conn.) Trust Co.	1,000,000
Brokaw & Co.	1,919,000
10. Brown Bros. Harriman & Co.	214,130,500
Geo. H. Burr & Co.	2,600,000
Central Illinois Co.	487,800
Central Trust Co. of Illinois	1,454,500
P. W. Chapman & Co. (Inc.)	7,345,500
5. Chase Securities Corporation	489,211,100
Chatham-Phenix Corporation	33,530,000
Coffin & Burr (Inc.)	1,300,000
Colvin & Co.	1,100,000
Continental & Commercial Trust & Savings Bank	2,000,000
6. Dillon, Read & Co.	824,080,750
Estabrook & Co.	12,500,000
First National Bank of New York	2,828,000
11. First National Old Colony Corporation	96,379,000
First Trust & Savings Bank	13,000,000
Harvey Fisk & Sons	1,543,750
Freeman, Smith & Camp Co.	125,000
A. G. Ghysels & Co. (Inc.)	1,980,000
Goldman, Sachs & Co.	8,377,500
G. V. Grace & Co. (Inc.)	250,000
Grace National Co.	14,847,500
Greenshields & Co.	3,000,000
2. Guaranty Co.	434,939,000
14. Hallgarten & Co.	216,572,840
Halsey, Stuart & Co. (Inc.)	51,644,300
Hambleton & Co.	700,000
13. Harris, Forbes & Co.	191,338,900

119

Hemphill, Noyes & Co. ....$	3,000,000
Hitt, Farwell & Co.	990,000
A. A. Housman Gwathmey & Co.	3,780,000
Howe, Snow & Bertles (Inc.)	12,287,500
E. F. Hutton & Co.	9,600,000
International Acceptance Bank (Inc.)	3,000.000
International Manhattan Co. (Inc.)	5,360,000
Interstate Trust & Banking Co.	1,980,000
A. Iselin & Co.	60,117,500
Jesup & Lamont	1,000,000
Kissell, Kinnicutt & Co.	45,775,000
Kountze Bros.	1,500,000
4. Kuhn, Loeb & Co.	384,738,700
Ladenburg, Thalmann & Co.	9,740.000
A. M. Lamport & Co. (Inc.)	820,500
7. Lee, Higginson & Co.	456,772,500
Lehman Bros.	20,375,000
F. J. Lisman & Co.	29,283,100
Lumbermen's Trust Co.	175,000
R. H. McClure & Co.	940,000
Marine National Co.	150,000
Marshall, Field, Glore, Ward & Co.	43,288,000
Merchants Trust & Savings, St. Paul	4,000,000
Minneapolis Trust Co.	4,000,000
1. J. P. Morgan & Co.	1,659,568,400
Morgan, Livermore & Co.	800,000
3. National City Co.	900,403,990
John Nicherson & Co. (Inc.)	3,365.000
Otis & Co.	4,487,500
Paine, Webber & Co.	11,353,500
Peabody, Houghteling & Co. (Inc.	18,500,000
Peabody, Smith & Co. (Inc.)	2,000,000
Potter & Co.	2,305,500
Redmond & Co.	4,612,500
C. B. Richards & Co.	1,307,000
E. H. Rollins & Sons	40,764,500
Scholle Bros.	2,362,500

J. Henry Schroeder Banking Corporation ....$	15,000,000
Schuyler, Earle & Co.	300,000
Schwababacher & Co.	2,000,000
15. J. & W. Seligman & Co.	128,854,500
Edmund Seymour & Co. (Inc.	2,000,000
J. A. Sisto & Co., New York	5,437,500
16. Speyer & Co.	237,411,300
Stone & Webster & Blodget (Inc.)	20,631,900
Jerome B. Sullivan & Co.	1,384,000
Taylor, Ewart & Co. (Inc.)	800,000
Lawrence Turnure & Co.	3,250,000
Union Trust Co., Pittsburgh	98,050,000
A. D. Watts & Co.	1,925,000
J. G. White & Co. (Inc.)	11,494,000
9. White, Weld & Co.	103,372,000
R. E. Wilsey & Co.	1,350,000
Wood, Gundy & Co. (Inc.)	35,000,000

Major banks and banking houses, with their banking affiliations

1. J. P. Morgan & Co.
2. Guaranty Co.
3. National City Co.
4. Kuhn, Loeb & Co.
5. Chase Securities Corporation.
6. Dillon, Read & Co.
7. Lee, Higginson & Co.
8. Bancamerica-Blair Corporation
9. White, Weld & Co.
10. Brown Bros., Harriman & Co.
11. First National Old Colony Corporation.
12. Bankers Trust Co.
13. Harris, Forbes & Co.
14. Hallgarten & Co.
15. J. & W. Seligman & Co.
16. Speyer & Co.

17. First Security Co.
18. Drexel & Co., Philadelphia.
19. Fifth Avenue Bank.
20. Corn Exchange Bank & Trust Co.
21. Bank of Manhattan Trust Co.
22. Continental Illinois Bank & Trust Co., Chicago.
23. Chemical Bank & Trust Co.
24. Morristown Trust Co.
25. First National Bank, Chicago.
26. International Acceptance Bank.
27. Irving Trust Co.
28. City Bank, Farmers Trust Co.
29. New York Trust Co.
30. Federal Reserve Bank, New York.
31. International Banking Corporation.
32. Provident Loan Society.
33. Lazard Freres.
34. National Shawmut Bank, Boston.
35. Goldman, Sachs & Co.
36. Central Hanover Bank & Trust Co.
37. Central Savings Bank.
38. J. Henry Schroeder Banking Corporation.
39. Empire Trust Co.
40. United States Trust Co.
41. American Acceptance Corporation.
42. Bond, Mortgage & Guarantee Co.
43. Spencer Trask & Co.
44. Chas. D. Barney & Co.
45. Overseas Securities Corporation.
46. Title Guarantee & Trust Co.
47. Tri Continental Corporation.
48. Bonbright & Co.
50. Aldred & Co.
49. American Continental Corporation.
51. Bank of New York & Trust Co.
52. Continental Securities Corporation.
53. G. M. P. Murphy & Co.

J. P. Morgan & Co.

J. P. Morgan, 17; Thomas W. Lamont, 17, 2; J. S. Morgan, Jr.,; E. T. Stotesbury, 18; Charles Steele; H. G. Lloyd, 18; Thomas Cochran, 12, 19; George Whitney, 2; Thomas S. Gates; R. C. Leffingwell; F. D. Bartow, 20; A. M. Anderson; William Ewing, 12; Harold Stanley; Henry S. Morgan; Thomas S. Lamont; S. Parker Gilbert.

Guaranty Co.

William C. Potter, president; Charles H. Sabin, chairman; Marshall Field, 21, 22, 49; Robert W. Goelet, 23, 46; Phillip G. Gossier, 24, 10; William A. Harriman, 10, 21; Albert H. Harris, 25; David F. Houston, 26; Grayson M. P. Murphy, 53; George E. Roosevelt, 23; Charles B. Seger, 26; Mathew S. Sloan, 27, 24; Joseph B. Terbell, 10; Thomas Williams, 23.

National City Co.

Guy D. Cary, 28; Cleveland E. Dodge, 28; John A. Garver, 29, 42; Joseph P. Grace, 28; Charles E. Mitchell, 28, 30; James H. Post, 28; Gordon S. Rentichler, 28, 31; Perry A. Rockefeller, 32, 10; Samuel Sloan, 28; Beekman Winthrop, 28, 31.

Kuhn, Loeb & Co.

Felix M. Warburg, 26, 21, 42; Otto H. Kahn, 5, 24; Mortimer L. Schiff, 23, 32; Jerome J. Hanauer; Gordon Leith; Geo. W. Bovenizer; Lewis L. Strauss; Sir Wm. Wiesman.

Chase Securities Corporation

Winthrop W. Aldrich; Frank Altschul, 33; Howard Bayne, 24; Hugh Blair-Smith, 34; Henry S. Bowers, 35; Newcomb Carlton, 26; Harold B. Clark, 9; Paul D. Cravath; Bertram Cutler, 24; Clarence Dillon, 6, 36; Fred H. Ecker, 32; Charles S. Hayden; Otto H. Kahn, 4; Charles S. McCain, 37; John McHugh, 38; Jeremiah Milback, 32; Geo. Welwood Murray, 24; Samuel F. Pryor, 10; Charles M. Schwab, 39; Thos. F. Vietor, 37; Albert H. Wiggin; Seward Prosser, 12.

Dillon, Read & Co.

Clarence Dillon, 5, 36; Wm. A. Phillips, 23; Dean Mathey,

29; J. H. Seaman; W. M. L. Fiske; Roland L. Taylor; Wm. A. Read, Jr.; E. J. Bermingham; J. V. Forrestal; A. M. Barnes; R. H. Pollard; Duncan H. Read; Westmore Willcox, Jr., Robt. O. Hayward; H. G. Ritter 3d; W. S. Charnley; Clifton M. Miller; R. E. Christie, Jr.

Lee, Higginson & Co.

Fred W. Allen, 29; Jerome D. Greene; Donald Durant, 28; Edward N. Jessup; Robert Grant, Jr.; George Murnane, 12.

Bancamerica-Blair Corporation

A. H. Giannini (chairman); E. C. Delafield (president); Elisha Walker (chairman executive committee); Frank Bailey, 42, 46; Frank L. Dame, 49; Henry J. Fuller, 50.11; Robert Law, 10; Sam Lewisohn; William D. Loucks, 10; Acosta Nichols, 43.

White, Weld & Co.

Harold T. White, 32; Francis M. Weld, 36; Farris R. Russell; Harold B. Clark, 5; W. J. K. Vanston.

Brown Bros., Harriman & Co.

James Brown, 36; James Crosby Brown; Thatcher M. Brown, 40; Moreau Delano; Ray Morris, 51, 52; Charles D. Dickey, 28; E. S. James, 34; W. A. Harriman, 2.21; E. R. Harriman, 28; M. C. Brush, 39.21.

First National Old Colony Corporation

J. E. Aldred, 50; Bernard W. Trafford; Phillip Stockton; Allan M. Pope; Nevil Ford; R. Paker Kuhn; F. Abbott Goodhue, 26, 21, 49; Paul M. Warburg, 21,26,49.

Bankers Trust Co.

Seward Prosser, chairman, 5; Albert A. Tilney; Cornelius Bliss, 40; Henry J. Cochran, president; Thomas Cochran, 1; S. Sloan Colt, 41; John I. Downey, 19, 42; William Ewing, 1; Walter E. Frew, 20, 46; Michael Friedsam, 21; Edwin M. Bulkley, 43; John W. Hanes, 44; Horace Havemeyer, 26; Fred I. Kent, 45; Ronald H. MacDonald 42, 46; George Murname,

7; Landon K. Thorne, 48.

Harris, Forbes & Co.

Harry Addinsell, 5.29; Lloyd W. Smith; E. Carleton Granberry, 49; Fred S. Burroughs; Don C. Wheaton, 49.

Hallgarten & Co.

Casimir I. Stralem, Max Horwitz, G. Merzback, Maurice W. Newton, H. Walter Blumenthal, Andrew J. Miller, Melvin L. Emerich.

J. & W. Seligman & Co.

Henry Seligman; Jefferson Seligman; Fred Strauss, 36, 47; Walter Seligman; John C. Jay, 19; Robert V. White, 47; Earle Baile, 47; Francis F. Randolph, 47.5; Henry C. Breck, 47.

Speyer & Co.

James Speyer, 21, 27, 32, 46; Edward B. Von Speyer; Herbert B. Von Speyer.

First Security Co.

George F. Baker, Jr., 32; Thomas W. Lamont, 1, 2; J. P. Morgan, 1.

Fifth Avenue Bank

Thomas Cochran, 1; John I. Downey, 12, 42; A. S. Frissell; John C. Jay, 15; Alfred E. Marling, 46; Fred Osborne, 53; Orlando F. Weber.

Corn Exchange Bank & Trust Co.

Francis D. Bartow, 1; Clinton D. Burdich, 46, 42; George Doubleday, 29; Robert A. Drysdale, 37; Walter E. Frew, 12, 46; Phillip Lehman; Robert Lehman; Charles W. Nichols, 46; Henry A. Patterson; Daniel Schnakenburg, 37; Richard Whitney.

Bank of Manhattan Trust Co.

John E. Aldred, 50, 11; J. Stewart Baker, 26; Stephen Baker, 26; Matthew C. Brush, 39, 10; Marshall Field, 49, 22, 2; Michael Friedsam, 12; F. Abbott Goodhue, 49, 11, 26; P. A. Rowley, 26; James Speyer, 16, 46, 32, 37; James P. Warburg,

125

49, 26; Paul M. Warburg, 26, 49, 11.

The foregoing, of course, does not begin to show all the interlocking relationship with many other important financial institutions in the United States, nor does it show these relationships which are tied in with the railroads and other leading industries, including water power, steel, oil, and chemicals.

I pointed out some further affiliations of this same group in two statements which I recently made before a subcommittee of the Senate Committee on Banking and Currency when I was opposing a further attempt of these same international banking interests to now take over and completely dominate the Federal reserve system.

I now place in the RECORD a letter in regard to the Mexican debt situation from Howard T. Oliver, of New York, a citizen of unquestioned integrity and standing, who has been a victim of these negotiators:

New York, January 27, 1931

Hon. Louis T. McFadden,
  Chairman Committee of the House on
  Banking and Currency, Washington, D.C.

My Dear Mr. McFadden: I beg to submit for your consideration certain facts and conclusions regarding the activities of the international committee of bankers on Mxeico, which I believe warrant an investigation by your committee. These facts have been enumerated concisely as possible commensurate with a comprehensive portrayal of a situation which is at variance with the public policy of the United States.

The facts and conclusions herein presented will, I believe, lead to the conclusion that the international committee of bankers on Mexico has exercised dominance over the Mexican policy of the State Department, attempted to influence the courts of the United States, drained the Mexican Government of much-needed funds, surrendered the rights of security holders, confused the titles of Mexico's foreign debts, enjoyed prefrence over other classes of Mexico's creditors, caused the reduction in value of Mexican bonds, minimized that nation's credit, aroused ill will toward the United States, and otherwise complicated our relations with Mexico.

I respectfully request that representatives of the International Committee of Bankers on Mexico be called to explain the statements herein and that I be given like opportunity to support them by evidence and data in my possession. I sincerely believe that the International Committee of Bankers on Mexico has outlived its usefulness and that it is the duty of your committee to terminate the activities of the bankers committee and to assist in bringing about a new constructive plan for the protection of the creditors of Mexico and the rehabilitation of Mexico's financial position.

I. The committee of bankers entered into contractual relations with the Government of Mexico at a time when recognition was being withheld from said Government by the Department of State. The resultant debt agreement was therefore in direct contravention of the public policy of the United States at that time.

II. A spokesman for the committee of bankers declared that the United States Government would be compelled to reverse its policy of nonrecognition of Mexico if the continuance of said policy should permit any interference with financial arrangements entered into by said committee with the Government of Mexico—the inference being that the bankers committee exercised sufficient dominanc over the State Department to force a change in the general policy of the United States toward Mexico. Within one month after the above declaration the State Department granted recognition to Mexico.

III. The bankers committee, in the person of its counsel, attempted to obstruct the due processes of the courts of the United States and to instruct said courts in the civil action of the Oliver American Trading Co. against the Government of the United States of Mexico and the National Railways of Mexico, although said committee was not a party thereto. Attempted dominance of the courts by a committee of international bankers is especially repugnant to American principles.

IV. The bankers committee, through the person of its

counsel, sought and succeeded in enlisting the interposition of the Secretary of State in the courts, contrary to the sharply defined principles of differentiation of the three branches of our Government as set forth in the Constitution of the United States. The susceptibility of the Secretary of State to suggestions of the bankers committee in the matter referred to emphasized the dominance of the bankers.

V. The bankers committee is a nonincorporated body, which assumed highly arbitrary powers, without responsibility, individually or collectively, to the United States, to any State therein, to Mexico, or to holders of Mexican securities. The addresses of the members are so published as to give the impression that the banking firms of which they are members appeared as sponsors for the acts of said committee, whereas less conspicuous statements refute this impression. Mr. T. W. Lamont, of J. P. Morgan & Co., is chairman and Mr. Frank L. Polk is counsel.

VI. The International Committee of Bankers on Mexico has at all times since its inception in 1921, and despite occasional protests to the contrary, maintained a dual capacity, namely, as agents for the Government of Mexico and as representatives of the holders of Mexican Government and national railway securities. The abuses possible under such dual roles are self-evident and constitute a jeopardy of the rights of unsuspecting holders of the aforementioned securities. Curiously enough, the committee of bankers continues to function despite the expiration of its self-alloted period of existence and the termination of the various contracts entered into. No public accounting has been rendered.

VII. In its self-assumed character as representative of the holders of Mexican securities, although it has never represented all of the bondholders, the International Committee of Bankers permitted the Mexican Government to believe that the latter's acquiescence in the terms of contracts with it would redound to the financial benefit of that country's finances and made a number of misleading statements justifying that Government in believing that loans or credits would result therefrom. No loans having been forthcoming, the deception of the Mexican Government has adversely affected the good will between the people of Mexico and the people of the United States, and is therefore of concern to our Representatives in the Congress.

VIII. As a result of the arguments and representations of the committee the Mexican Government was inveigled into straining its financial position far beyond its means in order to deliver to the said committee more than $48,000,000 destined for payment on account for her foreign debt. The efforts of the Mexican Government to comply with the contracts which she was induced to sign and ratify have frequently proven to be at the sacrifice of payments to school teachers, civil employees, the army, native and foreign merchants, and other creditors. The resulting preference enjoyed by the international committee has frequently aroused internal dissensions in Mexico which in turn constitute a menace to friendly relations with the United States.

IX. In the self-appointed role as representatives of the bondholders the latter were induced by the International Committee of Bankers to surrender rights stipulated in the original terms of their securities under erroneous representations that Mexico had at last achieved political tranquillity and would be able permanently to resume payments on her foreign obligations. That the committee erred in its judgment, acted contrary to the advice of others who were better informed on Mexican conditions, such as the Department of State, which was withholding recognition, is evidenced by the fact that two revisions downward of the original contract with Mexico have been signed. The ineptness of the committee has caused material injury to the rights of many American and European investors who had been led to have implicit confidence in the good will of Mexico and her capacity to pay. The resultant disillusionment has reduced public confidence in our southern neighbor and destroyed her credit. This is of practical concern to the people of the United States.

X. That each succeeding debt agreement waived further rights and reduced the value of the terms of the original bonds *indicates that the trust of the security holders in the personnel of the committee was abused beyond precedent. It was the practice of the committee first to commit the bondholders to reduce terms with Mexico and then induce the security holders to accept each succeeding reduction in their rights by intimations that Mexico was now capable of meeting the new terms. The effect of the arbitrary chiseling or whittling away of the terms stipulated in the original titles of the Mexican bonds and the nullification of some classes of bonds sets a most pernicious precedent tending to jeopardize $15,000,000,000 of American investments in other foreign government securities.*

XI.   The rights of 4,000 American claimants and other creditors of Mexico have been relegated to an inferior position due to the priority claimed and obtained by the international committee of bankers in behalf of the holders of Mexican securities. Holders of certain classes of secured bonds of Mexico have been protesting at the favoritism granted inferior classes by the bankers committee and demanding suitable recognition for their own. In other words, complete confusion has arisen as to the priority of various classes of bonds, the prior rights of claimants, and other classes of creditors. The resultant tangle of Mexico's external debts by this unofficial and unincorporated committee of bankers has set up a serious problem for the United States to unravel.

XII.   The bankers' committee has on hand, undistributed and undistributable to the bondholders, approximately $17,-000,000 received from the Mexican Government. There is no agreement in effect providing for its disposition, the title is not defined, and there is no one to demand an accounting for it, excepting the Committee on Banking and Currency of the House. About $33,000,000 have been paid to the bondholders and about $2,000,000 interest has accrued.

The preferred position heretofore enjoyed by the International Committee of Bankers on Mexico has contributed materially to the utter failure of the powers of diplomacy of the State Department to protect the rights of other citizens in Mexico either by direct representation or through the claims conventions.

The challenge herein presented to the people of the United States through their representatives in Congress, by way of you and your committee, is whether the power and authority of our executive department shall be subordinate to the influence and will of an unincorporated group of bankers at the expense of other citizens.

Respectfully yours,

Howard T. Oliver.

I now desire to refer to the last meeting of the International Committee on Mexican Debt, presided over by Mr. Thomas W. Lamont and which was held in New York, and to point out to you that in this agreement of July 25, 1930, it was proposed to make a refunding bond issue amounting to $267,-493,250. These bonds are to run for 45 years and pay 5 per cent interest under the law, but in the agreement the interest runs on a sliding scale for the first five years. The proposed issue is to be divided as follows:

Series A, $139,389,678; series B, $128,103,572.

The interest on series A is to be 3 per cent in 1931 and 1932, 4 per cent in 1933 and 1934, and 5 per cent in 1935 and thereafter.

The series A bonds are evidently intended to cover the secured debt of $68,806,000 and the total interior debt of $67,606,000, amounting to $136,412,000, mentioned in the schedule of debts accepted in the Lamont-De la Huerta agreement of June 16, 1922, page 41. It will be noted that the proposed issue of A bonds in the agreement under discussion is approximately $3,000,000 larger in amount than these same debts as set up in the agreement of June 16, 1922.

The interest on series B is to be 3 per cent in 1931, 1932, and 1933, 3½ per cent in 1934, 4 per cent in 1935 and 1936, and 5 per cent each year thereafter.

The series B bonds for $128,103,572 are evidently proposed to cover "the secured debt" accepted in the Lamont-de la Huerta agreement of June 16, 1922, which holds a lien of

131

100 per cent on the import and export taxes of the Mexican Government. (See memorandum of history of these bonds attached hereto.) This debt is stated as $128,684,000 in the Lamont-de la Huerta agreement of June, 1922.

The above items appear as follows under the title of "Schedule of obligations" on page 41 of the Lamont-de la Huerta agreement:

Mexican Government 5's, 1899	$ 48,635,000
Mexican Government 4's, 1910	50,949,000
⁴6,000,000 Mexican Government 6's, 1913	29,100,000
Total secured debt	$128,684,000
5 per cent municipal loan	6,769,000
Mexican Government 4's, 1904	37,037,000
Caja de Prestamos 4½'s	25,000,000
Total unsecured debt	$ 68,806,000
Mexican Government 3's, 1886	21,151,000
Mexican Government 5's, 1894	46,455,000
Total interior debt	$ 67,606,000

(No mention is made in this agreement of the Huerta bonds of 1913 and 1914 repudiated by Carranza but which were in a way recognized under the Lamont-de la Huerta agreement, as will be more fully explained further on. In the Lamont-de la Huerta agreement it was provided that the schedule of debts attached might be added to by later including "such other issues as the minister and the committee might jointly agree should be included in the Government external debt and railway debt." The repudiated Huerta bonds and about $118,000,000 in railway debts were the only items which had been omitted in this agreement.)

To cover the service of the new bonds to be issued under this agreemnt to refund the foregoing items the Mexican Government agrees to pay $12,500,000 in 1931 ($5,000,000 on account of which was paid as an evidence of good faith about

September 1, last), increasing this payment by $500,000 each year so that in 1936 and thereafter the payments are to be $15,000,000 annually. These payments during the first five years are to include a special fund of $11,755,003.38, which is to be used to take up all interest warrants and scrip and all interest due as of January 1, 1931, on the following basis:

	Value	Special Fund
(a) At 1 per cent of face value, receipts for interest in arrears, class B of the aggregate value of	$ 46,865,726.00	$ 468,657.26
(b) At 2 per cent of face value, receipts for interest in arrears, class A of the aggregate value of	64,223,446.00	1,284,46.92
(c) At 10 per cent of face value, current interest scrip of the face value of	13,219,207.00	1,321,920.70
Unpaid cash warrants, overdue coupons and interest on Government obligations, calculated to Jan. 1, 1931, of the aggregate face value of	61,214,608.00	6,121,460.80
	$185,522,987.00	$ 8,196,507.66
Current interest scrip on railway obligations of an aggregate value of	7,812,798.00	781,279.80
Overdue cash warrants on railway obligations "for which the Government stands responsible under the plan and agreement of June 16, 1922," etc.	17,772,159.00	1,777,215.90
	$211,107,944.00	$11,755,003.38

NOTE.—If this agreement should eventually go through the loss to security holders in connection with the first four items above, which refer to the bonded debt, would amount to $176,326,479.32. The last two items refer to bonds of the Tehuantepec Railway and cash warrants issued on railway obligations before the modifications of the Lamont-de la Huerta agreement made in October 1925, went into effect. These items aggregate $25,584,957. Taken up at 10 per cent these items would show a loss to security holders of $23,026,461.30. Otherwise under this agreement it is proposed to wipe out all interest in arrears, amounting to $211,107,944, by the payment of $11,755,-003.38 over a period of years, showing a net loss to security holders of $199,352,940.62. This is a far different attitude from that taken in the Lamont-de la Tuerta agreement of June 16, 1922, where all interest was calculated to January 1, 1923, and made a part of the recognized debt, while current interest from January 1, 1923, to January 1, 1928, was provided for, so far as it could be met in cash, by appropriation of the export tax on oil and a 10 per cent tax on the gross revenues of the National Railways.

This is but a brief outline of the present status of the Mexican debt situation which I have referred to in my opening remarks. A persual of Mr. Oliver's letter clearly discloses the position of the State Department in all of these negotiations.

I am now placing in the RECORD at this point a statement appearing in the Christian Science Monitor under date of January 31, 1931:

Gold Payments on Mexico's $500,000,000 Debt Suspended—
2-Year Postponement Necessary, Lamont Says, Because of
Peso's Decline—Equivalent Deposits in Silver
To Be Made in Interim

NEW YORK, January 31.—A suspension of transfer of payments of the Mexican foreign debt was announced yesterday by Thomas W. Lamont, of the banking house of J. P. Morgan & Co., and chairman of the International Committee of Bankers on Mexico.

Mr. Lamont said in a prepared statement that "a fresh

agreement" had been entered into which was supplemental to and in substitution of the debt agreement signed in New York City on July 25 last. It had been made necessary, he said, by the decline in value of the Mexican silver peso.

He added that the Mexican Government had stated that its capacity to pay in gold had decreased so greatly it could not possibly, within the limits of its budget revenue and requirements, provide the amount of gold called for under the July 25, 1930, agreement. This agreement provided for the consolidation of debt placed at $500,000,000 in gold.

Under the new agreement, signed in Mexico City by Montes de Oca, Minister of Finance, and in New York by Mr. Lamont, representing the bankers' committee, the Mexican Government may avoid for two years the obligation to make gold payments on its foreign debt.

The Mexican Government promises, however, to make deposits in silver equivalent to the gold payments. These silver deposits would be held in a "responsible depository" in Mexico City, and if within any time during the next two years the monetary situation in Mexico improves sufficiently to allow gold payments, Mexico promises that gold will be substituted for the silver.

The latest Lamont-Oca agreement also provides that the Mexican Government get back from the bankers' committee the $5,000,000 (gold) which it paid on its debt last August and substitute silver for it in the Mexican depository.

It was regarded as significant that Mr. Lamont's statement made no mention of the rate of exchange at which the silver would be turned in at the Mexican depository.

The agreement, if ratified, will have the effect of again postponing all payments on the Mexican foreign debt.

The history of the Mexican debt situation has been one of frequent "postponements" and evasions of payments by one means or another. The first "agreement"

135

between the Mexican Government and the international committee, called "the agreement of June 16, 1922," went into effect on December 8, 1923. Because of political disturbances in Mexico, which affected its financial plans, the Government issued an official decree on June 30, 1924, suspending the service of the foreign debt.

This suspension continued until the bankers' committee, after discussions with the then finance minister, Alberto J. Pani, arranged substantial modifications in the agreement, specifically separating the agreements as to the direct Government debt and the National Railways debt. The modified agreement, signed on October 23, 1925, became effective on January 1, 1926. Remittances on the Government debt under the modified plan were made for about two years, but when full payments under the original loan agreements were to be resumed on January 1, 1928, the service on the direct debt again was suspended, the Government declaring itself unable to pay in full.

Discussion was resumed on June 25 last and the "agreement" of last July was arrived at. The Mexican Government again finds it impossible to live up to it.

The special delegates who conducted the negotiations here with Mr. Lamont were Roberto Casas Alatriste and Francesco Valladares, who had not been members of the commission which negotiated the previous agreement.

I now desire to refer to the agitation, which seems to be taking very definite form in regard to the international debt situation and German reparation payments under the Young plan, wherein it is indicated that a move is on for the revision of war-debt payments. In this respect, I cite the speech of Philip Snowden, Chancellor of the Exchequer, on the British war debt settlement with America, on February 11, and reported in the New York Times of February 12, in which he predicted that posterity will curse those who were responsible for the British war debt settlement. The article reads as follows:

He named no person, but, of course, he had in mind only the United States and Stanley Baldwin, who as Chancellor of the Exchequer, negotiated the war debt settlement with the United States in 1922.

He is quoted:

We have the burden of the war debt. I don't want to give offense to anybody when I make this statement that when the history of the way in which that debt was incurred—its recklessness, its extravagance and its commitments made, which were altogether unnecessary at the time—when all that comes to be known, I am afraid posterity will curse those who were responsible.

I also direct your attention to a statement by a Member of Parliament, J. M. Kenworthy, who said on the same day in Parliament (and I am quoting from his speech as recorded in the New York Times of February 12):

There should be an international round table conference on the interallied war debts and reparations. We should consider a moratorium. The conference should be called by the United States, but that country apparently is afraid to make the move so England should take the initiative. Such a conference would be the best thing the world could have for the restoration of normal conditions.

Up to the present—

He continued—

Germany has only made small payments which we have passed on to America, and America has re-lent the money to Germany. Now Germany doesn't dare borrow any more high rates from America, and we will soon have a flood of German goods dumped on our markets and the markets of the world. All of eastern America and the American bankers are in favor of a policy of moratorium, but the Middle West has not come over and is still in favor of our policy of 1920, that the Germans must pay.

It is apparent that Mr. Kenworthy was receiving the bulk of his information from this international group of bankers.

This was followed immediately by a statement by Lady Astor. She declared that she would use such influence as she had in any part of the world to put an end to the tall and bulky laborite called "this impossible situation of inter-allied debts and reparations." The views of Lady Astor are significant because of her Virginian ancestry.

That we are on the eve of important developments affecting reparations and debt settlements in which these international bankers are involved was indicated in Berlin, Germany, during the present week when the new National Socialist Facisti Party, which is directed by Adolph Hitler, when its entire membership in the Reichstag left the Reichstag in bloc joined by the nationalist members of the Reichstag under the leadership of Doctor Hugenberg, and have refused to participate further, apparently, in the present session of the Reichstag as a protest against the financial program of the present administration in Germany.

This is significant when you take into consideration the fact that the main plan of the platform of the Hitler party is a reconsideration of the treaty of Versailles and the Young plan looking toward cancellation of a complete reconsideration of the debts owed by Germany.

In the midst of all of this international unrest we are advised that Lee, Higginson & Co. are now negotiating in Berlin and Paris for a new international loan to Germany, as is indicated by an article appearing on the financial page of the Washington Star, under date of February 11, as follows:

> Germany is seeking another loan. A small one this time—only a feeler—about $32,000,000; and France is expected to take a good slice of it. If it is popular, it will be followed by other loans, for Germany must have several times this amount this year to keep going.
>
> It is now well known that the last German loan of $125,000,000 did not receive any wide support from the

American people. It is not likely, therefore, that the United States will take any great amount of German issues for the next few months. Still, who knows? George Murnane, partner of Lee, Higginson & Co., the firm which handled the American end of the last loan, is at present in Paris working out, with other bankers, the details of the new issue, indicating, at least, that the United States will have an opportunity to subscribe for a part of the new issue.

George Murnane, named in this dispatch, is a partner of Lee, Higginson & Co., referred to here, and is also a director of the Bank of Manhattan Co. of New York and several other of the Warburg financial institutions. He has also been recently elected a director of the Marine Midland Bank of Buffalo, which is a part of the Marine Midland Corporation. This is the institution in which the Hon. Edmund Platt, former Vice Governor of the Federal Reserve Board, was recently made a vice president.

I have been pointing out in the past how the Bank for International Settlements was to serve the interests of these international financiers, and in this connection we are advised by the present head of the Bank for International Settlements, Mr. Gates W. McGarrah, former head of the Federal Reserve Bank of New York, under date of February 12, in a speech that he made in Paris on that date before the American Club, that more foreign loans are to be made. We read:

World bank head would reopen the great capital markets to external financing. Favors long-term credits.

In this article appears this most significant statement. I quote:

It is most appropriate that I should mention the subject before the American Club of the city of Paris, because it is upon Paris and upon New York that, owing to the special conditions now prevailing in London, the opportunity and obligation fall to help themselves by helping others through making long-term investments.

In this connection I have been repeatedly pointing out the fact that over 60 per cent of the world's gold is at the present time under the control of Paris and New York. I have been constantly stressing how and to what extent the Federal reserve system was being involved and dominated both in the United States as well as internationally by these two banking groups, J. P. Morgan & Co. and Kuhn, Loeb & Co.

These, with the other things that I have stated, are my reasons for calling this matter to the attention of Congress and to point out the danger that confronts this country by participating in the involvement through these international bankers either by the people of this country or through the investment in these loans, which if they do not now involve our Government will involve our Government in the end. I have been calling the attention of the Congress for some time past to the seriousness of this situation, and I can appreciate that at first to some of you these financial questions and these connections that I have been pointing out and am now making definite and complete are problems complex, but of which every Member of this Congress must now take cognizance and act before it is too late.

I desire again to emphasize some things that I have previously said, so let me begin with the conditions of to-day and our position among the nations of the world and then briefly trace their connection with the treaty of Versailles.

We know what we did not know for a good many years after the war, that our country now stands without comparison in the strength of its institutions and in the magnitude of its power and wealth. The consciousness of this fact has come to us only gradually and we have received it almost with incredulity.

We have been equally slow to realize how greatly the war there lowered the vitality and the political and economic power of the great European states. What students of history call the balance of power no longer exists, or if it were to manifest itself it would have to be some combination to offset the power of the United States.

Probably already in 1914 the power of the United States was far greater than we or others supposed, but it was latent, because under our institutions and conceptions of the functions of a government we did not direct it toward those aggresive foreign enterprises which then characterized the policies of strong European states. We did not enter greatly into their calculations except that they were quite careful to respect such rights as we claimed.

But great as was our real power in 1914, it is immensely greater to-day; actually, because we possess more than twice the gold stock we then had, which greatly strengthened our banking power, and relatively because of the weakening of the states of Europe.

It would seem, then, that we would be justified in feeling a sense of security and in relaxing the vigilance which patriotic men must feel in times of national insecurity, and that our noblest sentiments would express themselves in gratitude for our good fortune and in a determination that it should not engender in us an unbecoming spirit of vain-glory or national vanity.

But the conditions of to-day do not in fact, justify such a sense of security. We are not faced by a military menace. We are not at the moment threatened with war. But in the field of diplomacy and international finance forces of a subtle and obscure nature are at work, and with which we must reckon. The victories of the mind and of the wits are sometimes as great as those of the battlefield. Perhaps Sir Charles Addis, the British representative on the Bank for International Settlements, had this in mind when he said recently, *"True wisdom lies in the masterful administration of the unseen."*

I think the broad statement may be made that the governments of the industrial states of Europe do not reconcile themselves to the great industrial and financial preponderance that has come to America since the war. Stripped of their stored-up wealth by the war, it is impossible for them to reestablish their

141

industrial preponderance in its pre-war vigor. It would take two or three billion dollars more of gold than they have to give them financial resources adequate to the reestablishment of their pre-war power. It would also require a lowering of the industrial power of the United States before they could recapture the world markets which they formerly dominated.

There are evidences that the purposes of international financial activities are now addressing themselves to those general ends. There is a rapidly developing movement toward the control of our Federal reserve banking system by powerful groups of bankers who are equally at home in the United States and in Europe and who regard the vast credit facilities of that system as being available for use abroad as much as for domestic purposes.

You are aware that before the Federal reserve system was adopted in 1913 we had no single central pool of gold stocks and credit. Thousands of banking institutions throughout the country maintained their own gold reserves. Under these circumstances it was not possible for a few officials to grant credits of billions either at home or abroad. But under the Federal reserve system the reserves of all the member banks are in the possession of the Federal Reserve Board at Washington. The vast international credit operations that the prosecution of the war entailed brought the entire liquid wealth of the country under the control of that system and accustomed those who administered it to regard the dispensing of billions in credit at home or abroad as their own prerogative.

When the Federal Reserve Act was passed it was intended that the Federal reserve system should be a governmental agency and its policies under government control. With the passage of the years, however, it has tended more and more to become an autonomous body reflecting the will of the dominant financial interests, and acting independently of political authority. Claims are insistently made to-day that the Secretary of the Treasury should have no control over it and that the Comptroller of the Currency should be made an agent of the Federal Reserve Board and not of the United States

Treasury. Under this plan the Government would have abrogated its constitutional authority to coin money and regulate its value and surrendered it into private hands.

The usurpation of authority has already gone far. The Federal Reserve Bank of New York, with the permission of the Federal Reserve Board at Washington, has placed billions of dollars of credit at the disposal of New York banks to be loaned abroad by discounting foreign acceptances and permitting foreign loans of all kinds to be made, without the authorization of the United States Treasury.

If the powers which it is now exercising over credit in the United States are permitted, or are to be permitted by statute, then it is within the discretion of the Federal Reserve Board, if it so chooses, to shift the entire monetary wealth of the American people to the uses of the foreigner.

And the developments of recent years give color to the suspicion that it is the purpose of those who now control the Federal reserve system to move a considerable distance in that direction.

The Young plan, drawn up in 1929 and now adopted, created the Bank for International Settlements, located at Basle. It is obviously a central bank for Europe, through which the European states intend to conduct all business which they in common have with powers outside of Europe. It enables them to present a common financial front in dealing with non-European financial centers. It was set up with the active co-operation of the great international financiers of New York, and a former head of the Federal Reserve Bank of New York is now its president.

One of the primary purposes of this bank is to administer the distribution of German reparations as they were created under the treaty of Versailles. How rapidly its purposes have expanded during the course of its short history may be seen by the following dispatch from Basle on February 9 last:

A plan to solve the problem of world gold movements by making transfers on the Bank for International Settlements without physically transferring the metal itself was contained in a resolution adopted to-day at a conference of the international bank directors with governors of national banks of issue.

For some time international financiers have been pondering the tangle of gold reserves. They have been seeking some way in which the flow of the yellow metal can be diverted from such countries as France and the United States, which hold most of the world's supply, and started toward those nations with depleted stocks.

The scheme offered to-day appears to be that gold deposits should be made in the Bank for International Settlements. Then when gold must flow from one nation to the other it can be done merely by a transfer on the books, since the metal already will be in the vaults of the international bank, where both parties have accounts.

As soon as this provision goes into actual operation shipments of gold to the United States will permanently cease, while shipments of gold from the United States to Europe may be freely made.

I think it can hardly be disputed that the statesmen and financiers of Europe are ready to take almost any means to reacquire rapidly the gold stock which Europe lost to America as a result of the war. I think it can hardly be disputed, either, that the control of our gold and our credit power through the Federal reserve system has fallen into the hands of powerful international financiers who are willing to cooperate with the the Europeans in this purpose.

It is within the power of the Congress to take this power away from the private financiers and lodge it again in governmental agencies where it belongs, but public opinion must support the Congress if this is to be done. It is the right of the American people to require that the gold stock be protected by the Government and retained for domestic purposes if they so choose. So long as we have a favorable trade balance, which we have and will probably continue to have, the gold can not flow out of the country unless it is shipped abroad as a voluntary gift.

No foreign nation has a right to demand any part of this gold, as is being insistently urged in some quarters. There is no moral duty on the part of the United States to part with it upon foreign request. Yet under the state of the law to-day, with the Federal reserve system dominated by a nongovernmental power, a steady flow of gold out of the country might take place through the unchecked granting of loans and credits abroad.

Something of this kind is being devised to-day through the instrumentality of the Bank for International Settlements.

The Stresemann policy, having failed to accomplish what it was intended to do, some other means will be taken to accomplish the same end.

The Stresemann policy was devised to bring Germany and the allied governments into harmony in a plan to sell the German war reparation bonds in their billions outside of Europe. Until this was adopted as a common policy, Germany stubbornly refused to have her reparation debt commercialized and thus fixed irrevocably upon her. By the Stresemann policy she was offered a substantial share in the proceeds from the sale of the bonds, and this brought her into agreement with the reparation policy of the allied governments.

Under the Young plan a general European agreement was reached to commercialize these bonds, to the amount of $3,250,000,000 outside of Europe. The American investment market was the only market capable of absorbing them, and it was here that they were intended to be sold.

The Dawes plan of 1924 had precisely the same purpose, but it could not be put into operation in the United States because at that time Germany stubbornly withheld her consent to the commercialization of the bonds.

The reparation bonds had been created, and Germany had been forced to recognize their existence, by the London ultimatum of 1921 which fixed their total amount at $33,000,000,-000, twelve billions of which were intended to be commercialized upon the international investment market at once. If the twelve billions in bonds could have been disposed of in the United States at that time, it would just about have canceled the allied debts to the United States, and the United States would have become the sole collector of the German war indemnity.

The reparation bonds of the London ultimatum of 1921 were created in pursuance of the financial clauses of the treaty of Versailles which permitted each allied government to sell its right to collect a share in the German indemnity to private purchasers for cash. What was done in the London ultimatum, the Dawes plan, and the Young plan leaves small doubt that it was the intention of the makers of the treaty of Versailles that American investors in these bonds should pay the German indemnity to the allied states in cash, looking to Germany for reimbursements in annual payments over a long period of time. This has not yet been accomplished, but the purpose is still being pursued in the Young plan.

So it is not such a far cry from the international financial questions of to-day to the treaty of Versailles 13 years ago. Indeed, we are faced now with precisely the same situation as existed then. The war has never been liquidated fnancially in the way that the treaty of Versailles intended, and the same conditions which Lloyd George and Clemenceau presented for American acceptance then are presented for American acceptance to-day.

The Bank for International Settlements is to receive $500,-000,000 a year from Germany in reparation payments and is to place the money to the credit of the allied governments. The allied governments draw upon these sums to pay the annual interest on their debts to the United States. But the United States, according to the news of February 9, which I quoted just now does not receive the gold. The gold remains to its credit on the books of the Bank of International Settlements at Basle.

Simultaneously with these transactions the Young plan reparation bonds are being offered to the American investor.

There are $3,250,000,000 worth of them, if he chooses to purchase so many, and the gold which he pays for them may, in the discretion of the Federal reserve bank, be shipped continuously across the Atlantic to Europe.

There is one more point I wish to speak about which involves the legality of the treaty of Versailles, and consequently the legal sufficiency of these Young plan reparation bonds. It is of considerable military interest and was not generally known to our soldiers or to others at that time. The Germans signed the armistice agreement after a long series of negotiations between President Wilson and the German chancellor in October. These negotiations ended in a peace agreement which was binding on both sides when the armistice came into effect.

It provided for reparation payments which were less than a fourth of the sum afterwards fixed by the London ultimatum. The German agreement to the larger penalty was extracted from them by the pressure of a food blockade imposed upon them after the armistice and maintained while the peace conference was in session. This was a clear violation of the laws of war and of international law. It was an act of bad faith and is the explanation of the universal suspicion and distrust that animate international relations in Europe to-day.

To ask us to take a stake in the German reparations at this late date, as they are doing when they offer us the Young plan, is an absurdity. It is worse than an absurdity; it is a fraud, and an affront to our intelligence.

There is great need that these broad questions be taken up in the Congress and discussed openly, so that public opinion may arrive at intelligent conclusions upon all the considerations involved. It is not wise for us to leave our international fate in the hands of the international bankers.

The SPEAKER pro tempore (Mr. Tilson). The time of the gentleman from Pennsylvania [Mr. McFadden] has expired.

IX

PRESENT NATIONAL
AND INTERNATIONAL
BANKING SITUATION

Monday, March 2, 1931

Mr. McFADDEN. Mr. Speaker, under general leave granted
to Members to extend their remarks in the RECORD, I herewith
insert the following:

Banking deals with money and the money value of things,
and it is therefore in communities where there is much money
and many valuable things that banking reaches its greatest
magnitude. Needless to say that here in the United States, and
in the era in which we are living, more banking is being done
with real money and real things than was ever done anywhere
in the world before.

Financial transactions, including those which overlap
frontiers, are now carried on upon so great a scale that it
is no easy task, even for bankers engaged in extensive transactions, to perceive the larger tendencies and estimate their
probable results. Formerly we were accustomed to estimate
conditions about us and consider these as determining whether
business was likely to be good or bad. There is too much
tendency to do that now and to ascribe to local or domestic
conditions reasons for the state of trade or of credit at a
particular moment.

Before the Federal reserve system was established in 1913
thousands of banks maintained their own gold reserves. After

148

its establishment the member banks gave their gold reserves into the control of the Federal reserve banks and a vast central pool of credit was created under control of the Federal Reserve Board.

"Credit once brought into existence," some one has said, "is a natural fluid which can not be kept from flowing into the nearest channel available under the gravitational force of demand in the form of interest rates." The streams of credit which have flowed out of this central reservoir since its creation have brought changes and raised problems which were undreamed of in 1913. We have centralized the creation of credit and its uses.

The revolutionary character of the Federal reserve system was greatly magnified by the coming of the war in Europe in 1914. Historically, the central bank came into existence as a war instrumentality. The Bank of England was created in 1694 to establish a central pool of the nation's wealth upon which the government of William the Third could draw to defray the expenses of its wars upon the Continent, and since that date its resources have been primarily at the disposal of the British Government in its imperial and foreign enterprises. The central bank enables the Government to utilize, if it so desires, the entire credit power of the nation in enterprises abroad.

No doubt this was not in the mind of the Congress when it established the Federal reserve system. A status of peace seemed to be our normal condition, and it was the stabilization and equalizing of credit conditions in our domestic economy that was uppermost in the minds of the legislators.

From 1914 to 1917 our stimulated foreign trade gave us a large favorable trade balance which was offset by loans by private bankers to the Allies. After we entered the war the belligerent governments suspended shipments of gold. The allied governments asked and received credits from the United States Government sufficient to cover all debts, and these credits were raised here by the floating of the Liberty and Victory loans.

I would invite your attention to the way the "stream of credit," which we are likening to a natural fluid, has flowed during the past 14 years, viewed, as it were, from some stationary point of observation which ignores minor eddies or whirlpools, the rate of the current here or there, or the depths or shallows at a particular point.

Beginning with 1917 we see it sweeping eastward across our political boundaries "under the gravitational force of demand in the form of interest rates" and under the impulsion of a foreign war. For four years and more the vast current flowed unchecked. These four years of war did their devastationg work in Europe. Year by year on an ever-greater scale the warring states expended their stored-up wealth outside of Europe.

When the armistice came, and with it the reaction from war, all Europe was stunned and inert, but there existed an insistent demand for foodstuffs, goods, and commodities which had to be met. Europe presented a limitless consuming market, and the producing market was in the United States alone.

You will recall the enormous industrial energy with which America met this demand. And in order that the manufacturers, merchants, and workers might be paid without depending upon remittances from the foreign purchaser, the Government extended further loans to the allied states and, through the War Finance Corporation, advanced hundreds of millions of Government money to the banks so that the banks could continue to finance the producers.

Month after month this went on, with the credit inflation mounting far beyond that which would have been justified by the gold base, and during this period nobody inquired what the consequences would be if Europe could not settle its trade balance. Finally, in 1920, the Government became alarmed; it ceased making loans to the banks for the financing of exporters, called on the governments of Europe to settle their trade balance in gold, and induced the Federal Reserve Board to raise its rates.

Never was industrial activity on such an intensive and so

vast a scale so suddenly and so completely reversed. From one end of the country to the other bank credits were frozen, factories closed, and not only foreign but domestic trade brought almost to a standstill. This condition lasted through 1921.

Returning to our metaphor of credit as a natural fluid, the scene from our stationary point of observation is now changed. The rushing stream that had been pouring across our territorial borders has dried up as quickly as it had sprung forth. Where before had been a broad and swift-flowing current there appeared sandy wastes through which could be discerned a few trickling streams flowing from one stagnant pool to another. Credit for domestic purposes was as unavailable as for foreign.

This sudden industrial stagnation in the United States was as unpleasant as it was unexpected, but it was felt far more acutely in Europe, which for a year had been living upon the importations from the United States.

There was only one way to have these importations begin again, and that was by paying for what had already been sent so that the banks in the United States could again have sufficient reserves to allow them to make new loans to exporters. The allied governments, therefore, had to remove the embargoes which they had maintained on the exportation of gold so that the European trade balance with America could be settled.

The recovery in the United States in 1922 coincided with the receipt of continued importations of gold on an immense scale. Gold continued to flow into the United States until, as you will recall, our gold stock in 1924 amounted to $4,000,-000,000. It is on the basis of this gold cover that the great industrial activity of the past decade has been able to be carried on.

The influx of the gold refilled the great credit container of the Federal reserve system. Out of this container in 1922 innumerable small streams of credit began to flow throughout the United States. The sandy stretches and the stagnant pools disappeared and there was movement again everywhere.

If a governmental policy had been entered upon in 1922 of confining the use of Federal reserve credit to the needs of the domestic market and of foreign trade, business and financial conditions in the United States would have been stabilized upon a sound basis and the function of the Federal reserve system would have become more clearly defined.

If it were considered that the political and social structures in Europe might disintegrate without the aid of great loans from the United States, this would have been regarded as a political question which would have been given due consideration and regulated by legislation at Washington.

The belligerent states of Europe were entirely impoverished as a result of the war. Their industrial and financial potentialities were greatly and permanently lowered. Europe to-day is no better able to carry a foreign debt of $20,000,-000,000 than the states of South America would be. But this view has not prevailed at Washington.

The great international banking interests of the East have persisted in the view that the war in Europe was only an incident, although a grievous one, in the history of that continent, that the thread of European life and activity could be taken up after the war and followed under substantially the same conditions that had prevailed before 1914.

Under this appraisal, the ultimate financial resources of the states of Europe remain as great as they ever were and assurances are given the American people that investments in Europe are a good risk. Yet the German Government has been able to pay reparation annuities only out of the receipts of loans from America, the allied states groan under the payment of installments on their debts to America, and are protesting that they can not pay these installments unless they first receive the money from Germany. Most of the states of Europe are nearly denuded of gold, which is the only measure of monetary wealth, and their resources and those of private citizens are necessarily limited by the amount of the gold. It is probably no exaggeration to say that substantially the only monetary wealth in Europe to-day is the credits which are continuously flowing there from New York.

Since 1922 the air has been filled with schemes and plans for utilizing Federal reserve credit in Europe. In 1924 the international bankers devised the Dawes plan, which created negotiable German reparation bonds in the sum of $4,000,-000,000, the bulk of which was intended to be sold in the United States. The State and Treasury Departments of the United States Government actively participated in these negotiations, but they did not meet with the approval of President Coolidge and the bonds could not be offered on the American market.

Nevertheless an active propaganda here proclaimed the Dawes plan as a final settlement of the contentions in Europe, and with this propaganda as a basis the international bankers entered upon a policy of pouring the money of American investors into Europe through the purchase of governmental, municipal, and industrial bonds.

Nothwithstanding the fact that political, financial, and economic disintegration has steadily increased in Europe with the passage of the years, the propaganda of prosperity in Europe has been kept alive in this country in order that the international bankers might continue in their lucrative trade of selling European bonds here. The Dawes plan has been revived in the Young plan of 1929, under which negotiable German reparation bonds in the sum total of $3,250,000,000 are available for sale upon the American market.

In a speech which I made here recently I included a table showing the loans which the international bankers have made abroad since 1919 and the banking houses which made them. The total of these loans is nearly $8,000,000,000. Add to this $9,000,000,000 in loans made prior to 1919, making a total of $17,000,000,000, which, together with the public debts of $12,-000,000,000 that the European states owe the United States Government, makes a total debt of $29,000,000,000 owed by the foreigners to the people of the United States, and if the $3,000,000,000 in Young plan reparation bonds were disposed of in this country the total would be raised to $32,000,000,000.

This practice of the bankers of extending loans by billions of dollars to Europe began during the war and has continued under the Dawes and Young plans. They have been doing substantially what the Dawes plan would have accomplished if it could have been put into operation in the United States.

These vast loans gave Europe a renewed purchasing power here, and the greatly stimulated trans-Atlantic trade was the basis of the feverish financial optimism which centered itself in the operations of the stock market which culminated in the crash of 1929.

During those five years we saw once more the great stream of credit flowing eastward across our borders. And again we saw it suddenly terminate in 1929 and the sandy wastes and stagnant pools reappear. This time there was no gold stock in Europe to be shipped westward to settle the foreign debt. The billions advanced by the international bankers have not been repaid.

Under the Young plan it was the intention to post the first tranche of the reparation bonds on the American market in 1929. If the bonds had been acceptable and the way opened for the floating of successive tranches, the improvement in Europe's purchasing power would have been immediate, trans-Atlantic trade would have immediately revived, and industrial depression in the United States would have been checked. There would have been no collapse of stocks in 1929. It would, however, merely have been postponed. Stagnation here would have supervened at a later date, when European purchases here had exhausted the credit, just as it supervened here in 1920 and again in 1929.

If the international bankers now resume the practice of selling European securities here at the rate of a billion dollars a year, we will have several years of exaggerated industrial activity like those which followed the Dawes plan, followed likewise by a sudden stagnation like that after 1929, supervening when the European credit has been expended here. The great stream of credit flowing eastward across our borders will be

COLLECTIVE SPEECHES OF HON. LOUIS T. MCFADDEN

checked again and the sandy wastes and stagnant pools will reappear.

The longer this policy of the international bankers is followed the greater becomes the number of people throughout the country who hold foreign securities which the mounting debts of foreign governments make it less and less possible for them to repay, and the greater grows the proportion of the liquid wealth of the country which remains in the hands of the international bankers.

As an adjunct of this policy the eager support which the international bankers of New York have given to the Bank for International Settlements set up under the Young plan is entirely logical. It is in the nature of a central bank for Europe, through which the European States collectively may deal with financial centers outside of Europe. The receipts from the sale of more than $3,000,000,000 worth of Young plan reparation bonds outside of Europe were intended to fill its coffers with gold at an early date.

But there is no way in which gold from America can be made to flow into Europe through payment of balances because the balance of payments is so greatly in favor of the United States. The Stresemann policy, which I have discussed in the Congress, and which has guided every foreign office in Europe for years, is a plain notification to us that loans from the United States in billions is the sole basis upon which the European statesmen propose to reconstruct European affairs. Under the Stresemann policy many more billions were to have been received from America on balance. This would have caused a flow of gold from America to Europe.

The gravity of this for us lies in the fact that the Stresemann policy had the wholehearted support of the international bankers of New York. That it is their desire that gold in large amounts shall flow from the United States to Europe is evidenced by their support of this policy, and now that the Stresemann policy has failed it is being urged in New York by the leading international bankers that we should release a portion of our gold for the reserves of depleted central banks in Europe.

The relations of the Federal Reserve Bank of New York with the banks of Europe have become as intimate in the matter of extensions of credit as if these European banks were members of the Federal reserve system. One can but wonder upon what theory of banking this practice is based.

No bank ever existed except under the protection of some sovereign authority and for the furtherance of the purposes of that sovereign power. Without such sovereign protection its treasures would be at the mercy of any band of marauders. The practices which the Federal reserve bank and the international bankers of New York are following would indicate an assumption that a political alliance or a super-state has been created under whose sovereign will the safety and security of these international banking transactions is guaranteed. If there were, in fact, a single sovereign power dominating the United States and the states of Europe, and a bank of international settlements were set up by this power, then the gold reserves of the central banks could be kept in the Bank for International Settlements where they would remain permanently; credits and debits of gold would be entered upon its books in the manner in which this is done for domestic banks by the Federal reserve system.

Inasmuch as the creators of the Bank for International Settlements assume that some sort of political status quo exists in the world sufficiently powerful to guarantee the safety of gold deposits in the Bank for International Settlements, and are inviting our Federal reserve system to entrust a part of its gold stock to the custody of that bank, prudence would move us to inquire what is the political authority or sovereign power under whose protection the bank will operate.

It is located within the territorial limits of the small neutral state of Switzerland and it is not pretended that it derives its security from Swiss protection. It rests upon the security of the treaties at The Hague which put the Young plan into operation about a year ago. The Hague conference was not characterized by harmony and good will. It was one of the stormiest and bitterest international conferences ever held. It can hardly be denied that the sole motive for agreement was the mutual financial benefit which might accrue if the bulk of the $3,000,-000,000 worth of Young plan reparation bonds, there being created, could be disposed of in the United States. If the bonds can not be so disposed of in the United States, the motive which made the signing of The Hague treaties possible fails, and there is nothing to hold the parties to their agreements.

The centrifugal influences in Europe are dominant, as may be seen by studying the political relationships of any one state to the others. All are armed to the teeth, except those held in subjection by the treaty of Versailles.

Is there any interest which they may be said to have in common? There is one, and we may find it by examining the important international conferences there since the war.

The first important international conference after the treaty of Versailles was the London ultimatum of 1921. At this conference Germany assumed liability for the payment of $33,000,000,000 in negotiable reparation bonds—and, incidentally, pressure by the State Department here upon Germany had much to do with her signing of the treaty. Twelve billions of these bonds were to be commercialized immediately on the international market. It was the purpose to sell them outside of Europe, and the proceeds were to be divided between the allied governments.

The next important conference was that of Genoa in 1922, at which the presence of the United States was urged most insistently. The motive here was to facilitiate the marketing of the reparation bonds outside of Europe, but the absence of the United States caused the main purpose of the conference to fail.

The next great international conferences was the Dawes plan conference in London in 1924. This was for the fixing of the annuities which Germany should pay, but without reducing the total amount of her liabilities. The chief interest was in finding out how large a sum could be obtained by issuing negotiable reparation bonds to be sold on the investment markets of the world. That treaty provided for the issuance of $4,000,000,000 worth of these bonds, the proceeds to be divided among the allied governments. Secretaries Hughes and Mellon were present in London at the negotiating of these agreements.

The Dawes plan bonds, however, could not be sold in the United States, partly because of the bad relations on either side of the Rhine and partly because the Coolidge administration would not permit it here. The Dawes plan, therefore, failed in its main purpose, as the London ultimatum had done.

It was after the Dawes plan was signed that the international bankers of New York began selling German municipal and industrial securities here upon an enormous scale, the loans mounting, as you will recall, to more than a billion and a half dollars: Germany out of her own resources had no means whatever of paying the Dawes plan annuities. She paid them, and it was intended that she should pay them, out of these receipts from America.

Notwithstanding the failure of these various treaty adjustments in Europe to accomplish their purpose, there was so much encouragement from the international bankers of New York, and at times from administrations in power in Washington, that this one motive of common action among the states of Europe remained alive. In France it got into domestic politics and in 1927 aided in keeping Poincaré in power.

The chief interest at the time of the meeting of the Council of the League of Nations at Geneva in 1928 was a plan "for the final settlement of German reparations." This plan was to fix not only the amount of the annuities Germany was to pay but the total number of years over which they were to be paid. By treaty settlements provision was made for the appointment of a committee of experts to draw up a plan, and it was desired that an American should be the chairman. This was the origin of the Young committee, which met in Paris in February, 1929, and substantially rewrote the Dawes plan, reducing the amount of the commercializable reparation bonds to $3,250,000,000.

This plan was made effective by The Hague treaty the next year. Under the London ultimatum and the Dawes plan

Germany had held back when it came to issuing the commercialized bonds because the burden was too great for her to assume. At The Hague conference, however, she was assured of one-third of the receipts from their sale, and this assurance induced her to become a party to the treaty.

The Young plan bonds were offered here last July as "the German international 5½'s," but the venture was not successful. If the bonds can not be sold here on the scale intended, the entire Stresemann policy, as it is called—that is to say, the one policy which might unite the states of Europe in a common cause sufficiently strong to keep them at peace—fails and falls to the ground.

That, apparently, is what has happened in Europe. The defection of Italy leaves Britain and France in a close alliance to maintain the treaty of Versailles, with its reparation demands upon Germany, while in Germany there is a strong and growing purpose of radically revising the Young plan, and the Bruening Government holds on to power only by yielding more and more to this demand.

Tranquillity in Europe, therefore, seems more than dubious. These major conferences of which I have spoken have not been League of Nations conferences. The League of Nations is not a superauthority exercising sovereign power. It could not afford physical security to the Bank for International Settlements.

What, then, might be the fate of the gold stocks held in trust in the vaults of the Bank for International Settlements if this one motive of common action in Europe failed? If, as a result of a common policy in Europe, a continuous flow of gold and credits from America can not be secured, what is there to hold these states together in peace? There is nothing, unless they can bring themselves to a radical revision of the treaty of Versailles, which will eliminate the idea of German reparations to be commercialized outside of Europe, and which will undo the other injustices of that treaty.

It can not be said, then, that there is a stable status quo in Europe emanating either from comprehensive treaty agree-

159

ments or from the creation of a supersovereign power; and there is no territory in Europe where the gold reserves of a world bank would not be exposed to the vicissitudes of international strife. The site of the present bank has been chosen in the general locality of the territory which for centuries has been known as the cockpit of Europe.

I stated above that political, financial, and economic disintegration since the war have been increasing in Europe. I know of no disinterested observer who denies this. The following conclusions were expressed in an article by the well-known observer, Frank Simonds, just the other day:

In sum, the impression I gather from Geneva and from the public men of all European countries here assembled is this: With the exception of France, the condition in all continental countries has become such that the familiar issues and problems of the postwar era, problems political and military, have become actually side issues.

Disintegration within the countries has become so general and gone so far that one of the most familiar judgments one meets is that capitalistic and democratic civilization is endangered, if not doomed, and that Europe is drifting toward a general catstrophe, still continuing to murmur the old words of nationalism.

Or, to put it differently, there is a growing recognition that recovery from the World War has not yet even begun and that no one can now guess what the new Europe will be like, although more and more are convinced that it will be incredibly unlike the old.

In any event, what seems in America to have remained an economic crisis has in Europe broadened into a political, social, and intellectual crisis. Informed people are no longer discussing the question of return of prosperity, but whether old Europe can survive this final catastrophe.

To continue indefinitely to make loans to a debtor who can not pay is not good business and is not good banking. These vast loans which I have listed have been made practically without security for the scarcity of gold in Europe makes their

160

settlement in the customary way impossible.

It would seem that our experience in 1920, when a vast credit inflation was carried to a most perilous degree because of the delay abroad in settling an immense trade balance, would be a sufficient warning against jeopardizing a great part of the Nation's wealth in advances to an insolvent debtor.

In 1920 payment in gold, though dangerously delayed, could be and was made in time. But if inflation here were again carried to a similar excess in expectation of settlement from abroad, the consequences would not result so happily if the foreign debtor failed or were unable to ship gold.

There is a strong tendency here to exaggerate the total amount of our foreign trade in proportion to our domestic trade and its relative importance. It ought not to be forgotten that our entire foreign trade is normally less than 10 per cent of our domestic trade. The vast free-trade markets, producing and consuming, within our continental limits constitute the greatest business empire the world ever saw.

It can hardly be controverted that to preserve the health, energy, and activity of this great domestic market and to protect it from stagnation by the proper management of its currency is of the first importance to the American people. To divert or tamper with the flow of credit needed in this market in order to create and strengthen producing markets abroad is a policy not in the interests of the American people.

It would seem to be a sound principle that loans abroad should be in proportion to the value of our normal foreign trade, and limited by that measure. This is all that the outside world has a right to ask and is all that was ever undertaken by any other nation.

If the world were filled with communities possessing great monetary wealth, the organization of giant industrial enterprises in the United States for the purpose of exporting their products on a vast scale might be a logical development. But the world to-day is not filled with such communities, and it is precisely those communities which constitute the largest consuming markets for American export products that are without the means to pay for them. The extent to which foreign nations since the war have been consuming American-created products without the means to pay for them is measured by that enormous sum of $8,000,000,000 extended in foreign loans by private bankers to which I have referred.

There is a tendency, I may say here, to seek to discredit critics of the international banking policy which has prevailed here since the war, and to denounce their views as radical or unsafe. This criticism is wide of the mark when directed against efforts to guard and preserve the national wealth of the United States and to render the capital of its citizens secure under the protection of the laws of their own country. They are not to be confounded with any form of radicalism. In my own case I fear no comparison of motives with the motives of those who have dominated our foreign financial policy since the war and who have brought upon us successively the conditions of 1920 and 1930.

If it is admitted that what we have been doing is not good banking policy and is not based on business principles, it may be urged that the policy is justified on sentimental grounds. Here a subject of discussion is opened up which is outside the bounds of a discussion of banking and sound banking principles. We enter the realm of politics and international relations, of allied debts and reparations, and must discuss the question of whether, how far, and to what nations the financial assistance of our Government ought to be given.

This is in fact the field to which our inquiries ought to be turned not as bankers but as patriotic citizens. The unrestrained selling here of billions of dollars' worth of European securities by private bankers ought to come to a stop while the ideas of the Government and of the people are clarified on great fundamental questions which are essentially political in their nature. International rights and obligations ought to be fearlessly considered and definitely settled. Until this is done there are none who have the right to divert the credit of the Federal reserve system from domestic to foreign uses unchecked and on a scale which has twice imperiled the safety of the country, and which may imperil it in the future.

The Federal Reserve Board is not intended to be an autonomous body serving foreign banks, if it so chooses, precisely as it serves member banks in the United States. Nor should it expand credit without limit in order to facilitate the sale in this country of billions of dollars' worth of foreign securities. To relieve it of responsibility in this connection I recently introduced a resolution for the creation of a capital issues board to pass upon the issues of such securities.

The shifting foundations upon which our financial relations with the States of Europe now stand should be replaced by a stable base erected by political authority.

Efforts at treaty settlements between the states of Europe and the international bankers of New York like the Young plan, setting up a Bank for International Settlements at Basel intended to facilitate the transfer of credits and the shipment of gold from New York to Europe and to make possible the sale in the United States of German war reparation bonds to the amount of over $3,000,000,000, of which our State Department professes to remain entirely ignorant, ought to become a thing of the past.

This titanic flow and ebb of credit since the war has not been a matter of ordinary trade and commerce governed by the principles of political economy and of banking. It has been primarily political in its nature and has evidenced the desperate efforts of governments in Europe to regain the economic power they possessed before the war.

It has been the repercussion of these efforts upon our unregulated Federal reserve system that has disturbed our domestic conditions. The stream of credit was not properly regulated at the source; the great sluice gates of the dam were not properly guarded.

In conclusion, we have in the Federal reserve system an engine of stupendous power, whose destructive potentialities, perhaps, are as great as its constructive power. It is a governmental agency, and its action should be guided by definite governmental policy.

X

WAR DEBTS AND
REPARATIONS
THE HOOVER MORATORIUM

Wednesday, December 9, 1931

Mr. McFADDEN. Mr. Speaker, under leave to extend my remarks in the RECORD, I present an address delievered by me before the Bethesda (Md.) Chamber of Commerce, Monday night, December 7, 1931, as follows:

From one extremity of this country to the other commerce and industry are stagnant, agriculture is prostrate, and business of all kinds, big and little, is disorganized; capital has suffered heavy losses, the wages of labor have been lowered, there is much unemployment, and suffering and want are widespread. These conditions have prevailed for more than two years.

Where should we look for the causes of this condition? The expert diagnosticians have combed the domestic field and although some for interested purposes have striven hard to prove the causes to be domestic they have failed to find anything which furnishes an adequate explanation.

We live in a rich and fertile land, possessing almost every natural resource; our population is intelligent and energetic; our laws allow the broadest possible initiative to energy and enterprise; we have suffered no epidemic of disease or prostrating disaster of nature; and we are not harassed by wars or the fear of war. For the maintenance of our national welfare we are peculiarly free from the need of dependence on the foreigner; we could live, and live well, solely on the proceeds of our own resources. What, then, has suddenly brought this industrial paralysis throughout the land?

A belated admission was made only a few weeks ago by one of our leading bankers who appeared before a congressional committee that we have loaned too much money abroad, and that this is a major cause of the industrial stagnation. So it is causes coming from without and not those arising from within that we must examine if we would understand what has happened and know how to guard against it in the future.

Most of the money which we have loaned abroad has been loaned in Europe. The practice began with the making of the vast war loans. It would have seemed that our lending should have ended there, as indeed our public lending did, for a time; that private lending would have been upon a strict business basis, limited by the capacity of the borrower to pay. As we know now, loans upon this basis would have been relatively small.

We had a depression in this country in 1921, which was due to the fact that payment of a very large trade balance due from Europe in gold was unduly delayed. It was eventually paid, raising our gold stock to $4,000,000,000 and restoring our domestic economy to a sound and healthy condition.

This was our situation in 1924, and there is no reason why the facilities of the Federal reserve system and of the banks of the country should not have been conserved thereafter for a vigorous internal development, which should have been the chief preoccupation of Government and become a national policy.

But after 1924 this sound policy was deliberately rejected by our State and Treasury Departments and by our great private bankers. They all cooperated in the creation in Europe of German war reparation bonds, which they made negotiable, to the amount of $4,000,000,000, under what they called the Dawes plan, and the Federal Reserve Bank of New York devoted most of its energies to facilitating the desires of European borrowers, public and private, to monopolizing the resources of our Federal reserve system.

I have explained heretofore that there was a hitch in the plans to dispose of the Dawes plan bonds in the United States and that none of them were sold here, and that the international bankers thereupon began a most energetic campaign of vending European municipal and industrial bonds of all kinds.

This put billions in ready cash into Europe and gave it an enormous and artificial purchasing power here, which created the apparently prosperous period here between 1925 and 1929. When they had spent all that they had borrowed and could get no more, the overstimulated producing market in America was without a customer, a glut of unsold goods in our domestic market followed, and our industrial life was thrown into the disorder which is with us yet.

Now, the simple explanation of all this is that we were making loans which it was not in the power of the borrower to pay back, and we are having the same experience that an imprudent private capitalist would have under the same circumstances.

In the light of these facts, a careful scrutiny of the Young plan would seem to be advisable. In so far as it provides what they call "conditional" annuities, which are merely annual payments by Germany to the Allied States, it need not concern us. But it also provides what they call "unconditional" annuities, payments of $160,000,000 in cash which Germany must make under all circumstances. If that were all it, also, need not concern us. But that is not all. A bond issue is to be floated of $3,250,000,000 in negotiable gold bearer bonds for the benefit of the Allied States,and these unconditional annuities are to pay the coupons. Inasmuch as it was European bond issues totaling about $4,000,000,000, dumped in this country between 1925 and 1929 that has caused the present mischief, are we to face the same experience in the future when this $3,250,-000,000 in Young plan bonds is dumped here? Moreover, these are not commercial bonds; they are war-reparation bonds;

they are treaty of Versailles bonds; and they have their origin in a swindle.

Immediately after the armistice the supreme war council drew down a curtain between the realities in Europe and all on this side of the Atlantic, and before that curtain they proceeded to enact a drama for the benefit of the trans-Atlantic audience, an elaborate pageant called "War Reparations" which purported to be authentic history and which was so accepted here.

Since then continuously they have presented other acts of the play, and these acts also have been witnessed from here and accepted as true and authentic.

The drama opened immediately after the armistice with a chorus which hailed the armistice agreement as marking the conquest and unconditional surrender of the enemy. We say a victorious peace conference deliberating upon his fate. We heard the cry go up for just and condign retribution for his crimes. We heard the shrill recital of his treachery and his barbarous cruelty, and of his congenital incapacity for the observance of good faith; and we were told of the necessity of shackling him for generations so that his innocent and peace-loving neighbors might sleep in security at night. We saw the peace conference deliberating upon the confiscations and tribute to be imposed, and adopting the principle that the extreme maximum that could be exacted was less than the requirements of justice demanded.

And under the histrionic stimulus all this seemed just and right to us. Our President went to Paris, and we saw him moving across the center of the stage; we saw him with a noble gesture renounce all reparations on our account, and when he came home with the treaty which he had signed and recommended it to us, most of us accepted it as a reality.

So far as Germany was concerned, after watching the Paris drama for six months, we saw a ruthless enemy who had been fairly conquered in battle effectively and properly shackled. This met with our approval, and we practically dismissed Germany from our minds. Our fascinated eyes were fixed on the League of Nations, the most gorgeous spectacle of the peace conference drama. It seemed to illumine the international stage like a rainbow after storm.

Some among us, however, feared that by entering the league, as it was constructed, we would be granting away too much of our sovereign power. We had given full faith and .credit to the war settlement with the enemy, we harbored not the slightest distrust as to its honest character, but we were apprehensive that under this world charter of law we would be yielding too much. So the Senate did not ratify the treaty of Versailles, and in declining to ratify the treaty it incidentally declined to ratify the war settlement with Germany. This was a profound disappointment to the supreme war council.

But as the years passed, the supreme war council, not discouraged, continued to stage the elaborate drama of German reparations for the benefit of the trans-Atlantic audience. The second act was the London ultimatum of 1921 which created negotiable German reparation bonds in the sum of $33,000,-000,000, belonging to the Allied States, with a view to disposing of them chiefly in the United States. Most of the trans-Atlantic audience continued to look on interested and indeed, fascinated. The third act was the Ruhr invasion and the Dawes plan with its $4,000,000,000 in negotiable reparation bonds; and the fourth act was the Young plan with it $3,250,-000,000 in similar bonds.

For one reason and another the sale of the negotiable reparation bonds in America could not be gotten under way, and so, after the second act, the supreme war council began sending its ushers, the international bankers, through the trans-Atlantic audience, passing the hat, and leaving no section of the house uncombed. In this way, several billions of dollars were collected for which the ushers exchanged with the audience allied and German municipal and industrial bonds. This cash was needed to defray the expenses of the dramatic production.

As we meet here now, the ushers are offering to the audience the Young plan reparation bonds (those for which the unconditional annuities are to furnish funds for payment of the coupons). There are about $91,000,000 now being distributed through the aisles, and as soon as the audience is in a more liberal mood than it is just at present, there are more than three thousand million dollars worth of them resting on the shelves of the Bank of France ready for distribution. France having furnished the greater part of the histrionic talent which has kept the trans-Atlantic audience enthralled, the collections of the ushers to be derived from future sales of the Young plan bonds are, therefore, to go almost exclusively to France.

As I have explained before, if the Allied States can sell most of them here, we will have paid the German war indemnity to them in cash in exchange for the right to collect it in annual installments from Germany for the next half century.

When we have bought the bonds the play will be brought to an end, and the trans-Atlantic audience will be allowed to awaken from the spell; the curtain between them and reality which was lowered on November 11, 1918, will be raised again, and they will be permitted to gaze upon the stark realities which have been concealed from them for 13 years.

It is my purpose now to point to the realities which all along have lain behind the curtain. The armistice of November 11, 1918, did not mark the conquest and unconditional surrender of Germany. Germany was still capable of military resistance, and on November 11 had no thought of selling herself into slavery. On that date she had closed with President Wilson a preliminary treaty, definite and clearly understandable in its terms, and one in which the Allied States had only too willingly joined in order that their very existence might be preserved.

Under that treaty Germany, besides the cession of certain territories, would have paid war reparations amounting in all to about $8,000,000,000. If the treaty had been honestly carried out in letter and spirit the reparations would have all been paid by this time and the war would be over in Europe. The drama for the benefit of the trans-Atlantic audience would not have been invented and there would be no reparation question to-day into the forefront of which America has been thrust.

169

But this honest settlement would not satisfy the swindlers of the supreme war council. They wanted somebody to pay them the costs of Europe's war; they wanted somebody to buy from them the right to collect an enormous war indemnity from Germany. And the first thing to do was to transform the peace terms into a conquest so that Germany could be exploited.

Under the military armistice terms Germany was giving up her means of defense, and in a few weeks was disarmed. It was possible now to overcome her by military pressure and to substitute the terms of conquest for those of the preliminary treaty. Some form of ruthless force was needed to break an unconquered nation, even though disarmed, and for this purpose there is no force so effective as the continued pressure of starvation.

So, simultanously with the opening of the drama staged at Paris for the entertainment of the trans-Atlantic audience, the tragic and sordid reality of history took its course behind the curtain that hid it from the spectators. The systematic starvation of the German Nation began.

It is well to be specific about events of such magnitude. The necessary dispositions to effect the postarmistice conquest were taken at a secret three-day meeting of the supreme war council which opened in London on December 1, 1918.

These dispositions placed Germany in the hands of Marshal Foch and the armistice commission on the Rhine; and the armistice commission, with the assistance of the blockade commission, was given its orders to effect a conquest of Germany.

The day after the meeting in London adjourned notice was given of general British elections to be held on December 14, and the coalition government (notwithstanding its agreement with Germany on November 4) promised the people that if reelected they would go to the peace conference demanding the last farthing that could be extracted from the Germans.

On the next day orders in council sent the English Navy into the Baltic with instructions to blockade the German Baltic coast, and this naval blockade was maintained throughout the period that the peace conference sat. It completed the military encirclement which Marshall Foch had instituted by land, and it excluded the importation of any food whatever into Germany until after the treaty of Versailles was signed six months later.

These measures were all taken and put into operation while President Wilson was on the Atlantic Ocean, and they were concealed from him after his arrival in Europe.

The President went to Europe to put into effect the peace terms already agreed upon. He was no party to this new development. Again, in matters of such historic magnitude, it is well to be specific.

Some of us here may recall what the President said on November 11, 1918, when he addressed both Houses. Informing the Congress of the signing of an armistice and the ending of the war, he said that the war had been ended in a spirit of friendship to the German people under their new democratic government, and that a policy of good will and aid to them would be followed; that the first manifestation of this friendly attitude was a comprehensive plan for food relief, in which the allied governments had signified their purpose to join, to be carried out in the same systematic manner in which the relief of Belgium had been organized. "Hunger does not breed reforms," said the President, "it breeds madness and all the ugly distempers that make an ordered life impossible. They are now face to face with their initial test; we must hold the light steady until they find themselves." The same spirit permeated the entire address.

And on November 12 a note from the State Department was transmitted to Mr. Hans Sulzer, Minister of Switzerland, in charge of German interests in the United States, requesting him to transmit a communication to the German Government. The communication to the German Government was couched in the same terms as those which the President had used in addressing the Congress the day before, and assured the German Government that he was willing to consider favorably the supplying of foodstuffs to Germany and to take up the matter immediately with the allied governments.

So, as he stood here, there was no uncertainty or indecision in his purpose. But from the moment of landing in Europe on December 14 he found himself in an atmosphere which did not accord with his views. The first four weeks after the armistice had brought about a great change there. The spirit of vengeance blazed on every hand; the slightest suggestion of moderation toward the enemy was viewed as the act of a pro-German. The kahki election had just been held in England and the armistice agreement had been suppressed and forgotten in France. The supreme war council, now in full course upon its career of international perfidy, had done its work well among the peoples.

For a few weeks it let the President have his turn, knowing it was now safe to do so. He spoke in public addresses much in the way he had spoken to the Congress; he spoke of the great wave of moral force now running through the world, of the need of a people's peace, and of the need of the sense of brotherhood.

The official peace conference convened late in January, and in the meantime the supreme war council's conquest of Germany by the slow pressure of a food blockade, carefully concealed from the President and the trans-Atlantic audience, was well under way.

The Reparation Commission of the peace conference was organized on February 3, 1919. Here, in the most profound secrecy, these clashing purposes met for a showdown.

Mr. John Foster Dulles, legal adviser to the American delegation, arose and announced that it was the American position that the agreement signed by the Allies with Germany on November 4, 1918, constituted a limitation upon the right to impose reparations or penalties, and in successive meetings he maintained that the limitation was clear and unmistakable.

On behalf of all the Allies, and in arguments in successive meetings, Lord Sumner, legal adviser for England, took the opposite view. Upon this momentous point the Reparation Commission was in deadlock when President Wilson sailed for the United States on February 14, to be absent from the peace conference until March 15.

172

It was the President's parting instruction that the American delegation should maintain its position. Again, let me be specific in order that there may be no doubt of our historic facts. On February 16, as Mr. Baruch himself has told us, the American delegation on the Reparation Commission sent a wireless message to the *George Washington* telling of the deadlock and asking for instructions. The President replied with unequivocal directions to them to maintain their position, and if necessary to make it public.

Besides the legal adviser, John Foster Dulles, the American members of the reparation commission were Bernard Baruch, Norman Davis, and Vance McCormick. Why did they ignore their instructions from the President? Why did they fail to make their position public, as he directed?

It is obvious that the President wished this announcement to come from them and not from himself, and that if the announcement had been made, he would have proclaimed it as the position of the United States. It may be, also, that in sailing for the United States, he wished to be in his own country, in contact with the Congress and public opinion here, when this vital issue arose.

But the American delegation on the reparation commission did not make their position public, nor did they adhere to it as time passed, as is evidenced by what the commission did. The signal failed to come from Paris, and something sealed the lips of the President while in the United States. What it was must, perhaps, be left to the psychologists.

Meanwhile, in Paris, the reparation commission began its work of estimating Germany's capacity to pay upon the principle that there was no limitation upon their right to impose penalties. Marshall Foch and the blockade commission continued to withhold food from Germany and to wrest from the German Government the successive concessions which were finally to be written into the treaty of Versailles.

The treaty had already taken form when the President arrived again in Paris, and the rushing tide of events was beyond his power to turn or stay. It appears that he clung des-

173

perately to the letter of his peace agreement with Germany—
to the assertion that in accordance with it there must be only
reparations and not punitive damages; and that to meet his
wishes this was agreed to as a matter of form while the term
"reparations" was made to cover everything that could be
included in a conquest.

By the end of March the land and sea blockade of Germany was doing its work. The German Government asked upon
what terms the blockade would be lifted and food supplied,
and a conference was arranged at Brussels to fix these terms.
Once more, as this is history, let us be specific.

The conference was convened at Brussels on March 23,
1919, and there Germany delivered up all the gold in the
Reichsbank and all the negotiable securities which her people
possessed, and accepted the obligation to pay reparations in an
indefinite sum and for an indefinite future to be fixed by her
conquerors.

In return she received a contract for the delivery in her
ports of a fixed quantity of grain and foodstuffs per month for a
definite number of months. Thomas Lamont and Norman Davis
were the American members of this commission.

The Germans carried out the terms of this agreement, but
the peace conference did not. There was fear that if food now
reached Germany she might reject some of the terms agreed
upon and those yet to be imposed. No food ships, therefore,
were allowed to dock at German ports until after the treaty
of Versailles was signed on June 28, 1919.

This, in brief, is the history of the making of the treaty of
Versailles. That it is illegitimate under the law of nations in
that it violates the preliminaries of peace is evident. It affords
the only claim to legality that the London ultimatum, the
Dawes plan, and the Young plan, have and its illegitimacy
therefore taints these settlements also. It had as its motive the
sale to the American people of th right to collect an illegally
imposed war tribute.

Mr. Barney Baruch, in 1920, published his views upon the
peace settlement, and explained that the treaty was made

under the influence of blood-raw passions. He thought that under the circumstances it was as good a settlement as could have been obtained, and his American associates upon the Reparation Commission appear to have agreed with him.

It may be that the settlement was as good a one as could have been obtained in view of the fact that the American members of the Reparation Commission failed to make their position public. Speaking for the President they had declared that there was a limitation upon the right to impose reparations, and they had been directed by him to maintain this position and to make it public. What was it that palsied the tongues of these gentlemen, and why did they so readily fall away from the President at the most critical moment of his public career?

Our views of the war settlement need revision. I need but point to the London ultimatum, the Dawes plan, and the Young plan with their billions in negotiable German reparation bonds, not one of which was ever disposed of anywhere until, after the lapse of 10 years and a campaign of ceaseless intrigue on both sides of the Atlantic, a complacent administration at Washington has permitted them to reach their destination in Wall Street.

There are three profound betrayals which are the foundation of this war settlement—the betrayal of the enemy by the supreme war council after a preliminary treaty, the betrayal of President Wilson by his colleagues in the peace conference, and the betrayal of the American people by the allied governments, who sought to shift to American shoulders the cost of the war in Europe, notwithstanding the fact that America's military power had saved them from conquest by the enemy.

The classic annals of bad faith which darken the annals of human history pale into insignificance before the sinister spectacle of this wholesale repudiation of moral principle. Nations and monarchs have been betrayed before, as when Scipio betrayed Carthage and when Brutus betrayed Caesar or when at Senlac the Saxon thanes came not to King Harold's muster; great figures of history have been undone by men whom they had the right to trust and benefactors have been destroyed by

175

those whom they have saved; but the moral abasement of those who at one and the same time treacherously overcame the enemy, treacherously destroyed their own chosen leader, and treacherously plotted against the nation that had saved them from conquest is comparable only to that which 2,000 years ago betrayed the Leader with a kiss.

In this country the sordid history of these intrigues is identified with no political party. Under a Democratic administration an international financial power usurped the functions of the American delegation in the peace conference. Under the Republican administration which followed it, this same financial power entrenched itself in our State and Treasury Departments, and it has remained there ever since. Political leaders who serve this financial power are put forward as candidates for President. It is the part of patriotism for all of us to rid our parties of the dominance of this group and to retire them from leadership in American politics and in private American finance. We need leaders who are not in the service of foreign governments and of a foreign financial power; we need leaders who can comprehend the extent and scope of these foreign influences and who will deal with them from the standpoint of the interests of all the people.

The business before the Congress in the next few days will be the consideration of the Franco-American accord of last August. Its terms are not those of the moratorium proposed by President Hoover on June 20 last. They are as different from it as black is from white. The moratorium of June 20 proposed a postponement of payments on all war debts and reparations. The Franco-American accord was made expressly to save the Young plan by excluding the unconditional annuities from the operation of the moratorium.

In view of the origin, history, and nature of the commercialized reparation bonds, is it not an insult to the representatives of the American people to ask them to put their stamp of moral approval upon them? Are we by passing this measure to reverse our policy of 13 years and make the United States at last a party to Mr. Baruch's blood-raw peace?

176

Putting aside now the matter of German reparations and the moral and legal insufficiency of the European settlements based upon them, why should we grant a moratorium upon all allied debts? The proposal is too sweeping. If Great Britain desires such a moratorium, under the circumstances, we are justified in granting it. It would be a constructive measure. But gratuitously to offer a moratorium at this time upon the French debt is a measure of inexcusable folly, because there is no doubt whatever of the French capacity to pay.

If France refuses to enter a moratorium which includes the unconditional annuities, then let her take what course she chooses; but let her fight her own battles over them without leaning on the United States Government for support and assistance. The days are over for attempts at the integral execution of the blood-raw peace, and, without American support, this will quickly become evident in Europe. Let France awaken from her 13-year-old opium dream of selling to America for cash the right to collect the German reparations; and to signalize this awakening let her feed the three billions of negotiable Young-plan bonds into the same furnace in which a year ago the London ultimatum bonds were incinerated.

The monotonous reiteration through the years that the allied governments must first receive from Germany any moneys which they pay on account of their debts to the United States has no merit whatever. It is a part of the chorus of the reparations drama. The answer to it is the fixed and avowed position of the United States that there is no connection between German reparations and allied debts to the United States.

It is true, as a matter of fact, that for 13 years the allied governments have collected in reparations from Germany much more than they have paid annually to the United States. It is no less true that for the past seven years Germany has made these annual reparation payments out of money borrowed in the United States. Do the allied governments mean to tell us if America ceases to make loans to Germany and thereupon Germany ceases to pay reparations to the Allies that the allied governments will cease making annual payments upon their debts to the United States? Repudiation is the only name which could be given to such a policy.

When the European statesmen have divested themselves of the sickly dream of delivering a German slave state to America for a price of billions in cash, the motive and purpose involved in the conception of German reparations will logically follow. It is a sine qua non to the first steps toward a reconstruction of Europe.

As to the allied debts to the United States, it has not been demonstrated that they can not pay these debts out of their own resources, for thus far they have not had to do so. The United States will remain a fair and just creditor. It is conceivable that in future years these governments, or some of them, may not be able to bear the weight of the debts, for the fortunes and resources of nations rise and fall. In that case the burden can be lightened or the debts canceled, but in our policy there should be no connection between them and the German reparations.

This Franco-American agreement, which Mr. Mellon and Mr. Edge negotiated at Paris last summer, ought not to be ratified. Its rejection will serve the salutary end of making it plain to the governments of Europe that in orienting their policies for 13 years upon the hope that America will pay for the war by buying the right to collect the German reparations they have been following a will-o'-the-wisp; it will suggest to them the advisability of freeing themselves from the reparations hallucination, and of readjusting their mutual financial relationships upon a basis of reality. And once for all it will free American public policy and American private finance from association with the guilty intrigue of 1919 and from the moral degradation of a nearer association with the blood-raw peace.

XI

WAR DEBTS AND REPARATIONS
THE HOOVER MORATORIUM

Friday, December 11, 1931

EXTRACTS FROM DEBATES IN THE FRENCH CHAMBER OF
DEPUTIES IN REGARD TO THIS SUBJECT

Mr McFadden. Mr. Speaker, under leave to extend my remarks in the Record, I herewith insert the following.

Because of the colloquy that took place in the debate to-day between Representative Summers of Texas and his interpreters, I am placing in the Record an extract from the debate in the French House of Deputies pertaining to the matter.

One of the French Senators, Dominique Delahaye, did not mince matters when he spoke. Among other things, he said:

Gentlemen, every time you have been on the point of a capitulation I have ascended this tribune in order to say to you, "You are making a mistake."

I have never been able to convince you, and thus, from mistake to mistake, from capitulation to capitulation, you have come to the point of being led by the nose by a gentleman named Hoover, whom you confound with the United States, as if the United States and Mr. Hoover were not absolutely different.

COLLECTIVE SPEECHES OF HON. LOUIS T. McFADDEN

That is the confustion in which this debate has taken place. Now, we know already what we have experienced with a gentleman with a stepmother's smile who was named Wilson. You are going to have—I hope so—the same disenchantment, if Congress wishes to give to Hoover the lesson it gave to Wilson; but there is such an advantage for the bankers of the United States that I am afraid they will buy the Congress, as one says the practice is. If this is inexact, let the Congress correct it.

The French Chamber of Deputies met on June 26, 1931, and after a few preliminary matters had been disposed of, took up the discussion of the Hoover proposal in accordance with the order of the day. Premier Laval made a communication on behalf of the Government and was followed in turn by 11 deputies who had reserved the right to address the chamber on the subject, and also by M. Pierre Etienne Flandin, the Minister of Finance. At this point I desire to place before you and to have inserted in the CONGRESSIONAL RECORD a full account of the proceedings, as they are recorded in the Official Journal of the French Republic and as they have been translated in my office for your convenience.

COMMUNICATION FROM THE GOVERNMNET

The PRESIDENT. The President of the Council has the floor for a communication from the Government.

M. PIERRE LAVAL, President of the Council, Minister of the Interior. Gentlemen, before the debate on the interpellations begins, I have considered it to be my duty to place before you three documents. I shall read them without making any comments, reserving the right to answer the interpellators later.

Here is, first of all, the message from President Hoover:

The American Government proposes the postponement during one year of all payments on intergovernmental debts, reparations and relief debts, both principal and interest, of course, not including obligations of governments held by private parties.

Subject to confirmation by Congress, the American Gov-

180

ernment will postpone all payments upon the debts of foreign governments to the American Government payable during the fiscal year beginning July 1 next, conditional on a like postponement for one year of all payments on intergovernmental debts owing the important creditor powers.

This course of action has been approved by the following Senators: Henry F. Ashurst, Hiram Bingham, William E. Borah, James F. Byrnes, Arthur Capper, Simeon D. Fess, Duncan U. Fletcher, Carter Glass, William J. Harris, Pat Harrison, Cordell Hull, William H. King, Dwight W. Morrow, George H. Moses, David A. Reed, Claude A. Swanson, Arthur Vandenberg, Robert F. Wagner, David I. Walsh, Thomas J. Walsh, James E. Watson, and by the following Representatives: Isaac Bacharach, Joseph W. Byrns, Carl R. Chindblom, Frank Crowther, James W. Collier, Charles R. Crisp, Thomas H. Cullen, George P. Darrow, Harry A. Estep, Willis C. Hawley, Carl E. Mapes, J. C. McLaughlin, Earl C. Michener, C. William Ramseyer, Bertrand H. Snell, John Q. Tilson, Allen T. Treadway, and Will R. Wood. It has been approved by Ambassador Charles G. Dawes and by Mr. Owen D. Young.

The purpose of this action is to give the forthcoming year to the economic recovery of the world and to help free the recuperative forces already in motion in the United States from retarding influences from abroad.

The world-wide depression has affected the countries of Europe more severely than our own. Some of these countries are feeling to a serious extent the drain of this depression on national economy. The fabric of intergovernmental debts, supportable in normal times, weighs heavily in the midst of this depression.

From a variety of causes arising out of the depression, such as the fall in the price of foreign commodities and the lack of confidence in economic and political stability abroad, there is an abnormal movement of gold into the United States which is lowering the credit stability of many foreign countries. These and the other difficulties abroad diminish buying power of our exports and, in a measure, are the cause of our continued unemployment and continued lower prices to our farmers.

Wise and timely action should contribute to relieve the pressure of these adverse forces in foreign countries and should assist in the reestablishment of confidence, thus forwarding political peace and economic stability in the world.

Authority of the President to deal with this problem is limited, as this action must be supported by the Congress. The President has been assured the cordial support of leading members of both parties in the Senate and the House. The essence of this proposition is to give time to permit debtor governments to recover their national prosperity. I am suggesting to the American people that they be wise creditors in their own interest and be good neighbors.

I wish to take this occasion also to frankly state my views upon our relations to German reparations and the debts owed to us by the allied Governments of Europe. Our Government has not been a party to or exterted any voice in determination of reparation obligations.

We purposely did not participate in either general reparations or the division of colonies or property. The repayment of debts to us from the Allies for the advance for war and reconstruction were settled upon a basis not contingent upon German reparations or related thereto. Therefore reparations is necessarily wholly a European problem with which we have no relation. [Exclamations and various movements.]

I do not approve in any remote sense of the cancellation of the debts to us. World confidence would not be enhanced by such action. None of our debtor nations has even suggested it. But as the basis of the settlement of these debts was the capacity under normal conditions of the debtor to pay, we should be consistent with our own policies and principles if we take into account the abnormal situation now existing in the world.

I am sure the American people have no desire to attempt to extract any sum beyond the capacity of any debtor to pay, and it is our view that broad vision requires that our Government should recognize the situation as it exists.

This course of action is entirely consistent with the policy which we have hitherto pursued. We are not involved in the discussion of strictly European problems of which the payment of German reparations is one. It represents our willingness to make a contribution to the early restoration of world prosperity in which our own people have so deep an interest.

I wish further to add that while this action has no bearing on the conference for limitation of land armaments to be held next February, inasmuch as the burden of competitive armaments has contributed to bring about this depression. ["Very good! Very good!" from the extreme left.] We trust that by this evidence of our desire to assist we shall have contributed to the good will which is so necessary in the solution of this major question. [Various movements.]

The President of the Council. This is the reply which the French Government has made to Mr. Hoover's message:

"The French Government has taken cognizance, with a lively interest, of the proposal of the President of the United States, and it declares itself in cordial accord with the elevated sentiments which inspired that proposal. [Various movements.]

"The French Government is, more than any other, desirous of seeing affirmed in the acts for the economic restoration of the world a solidarity with which it has always been inspired, whether in accepting successive reductions of the German debt or in executing the anticipated evacuation of the third zone of the Rhineland in exchange for a complete and definitive settlement of the program of reparations, decided at Geneva September 16, 1928.

"It must emphasize before the opinion of the world the extent of the new sacrifice which is asked of France after all those to which she has already agreed.

In order to reply to the suggestion of President Hoover, the French Government is ready to ask the French Chambers, of which the intervention is indispensable and the decision sovereign [applause], that France abstain, provisionally and for a delay of one year, from conserving any payment on the part of the Reich. [Fresh applause].

183

"But, being given the nature of the engagements of the Young plan, freely accepted and quite recently subscribed to, the solemnity with which was recognized the definite and unalterable character of the unconditional annuities by which necessary permanence of the principle of reparations was expressed [very good! very good!], the risk of shaking confidence in the value of signatures and of contracts [very good! very good!] and thus of going against the end aimed at would be great, if, in the proposed suspension of payments, the unalterable annuity were treated like the conditional annuity. [Applause.]

"The French Government emphasizes in particular that a formal assimilation has been established between the private debts of the Reich (Young loan and Kreuger loan) and the unconditional annuities not yet mobilized. To suspend the payment by Germany of the unconditional annuity while admitting that the Young loan placed with the public should continue to be served would go directly against a fundamental principle and express stipulations. [Very good! Very good!]

"The Government, then, considers that a moral interest of the first order is attached to this: That, even during the delay provided for by President Hoover, the payment of the unconditional annuity should not be altered in any way.

"The French Government, desirous of collaborating generously in every effort made to lessen the consequences of the present crisis, believes that it ought to point out, even in the interest of the success of this effort, that the general suspension of payments alone would not offer a sufficient remedy. The dangers threatening German economy and more generally European economy at the present time have a different origin and are related, notably, to important restrictions of credit or to withdrawals of foreign funds. The solution of the German crisis does not seem, therefore, to rest only in a diminution of the charges in the budget of the Reich but in an extension of credit.

"This is why the French Government declares itself ready, under the reservation of the approbation of Parliament, to put at the disposal of the Bank for International Settlements a sum equivalent to its part, for one year, of the unalterable annuity, under the single reservation of the sums necessary for the execution of the remainder of its contracts of loans in progress at the present time, which is, furthermore, useful for German economy.

"In making this proposal the French Government expects that the other beneficiaries of the Young plan will take the same decision, and it even hopes that other measures may be taken to favor the useful reestablishment of credit and of confidence in the world.

"The funds thus paid to the Bank for International Settlements may be immediately utilized for the amelioration of credit in Germany, as well as in the countries of Central Europe, and notably in those in which the suspension of the Young plan, during one year, might create financial or economic distress. [Very good; very good.] It goes without saying that the amounts thus employed will become payable again at the expiration of the period of one year provided for as the limit of the provisional suspension of the Young plan.

"The French Government is equally of the opinion that all useful precautions should be taken so that these sums, as well as those to come from the lightening of the budget of the Reich resulting from the suspension of one year of the payments of the Young plan, can not be utilized save for economic ends [very good; very good], all danger of the financing of dumping being set aside. [Very good, very good.]

"Finally, it would be opportune to provide, before the expiration of the delay of one year, for an examination of the measures to be taken by Germany for the resumption of her payments.

"The proposals of the French Government and the adjustments which the putting into practice of the American offer will suggest and which will necessarily form the subject of a further exchange of views thus appear perfectly compatible with the dominant idea of the proposal of President Hoover.

"In placing at the disposal of the Bank for International Settlements, upon the conditions stipulated in regard to this

185

matter, her part of the unconditional annuity, France will be deprived during the period of suspension of what was assigned to her by virtue of the expenses she had to undergo for the restoration of her devastated regions.

"Without wishing to insist on the difference between the sums she has received and the sums she should have received, France recalls the fact that the total of her public debt amounts to-day to about four times that of the debt of the Reich and that her attempt at financial rehabilitation, pursued and realized by her own means, barely four years ago, should not be placed in jeopardy. [Applause.]

"The French Government is, then, able to affirm the solidarity of the French Republic and of the Republic of the United States, in the moment in which, faithful to their traditions, the two countries are cooperating in measures of safety in a crisis considered to be grave. They have the right to hope that their international good will will be answered by respect for treaties and by the restoration of confidence among peoples — conditions of the future of peace." [Applause.]

M. HENRY FRANKLIN-BOUILLON. And now, Frenchmen, pay three milliards more of taxes!

The PRESIDENT OF THE COUNCIL. Here, now, is the letter which the ambassador of the United States has addressed to the Minister of Foreign Affairs:

PARIS, *June 26, 1931.*

Mr. MINISTER. I have to-day received from my Government a telegram reading as follows:

"The American Government appreciates the cordiality with which the French Government has replied to the proposal of the President. It hopes that the French Government will profit by the presence of the Secretary of the Treasury, in order to discuss with him and with the ambassador the different problems raised by the original proposal of the President and the French reply. The ambassador and Mr. Mellon have received full information concerning the views of the American Government."

186

Accept the renewed assurance of my high esteem and my best sentiments.

WALTER E. EDGE.

M. GRATIEN CANDACE. There is no further need for debate.

DISCUSSION OF SEVERAL INTERPELLATIONS ON THE AMERICAN PROPOSAL CONCERNING WAR DEBTS

The PRESIDENT. The order of the day calls for the discussion of the interpellations:

1. Of M. Margaine on the situation created by the decision taken by the Government of the United States to propose the suspension during one year of the payment of war debts;

2. Of M. Dubois on the attitude which the Government expects to adopt toward the American proposal relative to the war debts;

3. Of M. Louis Marin on the participation of France in the negotiations which have resulted in the declaration of the President of the United States, on the exact sense of the proposals which it contains, on the negotiations which are the result of it, and on the procedure which the Government will adopt in order that the chamber may pronounce its views with a knowledge of the matter before any engagement is made, conformably to the recent promise of the president of the council;

4. Of M. Nicolle on the proposal of President Hoover in view of our economic situation;

5. Of M. Pierre Cot on the measures which the Government expects to take in order to insert the proposal of Mr. Hoover in a plan for the economic reorganization of Europe;

6. Of M. Camille Planche on the opportunity for France to avail herself of the proposal of President Hoover in order to bring about an effective policy of disarmament;

7. Of M. Leon Blum on the situation created by the offer of President Hoover;

8. Of M. Bergery on the measures to be taken to attach

187

the reply to the American proposal to a common policy in regard to Germany;

9. Of M. Marcel Heraud on the attitude which the Government expects to take in regard to the proposals formulated by President Hoover relative to a suspension of the payment of war debts;

10. Of M. Xavier Vallat on the exact practical significance of the proposal of Mr. Hoover and of the reply which has been given to him by the French Government;

11. Of M. Pezet on the spirit and the positive plan according to which the Government intends to reconcile respect for our rights and the balance of our economy with a policy of economic collaboration between peoples and of moral disarmament, which are equally indispensable to perfect international security, a policy which would be the justification of the sacrifices conceded in the reply to the proposal of President Hoover;

12. Of M. Thebault on the inspiration, the exact sense, and the result of the American proposal of President Hoover.

M. Jean Mistler. We request a suspension of the session.

The President. M. Mistler requests a suspension of the session.

M. Mistler has the floor.

M. Jean Mistler. I should like to justify, in a few words, the request for suspension which we have presented.

The Chamber has just listened with great calm and extreme attention to three very important documents, two of which, at least, are entirely new.

My colleagues will undoubtedly be unanimous in judging, with me, that it is not sufficient for us to have heard such documents read once in order to form an exact opinion concerning their contents and that at least a summary examination of their text is indispensable to us before taking the exceedingly grave decision before which this assembly will find itself placed. [Applause.]

Numerous voices. Suspension!

From various benches. Till Tuesday!

The President. The president of the council has the floor.

M. Pierre Laval, president of the council, minister of the interior. If it is simply a question of suspending the session in order to permit the Deputies to acquire a more complete knowledge of the documents which I have just read, I declare myself in full accord with the Hon. M. Mistler. [Very good! Very good!]

If, on the contrary, it were a question of postponing the debate to another day [No! No!], I declare that the Government, being in the midst of negotiations, could not admit anything but that an immediate solution should be given to this debate.

We wish to know what the principles are which Parliament intends to establish for the conduct and accomplishment of the negotiations which are in progress. [Very good! Very good!]

The President. Until what hour does the Chamber wish to suspend the session?

Numerous Voices. Until 4 o'clock.

The President. There is no opposition? The session is suspended until 4 o'clock.

(The session, suspended at 25 minutes past 3, was resumed at 4 o'clock.)

RESUMPTION OF THE DISCUSSION OF THE INTERPELLATIONS ON THE
TEMPORARY SUSPENSION OF THE SETTLEMENT OF WAR DEBTS

The President. We return to the discussion of the interpellations.

M. Margaine has the floor, in order to develop his interpellation.

M. Margaine. My colleagues will be kind enough to permit me, in the interests of clarity, to which I am particularly attached, to define in the most precise manner possible the position which I wish to take in this debate.

I will not examine the basis of the proposal of Mr. Hoover. Just as Mr. Hoover can do nothing without his Congress, so the French Government, since the Young plan is the result of a law, can do nothing without Parliament. I will, then, wait for the proposed legal bill in order to discuss the basis.

What I should like to examine to-day is the entirely novel situation resulting from the abrupt intervention of Mr. Hoover. There are, to begin with, surrounding that intervention, particular circumstances, certain obscurities, which I hope the Government in time will be so good as to undertake to elucidate.

The Ambassador of the United States called Tuesday evening to state to the president of the council that there had been no discussion preliminary to the intervention of Mr. Hoover. If the heads of States have sometimes a language which is somewhat brutal, diplomats, on the other hand, have a language which is particularly flexible. For, indeed, there are certain facts which one can not do otherwise than to underline and which do not completely harmonize with such a declaration.

Mr. Mellon disembarked in England on the 16th. The following morning he took care to make a declaration, in which he stated that he was making a purely private journey, his only object being to pass some days with his son, a student at the University of Cambridge.

Nevertheless, that same day the officious newspaper—I may well call it that—of the Labor government, the Daily Herald, explained that the American minister had come to Europe because Mr. Hoover was convinced that it was necessary to do something in regard to what concerned the war debts if one wished to avert a collapse disastrous for American financial interests.

The paper added that Mr. Hoover had in mind the idea of a suspension for two years of all payments of reparations and war debts. As this subject had been abundantly treated at Chequers between the English and the German ministers, it seems to me impossible that there had not been, between Chequers and the departure of Mr. Mellon, negotiations, communications, between the American Government and the English Government. The least that one could say is that the facts show that the newspaper, the Daily Herald, was particularly well informed.

On the other side, Mr. Mills, Assistant Secretary of the Treasury of the United States, saw the ambassador from England to the United States on the morning of June 20. It was after this visit that he returned to see Mr. Hoover and that the communication was made. I have difficulty in believing that the ambassador from England was summoned at that moment in order to be advised of a matter of which he knew not the first word, after the communications whose certitude I have just made manifest.

Consequently, for my part, until proof of the contrary—and I will presently return to it—there were, in regard to the facts which have surprised us, conversations covering 20 days or so between the English and American Governments.

Contrary to what evil-intentioned characters have claimed, Mr. Hoover is far from being an impulsive person. He is a man whose character is well known. He studies much; he reflects much. All his past is the proof of it. If he has placed France before an accomplished fact, it is because he was told that it would be necessary for him so to act in order to succeed quickly and well.

But Mr. Hoover has done much more than that, and he has certainly not done it lightly: He has broken with the traditional policy of the United States. Permit me to emphasize the importance of such an attitude on the part of the President of the United States.

The American, the man in the street, does not trouble himself with questions of external policy. For him Europe is a small continent in which little nations, so numerous that one can not remember all their names, engage in rivalry, are jealous of one another, and fight, instead of bringing themselves into agreement as the States of the great Republic of the United States have done.

The man in the street is satisfied, so far as external policy is concerned, to know that his Government is remaining faithful to certain doctrines which I will summarily recall: The Monroe doctrine, the doctrine of Washington, the doctrine of John Hay.

Quite recently the Government of the United States, with

a certain solemnity, on several occasions, declared that it would not concern itself in European affairs. Permit me to recall some of the circumstances in which this affirmation has been made.

When the Europeans asked the Government of the United States to have itself represented at the Genoa conference, the American Government officially replied that it did not wish to take cognizance of the affairs of Europe.

In 1922, when Lord Balfour sent the well-known note in which he proposed the annulment of war debts, the American Government replied that the affairs of Europe did not concern it; that the States of Europe had, to America, certain debts of an exclusively commercial character and that it would discuss them with each of the countries separately.

I can not admit that the Executive power of a country which is attached to such an extent to traditional doctrines could have overturned all its traditions simply because Mr. Mellon, making a pleasure journey, had a conversation, by accident, with Mr. MacDonald. No. There is—let us say it and let us know how to see it—something quite different.

Besides the man in the street of whom I have been speaking, there are American business men who have dealings with Europe and, above all, with Germany, and who, since a very short time ago, have had serious reasons for disquietude.

In the United States itself there have been some characteristic occurrences, with which the press has concerned itself and of which I shall permit myself to cite some examples showing that in that country there is an internal evolution which is not without a certain gravity.

All these events, of which I shall cite some, have been set forth by the Democratic press.

Recently in the Pittsburgh basin at Westland a thousand striking miners fought with mounted police. A policeman was beaten. His comrades fired. Two miners were wounded.

At Ellsworth a veritable battle took place between the miners and the police of the coal companies. The women and children fought with particular fury.

In Kentucky, at Evarts, miners and mine police had a

pitched battle. There were killed on one side and on the other.

In the State of Virginia 1,500 miners came to Charlestown and marched through the streets, demanding bread for their children.

The Democratic press has seized upon these facts. It denounces the activities of the magnates of the industry, and since his name is spread throughout its columns, I may well remark that at their head it inscribes Mr. Mellon.

It was necessary for the United States that this situation should not grow worse, and it would have grown worse if in Germany events had entered upon an acute phase. It is at the bottom the German situation which is the origin of everything.

I shall not return to the explanations given in this very place at the end of 1929, before the Government left for The Hague, when we put it on its guard against the constitution of a German-American industrial bloc, which was beginning to take on a certain solidity.

Germany, thanks to the formation of this bloc, made important appeals to American capital. The statistics show us that from 1926 to 1930 the public emissions of Germany abroad—almost all in America—attained the sum of six milliards and a half of reichsmarks, and this sum does not include the direct investments of Americans in German industry.

I find, in the same statistics, that in 1928 the total of foreign capital invested in that manner in Germany was four milliards two hundred and fifty millions of reichsmarks; in 1929 two milliards seven hundred and fifty millions.

Certain American financiers some months ago began to be alarmed by this constant outflow; their apprehensions are revealed in the fact that in 1930 the capital funds thus placed in Germany barely attained the sum of half a milliard.

On the other hand, Germany has made a great deal of noise about her budgetary difficulties. One saw M. Hilferding give way to M. Moldenhauer, then M. Moldenhauer give way to M. Dietrich, always because of the impossibility of establishing a budget, all this in the space of eight months. In spite of

193

all these changes the budget could not be established, save by making use of article 48 of the constitution of Weimar; there was a legal decree on the 1st of August, 1930, another on the 1st of December, 1930, and a third quite recently. All these facts have powerfully shaken the confidence of the Americans.

Just at the moment in which Mr. Mellon arrived in England the Reichsbank proceeded to enormous sales of gold and of exchanges. It sold in the first fortnight of June one milliard fifty millions of reichsmarks, keeping only one milliard six hundred millions! the legal reserve of the Reichsbank was very close to being reached.

During these same days in Berlin panic reigned. In the banks one sold, not banknotes—they had no more of them—but promises of banknotes to be delivered in a fortnight.

All this caused superficial observers to believe that Germany was struggling in the midst of grave budgetary difficulties. I say "superficial observers," for if the Americans had given themselves the trouble to read over the reports of their compatriot, Mr. Parker Gilbert, notably the last, which is of May, 1930, they would there have seen the affirmation, many times repeated, that the Germans will put order into their budget when they wish. [Very good! Very good!] But they do not wish it yet, because in order to make an end of the payments of the war debts it is necessary that their budget should remain in disorder. [Applause on the left, in the center, and on the right.]

M. Lionel de Tastes. It is useful to recall it.

M. Margaine. One speaks much in order to impress the world of the considerable Germans unemployed.

Consider what happens in the German villages. The children do not work with their parents, as is the case in France. They always go to work for a neighbor; exchanges are made and the young people are engaged by a contract of labor. They are salaried, only the salaries balance each other. When they return home, the work in the fields being finished, they are unemployed. This makes up a certain number. [Various movements.]

194

Consider, on the other hand, building workers. At all times in Germany these workers have never worked in the winter, even on the interior of houses, and their salaries have always been calculated in such a manner that in winter they might live on their reserves. To-day these are among the unemployed.

The Germans make a great matter of their figure of 5,000,000 of unemployed. I am sure that when they come to regard it more closely they will immediately reduce it by a million or a million and a half at least.

But all this Germany does not intend to change. For, if, underneath, she is tranquil, by this means she disquiets the world; and we perceive that she does so.

Let us then take into account the fact that the economic situation of Germany is, at bottom, excellent.

The balance of German foreign trade is characterized, in the course of these last years, by a permanent active surplus. Of a total volume of business of twenty-two milliards three hundred millions of reichsmarks in 1930, the importations represent ten milliards three hundred millions, the exportations twelve milliards, in which are included the reparations in kind, for a sum of seven hundred millions. With reference to 1929 there is certainly a slight lowering of exportations—twenty-six milliards eight hundred millions—but, on looking closely, one sees that this diminution is due to the lowering of prices and that the diminution of quantities is excessively small, contrary to what is taking place in almost all the industrial countries.

The part which has diminished least among the importations is that of manufactured products. This is a result contrary to that which is reported in all the other industrial countries.

In 1931, from the very first months, the rising movement of German exportations began again. In the month of January, 774,000,000 of reichsmarks; in February, 778,000,000 of reichsmarks; in March, 867,000,000 of reichsmarks. The increase affects especially manufactured products: January, 575,000,000 of reichsmarks; February, 591,000,000 of reichsmarks; March,

195

662,000,000 of reichsmarks.

Germany, in spite of the world crisis, has attained the second rank among the exporting countries of the world, passing England, and she is not far from having first place.

Where, then, does she sell all the products which she exports? She sells them, above all, in three countries: England, Holland, and France. The United States comes far behind. The third country, France, buys from the Germans to the extent of 1 milliard 149,000,000 of reichsmarks; the United States to the extent of 685,000,000 only.

Where, then, does Germany buy all she needs in order to work? From us? Not at all. She buys from the United States.

For importations the United States is at the head with 1 milliard 307,000,000 of reichsmarks. England comes next, but far behind, with 639,000,000 reichsmarks.

Thus Germany, with an industry always more prosperous, sells to Europe, buys from the United States. It is natural enough that the United States should concern itself in a particular manner in regard to her situation.

For that country, before committing yourselves, understand well that, at bottom, there is nothing to fear. Her foundation is solid—it is of rock. That which is floating is appearances, and they will disappear when she wants them to. [Applause from the left, from the center, and from the right.]

Her industry is the best equipped. Her trade is the best organized, technically. For her economic storms are only transitory.

But she has sworn, first of all, not to pay reparations; next, to rectify her eastern frontiers. You will not bring her out of that idea. [Applause from the same benches.]

I have said—for I am convinced of it—that there has been, at least in the general outlines, concert between England and Germany unknown to us.

Why, then, has England, our ally, our faithful ally, taken this position?

Whatever our Government may have said concerning it, in the course of a recent interpellation, the Anschluss was not, at bottom, considered as a catastrophe by England. England is playing her accustomed game—to maintain balance between the nations. She does not care to have one nation surpass the others too much. At bottom, the Anschluss was a perspective which she was willing to contemplate.

Only in regard to this performance—I do not wish to call it either a drama or a comedy—something particular took place.

You have all heard talk of the very grave crisis of the Kreditanstalt.

I do not wish to enter to-day into too many details. Some other day, I hope, the Chamber will give me permission to show that the gravity of the crisis of the Kreditanstalt does not rest only in the fact that a financial establishment has suffered passing difficulties, but in the fact that Austria, as she is constituted, can not live. This must be said. [Very good! Very good! from various benches.]

However it may be, there was a crisis in the Kreditanstalt.

I heard the Minister of Foreign Affairs say from this tribune that it was necessary in this matter to take account of the fact that all financial centers depend upon one another and that the crisis of the Kreditanstalt could not in any way leave us indifferent.

I note with satisfaction that our financiers here in Paris are at least a little better informed and that they did not attribute to that event the dangers for France in which our minister seemed to believe.

When our Government asked them not to agree to lend their support in order to save the bank except on condition that Austria should reassure us in regard to her intentions concerning the German-Austrian customs union, they replied that that was the most natural thing in the world and they very firmly and very patriotically took that position.

Unfortunately England did not agree that one should make the abandonment of the project for an Austro-German customs union a condition of the saving of the Kreditanstalt, and, in order to settle the matter she took upon herself alone the burden of putting the bank back on its feet, but she found

197

out by experience that it would cost terribly dear, more dearly than she had expected.

The Bank of England on the 18th of June made to the National Austrian Bank, in order to sustain the Kreditanstalt, an advance of 150,00,000 schillings, or £4,286,000. Unfortunately for her, she was to discover that, on the one hand, it was very difficult for her to maintain for a long time that lending position, and, on the other hand, that even that sum, considerable as it was, would not be sufficient, for the engagements of the Kreditanstalt represented from 800,000 to 1 millard of schillings; that is to say from £24,000,000 to £30,000,000.

This burden which the English attempted to assume alone in order to hinder us from accomplishing our object bore heavily upon them; they were, naturally, not grateful to us for it, and it was not with displeasure that they saw impending an incident in which we would find ourselves placed in a disagreeable position; thus they awaited events tranquilly, taking care to say nothing to us concerning them.

Here, then—and I must excuse myself for having taken so long—is the description of the European setting at the moment when the proposal of Mr. Hoover arose abruptly.

All in all, we are asked to deprive ourselves of important resources which are an appreciable element in our budget, but there is in that an aspect which I do not wish to take up until we are faced with a legal project.

What I derive from the reply of the president of the council is that we are yielding. Very well. Only we yield very often, and it would perhaps be time to think of stopping.

And I will permit myself to say to the president of the council, although it is too late, since he has already replied to the United States, that I should have preferred to see a prejudicial question put to Mr. Hoover: Is the United States, yes or no, disposed to return to involve herself in the affairs of Europe? [Lively applause from the left, from the center, and from the right.]

If yes, let them send an official delegate; we will enter into discussion. If not, let them say so once and for all. Because—I ask permission to state my whole thought [Speak! Speak!]—it is not possible for us to remain exposed every four years, when a presidential election is approaching, to interventions of this kind. [Lively applause from a large number of benches.]

Oh, gentlemen, I know well that there is the immense service which the head of the United States says he has rendered to Europe. He has saved Germany from certain collapse, in which, evidently, a good part of Europe would have been involved.

But from where did that threat of collapse come? From the fact that Germany has been living for some years past on the short-term credits which the financiers of New York have been so good as to grant her, and the danger has come from the fact that these same financiers have withdrawn those credits in enormous amounts.

M. HENRI PATENOTRE-DESNOYERS. There is the truth.

M. MARGAINE. Well, could not Mr. Hoover, the head of the United States, have begun by asking the American financiers to stop the enormous withdrawals they were making? [Applause from the left, from the center, and from the right.]

After all, it is the affair of the United States. They should, perhaps, have been able to begin by acting at home.

And even since, in letting things proceed normally, the United States receives important payments from Europe, Mr. Hoover might perhaps, have been able to use these payments for loans to Germany. [Very good! Very good! from various benches.] Only, in the United States, a gesture of that kind would not have been enjoyed in the same manner. [Applause.]

So much for to-day. Will you permit me to examine what will happen to-morrow?

Herr Bruening, we are told, is coming to Paris. So much the better! The more we have frank conversations with our neighbors the better it will be. [Applause.]

I imagine willingly enough the sense of these conversations. Herr Bruening is going to explain the situation of his country. He will say that the war, the revolution, the occupation of the Ruhr have caused capital to disappear in Germany.

199

M. HENRI PATENOTRE-DESNOYERS. There is still enough for the construction of cruisers.

M. MARGAINE. While there is, he will say, so much available capital in the world, she lacks current funds.

He will explain that she can not find capital otherwise than at short term unless she lives in a good understanding with France, because then the world would feel itself reassured.

What shall we reply to Herr Bruening? We will speak to him of Poland [Very good! Very good!]; we will tell him that the manifestations to which Germany has lent herself in regard to that country in the neighborhood of her frontiers are giving rise to profound trouble there, that this trouble spreads throughout the whole of Europe, and that it is because of this very trouble that the world does not feel itself secure; that Germany can not find long-term credits.

I hear the answer of Germany. She will object that if, in the question of Poland, there were for the Germans only a question of national pride, one could still come to the end of it. But she will represent that, unfortunately, there are material questions which themselves keep constantly alive that sentiment of national pride.

Herr Bruening will tell you that the city of Danzig was formerly the natural outlet of eastern Pomerania and that it is now irremediably separated from it.

He will tell you that not only does Danzig on her side see her situation profoundly altered, but that on another side—and thanks to French capital—Poland is building at Gdynia a new harbor which will end by ruining the city of Danzig.

He will tell you, again, that the fishermen of the coast of eastern Pomerania formerly supplied the Catholic population of Poland and that now they no longer have any customers save the Protestants of Germany who hardly eat any fish, so that they are reduced to black poverty. And thus you will be led to see that there are these comprehensive questions, European questions. You will approach others, you will make the tour of them, and everywhere you will run against the obstruction of European questions. Would it not be better to begin at once by examining a European organization, of which M. Briand first spoke, but which, for reasons I do not wish to analyze, he has not been able to realize?

I have been very much struck by the remarkable results which the ministers of the States of central Europe obtained when, in their distress they met in a series of conferences which lasted only three months, which were terminated at Warsaw, and which achieved the result that each of the governments recognized the necessity of organizing the exportation of its agricultural products and immediately succeeded in it.

Only, in these conversations, they were not embarrassed by a secretariat general, thinking, hindering, composed of functionaries who were paid their weight in gold. They did not invite, in order to ask their opinion, representatives of Japan, of Chile, of China, and of Peru. [Very good! Very good, from the right.] They talked between themselves, between men who are putting their affairs in order.

Let us do the same for the affairs of Europe. Let us understand ourselves directly, in silence. I may dare to say, I will even go so far as to say, renouncing noisy acclamations, let us undertake simple and practical conversations. It is only thus that we shall be able to obtain the peace of Europe.

And if the journey of Herr Bruening can only end in this result, gentlemen, we shall be able to felicitate ourselves upon it. [Lively applause from the left and on numerous benches. The orator, returning to his place, receives felicitations.]

The PRESIDENT. M. Louis Dubois has the floor, in order to develop his interpellation.

M. LOUIS DUBOIS. Gentlemen, I have asked to interpellate the Government on the attitude which it expects to take in regard to the American proposal relative to war debts.

The Government has made a first reply to the American proposal. It is not my intention to study that reply, which in a certain measure, would be of the nature of giving myself satisfaction.

My intention is to place as clearly as possible before the Chamber and before French public opinion—I do not dare to say world public opinion—the question of the Young plan and German reparations as it presents itself at the present time.

What does President Hoover ask of us? What does he propose?

Knowing the difficulties in which Germany is struggling, financial difficulties and not, as M. Margaine has just demonstrated in a remarkable manner, economic difficulties, financial difficulties in which his American nationals were gravely interested, President Hoover, penetrated, I doubt not, by sentiments much more elevated and very generous, inspired by his passion for universal public welfare and for peace, makes certain proposals to Europe.

He declares himself prepared to give up for the benefit of Germany the amount of the payments which she makes, for the account of her European creditors, to the Bank for International Settlements, and which it pays to the United States in order to extinguish the war debts of the former associates of that country. He proposes this for one year only.

It is a gesture, to consider it only as a gesture, which is undeniably generous. He does not make it, however, without asking from Europe, particularly from France, a return.

Germany, he tells us, pays important sums, some of which come to me, America, some of which remain in Europe, all under the head of reparations.

I ask that all the creditors of Germany, for the total amount of their credits and for one year, give up receiving these sums from Germany, who, thus relieved of the burden of her war debt, will be able to return to the financial prosperity which is lacking to her at the present time.

That is the thesis of President Hoover. I do not wish to study it or to discuss it. I ask myself simply what the repercussion of a consent given to the thesis of President Hoover and to his proposals may be for us, as much from the financial point of view as from the political point of view. [Very good! Very good!]

In order to expound the question clearly to bring out the essential principles which are at stake, it is indispensable to go

202

back a little. It will not be long. [Interruptions on the extreme left and on the left. Applause on the right and in the center.]

The Young plan is an accomplishment. One can not understand it unless one knows what preceded. And we should keep present in our memory in order to judge the situation and the concessions which are asked of us.

For the origin of the Young Plan, it is necessary to go far back.

In 1914, the invasion of Belgium, in violation of the treaties of Belgian neutrality; the war during four years, accompanied by formidable and, to a large extent, systematic destruction on the part of Germany [applause]; the treaty of peace of Versailles; the message from President Wilson of the 8th of January, 1918, specifying the evacuation of the invaded regions of Belgium and France and their restoration, a message followed in reply to an interallied memorandum, by the declaration of November 5, 1918, from Mr. Lansing, American Secretary of State, speaking in the name of President Wilson, confirming again the fact that Germany, in any case, should repair the material damage done in the invaded countries; clauses of the armistice of November 11, 1918, clause 9: "Reparation of damage"; finally, the treaty of peace, Parts VIII and IX, establishing the obligation of Germany to pay for the damages which the Allied nations, especially Belgium and France, had been the victims of, through her action.

The treaty of Versailles, Parts VIII and IX: "Reparations and financial clauses," articles 232 and the following define the damages which should be repaired.

Here I will permit myself to call to your attention, in passing, the fact that the word "reparations" in the treaty has regard, without distinction, to the payment of damages to goods and damages to persons, these last taking the form, most generally, of pensions to assist the wounded and mutilated, the former soldiers, or their dependents.

The amount of these damages for which Germany was responsible was fixed, according to the terms of the treaty, by a commission called the Reparations Commission April 27, 1921, not at the London conference, as it is unceasingly repeated, but by the Reparations Commission itself at Paris, after a very detailed study, at 132 milliards of gold marks—802 milliards of present francs—which by the terms of the treaty should have been paid in 30 years.

You will say to me: "A fantastic figure," and so forth. That is not the question.

That is the amount by virtue of the treaty of the German reparations debt, and that is the initial figure of that debt.

Then the manner in which Germany was to discharge it was established. This was the schedule of payment called that "of London," which was, in fact, more or less elaborated at London, but which was equally established by the Reparation Commission and notice of it was given to Germany by the said commission at Paris May 5, 1921.

The schedule of payments provided for very substantial payments by Germany, the delivery by her of bonds, of obligations capable of being negotiated. The annuity, which was to vary according to the extent of the exportations of Germany, would have been actually in the neighborhood of 5 milliards of gold marks.

You know what became of this schedule of payments and of the obligations of Germany. Repeated defaults on the part of Germany, occupation of the Ruhr, international difficulties, Dawes plan, and London conference.

The Dawes plan lightened considerably the obligations of Germany. Without determining their number the annuities were established as very moderate in the beginning and becoming fixed, from 1928-29, at the figure of two thousand five hundred millions of gold marks, which was susceptible to increase later, according to a certain indication of prosperity.

You know that Germany discharged her obligations during the first years, in which the annuity was very slight. But, from the year 1928, in which the so-called "normal" annuity was to begin to run—2,500,000,000 of gold marks—Germany protested so strongly that, on the 16th of September, 1928, at Geneva, the constitution of a committee of experts charged with the duty of examining again the problem of reparations was decided upon.

This was the Young committee, in which the United States, in the person of her representatives, and particularly its president, Mr. Young, played one of the most important roles.

From this came the Young plan, which, by virtue of the very mandate given to the committee and by virtue of The Hague accords, constitutes the "complete and definitive settlement of the problem of reparations."

From the financial point of view, the Young plan appears as follows:

Germany is to discharge her reparations debt in 58 annuities paid into the coffers of the Bank for International Settlements, the trustee for her creditors.

The figure of 59 annuities was chosen to fit the number of annuities remaining to be paid to the United States of America and to England for the settlement of their war debts due from their former allies and associates.

Thirty-seven annuities are of a mean value of 1,988,000,000 of reichsmarks—once and for all, I will recall the fact that the value of the reichsmark is 6.8 francs at par—and 22 annuities are of a mean value of 1,564,000,000 of reichsmarks.

For the moment, there is no question except as regards the 1931-32 annuity, but, before speaking of it, it is indispensable to lay stress on a particular point, the crux of the question which is to be placed before you; that is, the very clear distinction which was established for the first time in the debt of Germany, one part corresponding to the partial reparation of the damages done to property, otherwise said to be for the restoration of the invaded and devastated regions.

This was the first time that a kind of priority was thus established to the benefit of debts relative to reparations properly so called. I shall return to it presently, in a few words, in order to show you the full significance of this decision, which was taken, not only by the reporters of the Young plan, but by the governments met at The Hague in the month of August, 1929, and in the month of January, 1930.

How, then, is the Young annuity divided?

In reality there are two annuities; the one called "conditional," the other called "unconditional."

"Conditional" annuity—that is to say, subject to being suspended—in stated conditions, whether for the transfers to the creditors in foreign exchanges, or even, in conditions equally stated, for the payment in reichsmarks.

"Unconditional" annuity, payable in foreign exchanges and not, in any case, subject either to suspension of transfer or to suspension of payment.

The "unconditional" annuity is 660,000,000 of reichsmarks a year during 37 years, and even, if the letter of the plan is observed, during the 59 years.

Of these 660,000,000 of marks, France receives 500,000,000 of marks. I will say at once that from the 660,000,000 there must be deducted the service of the annuity of the Dawes loan of 1924; that from the share of France, 500,000,000 of marks, the service of the annuity of the Young loan contracted by Germany in 1930, of which a part was placed in France in accordance with her rights in the mobilization of the unconditional part, must be deducted.

How will acceptance of the proposal which is made to us by President Hoover affect us?

Before answering that question it is indispensable for me to establish the good foundation of our claims as regards the unconditional part; in other words, of the absolute right, going far back, which we have to receive that part.

One might go back, in fact, to the message of President Wilson, which established a true priority in favor of the restoration of the devastated regions; to the Lansing declaration of the month of November, 1918, which confirmed this point, defining it clearly.

One might take up various articles in the treaty of peace:

"ART. 232. * * * The allied and associated Governments require in any case, and Germany accepts the obligation, that all the damages caused to the civil population of each of the allied and associated powers and to their property during the period in which that power was in a state of war with Germany by the said aggression by land, by sea, and by the air shall be repaired ° ° °."

"ART. 235. In order to permit the allied and associated powers to undertake at once the restoration of their industrial and economic life, while awaiting the definitive established of the total of their claims, Germany will pay, before the 1st of May, 1921, 20 milliards of gold marks ° ° °."

The twenty milliards of gold marks have not served for that at all. But it is none the less a right which is written in the treaty.

The same article 235 refers to annex 2, which, in paragraph 12, specifies:

"° ° ° In order to facilitate and to pursue the immediate restoration of the economic life of the allied and associated countries, the commission, as provided in article 235 ° ° °"

Article 237, a vital point which seems to have been forgotten until the Young Plan:

"The successive payments ° ° ° made by Germany to satisfy the claims above stated shall be divided by the allied and associated Governments according to the proportions fixed by them in advance and founded in equity and the rights of each ° ° °."

It is here that an absolute priority should have been specified in favor of the damages to property, of the restoration of the devastated regions. [Very good! Very good!]

That priority was imposed in an absolute manner, even financially.

Consider the situation of the invaded countries, of the countries on the soil of which during four years the war was waged.

There was there a right all the more absolute because the north and the east of France had served, not only for Germany but equally for our Allies, as the field of battle, and thus the sufferings and devastations which we endured in the common interest were spared to our Allies. [Applause from the right.] There, then, was the beginning of a priority.

But there was another reason, a reason of a financial character. These regions, as President Wilson said, as the treaty

207

of peace said, it was necessary to restore immediately. It was indispensable, not only for the prosperity of the invaded countries, but for justice; and even to the interest of Europe and of the world. It was necessary to restore them immediately; to lay out immediately, in consequence, the necessary sums. This is what we have done.

While it is only with a long maturity and by annuities extending over a great number of years that damages to individuals are repaired, in regard to damages to property, on the contrary, there was an obligation for the immediate restoration of the devastated regions. That is why a priority was imposed for the reparation of damages to property.

Why was that priority not stated at the time of the treaty of peace and of the first conferences which followed it?

To answer that question would lead me too far afield. Various interests intervened. Belgium has obtained satisfaction in part. France has found herself injured, and all the more gravely injured because the debt of Germany has been diminished. If Germany had paid within 30 years, as the treaty stipulated, the total amount of her debt, one would not perhaps have been able to examine it too closely. We would have received substantial sums from the very first years. You know that that was not the case, since on the eve of the application of the Young plan, under the heading of reparations we had not yet received one sou from Germany. All her payments had been assigned to the payment of certain advances made by the Allies other than ourselves to Germany; to the payment of the expenses of the army of occupation; to the payment of reparations, for example, to Great Britain. But we had not at that time received one centime under the heading of reparations.

And nevertheless how many milliards had we not already spent!

Let us see now what the Young plan assigns to us.

But perhaps a part of the Assembly is about to manifest some impatience.

Undoubtedly, the great number of our colleagues know by heart the texts and figures of the Young plan, but the public

208

does not know them, and it is indispensable to us it know them. [Interruptions on the extreme left.] Perhaps there are even some among you who do not know them. [New interruptions on the extreme left.]

FROM THE EXTREME LEFT. We have never heard them.

M. LOUIS DUBOIS. You have not heard them for the very good reason that it was not possible at the time of the discussion of the Young plan for the speaker who is now on the tribune to expound his manner of looking at the Young plan and its economy. [Applause on the right.]

The Young plan comprises, in reality, two parts: A report of the experts and a series of annexes.

This is how, in their report, the experts express themselves in regard to the unconditional part of the German annuity:

"ARTICLE 33. At this moment it is equally admitted that the possibility of accepting annuities inferior to those which were established by the Dawes plan depended upon the certitude and the facility with which the creditors might commercialize obligations withdrawn thenceforth from the influene of politics."

"ARTICLE 89. Of the annuities above mentioned, the amounts stated hereafter shall be unconditional; that is to say, payable in foreign currencies, by means of equal monthly installments, without any right of suspension whatever: Six hundred and sixty millions of reichsmarks a year, the sums which the service of the German external loan of 1924 requires being included therein."

That is, 660,000,000 less 48,000,000—612,000,000, the actual total of the unconditional annuity.

"Article 115.—The part of our task which was not the least difficult, was to determine the sum which Germany might immediately undertake to pay under the heading of the definitive unconditional obligation. One can not establish in advance with precision the moment at which the difficulties of proceeding to the transfer in foreign exchanges may appear. However, great care has been taken to remain so far below that limit that all possibility of error is eliminated."

It is not only in the report that this point is made; it is also made in the special annexes which are attached to it.

Notably, this is what Annex III, article 137, states:

"The sums corresponding to the service of the interest and to the amortization of the mobilizable and mobilized fractions of the annuity coupons shall be paid to the Bank for International Settlements by the German Reich, without any reservation, that is to say, on its sole responsibility. The financial service of these mobilizable or mobilized fractions shall constitute a definitive international obligation, absolute and unconditional in the financial sense of the word." [Applause from the center and on the right.]

And The Hague accord of January 20, 1930, which adopts in its entirety the Young plan, report, and annexes, with some slight differences, this accord, in its first article, specifies that 'the experts' plan of June 7, 1929, together with this present agreement and the protocol of August 31, 1929 (all of which are hereinafter described as the new plan), is definitely accepted as a complete and final settlement, so far as Germany is concerned, of the financial questions resulting from the war.

"For that acceptance * * * the German Government undertakes, as regards the creditor powers, the solemn obligation of paying the annuities provided for by the new plan in conformity with the stipulations it contains."

You know of what these stipulations consist for the unconditional part.

The matter is so important, the engagement made by Germany is so vital and so definitive, that it is even reproduced on the certificate of debt of the Reich.

Here are the terms of Annex III of the accord of The Hague of January 20, 1930, Article 4, first paragraph:

"The sums corresponding to the service of the interest and to the amortization of the mobilizable and mobilized fractions of the annuity coupons shall be paid to the bank in money other than the reichsmark by the German Government, without any reservation; that is to say, on its sole responsibility."

You will please notice that the same privilege applies as

well to the "mobilizable" fractions as to the "mobilized" fractions.

I continue the quotation:

"The financial service of these mobilizable or mobilized fractions of the annuities shall constitute a definitive international obligation, absolute and unconditional in the financial sense of the word." [Applause from the center and on the right.]

That being stated, the character of the unconditional part of the annuity being clearly defined and determined, as I have indicated, by the Young plan and the international accords, what is our position and what would be the effect for us, from the financial point of view, of the acceptance of the Hoover proposal?

The only question is that of suspending or adjoining—it would certainly be necessary, on this matter, that we should have some precise details—the payment of the 1931-32 annuity.

The 1931-32 German annuity is figured at 1,685 millions of reichsmarks. Of this amount 838.4 millions comes to France, of which 338.4 are under the conditional heading; under the unconditional heading, 500,000,000 less the service of our part of the slight amount already mobilized, 44.5 millions, which reduces the sum to be received to 455.5 millions of marks.

But it is further necessary to deduct eighty millions of marks which are indispensable to make up the sum which we owe to the English and to the Americans by way of our war debts.

For the part which comes to us under the conditional heading is not, to the extent of about this amount, sufficient to pay our part of the war debts to the English and to the Americans, and it is further necessary that we should take from our unconditional part the sum of 80,000,000 reichsmarks. [Various movements.]

So that there remains to us a substantial sum, which can be—let us speak now of French francs—represented by two thousand two hundred and eighty-three millions. In other words, for the year 1931-32 would have the disposition of two thousand two hundred and eighty-three millions of actual francs under the heading of reparations properly so called for material damages above the sums employed for the payment of our war debts. That sum is going to fail us.

A note has been published which seems to me to be very well established, from which it appears that the French budget will only have to support a loss of one milliard nine hundred and some millions.

The budget, perhaps; but, apart from the budget, there are other payments to be made, on which I will not dwell. In reality it is two milliards two hundred and eighty-three millions of francs which we are going to lack.

It is evident that it will be necessary to get them somewhere and our minister of the Budget will find himself very much embarrassed. To what reources will he have recourse? This is not the moment to ask that.

Then, it has been said—and the Minister of Finance in a note has replied well enough to this objection—"You know very well that Germany was going to declare a moratorium on transfers. By that very fact you would have been obliged to make up the guaranty fund of 500,000,000 of reichsmarks; in other words, three milliards of francs, which you were to establish in order to guarantee the payment to your cocreditors of the conditional part which should be paid to them."

You know, in fact, gentlemen, that by virtue of the advantage which gave to us, but which was very largely justified, the attribution of 500,000,000 of reichsmarks of the unconditional part, we were asked, as a compensation, to answer, to a certain extent at least and to a substantial one, for the payment to our cocreditors and not to ourselves of the conditional part.

Now, there would remain for us to pay two thousand seven hundred millions to this guaranty fund. But who says that we shall not be obliged to pay them?

That which I declare, for the moment, is that already we are deprived for one year of two thousand two hundred and eighty-three millions of francs.

If next year, if even in the course of the present year, Germany comes to tell us, "In spite of all my good will, I am obliged to declare a moratorium on transfers," we would still be obliged to pay in addition to the Bank for International Settlements 2,700 millions, or in all and in round numbers a deficit of 5 milliards of francs.

I do not wish to envisage the rest, for I fear that if on this ground we yield, be it ever so little, to Germany, who expects it, her demands will not be finished.

It is therefore indispensable that we should be very clear in regard to the matter. As M. Margaine has just shown very well, Germany is not, from the economic point of view, in the condition one would like to say she was in.

If, financially speaking, she is in a bad condition, it is sufficient to refer to the report of June 30, 1930 ,of Mr. Parker Gilbert to know that it is her fault, exclusively her own fault. It is not for us to pay for the faults of Germany. [Applause from the center and on the right.]

That is why I insist, in regard to the Government, that it should be intransigent in this connection.

That, temporarily, it should grant some relief; I do not wish to say that I shall oppose that. I know nothing about that; it will depend upon the declarations that are made to us. But it is indispensable that we should maintain our imprescriptible rights, not only as regards the unconditional part but also the conditional part.

Notice that the amount in full of the conditional and unconditional annuities, of the global annuity paid by Germany represents only one-fifth of what we have spent—I do not say of what was due to us—for the devastated regions and for the pensions, without counting the interest.

As we are giving up the total of what we receive as the conditional part, in order to pay our war debts, it is only one-tenth of our expenses for the restoration of our devastated regions which we shall receive, admitting that Germany pays regularly the annuity for which the Young plan provides.

But it is not only the unconditional annuity which is neces-

213

sary to us; it is also the conditional annuity, for how shall we pay the English and the Americans?

In the case of a simple suspension I know well that we also to a certain extent can suspend our payments temporarily.

But if at the end of the account Germany gets out and does not pay, shall we pay the English and the Americans?

FROM VARIOUS BENCHES. No! no!

M. JEAN FABRY. There will not be a French Chamber to vote the credits.

M. LOUIS DUBOIS. There is the question as it stands, with all its gravity, all its extent. I believe that I have submitted it clearly enough to the Chamber. [Applause from the center.]

I now ask the Government to tell us what its position will be. For the answer which it has made is not an answer to the question which I have permitted myself to put to it.

I dare to hope that the Government will know how to sustain the interests of which it has the care. [Applause from the center and on the right.]

XII

WAR DEBTS AND REPARATIONS
THE HOOVER MORATORIUM

Tuesday, December 15, 1931

Mr. McFADDEN. Mr. Chairman, ladies and gentlemen of the committee, at this hour the Ways and Means Committee of the House is taking up the discussion of the moratorium bill. I understand that the Under Secretary of the Treasury is at the present moment presenting to that committee the administration's ideas as regards the Hoover moratorium.

I am greatly indebted to the majority leadership of the House for granting me this time to discuss minutely this question of the moratorium. I desire also to observe that at this time, before the bill is under consideration in the House and before the bill has been discussed except by the presentation of the administration's plan in the Ways and Means Committee, the full force of the administration's influence is being exerted to exact the pledges of the Members of the House as to how they are going to vote on the moratorium.

The particular situation I want to mention at the outset is that at the present time the Hoover moratorium has been succeeded by the operations of the Young plan, brought about by the recent conference in Washington of the Premier of France, M. Laval, and the President of the United States. Under that plan the Germans have asked for a moratorium as provided by law, and the committees appointed under that

215

plan by the Bank for International Settlements have been engaged for the past week in determining Germany's capacity to pay. In addition to that the committees of the international bankers are also at work studying the short-time debt situation and Germany's capacity to pay the short-term debts. It is well for you to keep in mind that there is much confusion as regards the short-term debts. The matters in which the international bankers are particularly interested at this time are the acceptance credits. Those are the short-term debts that are referred to.

On June 20, 1931, while Congress was not in session, the President of the United States, acting without any legal or official authority, for the benefit of a foreign country with which we had lately been at war, proposed and virtually brought about a loss to this country of $245,000,000 in one single year and paved the way for much greater losses for this country to sustain in all the years that follow after. Worse than that, he proposed that the Congress of the United States should unlawfully dissipate the resources of this country by giving the money which was due to us under contract, and which should have been paid to us and of which we are the trustees for the people, to foreign nations which have no claim upon us and through them to that foreign nation with which we have lately engaged in war. In short, he proposed that we should take money away from the men and women and children of this country and give it to Germany. This, in my opinion, was an infamous proposal.

Because it was an infamous proposal, the President of the United States endeavored to find support for his intended action. He was afraid to do this thing alone at the bidding of the German international bankers—the Warburgs; Kuhn, Loeb & Co., of New York; and their followers—all of whom have been engaged in bleeding this country white for the benefit of Germany and themselves ever since the World War came to an end. He was afraid to do it on his own responsibility, because he had no authority to do it in law, either in domestic law or in international law, in morals, in good faith, or under his constitutional oath of office. In fact, it was a violation of his oath of office and a breach of international law for him to do it at all. So, what does he do? He forgets himself and goes so far as to summon the leaders of Congress by telegraph and telephone and asks them to signify their consent to his proposed illegal action in advance. He asked them to give him their votes to sustain his illegal action. He proposed to commit an unfriendly act toward France and he asked certain members of both parties in Congress to sustain him in that course of conduct. He asked them to promise to legalize his unfriendly act. And in advance of the assembling of this Congress which alone has power to make law for this country.

Those of you who were not consulted in this crude attempt at usurpation of legislative power were in effect foreclosed in advance. You were, perhaps, men of no importance in the eyes of President Hoover. Has any President ever so far forgotten the dignity of his office and the limited place of the Executive in this Government as to do a thing like that before? Could anything be more distressing to American pride than such a message to the powers? What constitutes leadership in Congress? Does leadership mean that men of both parties from States where international bankers have their head offices can upon occasion go into a secret conference with the President of the United States, the agent of those bankers, and tell him the little fellows do not count, that they can be held in line and forced to vote "yes" when they might be expected to vote "no"?

Mr. Hoover is not running a coal mine here. He is not a dictator.

I have been here for a good many years. For the past 17 years I have been a member of the House Banking and Currency Committee. For that reason, I presume, I received a telegram last June from the President of the United States asking my consent to the course he wished to pursue. I did not answer that telegram. I am standing here as the representative of the fifteenth congressional district of my native State, and my vote has not been cast in secret upon a matter concerning which my constituents have had no information and no chance

217

for discussion. This is the place where we make the laws. This is the place where my vote is cast for the fifteenth district of Pennsylvania. [Applause.] I do not vote on matters concerning the welfare of the United States in a telephone booth or in the office of a telegraph company. Consequently, I stand here free. I have made no bargain to vote for the proposal of the German international bankers and the deal Herbert Hoover is trying to put through for them.

But were it otherwise, had I yielded to the importunate demand of the President of the United States, had I been misled by the specious plea of urgency or by any other consideration, and had I afterwards found out what I propose to unravel for your consideration here to-day, I would not feel bound to vote in accordance with a promise that had been wrung from me by unfair means; I would take back such a promise and I would examine the question on its merits and vote according to my conscience and the interests of my constituents.

Do you remember what happened in this country when President Wilson asked the voters to elect a Democratic Congress so that his policies might be put into effect? It was nothing like this bold-faced attempt to usurp legislative functions, to make a law in a small group, and then to peddle it to legislators for their approval. President Wilson's request was nothing like this, and yet the country resented it and refused it and sent us a Republican majority instead of a Democratic one.

After completing his underhanded arrangements by telegraph and telephone, arrangements which savored more of the ways of an oriental potentate drunk with power than of conduct proper for a President of the United States to pursue, Mr. Hoover, with a dramatic flourish, made his proposal, linking it as usual with a lot of false and insincere humanitarianism.

One of the most significant things about the Hoover moratorium was the suddenness with which it was proclaimed. There was nothing accidental about that suddenness, however. The present administration never makes a move of this sort without ordering a spot light beforehand. Months may go into the excited preparation of a deal, but when the moment comes to give the people an official version of what is happening the electricians are ordered to drag in the spots; the sound apparatus is sent for, and the photographers may be seen hurrying toward the White House.

Behind the Hoover announcement there were many months of hurried and furtive preparation both in Germany and in the Wall Street offices of Germany's bankers. The groundwork had to be prepared. The German budget had to be doctored and left unbalanced. Germany, like a sponge, had to be saturated with American money. Mr. Hoover himself had to be elected, because this scheme began before he became President. If the German international bankers of Wall Street— that is, Kuhn, Loeb & Co., J. & W. Seligman, Paul Warburg, J. H. Schroeder & Co.—and their satellites had not had this job waiting to be done, Herbert Hoover would never have been elected President of the United States. They helped select him. They helped elect him.

The Hoover proposal originated in the offices of the German international bankers in New York. William Randolph Hearst has lately made the following statement:

> This plan for revision of war debts, with America paying the piper while war-mad Europe dances, is purely a plan of international bankers, who make money through commissions out of spoliation of their countrymen. One of those bankers wrote me the whole plan months before it was made public and asked my support of it.
>
> I refused support and I pledged unending opposition to this plan to plunder the American people in the interests of foreign nations, for which most of these international bankers are financial agents.

[Applause.]

You will notice that Mr. Hearst says the plan was presented to him in writing by an international banker months before it was made public. This ought to convince you that it did not originate in the mind of President Hoover. It ought to convince you that it was presented to President Hoover by

219

the same international bankers or one of his followers who presented it to Mr. Hearst and who was rebuked by Mr. Hearst for his cheek and impudence. This international banker was not rebuked by Mr. Hoover. Mr. Hoover, it appears, promised to support the plan, although in his campaign speeches and in other addresses made by him he continued to deny that he was in favor of the object of the outrageous and unpatriotic German banker propaganda for cancellation of war debts and the binding down of American labor to the task of paying the entire cost of the World War.

We have other evidence that this is true. Unknown to the President and his banker friends, an account of the plan was brought to Washington in the summer of 1930, nearly a year before the President appeared before the footlights, and, as master of ceremonies for the German international bankers, made his public announcement. If there was a crisis in German financial affairs in July, 1931, and if there is one in those affairs now, that crisis was well arranged in advance by the German international bankers and no one in Germany took any steps to prevent its occurrence. The plan was brought to Washington and it was divulged to Senators. Closely as the secret was guarded it leaked out nearly a year in advance. This ought to convince you that it was not the result of any sudden emergency in Germany or elsewhere. This ought to convince you that it was a put-up job.

But we have other and equally convincing evidence in regard to the origin of this plan. On October 23, 1931, the German Minister of Communications, Herr Treviranus, publicly stated in Germany that President Hoover began secret conversations with Germany in regard to this plan in December 1930. That was last December, when our people were suffering from starvation in Arkansas. That was during the last session of Congress when we were struggling to obtain help for the victims of the great drought and the depression. While our minds were occupied with those matters, while our men were walking the streets in a vain search for employment, while the suicide total was mounting, the President of the United States secretly approached Germany and asked her if he could do anything for her in the way of getting her reparations obligations lightened. The German minister, Herr Treviranus, has stated that one of the chief intermediaries in this matter died and it seems as if that chief intermediary might have been Joseph P. Cotton, who died at Baltimore this year. Herr Treviranus has stated that Hoover's negotiations were carried on with the utmost secrecy and we may well believe it.

The Public Ledger of Philadelphia published the following dispatch on October 24, 1931:

[Public Ledger Foreign Service]
GERMAN REVEALS HOOVER'S SECRET—MINISTER SAYS
PRESIDENT STUDIED MORATORIUM MONTHS BEFORE ASKING IT,
SLOW PAYMENT HINTED

BERLIN, October 23.—Minister of Transportation Treviranus revealed in an address here to-night that, contrary to the general impression that President Hoover's moratorium was the result of a sudden decision, the American President was in intimate negotiations with the German Government regarding a year's debt holiday as early as December, 1930.

The President, according to Treviranus, who has long been intimate with Chancellor Bruening, did not even let his Cabinet members know what was going on. The negotiations, the German minister said, were made more difficult and the result was delayed considerably by the death of the "middle man" the first part of this year. Several of the minister's auditors recalled that the Under Secretary of State, Joseph Cotton, a personal friend and adviser of President Hoover, died about that time.

Previously it was believed that when Mr. Hoover returned from his western trip last June he learned for the first time the real seriousness of Germany's financial situation.

I might state in that connection that the hearings held by

the Banking and Currency Committee a year ago last summer, when we were considering this question of the sale in the United States of commercialized German reparation loans, this same Joseph P. Cotton, now deceased, appeared before that committee and gave testimony supporting the issue and sale in this country, as did the Treasury Department, of those commercialized bonds. They were put out in this country by this same group of international bankers at 91¼ and they are selling now between 25 and 30.

Mr. Cotton, not in the record, but in discussion with members of the committee, at the close of the hearings, told of his interest in Germany and the fact that he had a law firm, of which he was a member, with offices located in Berlin.

Here we have the German Minister of Communications, Herr Treviranus, telling us that Hoover did not let his Cabinet officers know what he proposed to do. He worked on his plan under the guidance and at the direction of the German international bankers and he thought he had his secret so closely guarded that the people of the United States would never be able to find out his part in the plot that was being concocted against them.

Mr. STAFFORD. Will the gentleman yield?

Mr. McFADDEN. I am sorry, but I prefer not to yield.

Mr. STAFFORD. The gentleman is making very serious charges against the President of the United States, and I was going to ask him the basis of his authority for stating that he was acting secretly with German international bankers.

Mr. McFADDEN. I think the gentleman will be satisfied by the time I finish.

The CHAIRMAN. The gentleman declines to yield.

Mr. McFADDEN. He proposed to sell us out to Germany. If he had looked about him, he would have seen on all sides the havoc that had been wrought by the exportation of American wealth to foreign countries. He could have seen mortgaged land, bare of goods, with mile-long bread lines in every city, and that havoc and that desolation and those homeless ones would have shown him that the time was ripe, that the international German bankers had got his country down, and would hold it down in the interest of Germany until it capitulated.

In January, 1931, in the city of Berlin, the Hon. Frederick Sackett, the United States ambassador, began and carried on further secret conversations with the German Government in regard to the obtaining of a moratorium for Germany. Subsequently, Sackett came to this country and looked around. He came and saw and, like a conquering hero, he went back to Berlin and told the German Government, with a diplomatic smile, that the time was auspicious. Mark that word auspicious! It was not auspicious for the people of the United States, but it was auspicious for Germany and it was auspicious for the German international bankers.

Now you have the facts and you can see how preposterous it was for the President of the United States to make a calculated entry before the footlights announcing his plans as if it were a sudden response on his part to a sudden emergency. You can see how preposterous it was for him to do that.

The 16th day of June was the date set by the German international bankers, the Bruening cabinet, Mr. Sackett, Mr. Hoover, and his associates for the opening of the great financial offensive against the American people. And how did they begin it? The head of Kuhn, Loeb & Co., Otto Kahn, was in Italy in June on international financial business. The first shot was fired from Italian ground. It was in the form of propaganda —the great weapon of those who do wrong. It appeared in the form of an article in the Christian Science Monitor. I shall read it to you.

[Christian Science Monitor, June 16, 1931]

ITALY OFFERS TO EASE REICH'S HEAVY REPARATION PAYMENTS, ALTHOUGH EUROPE LOOKS TO UNITED STETES TO CUT GORDIAN KNOT OF WAR DEBTS, THIS OFFER FROM ITALIAN SOURCE ATTRACTS ATTENTION

(By radio from the Christian Science Monitor Bureau)

LONDON, June 15.—A sample of European self-help calculated, it is thought here, to make a favorable impression in the United States is a proposal of Italian origin.

The plan put forward is that those powers receiving an amount from German reparations over and above the amount necessary to discharge their debts should forego this "indemnity," thus giving Germany the necessary immediate alleviation and providing a significant gesture of moral disarmament.

The position is that, whereas Britain, on the basis of the Balfour note, only demanded from its debtors sufficient to cover its payments to the United States, France, Italy, and Belgium, and to a limited extent the smaller reparations creditors, receive payments from Germany markedly exceeding their payments stipulated by funding agreements to Britain and the United States.

Italy, for example, receives on an average $53,425,000 annually on reparations account and has to pay to Britain approximately $20,000,000 and to the United States $22,-657,000, leaving a margin of $10,750,000, equivalent to 43,000,000 marks.

A corresponding margin exists in the receipts and payments by France and Belgium, and, therefore, any such remission would supply a handsome measure of relief to Germany's burden.

On the basis of the Spa percentages, which is the system of apportionment, France receives the lion's share of reparations, roughly 52 per cent, as compared with Italy's 10 per cent, and Belgium's 8 per cent. The annual sum accruing to France amounts to $261,625,000.

The Italian offer in a nutshell—believed to have official approval—is, that she is prepared to waive a portion of the reparations receipts if the other beneficiaries do likewise. Its policy is exactly parallel with the position taken on disarmament, namely, Italy is prepared to cut armaments to any figure if other European powers undertake a corresponding cut.

Opposition may be expected from France on the reparations as on the disarmament issue, but if The Hague settlements and the Young plan are to mean what they were designed to mean, namely, final liquidation of financial questions arising out of the World War, there is no doubt Italy has an unexceptionable case.

While opinion here adheres to the notion implicit in the Balfour note, namely, that the United States alone can cut the Gordian knot of international indebtedness, it welcomes the Italian proposal and would surely support any official move in this sense.

This article is misleading. I shall come to facts and figures presently and when I do, I will show you the contract executed by Germany in the Young law and I will show you the force of the settlement to which Germany solemnly set her hand and seal.

Now, why did Italy advertise herself at London as an international philanthropist, a canceller of debts, on June 15, 1931? She did it because she was told to do it. She did it because the German international bankers from whom she is receiving great favors at our expense in the future ordered her to do it. Mussolini is not the iron man. Otto Kahn is the metalliferous man. Mussolini is the needy man. Otto Kahn and his associates are the men who have measured Mussolini's need and who have promised to supply it if he will help them to break the contract Germany made with her creditors and which she now seeks to dishonor and to treat as a mere scrap of paper. Do you think France and her allies will permit the Young law, signed by Germany and other responsible powers, to be torn up in the German fashion of tearing up treaties and laughing at debts? France is saying no and in doing so is saying that it will be a bad day for Italy, or for any other country when it joins hands with Germany in breaking what France believes to be a legal contract and protests in setting at naught that international law which goes back through the treaty to the armistice.

Some people no doubt would have been better satisfied if Germany had whipped the United States and maimed another hundred thousand of our soldiers. Some of them think that the treaty of Versailles was not a good treaty. I share that view. The allied armies had a right to march to Berlin and the French could hardly have been blamed if they had set the torch to some of the German factories on the way. Instead of such a proceeding, the Allies made a treaty which embodied great concessions for Germany, all of which were predicated upon her expressed willingness to pay for the damage she had wrought. So far as the war is concerned, and the end of the war, I am satisfied to say that we sent our army to France for a purpose; that it achieved the purpose for which we sent it; and that the American cemeteries in France bear witness alike to our sacrifice and to our victory. I will also say that the present condition of this country and the Hoover proposal bear witness to the revenge that the German bankers have taken on us for the decisive part we took in the World War.

Over yonder across the river lies the Tomb of the Unknown Soldier. Hoover might almost have seen it from the window of the Lincoln study, where, with German emissaries, he planned to nullify the part our soldiers took in the World War and to set at naught the claims of our people to the money they showered upon this Government for the prosecution of the war. It seems prophetic when we remember that Lincoln wrote—and possibly in that very room—the following words:

Yes; we may congratulate ourselves that this cruel war is nearing the close, but I see in the future a crisis approaching that unnerves me and causes me to tremble for the safety of my country. As a result of the war corporations have been enthroned, and an era of corruption in high places will follow and the money power of the country will endeavor to prolong its reign by working upon the prejudices of the people until wealth is aggregated in a few hands and the Republic is destroyed. I feel at this moment more anxiety for the safety of my country than ever before in the midst of the war.

I am concerned now with the offensive against the French

226

and the American people and against the friendship which has for so long existed between them. I am concerned with the German offensive as it was developed by the German international bankers. Why do I call them German international bankers? I do so because I wish to emphasize the fact that international finance is almost exclusively German. Most of the international bankers are of German origin.

On the very day the propaganda from London announcing Italy's heroic pose was published in the Monitor a second article appeared in that sheet. I shall read it to you.

[Special from Monitor Bureau]
UNITED STATES RESERVES RIGHT TO RECONSIDER
POLICY ON WAR DEBTS

WASHINGTON, June 15.—The United States Government has an "open mind" on foreign war debts, it was authoritatively stated at the State Department Saturday, in connection with the discussions in Europe over the possibility of downward revision of the Young plan.

It was explained that the United States Government's policy on war debts and reparations is clearly established, but that in case of a serious crisis, it would "obviously have to consider temporary changes in policy, if that was necessary."

The administration is cognizant of the seriousness of the economic situation in Germany. It is keeping in close touch with developments and is fully informed of conversations going on abroad.

Initiative for action must come from European sources, however. Andrew W. Mellon, Secretary of Treasury, and Henry L. Stimson, Secretary of State, are going abroad this month and will meet European leaders, but without any proposal. Their purpose is wholly informative, it is declared.

You will notice the statement in the article I have just read:

Initiative for action must come from European sources, however.

It will be interesting when this matter goes to trial before the Permanent Court of International Justice to find out whether Herbert Hoover was acting as a legal agent of Germany or as the President of the United States when he made his proposal. If he was the agent of Germany, then Germany violated the solemn covenant of the Young law by procuring his assistance. If he acted on his own initiative as the President of the United States, then I think he is personally liable to the people of this country in a legal way and that those who acted with him are liable also. We can not have an agent of Germany acting as President of the United States.

But the sting of this article is in the tail. It lets us know that Mellon and Stimson are "going abroad this month." They are going to meet European leaders. They are going without any proposal. Their purpose is wholly informative. Mark that word "informative." They are going to Europe to give information. Their purpose is informative. They were not going to Europe to rest.

When Secretaries Mellon and Stimson went abroad they did not travel to Europe on the same ship. Mr. Mellon was the first to depart. By a coincidence he arrived in England on the very day the Italian gesture was reported in the Christian Science Monitor. And here, having told you that the 15th of June was the appointed day upon which the President of the United States ordered the forces who were acting with him to begin the offensive, I will tell you why that day was selected. On the 15th of June France paid this country a large sum of money. Prudently and with a kind of low-class cunning, this payment was gathered in, although the document which was intended to deprive France of her rights under the Young law was fully prepared and ready for emission to the world powers. Do you think that act of cunning escaped the attention of foreign statesmen? Do you think it has increased their respect for the United States?

Mr. Mellon raced through the next few days at high pressure and somebody in London who appears to have been interested in the dissemination of information gave news to the press that he had been invited to come to England by the British Government. This statement was vigorously denied by the private secretary to Ramsay MacDonald, who asserted that the British Government had addressed no invitation to Mr. Mellon and that it had not sent a communication to the Government at Washington to invite it to discuss revision of war debts, or any other question.

Nevertheless, Mr. Mellon, upon his arrival in England, lost no time in entering into a secret conversation with Mr. Ramsay MacDonald and with Montagu Norman, the governor of the Bank of England.

It is a little strange that Mr. Montagu Norman should have been there. As Henry de Jourvenel says, in speaking of this interview:

> Among the personalities present there was one not generally invited to conferences between prime ministers and foreign statesmen. This was the governor of the Bank of England.

You all know who Montagu Norman is and how closely he is linked with certain sinister figures in the banking world. You know that he comes here occasionally and that he transacts secret business with the Federal Reserve Board and the Federal Reserve Bank of New York. You know that he was suddenly taken ill when the old Tories in England found out what had been happening there and formed a national government and gave up the gold standard. You may remember that without allowing his name to appear on the passenger list Mr. Montagu Norman took ship for Canada and did not return to England until the storm blew over. I presume you know that the Federal Reserve Board and the Federal reserve banks are the agents of the Bank of England and that of late years Mr. Montagu Norman has had a great deal to do with George L. Harrison, governor of the Federal Reserve Bank of New

York. Mr. Montagu Norman did not come down to New York from Canada during his last visit to this continent. Instead of that, Governor Harrison went up to Canada to see him.

Let us leave Mr. Mellon in London for a while and return to Washington sweltering in the heat.

It is the 16th of June. The President of the United States is spending the summer in Washington. He has been hard at work with Henry M. Robinson, who is the Colonel House of this administration, and, like Colonel House, a secret emissary of Kuhn, Loeb & Co., Paul Warburg, and other German international bankers. Robinson's ostensible business is in California, but his real business is here, where he can see the President of the United States every day. Somtimes he goes to the Rapidan. Sometimes he spends several days at the White House. He passes for a Californian friend of President Hoover. I will tell you whose friend he is. He is the bosom friend and intimate of Paul M. Warburg, the man who engineered the great depression, the man who is the chief beneficiary of the losses sustained by the farmers and the wage earners of this country, the man who has stuffed this country full of worthless German acceptances, so that Germany might use them against us to trick us into breaking an international law in her behalf. More of Paul Warburg hereafter. For the present let us keep our eyes on Henry M. Robinson, the Colonel House of the present administration.

It is the 16th of June and the Monitor has published its little story about the generous Italians.

It is the 16th of June and here comes an Associated Press dispatch reading as follows:

[Washington Post, June 16, 1931]
Always holding reparations and war-debt payments as distinctly separate, the Treasury yesterday made known that recent events in Europe had caused no change in its attitude.

What recent events had caused no change in the Treasury's attitude? There had been no recent events in Europe which could have caused a change in the Treasury's attitude. This article further makes known that speculation having been aroused by Mr. Mellon's departure for Europe and by Mr. Stimson's prospective European trip, Mr. Mills, of the Treasury, and Mr. Castle, of the State Department, gave assurances that no official business was involved.

I am loath to accuse any man of toying with the truth, but candor compels me to say that, in my opinion, the assurances so given by Mr. Mills and Mr. Castle were intended to deceive the American people. Can we afford to trust our governmental business to men who lend themselves to this kind of deception?

This is a free country with what is supposed to be a free press. Whence came this custom of deceiving the people with carefully prepared misleading statements, artfully contrived releases, and all the other devices of overlordship looking down from a high place with contempt for the wage earner, the farmer, and the man of little or no property?

It is the night of the 16th of June in Washington. The President of the United States is out of town. That, too, was foreseen and provided for. It was a kind of alibi intended to make it easy for him to pretend that a certain crisis had come about in his absence. Now, comes the 17th of June and on that day, as if without knowledge of what was about to happen at Washington, the German ambassador to France goes to the French Minister of Foreign Affairs and to the French Minister of Finances and says that the German Government will soon be obliged to ask for a moratorium. This was a calculated move and Mr. Sackett was fully aware of it. It was done for the purpose of working on French nerves, to try to frighten and unsettle the French so that they might be startled out of their customary caution when they received the communication that the President proposed to make to them and upon which he had been hard at work with Breuning and Sackett and the Warburgs through their emissaries for so many months.

On the 18th of June the President returned to Washington

from the tomb of our late President Harding, where he had just descanted upon the infamy of anyone who betrayed the trust of the people in money matters. I call your attention to his words:

"BETRAYAL" IS CASTIGATED

There are disloyalties and there are crimes which shock our sensibilities, which may bring suffering upon those who are touched by their immediate results. But there is no disloyalty and no crime in all the category of human weaknesses which compares with the failure of probity in the conduct of public trust.

Monetary loss, or even the shock to moral sensibilities, is perhaps a passing thing, but the breaking down of the faith of a people in the honesty of their government and in the integrity of their institutions, the lowering of respect for the standards of honor which prevail in high places, are crimes for which punishment can never atone.

On the following day, as a part of this conspiracy, the Secretary of State, Mr. Stimson, sent for the French ambassador, Mr. Paul Claudel, and told him what the President was going to do. This, we understand, was about one hour before President Hoover gave out his statement to the newspapers.

Was this fair to the French ambassador when we know that the President had been working on this plan since the previous December; that is, December, 1930, and the plan he gives out is the one that was disclosed to William R. Hearst by an international banker several months before, that it is the same plan that was divulged here in secret to the Senators in the late summer of 1930. It is the same secret plan that the German Minister of Communications referred to in his statement which I have read to you. It was the international German bankers' plan for having the burden of reparations removed from her triumphant march toward world domination. Germany has already surpassed the United States in trade activity. She has had a favorable balance of trade every month so far this year. That can not be said of us who are asked to break the law of nations for her benefit. But the next time Mr. Hoover talked to France he had to talk on a different key. When baffled and humiliated he had to prostrate himself at the feet of Premier Laval and ask him to leave the balances of France in New York because the Federal Reserve Board and the Federal reserve banks and the international bankers and the New York bankers were headed for trouble through the loss of gold to the extent of $1,800,000,000 and perhaps more. It was then that the President of the United States did not appeal to the German international bankers who were then engaged in speculation in international exchanges, but it was then that he did appeal to the French Premier, Laval, to save him and his country from the sequences of his folly—the effects of the Hoover moratorium.

One hardly knows which is worse, the revolting dishonesty or the shocking bad taste. Do you wonder that his announcement of his plan created a sensation in France? As one of the French editors politely said, "The declaration of President Hoover is the most disconcerting impromptu diplomatic document imaginable. Leaving aside all sentimental considerations, it must be admitted that this rough brick hurled at Europe runs a strong risk of upsetting the whole edifice so laboriously erected by experts and governments for the parallel settlement of reparations and war debts. The American document was transmitted to our ambassador at Washington at the very time it was being made public like a simple harangue at a campaign rally."

After President Hoover had so unceremoniously informed Ambassador Claudel that he was at the moment giving out his plan, he is said to have telegraphed to Hindenburg, the President of Germany, begging him to telegraph him with the utmost haste a German request for a moratorium. We shall hear more of Hindenburg's telegram later on.

Simultaneously with this move on the part of their agent, Hoover, the German international bankers and others who followed their lead bought heavily in the stock exchanges and

233

this buying caused stocks to rise in price. As the editor above mentioned expressed it—

A dose of very uncommon simplicity would be needed to cause one to believe that the Anglo-German American banks, which had been preadvised of the arrangements made at Washington, did not seize the opportunity to start a financial maneuver to take place on all the world financial markets in order to give a consecration of fact to the policy of the President, obliged to reckon with the susceptibilities of the American Congress.

At this point I wish to insert in the CONGRESSIONAL RECORD a copy of the French reply to Hoover's proposal.

The CHAIRMAN. The gentleman from Pennsylvania asks unanimous consent to extend his remarks as indicated. Is there objection?

There was no objection.

Mr. McFADDEN (reading):

First. Repayment to France and other creditor nations within five years by Germany of the credits to be extended to the German economic system through the Bank for International Settlements. The original idea of the French Government had been to ask for the repayment within two years.

Second. Should Germany within five years enforce the moratorium as provided for under the Young plan the guarantee fund which is provided for by the Young plan would not be paid out by France, but would be built up by making use of the untransferred unconditional annuity.

Third. Allocation of part of the credits created upon the basis of the untransferred, unconditional annuity to such European States as Yugoslavia and Greece, which might be stripped financially, owing to the suspension of payments of all intergovernmental debts, the net loss of Yugoslavia being about $16,000,000 and of Greece $700,000.

234

[Here the gavel fell.]

Mr. Greenwood. Mr. Chairman, I yield the gentleman 15 additional minutes.

Mr. Stafford. Will the gentleman yield?

Mr. McFadden. I am sorry, but I have a connected statement which I want to complete. I would like to yield, but my time is limited.

Mr. Stafford. I see there is no trouble about the gentleman securing additional time, and I thought perhaps the gentleman would yield.

Mr. McFadden. If the gentleman will yield me more time to complete my address, I will then be only too glad to yield to the gentleman.

You will notice that the French in this reply expressly refused to give priority to private obligations. The bankers had endeavored to obtain this concession. President Hoover had tried to have the service on private obligations maintained. He wished to have the service on the Kruger & Toll Swedish loan kept up. (Kreuger & Toll and the Swedish Match Trust are a Warburg outfit, but this is another chapter.) This the French refused to allow, and I call your attention to their statement that—

A formal assimilation has been established between the private debts of the Reich (Young loan and Kreuger loan) and the unconditional annuities not yet mobilized. To suspend the payment by Germany of the unconditional annuity while admitting that the Young loan placed with the public should continue to be served would go directly against a fundamental principle and express stipulations.

The Government considers, therefore, that a moral interest of the first order attaches to the fact that, even during the delay provided for by President Hoover, the payment of the unconditional annuity should not be in any way postponed.

The Germans do not wish to pay reparations. Nobody likes to pay a bill for damages.

The whole world knows what the Germans did in France. There are districts in France which will never be as they were before. I believe that the mass of the German people were willing to pay their indemnity as France paid her indemnity after the Franco-Prussian War, but something happened to Germany which prevented the full and free execution of her obligations. I will tell you what it was. After the World War Germany fell into the hands of German international bankers. Those bankers bought her and they now own her, lock, stock, and barrel. They have purchased her industries, they have mortgages on her soil, they control her production, they control all of her public utilities. There is no country in the world to-day of which the inhabitants are so enslaved as are the Germans.

The international German bankers have subsidized the present Government of Germany and they have also supplied every dollar of the money that Adolf Hitler has used in his lavish campaign to build up a threat to the government headed by Bruening. When Bruening fails to obey the orders of the German international bankers, Hitler is brought forth to scare the Germans into submission. The German international bankers have worked up great resentment in Germany, and their hired agents have prompted the Germans to unite in order to free themselves from their war obligations. But resentment, the bankers knew, was not enough. They had to put a weapon into the hands of Germany which could be used against the society of nations in general and against the United States in particular. They conceived the idea of robbing us by stealth, by fraud, and by trickery, and they have succeeded. Through the Federal Reserve Board and the Federal reserve banks over thirty billions of American money over and above the German bonds that have been sold here has been pumped into Germany. When these Federal reserve loans began, Germany used to repay them. She established herself as a fairly good risk. Then her borrowings became larger and larger. You have all heard of the spending that has taken place in Germany. You have heard of her new modernistic dwelling

236

houses, her great planetariums, her gymnasiums, her swimming pools, her fine public highways, her perfect factories. All this was done on our money. All this was given to Germany through the Federal Reserve Board and the Federal reserve banks, and, what is worse, Federal reserve notes were issued for it.

A Federal reserve note is an obligation of the United States and here you have a banking system which has financed Germany from start to finish with the Federal reserve notes and has unlawfully taken from the Government and the people of the United States. The Federal Reserve Board and the Federal reserve banks have pumped so many billions of dollars into Germany that they dare not name the total. I have repeatedly asked the Federal Reserve Board to send me a list of the acceptance credits granted by the accepting banks of this country by and with the consent of the Federal Reserve Board, and they have not. They can not and they dare not divulge the total. This is the Congress of the United States, but you have no information concerning the amount of Federal reserve currency that has been issued for the benefit of Germany on trade bills or acceptances. How, then, do you propose to proceed? Are you going to throw away our resources under the debt settlements we have with foreign nations in order to help Germany do that which is forbidden in the Constitution of the United States? Are you going to make this Government a defendant in a million suits for damages brought on American citizens, whose property you propose to throw away?

Do you know that Germany has been lending our money to Soviet Russia as fast as she could get it out of this country from the Federal Reserve Board and banks? Do you know that she is the author of the 5-year plan; that she has armed and supplied Soviet Russia with our money? Do you know that Germany and Soviet Russia are one in military and industrial matters? Do you know that Germany is well armed and that we paid for her rifles and uniforms, her commercial trucks which can be converted for military uses inside of 24 hours?

She leads the world in aviation. Why not, when the Federal Reserve Board and the Federal reserve banks have been secretly financing her for years. I challenge the Federal Reserve Board and the Federal reserve banks to come in here and submit to an examination and an audit of their accounts. Do you know that the Federal Reserve Board and Federal reserve banks have also been financing Soviet Russia and that Russia owes an immense sum, of which $150,000,000 is due by January 1, 1932, and that Russia has no money wherewith to pay it and will presumably be unable to pay it?

There are 9,000 German officers in the Russian Army. The Krupps are manufacturing war munitions in Moscow, and the manufacture is going on day and night. Thousands of armored trucks and tractors, currently used in Germany for commercial purposes, are convertible into war tanks within 60 hours. But the most important activities are in the fields of aviation and chemistry. The Germans and Russians are working unremittently on war gas and war flame in soviet-owned laboratories.

In addition to their debt to us, Soviet Russia has borrowed 535,000,000 reichsmarks from Germany, and that was our money, too. For the first nine months of this year Russian orders to German manufacturers amounted to 851,000,000 reichsmarks more than the entire amount Germany is legally bound to pay to France. These Russian orders, which, roughly speaking, amount to about $202,620,000, were for general machinery, tool machines, and electrical supplies. Do you not think that Germany is doing a handsome business on the free paper Federal reserve notes unlawfully given from this Government for her benefit?

You have been informed that there is an alternative before the United States—that Germany will pay her commercial obligations if we effect her release from the payment of reparations. I say that Germany will not pay her commercial obligations. I say that the Federal reserve banks have purchased and rediscounted false, worthless, fictitious, and uncollectible acceptances drawn in Germany, and that those false papers are in the vaults of the Federal reserve banks, in the vaults of the designated depositaries as security for money taken from the citizens of this country by taxation, and in other banks, and I say that they are worthless. It is a mere figure of speech to call them frozen assets. They are dead losses. The Government's money in the designated depositaries is gone, leaving nothing but this worthless paper behind it. The Hoover proposal has already cost us $1,500,000,000 in gold credit. How much more are we going to throw away? For my part, I say, "Not one cent." "Millions for defense, but not one cent for tribute."

We were called to the White House on October 6, and the President told us we were facing a national emergency. What was the emergency? It was a condition brought about by Herbert Hoover himself when he agreed to put this scheme across for the benefit of the international German bankers who control this country through the Federal Reserve Board and the Federal reserve banks.

Last year there was some inquiry into the Federal Reserve Board and banks, and George L. Harrison, governor of the New York Federal Reserve Bank, was asked to state the amount of acceptances purchased by the Federal reserve banks in foreign countries. He was unwilling to answer in public. He was permitted to answer in secret. Why was that? It was because the Federal Reserve Board and banks are the duly appointed agents of the foreign central banks of issue and they are more concerned with their foreign customers than they are with the people of the United States. The only thing that is American about the Federal Reserve Board and banks is the money they use. The money is American but the contacts are European.

Who gave the Federal Reserve Board and banks the right to permit the German international bankers to loot this country and to take everything we had away from us? I say we will have an audit of these accounts and every Federal reserve bank and every director will be held liable for his acts in so far as he has been responsible for the exportation of American wealth to other countries and for the redistribution of wealth

239

which has taken place in this country.

Do you think the stock-market collapse was accidental or, as some wiseacres say, that the American people changed their minds overnight? It was not accidental. It was a carefully contrived occurrence, and it was a part of this same Hoover moratorium which was the first move of the drive to cancel debts. The international bankers sought to bring about a condition of financial despair and anarchy here so that they might emerge as the rulers of us all, and the next step they hope to take with Hoover's assistance is the establishment of a new kind of war finance corporation under the control of the notorious short seller, Bernard Baruch, or another of the same stripe. Then you will see fascism here instead of the Constitution of the United States; then you will see a dictator controlling industry and production as we now have a dictatorship controlling money and credit. Do you want that to happen? No? Then you had better watch the manner in which you are being led by Mr. Hoover with his explanations as to where his leadership is taking you and the other people of this country.

[Here the gavel fell.]

Mr. GREENWOOD. Mr. Chairman, I yield to the gentleman 15 additional minutes.

Mr. McFADDEN. I thank the gentleman.

Now, let us consider the Young law, which this moratorium will break for the benefit of Germany. After the war came the treaty of Versailles. Whether it was good or bad is beside the point. It was Germany who asked for an armistice. It was Germany who was defeated. The treaty is what saved Germany. But was Germany completely honorable in her observance of that treaty? She was not. The world re-echoed to her lamentations. Her propaganda kept up its work. When the Germans depreciated their currency they wiped out their internal debt. The losses in this country were enormous. So, too, were the losses in France.

At the present time the public debt of Germany is the least of the debts of the large European countries. By manipulation of her currency Germany freed herself of her internal debt. This is less than the other nations have to pay on their public debts. The other nations have already paid the internal public debt of Germany when they had their holdings of German currency wiped out by the manipulations of German bankers.

If Germany had sustained the burden of her own debt, as the Allies have done, and not obliterated it by inflation she would have had to raise 4,500,000,000 to 5,000,000,000 per annum in addition to her domestic expenditure. This would make it both just and practicable to add a provision in her budget which should bear some correspondence to the provision made in the Allies' budgets for their war expenditure.

Let us now consider the payments which are lawfully due from Germany under the Young law. Under this law Germany is required at the present time to pay a yearly annuity of 1,685,000,000 reichsmarks; of this amount France receives about half, or exactly 838,400,000 reichsmarks. This amount so payable to France divides into two classes: First, there is the conditional annual payment which amounts to 338,400,000 reichsmarks; secondly, there is the unconditional annual payment which amounts to 500,000,000 reichsmarks. The unconditional sum is subject to a heavy deduction for service of the amount already mobilized—Young bonds, and so forth. That amount is 44,500,000 reichsmarks. This leaves the unconditional amount for France at 455,500,000 only. Now, of this sum France has to take 80,000,000 reichsmarks and add it to the conditional amount in order to meet her payments to England and the United States. That leaves her an unconditional sum of 375,000,000 reichsmarks.

France receives no punitive damages under the Young law. The unconditional payments represent for France less than half of the interest on the sum she has had to expend for the reconstruction of the devastated regions. It seems not unreasonable, therefore, for the French to say that no arbiter and no court of international justice would tolerate such an indignity as the suppression or cancellation of these unconditional payments which are lawfully due to her. At this point

241

I wish to insert in the RECORD a copy of Annex I of the Young plan.

ANNEX I

Exchange of declaration between the Belgian, British, French, Italian, and Japanese Governments on the one hand, and the German Government on the other.

The representatives of the Belgian, British, French, Italian, and Japanese Governments make the following declaration:

Th new plan rests on the principle that the complete and final settlement of the reparation question is of common interest to all the countries which this question concerns, and that the plan requires the collaboration of all these countries. Without mutual good will and confidence the object of the plan would not be attained.

It is in this sense that the creditor Governments have, in The Hague agreement of January, 1930, accepted the solemn undertaking of the German Government to pay the annuities fixed in accordance with the provisions of the new plan as the guaranty for the fulfillment of the German Government's obligations. The creditor Governments are convinced that, even if the execution of the new plan should give rise to differences of opinion or difficulties, the procedures provided for by the plan itself would be sufficient to resolve them.

It is for this reason that The Hague agreement of January, 1930, provides that under the regime of the new plan the powers of the creditor powers shall be determined by the provisions of th plan.

There remains, however, a hypothesis outside the scope of the agreements signed to-day. The creditor governments are forced to consider it without thereby wishing to cast doubt on the intentions of the German Government. They regard it as indispensable to take account of the possibility that in the future a German government, in violation of the solemn obligation contained in The Hague agreement of January, 1930, might commit itself to actions revealing its determination to destroy the new plan.

It is the duty of the creditor governments to declare to the

German Government that if such a case arose, imperiling the foundations of their common work, a new situation would be created in regard to which the creditor governments must, from the outset, formulate all the reservations to which they are rightfully entitled.

However, even on this extreme hypothesis, the creditor governments, in the interests of general peace, are prepared, before taking any action, to appeal to an international jurisdiction of incontestable authority to establish and appreciate the facts. The creditor power or powers which might regard themselves as concerned would therefore submit to the Permanent Court of International Justice the question whether the German Government had committed acts revealing its determination to destroy the new plan.

Germany should forthwith declare that, in the event of an affirmative decision by the court, she acknowledges that it is legitimate that in order to insure the fulfillment of the obligations of the debtor power resulting from the new plan, the creditor power or powers should resume their full liberty of action.

The creditor governments are convinced that such a hypothetical situation will never in fact arise, and they feel assured that the German Government shares this conviction. But they consider that they are bound in loyalty and by their duty to their respective countries to make the above declaration in case this hypothetical situation should arise.

The representatives of the German Government, on their side, make the following declaration:

The German Government takes note of the above declaration of the creditor governments whereby even if the execution of the new plan should give rise to differences of opinion or difficulties in regard to the fulfillment of the new plan, the procedures provided for in the plan would be sufficient to resolve them.

The German Government take note accordingly that under the regime of the new plan the powers of the creditor powers will be determined in accordance with the provisions of the plan.

As regards the second part of the declaration and the hypothesis formulated in this declaration, the German Government regrets that such an eventuality, which for its part it regards as impossible, should be contemplated.

Nevertheless, if one or more of the creditor powers refer to the Permanent Court of International Justice the question whether acts originating with the German Government reveal its determination to destroy the new plan, the German Government, in agreement with the creditor governments, accepts the proposal that the Permanent Court should decide the question, and declares that it acknowledges that it is legitimate, in the event of an affirmative decision by the court, that in order to insure the fulfillment of the financial obligations of the debtor power resulting from the new plan the creditor power or powers should resume their full liberty of action.

The French, German, and English texts of the present annex are equally authoritative.

CURTIS.	PAUL HYMANS.	A. MOSCONI.
WIRTH.	E. FRANCQUI.	A. PIRELLI.
SCHMIDT.	PHILIP SNOWDEN.	SUVICH.
MOLDENHAUER.	HENRY CHERON.	ADATCI.
HENRY JASPAR.	LOUCHEUR.	K. HIROTA.

As you see, under the Young law, the French, acting singly or with others of the following powers—that is, British, Belgian, Italian, Japanese—can appeal to the Permanent Court of International Justice, where, upon a showing that Germany had committed itself to actions revealing its determination to destroy the Young plan, the French and other nations would, by a decree in their favor, have full liberty of action restored to them. Of course, Germany was guilty of those actions by using the President of the United States as an agent instead of acting for herself, according to the procedure laid down in the Young law, which procedure was binding upon her. After the visit of Premier Laval to this country President Hoover agreed that whatever is done must take place within the structure and provisions of the Young law, consequently there is no use in hoping for the Hoover moratorium now. It is a dead letter. It will do nobody any good and it will do the United States a great deal of harm.

In discussing this matter in the French Parliament, Premier Laval said:

> But, given the nature of the engagements, freely accepted and quite recently subscribed to, of the Young plan, the solemnity with which the definitive and unalterable character of the unconditional annuities by which the necessary permanence of the principle of reparations is expressed was recognized, there would be great risk of unsetting confidence in the value of signatures and of contracts and thus to go against the end aimed at if, in the proposed suspension of payments, the unalterable annuity were treated like the conditional annuity.

XIII

WAR DEBTS AND REPARATIONS

THE HOOVER MORATORIUM

December 18, 1931

Mr. McFadden. Mr. Chairman, ladies and gentleman of the committee, I observe by articles appearing in the public press of yesterday afternoon and this morning, published quite generally in the newspapers throughout the country, that I have been singled out as a victim of punitive measures to be administered to me by my Republican colleagues of Pennsylvania in the House and Senate of the United States.

I have serious objection to being tried in this ex parte manner and having an ex parte judgment rendered against me by this self-constituted board of inquiry concerning utterances made by me on the floor of this House. Whatever I said on the floor of the House upon any subject, I said in the performance of what I conceive to be my full duty in giving to the Members of the House such information as I had concerning matters then pending before the House, in order that they might have the same opportunity of considering and weighing the evidence that I had before voting upon such measures.

I submitted documents and was prepared to submit further documents were I permitted, but, unfortunately, on account of the insistence of the time restrictions I could not submit the other documents, all of which were of evidential value in determining the weight to be accredited to any remarks I was then making.

I was appearing in the performance of my official duty, as it is the duty of every Member in this House to give such information as he may have acquired to the House on any matter pending before the House that he believes will be to the best interests of his constituents and his country.

The truth of the allegations made by me in the speech that I made on the floor of this House seems to be the subject of inquiry of this cabal of my State associates in the Congress of the United State. If in the wisdom of this House, they desire to further consider this matter, I shall hold myself in readiness to furnish such additional information as I may have to offer, supplementary thereto, and all referred to therein.

Now, I want to discuss for a moment some phases of the bill that is now before us. I appeared before the Ways and Means Committee the other day and pointed out two or three things in connection with this bill. I have repeatedly been calling the attention of the Members here to one phase of this particular bill which, it seems to me, it is important for us to consider. I refer now to the fact that the ratification of this moratorium affects seriously the Young plan, in that it opens up the debt question.

I would also like to call the attention of the House to the fact that after the moratorium declaration, France, after several days of consideration, objected to that declaration and refused to concur. France finally entered into an agreement known as the Franco-American agreement, in which France changed completely the question of the moratorium. The subsequent visit to this country of Premier Laval, of France, brought back the Young plan into operation, which had been seriously affected by the moratorium, and France was assured, as a result of the Laval conference, if we can believe the reports of the French House of Deputies, that the United States was willing that France should deal with Germany.

Now, I want to call the particular attention of the House to the fact that the Franco-American agreement was an additional agreement, and I want to again call to the attention of the House, as I did to the Ways and Means Committee, the London protocol, and I want to state to you men here, many of you are lawyers—I am not—that there is a treaty involved in this transaction, and it is a matter for the United States Senate to handle.

There are conditions set forth in that treaty which have to do with international finance. There are matters in that treaty which affect international finance seriously.

I also want to call your attention to the fact that in the Young plan there were provisions set up whereby Germany was given a course to pursue in case she found herself unable to pay. The machinery was set up and was completely set up, so that if Germany found she could not pay her course was clear, and that course was that she should apply to the Bank for International Settlements for relief.

For some reason or other Germany did not see fit to operate under the Young plan. I have just been wondering, from the reports that are emanating from Basle, Switzerland, and Berlin in the last few days, referred to by the gentleman from Mississippi [Mr. RANKIN] and published in all the papers, where, under the terms of the Young plan, under which Germany is now operating, and you must understand in this connection that Germany is operating under the Young plan and not under the Hoover moratorium. Germany was given, since the the Hoover-Laval conference, the right to a 2-year moratorium by asking for it, under the Young plan, through the Bank for International Settlements. The Bank for International Settlements was directed to operate under the Young plan and set up a committee to study Germany's capacity to pay; but, as I say, for some reason they did not want to do this.

Now, as a result of what has happened since the Hoover-Laval conference, Germany has been told, not only by France but by the international bankers of New York, speaking for financial America, that they expected her to ask for a moratorium under the Young plan, as France was asking.

This committee has been working, and alongside the committee has been a committee representing the international bankers who have been responsible for the flotation in the United States of probably between seven and eight billion dollars' worth of German bonds and what is now known to be two billion and a half dollars of acceptance credits.

Why did Germany refrain from acting under the moratorium clause until she was forced to do so after the Hoover-Laval conference? It seems to me that these financial and economic committees which have been investigating her capacity to pay have discovered the reason why Germany did not operate under the Young plan. They would know that Germany was holding out. We have proof of that by the Wiggin report of last summer, which estimated $1,250,000,000 of acceptance credit, which was underestimated by 50 per cent.

The Germans apparently wanted to operate under some plan where their financial situation would not be gone into so carefully. The Wiggin report must have accepted the Reich's figures without a careful check.

The present committee, composed and dominated largely by England and France, have been watching the financial operations of Germany closely. They are in a position to understand the peculiar make-up of the minds of their neighbors.

I have referred to the fact that there was nothing new or pressing about this particular moratorium. I have pointed out the fact that it was known in the United States as long ago as the fall of 1930.

In that connection I want to call attention to a visit in the United States of a very important German, and I want to refer to an article which is reported in the *Baltimore Sun*—all the papers at that time had this—under date of October 20, 1930.

This article is written by Drew Pearson, the Washington Bureau, *Baltimore Sun*. It says:

Moratorium on Allied Debts to United States Unofficially Studied—New York Federal Reserve Bank Head Drafting Tentative Plan in View of Possibility Germany May Default on Reparations

Dr. Hjalmar Schacht, the man who stabilized the German mark, has placed an extremely frank and extremely gloomy picture of Germany's economic plight before the highest officials of the Hoover administration during the week-end.

Coincident with this it was learned to-day that George Harrison, governor of the Federal Reserve Bank of New York, has been working on tentative plans for a moratorium on allied debt payments to the United States in case Germany declares a moratorium on her Young plan payments to the Allies.

Mr. Harrison was in the Capital yesterday and to-day and had luncheon yesterday with Doctor Schacht at the home of the Secretary of State Stimson.

SUGGESTED DEBT REVISION

Because of this fact Germany made informal suggestions to Great Britain as early as last summer that a compaign be started for the scaling down of allied debt payments to the United States.

The officials with whom Doctor Schacht conferred over the weekend included President Hoover, whom he saw this morning; Secretary of the Treasury Mellon, whom he saw both yesterday and to-day; Eugene Meyer, chairman of the Federal Reserve Board; Joseph P. Cotton, Under Secretary of State; George Harrison; and Secretary of State Stimson.

In his conversations with some of these Doctor Schacht went into the German situation very thoroughly and was extremely frank.

I want to point out to you and call to your attention the fact that the ratification of the moratorium opens up the debt-settlement plan. The position of this administration has been reiterated by very high authorities that there was no connection between the war debts and reparations.

In the remarks I made the other day I referred to an editorial appearing in the Hearst papers to the effect that a plan had been submitted to Mr. Hearst in the fall of 1930.

Mr. RANKIN. What is the date of the paper that the gentleman is reading from?

Mr. McFADDEN. October 20, 1930.

Mr. BEEDY. A plan for what?

Mr. McFADDEN. A plan for the moratorium, as I just stated, reading from the article.

Mr. BEEDY. But the article does not so state. As the gentleman quoted it, it was a plan for debt revision.

Mr. McFADDEN. I shall put the article in the RECORD so that it can be seen for itself.

Mr. BEEDY. The gentleman inserted it in his original speech, and I called attention to it in my reply, and the gentleman will find that the language of the article stated that the plan submitted at that time was for debt revision and the word "moratorium" was not used.

Mr. McFADDEN. I have other articles here where the word "moratorium" was used. I think it is immaterial here, and I think the gentleman will appreciate that fact before I finish.

Mr. RANKIN. And Congress was in session after that.

Mr. McFADDEN. Oh, yes; Congress was in session until the 4th of March, 1931.

Mr. RANKIN. And it was never brought to the attention of Congress by the Executive.

Mr. McFADDEN. It was not at that time. I have several articles here covering the question of Dr. Hjalmar Schacht. In respect to Doctor Schacht's visit, I might say that I was advised of his contemplated arrival and purpose. I was told that Doctor Schacht, because of some activities of mine in connection with war debts and reparations and some speeches that I had made, desired to see me in regard to the question of a moratorium.

251

A friend of his came to me and asked me if I would see him. He apparently obtained my views as regards this particular matter and I did not have the pleasure of seeing Doctor Schacht on his visit here.

I want now to call attention to the correspondence appearing in the *Washington Herald* of December 17, 1931, being a copy of a letter addressed by Jules Bache, of the firm of J. S. Bache & Co., members of the New York Stock Exchange, of New York City, which firm is probably the second largest stock-exchange house in the city of New York. The letter is dated November 6, 1930. Note the dates in regard to Doctor Schacht's visit, which I have just referred to here, and this letter. Permit me to say also that Mr. Bache, besides being a member of the stock exchange, is an international financier, closely associated with the group of international financiers who have floated these large issues of German securities in the United States. His letter addressed to Mr. Hearst is as follows:

LETTER FROM MR. BACHE TO MR. HEARST

42 BROADWAY, NEW YORK, OCTOBER 21, 1930.

WILLIAM RANDOLPH HEARST, ESQ.

SAN SIMEON RANCH, CALIF.

My Dear Mr. Hearst: Some time ago at the request of some friends I drew up a memorandum of some views in regard to German reparations—which are not novel—with a view that an intensive campaign would be necessary in this country in order to influence the Washington atmosphere and educate the man in the street, realizing that any such ideas if fostered by Wall Street interests would be thought to be based on a desire of the banking interests to make their loans in Germany better and would prejudice political thought.

There is no such idea in my mind, but I am guided entirely by a desire to help the general depressed situation. I do not know whether your ideas coincide with mine, but I can not conceive of any better way of awakening public interest in this country in any such movement, as I am recommending, than to have it supported by the Hearst publications.

In addressing you I am reminded of the magnificent manner in which you took up the idea of the sales tax when I first discussed it with you, and I am wondering whether you are sufficiently interested in this subject to seriously consider the idea of having your publications lead in this matter.

Any such move by the United States can not help but elicit an enthusiastic reception by the nations interested, and while on the face of the proposition, it would appear as though we were making a present of part of our legitimate war loans, I am convinced that we are never going to be able to collect all of these war loans, and in fact I am inclined to think that we are likely to get a great deal more of our money back by this method than in any other way.

Asking your indulgence for this communication, and with cordial greetings, believe me

Very sincerely,

Jules S. Bache.

INCLOSURE IN MR. BACHE'S LETTER

October 1, 1930.

It seems to me that the United States has in its power by prompt action to change the entire current of sentiment throughout the world and that practically no cost to itself, but with the possibility of enormous indirect gain in the benefit that will accrue to the income of its citizens and its business community, by lifting the cloud of depression now weighing so heavily on the business world.

Doctor Schacht, since his arrival in this country, has been outspoken in expressing his unofficial opinion that it is only a question of time when Germany will be compelled to ask the Allies for a moratorium on its reparations payments. Any economist who will carefully review the situation and inform himself of the condition of German finances, will concur with Doctor Schacht. In fact, figures show that Germany has never paid any reparations in excess of the actual money loaned to it by other nations.

It has no resources of its own out of which to pay these reparations, which in the final analysis can only be paid out of an export balance, which Germany has not yet acquired to any extent.

The day that Germany ceases the payment of reparations the Allies, with the exception of England, which have contracts under the war loans to pay money to the United States will cease payment under those contracts, and we have no way to enforce payment thereunder. It seems, therefore, patent that beyond the English payments we have little to hope for from the German reparations once payment stops. It is unlikely that France will endeavor to compel payment by force, since a renewed invasion of Germany by French troops would so demoralize the German situation as to make payments still more hopeless.

I have, therefore, arrived at the conclusion that if the United States were promptly to call a conference of the Allies represented in Paris when the Young plan was evolved and offer to its debtors, including England, to reduce their payments in proportion to each of their debtor's share in the conditional payments contemplated by the Young plan, on condition that these debtors cancel those conditional payments, the very fact that Germany would thus be relieved of one-third of the amount fixed as indemnity under the Young plan would so improve the morale of the German nation, as well as its credit, that it would make it quite probable that the unconditional payments could be made, and the United States would thus recover far more from these war loans than under present conditions it is ever likely to receive.

The effect of the announcement of such a program would be so inspiring as to immediately dissipate the heavy clouds hanging over the financial future of the world. In fact, it would bring moneys to the United States which personally I am convinced it would otherwise never receive. It would so immeasurably improve the standing of the United States in the community of nations that such action by us would become an asset and remove a liability.

The unconditional payments agreed upon in the Young plan are $163,000,000. The conditional payments amounted to $314,800,000. It is these latter, which at best will never be collected, which I am asking the United States to lose.

I appreciate that politically this program is seemingly impossible of fruition. So did the repeal of the Volstead Act appear less than 12 months ago. There is only one way by which such a program could become successful. It would be by the formation of a group of great industrialists, if possible headed by Mr. Owen D. Young, the expenses of which everyone would gladly contribute, to educate the voting public of the United States into a realization that at best the man in the street has little interest in the sums which the United States might recover from these German indemnities.

　　　*　　*　　*　　*　　*　　*　　*

Right there I desire to call the attention of the House to the close relationship which big business not only in the United States but big business in Germany has; how closely it is related to the international financial group, which I am referring to in this debate. [Continuing reading:]

Since the great mass of the people do not pay taxes, whereas every factor in our community is interested in securing a better price for what he has to sell, whether commodity or labor, which would surely result in the improvement of the world's status. This movement must come from the great industrialists, whose following can be counted in the number of voters they employ.

This is a very practical letter to the Members of Congress as to how legislation is promoted by the interests that want to put something across. [Continuing reading:]

It can not come from the bankers, who would be accused of trying to make their loans good. It is a movement worthy of great leaders. Once started, it is bound to succeed.

I want to call attention to the fact that the international banking group, and this big international industrial group, have been carrying on a campaign intensively for the purpose of reducing and canceling these debts.

The announcement of the formation of such a committee would immediately start to improve world sentiment.

I am not going to read Mr. Hearst's reply, but I will ask unanimous consent that it be inserted in the RECORD at this point.

The CHAIRMAN. Is there objection to the request of the gentleman from Pennsylvania?

There was no objection.

The matter referred to is as follows:

LETTER TO MR. BACHE FROM MR. HEARST

NOVEMBER 6, 1930.

My Dear Mr. Bache: I advocated the sales tax because I believe in it. I can not advocate your present plan of the United States cancelling any more of the debts of the Allies for the simple reason that I do not believe in the plan.

I think the United States has already canceled too much of the debts owed to us by the Allies. My plan would be to insist upon the Allies paying their obligations and to deprive any country that would not pay its obligations of the favored-nations privileges.

I quite agree with you that politically your program is impossible of fruition, but I do not see any analogy between your plan of cancelling the debts of the Allies to the United States and the repeal of the Volstead Act.

The repeal of the Volstead Act did not seem at all impossible of accomplishment to those of us who were advocating the repeal. We felt that it ought to be accomplished, could be accomplished, and would be accomplished.

In regard to the further canceling of the debts to America by the Allies, about nine-tenths of the people of the United States feel that a proposition of that kind as an American measure can not be accomplished, should not be accomplished, and will not be accomplished.

I think the same banking policy should be followed toward nations as is followed toward individuals; and from what I know of banks and bankers, they do not as a rule cancel their loans to people who are able to pay, but unwilling to pay. The Allies are able to pay the United States and are merely unwilling to pay.

The ability of the Allies to pay does not depend on the German indemnity. The German indemnity should of course be reduced by the Allies, but not by us, who have neither received nor demanded indemnity from Germany.

Moreover, the territorial question is just as important as the financial question in dealing with the iniquities of the Versailles treaty—more important in fact. The plan of France was to crush Germany by dismemberment as well as by an impossible indemnity.

If America gets into the question of rectifying the iniquities and injustices of the Versailles treaty, we are likely to get into a vast amount of trouble and probably be involved in the war, which is almost sure to come as a result of that treaty.

My opinion, Mr. Bache, is that we are out of those complications and ought to stay out. We have asked for no direct indemnity from Germany. We have asked for only part payment of the debts which the Allies owe us.

The whole situation has been settled on this basis and the only advantage that we get out of the situation is that it has been settled.

I not only do not intend to advocate any further reductions in the debts the Allies owe this country but I will certainly vigorously oppose any such proposal.

Of course you realize perfectly that there is nothing per-

sonal in my attitude. I would be very pleased to do anything to oblige you if it did not involve a principle which I can not compromise.

Sincerely,

W. R. HEARST.

Mr. McFADDEN. I also want to call the attention of the House at this time to the struggle of these committees—the bankers' committee and the Young committee—that are dealing with Germany's capacity to pay. I want to make as clear as I can to you the fact that these international bankers are asking priority over the reparation debts which are owed to the Allies, principally to France. I also want to emphasize the fact that the Germans have agreed with these international bankers to give them a preference on their private debts. I want to also call attention to the fact that between the time Mr. Wiggin came back from abroad, in which he made his first report, that he and his New York committee of bankers have been very active in promoting a proper settlement that would inure to the benefit and protection of these private debts. They have evidenced interest, and they are on record in favor of the reduction and cancellation of German reparation obligations.

I want to call your attention to a statement that was left with the State Department on December 10. I am quoting now from the *Financial Chronicle* of New York under date of December 12, 1931. This article appears at page 3891, and the heading is as follows:

FRENCH GOVERNMENT'S MEMORANDUM TO STATE DEPARTMENT ON REPARATIONS

Associated Press dispatches from Washington on December 10 reported that the French Government had formally notified the United States of its position that reparations revision must be accompanied by a comparative scaling down on war debts.

The dispatch added: "Ambassador Claudel, of France, on instructions of the Paris Government, notified Secretary Stimson of the French attitude."

258

[Here the gavel fell.]

Mr. SANDERS of Texas. I yield to the gentleman from Pennsylvania [Mr. MCFADDEN] 10 additional minutes.

Mr. MCFADDEN (reading):

It was understood that French commissions in other interested countries were also instructed to advise nations to which they were accredited of the French position.

In th *New York Tribune*, under the same date, December 10, 1931, appears the following:

William R. Castle, Jr., Under Secretary of State, confirmed to-day the report that Paul Claudel, French ambassador, transmitted the views of the French Government on reparations to Henry L. Stimson, Secretary of State, yesterday. Mr. Claudel explained these views orally and then left a memorandum summarizing his conservation.

Later on it says:

Mr. Castle said he had read of the suggestion of J. Ramsay MacDonald, British Prime Minister, for a conference on economic conditions;

And it was informally placed before him.

It also says:

The French Government also advanced the view that any readjustment of reparations would have to be accompanied by a general rearrangement of the intergovernmental debts, which means the war debts owed to the United States.

I want to call your attention to a clause in the Young plan, inserted by France, not agreed to by the United States, but notice of which was given to the United States at the time of th signing of the Young plan. This stipulation provided, not in these words, but in substance to the effect that any lowering of German reparations payments would result in a like reduction of the debts owed to the United States by France. This is the reaffirmation on December 10, which the French Republic has served through their minister on the State Department of the United States.

Yesterday, when this came to my attention, I took occasion to call Mr. William R. Castle, Jr., of the State Dpeartment, on the telephone, and I read to him extracts of this article, and I asked him whether or not Mr. Claudel, on behalf of the French Republic, had left that notice with the State Department. He told me they had. I said, "Did Mr. Stimson, in his appearance before the Ways and Means Committee, present that information?" He said,, "No." I said, "Why not?" He told me that it was a communication from a foreign government, and we had no right to present it. I called on my colleague, the chairman of the Ways and Means Committee, then in executive session, and repeated to him what I have repeated to you here, and with all of the emphasis that I possessed, I insisted that they call Mr. Castle in executive session and get that statement.

I do not know whether they got it or not. I hope they did and I hope they gave proper and careful consideration to it, because that is their position.

I want to repeat in closing that when this moratorium is passed you are changing the Young plan. You are reversing the former opinion of all the administrations that have dealt with this debt plan, and you are opening up to a future conference the question of governmental debts owed the United States as well as reparations.

Mr. BEEDY. Will the gentleman yield to a question for information?

Mr. McFADDEN. Yes.

Mr. BEEDY. The gentleman has been discussing the question of debt revision or the cancellation of debts, which is one issue. Now, do I understand that the gentleman is opposed to the proposed moratorium, namely, the delay of a year in the payment of war debts? Am I correct in my understanding?

Mr. McFADDEN. I am opposed to this moratorium because it opens up the whole question of war debts and reparations.

Mr. Beedy. That is the gentleman's opinion, but the gentleman is opposed to a moratorium for a year and he has been consistent in that attitude, has he not?

Mr. McFadden. Because of the fact that Germany had a legal method under international law, which for some reason she saw fit not to exercise but which she has been forced to exercise now, and the committees are finding out the condition of Germany, and I am beginning to believe that we should not be aiding Germany in avoiding the just obligations she has entered into under an international agreement. [Applause.]

Mr. Beedy. And in the gentleman's opposition to a moratorium he stands to-day just where he has stood for two years; is that true?

Mr. McFadden. Oh, no.

Mr. Beedy. Has the gentleman changed his mind about it?

Mr. McFadden. I have learned a lot in two years. I have learned a lot in the last two weeks and I am learning every day.

Mr. Beedy. Has the gentleman changed his mind about the desirability of a moratorium at any time?

Mr. McFadden. I think I have answered the gentleman on that. I am opposed to a moratorium, if the gentleman wants to know; yes.

Mr. Beedy. Has the gentleman been opposed to it consistently?

Mr. Stafford. Will the gentleman yield?

Mr. McFadden. Yes.

Mr. Beedy. The gentleman yielded to me, and I think I am entitled to an answer.

Mr. McFadden. I said I have learned a lot about this in the last two or three weeks. I suppose the gentleman is referring to an interview which perhaps I gave out some time ago in New York.

Mr. Beedy. A year ago the gentleman announced that he favored a moratorium.

Mr. McFadden. But conditions have completely changed.

Mr. Beedy. How?

Mr. McFadden. I have been reciting to you what kind of

261

methods have been taken to bring about this moratorium, and I have learned more than I knew a year ago about this whole subject.

Mr. BEEDY. Are we not in more dire straits, Germany included, than we were in the fall of 1930?

Mr. McFADDEN. I think it is due largely to our intermeddling in this whole international situation. [Applause.] And let me say this: That this means also that we are going to be called into conference at a round table, on one side of which will sit Uncle Sam and on the other side of the table are going to sit the countries who owe us, and they are determined that these debts shall be reduced or cancelled. It means this: That these international bankers in order to protect their situation—and we have evidence of it in all the reports that come along—are planning now to organize international financial institutions comparable to those which are being organized or proposed to be organized here, for the purpose of taking bad debts out of one pocket and putting them into another, and then tying them up with a blue ribbon and selling them to the innocent public as something else when, as a matter of fact, they are nothing but bad debts.

Now, I say the quicker we get out of Europe and attend to the economic and financial conditions of this country, the better. I say, also, that the finest and best thing that can be said by this Congress would be to serve notice on these international bankers, that they must turn their backs on Europe and come back here and help us out of this disastrous economic and financial condition which they have brought about. [Applause.] I would also challenge the great industrial leaders of this country, like Owen D. Young and the heads of other big industrial institutions much in the same manner. I would say, "Gentlemen, we have confidence in your ability and your integrity, but you have been paying too much attention to international operations. You have brought about great unemployment in the United States; you have upset the whole economic condition of your country. Come back here and attend to the business of this country, in which you are engaged as leaders, and the Congress of the United States will support you to the limit, but when, by your actions and your operations, and through the sale of your securities, and through the use of the credit of the Federal reserve system you are depriving our people of their savings, their funds, and their right to do business, you are wrong."

Why, gentlemen, you would not stand for it one moment if you knew that international trade transactions were using the credit of the Federal reserve system at current, prevailing Federal reserve rates, when the people of the United States can not get access to the Federal reserve system at anything but exceptionally high rates. I say it is time we began to inventory the situation and find out where we are going.

Gentlemen, I have no sinister motives in what I am trying to do. What I am trying to do here is to do that which is best for the American people. [Applause.] Anyone who challenges that right I defy.

Mr. GOLDER. Will the gentleman yield?

[Here the gavel fell.]

Mr. SANDERS of Texas. I yield the gentleman from Pennsylvania 10 additional minutes.

Mr. McFADDEN. I yield to the gentleman from Pennsylvania.

Mr. GOLDER. I desire to make a statement in justice to the the gentleman from Pennsylvania [Mr. McFADDEN]. The newspapers have carried a story to the effect that the gentleman from Pennsylvania has been repudiated by his colleagues from that State. I desire to state that while the gentleman's colleagues from Pennsylvania have disagreed with the expressions of our colleague relating to the President of the United States, I believe there is not a member of our delegation who has the affection or the respect of his colleagues to a greater extent than my colleague from Pennsylvania [Mr. McFADDEN].

Mr. SANDERS of Texas. Mr. Chairman, I make the point of order I yielded to the gentleman from Pennsylvania [Mr. McFADDEN].

Mr. GOLDER. The gentleman from Pennsylvania yielded to me, and I felt, in justice to him, that it ought to be understood by his other colleagues in this House that I, at least, as his colleague from Pennsylvania, have the same regard and respect for his ability and his courage that I had three days ago, though disagreeing entirely with his references to our President. [Applause.]

Mr. McFadden. Gentlemen, I have been seriously criticized here, and, in addition to what I have already said, I have heard the lip-to-ear conversation that has been going on around this House. I have heard all kinds of stories issued for the purpose of discrediting me. I am not on trial here, gentlemen. I am ready to answer any questions, and I am surprised that my colleagues here would listen, without even discussing these matters with me in order to get the facts. It is regrettable.

Mr. Stafford. Will the gentleman yield?

Mr. McFadden. I yield.

Mr. Stafford. The gentleman in his speech stresses the fact that Germany did not apply for a moratorium, under the Young plan, as it might have done. I wish to ask the gentleman whether or not under the terms of her agreement Germany could only ask for a moratorium of the conditional payments and not the unconditional payments, and is it not a fact that France refused to accede to the position of the President in granting a complete moratorium, and that prevented, as a psychological matter, a revival of business in general?

Mr. McFadden. My answer to the question is this: Since the visit of the French premier to Washington, Germany has gone under the Young plan and has asked for this relief as the right and proper and orderly way to proceed.

Mr. Stafford. But under the Young plan——

Mr. McFadden. I do not yield any further. I think I have answered the question.

XIV

WAR DEBTS AND REPARATIONS

THE HOOVER MORATORIUM

Radio Address of Hon. Louis T. McFadden

January 6, 1932

IN DEBATE WITH NORMAN THOMAS, OVER STATION WOR, DECEMBER 27, 1931

Mr. Woodruff. Mr. Speaker, under the leave to extend my remarks in the Record, I include the following remarks of Hon. Louis T. McFadden, in debate with Norman Thomas on the subject of the moratorium, over station WOR Sunday afternoon, December 27, 1931, between 3 and 3:45 o'clock:

As a text for this discussion, I desire to quote from an eminent authority, Calvin Coolidge, who, on October 22, 1930, said:

"Those who are constantly agitating, either for political or publicity purposes, for a revision of German reparations, and who are trying to connect them with the European debts owed the United States, are doing distinct injury to the world economic situation. They arouse new uncertainties and inflame old animosities. We should regard these questions as settled. Let Europe adjust its own difficulties. The present rates of payment can be met by all countries concerned.

265

"Those saying that if Germany defaults reparations other countries can not pay the United States' debts are overreaching themselves. That means that if reparations are not collected from Germany they must be collected from the taxpayers of the United States."

The principles of a republic are those of liberalism, and it fosters the spirit of equal justice among its citizens and of fair dealing with foreign states. Throughout our own history public opinion has manifested its sympathy with the growth of liberal institutions abroad and with foreign causes which appeal primarily to the principle of justice.

In formulating national policy, therefore, when a new question rises in our relation to foreign states public opinion here is not inclined to override the promptings of calm and fair judgment and act hastily in an arbitrary spirit of self-interest. The public judgment at times may be at fault because of insufficient information, but the fault is more likely to arise from this cause than from a deliberate intention to ignore standards of right conduct.

The war in Europe left us a legacy of complicated international questions, and because of their complications there has been much diversity of opinion as to their proper solution. Public opinion has given much attention to them and has been patient and conscientious in its desire to formulate a judgment.

We have heard all that our former allies have had to say about the war debts which they owe us and about the German war reparations. We have been urged as a duty to join the League of Nations and the World Court. Voices from Europe and voices here have urged us as a duty to cancel the allied debts and to forsake the principle of political isolation which they tell us is an ignoble and selfish one.

For some years after the war the situation was so confused that it was impossible for public opinion to reach a judgment. But 13 years have passed now since the war ended, and things have transpired both here and in Europe that tend to simplify the problem.

We know that when the allied war debts were funded we

canceled more than half of the amount of those debts. We know that we took no share in the reparations exacted from Germany, and that there is no logical reason why we should have any concern with them to-day. We know, too, that the German reparations have been a cause of frightful disorganization in Europe ever since the war and that the Allied Governments have persistently sought to make the payment of their debts to us dependent upon the receipt by them of reparations from Germany. We are conscious of a strong determination in Europe to involve us intimately in the interminable controversies which convulse that continent. Just as long as Europe can keep us in these international conferences on war debts, reparations, and all world affairs, just that long has she hopes of involving us in the League of Nations, the World Court, and the world bank—all instruments concocted to take away our freedom in Government and finance.

We know that in the normal prosecution of our domestic and foreign commerce we prospered after the war and that in 1924 the country was in a sound condition financially and industrially. There was nothing in our domestic condition that menaced or threatened this prosperity. But in little more than five years thereafter our financial and industrial structure was shaken to its foundations, chiefly because of the dislocations caused by the enormous loans made to Europe on a scale far beyond Europe's capacity to repay.

We are told that we must postpone or cancel payments on our foreign debt to restore our export trade. In other words, if we give our foreign customers money with which to purchase merchandise they may buy it from us.

In the 10 years ending with 1929 our total of exports to all countries was $49,609,677,114. In the same period our total of money sent abroad was over $60,000,000,000, including foreign loans, investments, debt-funding settlements, gifts, ocean freight bills, travel expenses, and foreign remittances. Exports for the war period were more than covered by our direct war expenditures, which last was also a contribution to foreign interests.

We, ourselves, paid for every dollar of merchandise sold abroad by exporting money which we are now told is never coming back to us. This economic absurdity finally collapsed under its own weight; our alleged "prosperity" ruined us. We can not afford to restore a foreign trade in which we pay for our exports as well as for our imports.

"Hands across the sea" are always palm up when westbound.

We realize now that, far from having followed a policy of isolation, we have to a great extent made Europe's problems our own and in doing so have sacrificed our own interests and imposed unjustified burdens upon our own people. To do more than we have already done would endanger our present safety and jeopardize the Nation's future.

The only good thing about the joint resolution authorizing the Hoover debt moratorium was the amendment which expressed the will of the Congress that there shall be no reduction or cancellation by the United States Government of the debts owed the United States by the foreign countries.

Apart entirely from the international debt question, the method by which the matter was put before the Congress for action sets a dangerous precedent in the negotiation of agreements with foreign governments. If, when Congress is not in session, a President can call in congressional leaders, or even communicate with a majority of the Members of both Houses, telling them that a certain proposed agreement with foreign governments is desirable and urgent, and upon these representations can obtain their promises to ratify it when it is later presented to the Congress in session, the independent power of the Congress under the Constitution is virtually destroyed. I will here and now venture the definite opinion based upon the discussion and expressions of the Members of both Houses of Congress during the consideration last week of the Hoover moratorium that if they had not been pledged last June they would have voted against ratification of the Hoover moratorium.

In the first place, the President is enabled to assure the foreign governments that the Congress will ratify what he does and this places the Congressmen in an embarrassing position if they subsequently see reasons why ratification should be withheld. The finished product may bear a different aspect from that which it first presented, but, conceiving themselves bound by their promises, the legislators may find themselves unable to reconsider their position and, against their better judgment, will vote for ratification.

This is as true with reference to treaties which come only before the United States Senate for ratification, as for agreements affecting revenue, like this one, which must come before both Houses of the Congress.

In this case the information contained in the executive message asking for ratification was entirely inadequate and misleading. It asked for the ratification of an agreement proposed on June 20 last, for which a certain number of Senators and Representatives had promised approval.

But the agreement of June 20 had, in fact, been materially changed by a subsequent agreement made with France on July 6. Several nations which had immediately ratified the agreement of June 20 had to reconsider their action, and on August 11 they met in London and signed a protocol binding themselves to the terms of the American agreement with France and making Germany a party to it also.

Yet the Executive message on the 10th of December asked for ratification of the moratorium proposed on June 20 and said not a word about the subsequent changes.

The report of the Ways and Means Committee to the House stated that the Franco-American agreement and the London protocol had been before the committee when considering its report. How these documents came before the committee I do not know; they did not accompany the message of the President, and they were never at any time presented to the House itself for its consideration. They together contained the real moratorium agreement, and they ought to have been submitted formally to the Congress.

The whole thing was done in a loose and inadequate manner which showed small regard for the dignity of the Congress and which was a blow to the treaty-making processes of the Constitution.

The general impression, both in and out of Congress, appears to be that Congress has ratified an agreement for the temporary suspension of payments of all war debts and reparations as proposed on June 20 last, the subsequent changes being of only minor importance. This impression is erroneous.

The Franco-American agreement of July 6 excepts the unconditional annuities from the operation of the moratorium; it leaves them in full force, and it rivets them more firmly upon Germany by reason of the agreement of the United States with France that they must be paid. Moreover, when a little later Germany was made a party to this agreement by the London protocol, instead of lessening the amount of the reparations which Germany must pay unconditionally, it increased that amount, because it provided that the conditional annuities suspended for one year are to be funded over a 10-year period and that these payments must then be met unconditionally.

Under the Franco-American agreement the amount that Germany must pay annually without the right of postponement is a larger sum than if the Franco-American agreement had not been made. The moratorium has not lightened the absolute burdens of Germany; it has made them heavier.

If there was any merit at all in the original proposal of June 20, that all payments between governments be temporarily suspended, it would have consisted in holding the critical situation in suspense long enough to give the European governments time to agree upon mutual concessions. But the original proposal was entirely discarded, and under French insistence the absolute obligations of Germeny were made harder and more rigid. It can not be said, therefore, that the final agreement has improved conditions in Europe.

It is claimed that the proposal of June 20 prevented a financial collapse in Germany which would have been catastrophic in its influences elsewhere. This was what it was intended to do, but did not accomplish. To accomplish this, immediate ratification by France, as well as by the other nations, would have been necessary.

But it will be recalled France refused to ratify it, and insisted upon the new agreement which I have just described. Instead of the financial conditions in Germany improving they immediately became more critical, and the bankruptcy, which was only threatened on June 20, became actual when later in the summer the great Danat Bank and the banks generally in Germany were thrown into bankruptcy and the Reichsbank had to close its doors. This brought on the financial collapse in England and the fall of the pound, which carried down with it the currencies of numerous of the smaller European countries. If financial catastrophe in Europe has not supervened as a result of the Franco-American agreement it is hard to understand what financial catastrophe is.

The trouble with Europe to-day is that its international financial structure is grotesquely inflated with a fraudulent asset of $10,000,000,000 in German reparations with which the allied governments seek to pay all their debts. This asset has no value because it is an asset only if Germany pays punctually the annual interest and sinking fund upon it. Germany has not paid these annual sums out of her own resources. After the war she paid $9,000,000,000 in reparations which was in fact all that she justly owed. Since then she has not paid reparations out of her own resources, she can not so pay them, and she does not intend to try to do so.

The entire inflated financial structure since the war has been predicated upon the theory that Germany could pay the charges upon billions in reparation bonds held by the allied governments; and there has been an iridescent hope that the American public might be induced to buy these bonds from them. The allied treasuries would thus be filled, and the job of patrolling Germany would be transferred to the United States Government.

It is upon this grandiose financial coup that the allied governments and the international bankers have for years unsuccessfully lavished the intellectual treasures of their minds, and it is because they have made this plan their chief pre-occupation that genuine reconstruction in Europe has been at a standstill for 13 years. It is time that this conception be abandoned.

To come back now, in closing, to the amendment which accompanied the passage of the joint resolution by the Congress the other day.

The amendment makes it plain that it is the will of Congress that there shall be no cancellation or reduction of the allied debts to the United States. We believe that these are just debts and that the allied governments are able to pay them out of their own resources and without reference to receipts from German reparations.

Heretofore the allied governments have contrived to get the money from Germany, and there is plenty of indication that they are unwilling to pay us any sums that they do not first collect in this way. One thing is sure, namely, that Germany is going to stop paying reparations, because the American bankers are going to be made to stop lending billions to Germany with which to pay them.

The allied governments will therefore have to make their payments to the United States out of their own resources. The decision whether they will do so is for them alone to make. We can be of no assistance to them in making up their minds. But we will not accept German reparation bonds from them in lieu of what they owe us, nor will we permit them to negotiate them upon the American investment market. In the future, as in the past, it will remain the American position that there is no connection between German reparations and allied debts to the United States.

Mr. Thomas, in answering your presentation I desire to make a constructive suggestion, one that will go further than any other in laying the basis for a justification of real disarmament in the United States, and this suggestion should receive the careful thought and attention of those people in the United States who are so active in agitation looking toward disarmament.

I have pointed out that international bankers and diplomats contend that Europe can not pay the debts it owes to the United States. Our former allies insist that they will pay us only if Germany pays them, and they add that Germany can not pay. According to this contention, American taxpayers are expected to pay Germany's so-called "reparations" to the European nations, which, with our aid, defeated her in the World War.

The allied nations have received substantial material benefit from the war. They have annexed large areas of colonial and other territory which belonged to Germany, Austria, and Turkey. They have persuaded us to cancel the debts incurred for money and material advanced them during the war. The present debts owed us are for money loaned Europe for reconstruction purposes and property sold them at 20 cents on the dollar.

They now claim that world-wide deflation makes the whole or partial cancellation of the postwar debts, amounting to eleven and one-half billion dollars, necessary. The United States is asked to assume the entire burden of this deflation, Europe assuming none. The question of "ability to pay" has been brought to bear on every nation and people involved except the United States and the American taxpayer.

It is only fair that Europe should share in this deflation. It is perfectly practical for England and France to do this without financial expenditure of any kind; since they are our principal debtors it is fortunate that they are the best equipped to share the burden with us.

England is possessed of numerous island and mainland colonies close to our coasts. No reference to Canada is here intended. Canada is a self-contained Dominion, virtually an independent nation and a most excellent neighbor. Canada is the most virile part of the British Empire to-day and brightest hope for the growth and continuance of British power and influence in the world.

There are other British possessions which do not enjoy the status of Canada. Many of them are the seats of strongly forti-

273

fied British naval bases and by their location can be designed for no other purpose than possible hostilities against the United States. Bermuda is a case in point. That group of islands has large dockyards and extensive fortifications, barely 30 hours by fast steamer from New York City and hardly 4 hours by airplane. It is only 5 hours by airplane from Hamilton in Bermuda to the Capitol of our Nation at Washington.

The Bahama Islands are not fortified but provide a splendid base for aerial operations against Florida and our south Atlantic seacoast. Jamaica dominates the Caribbean from the center and is an effectual naval and aerial "cover" for the Panama Canal. The Windward and Leeward Islands wall in the Caribbean on the east, British Guiana providing a mainland "anchor" for the long chain of islands which run north to Porto Rico and Haiti. On the western side of the Caribbean, British Honduras occupies a position of great strategic importance.

Trinidad, almost touching the South American Continent, has a strong naval base; so has Kingston, in Jamaica. I would point out that no possible enemy threatens British interest in our home waters, unless Britain regards the United States as an enemy.

May I suggest that it would be a welcome gesture of intended friendship if England should offer to transfer to the United States in part payment of her debt to us the colonial possessions which she holds in waters which wash our coasts from Florida to Maine. It would provide a partial settlement of the debt burden which England finds so heavy, and it would give us a feeling of security, besides strengthening the friendship between the two nations. It would be the most effectual step in the direction of real disarmament which could be taken in the present state of the world. I commend this suggestion to all those groups in the United States who are so active at this time in disarmament—in both our Army and Navy.

I desire to point out that a large part of our national territory in the past has been acquired by purchase. The Louisiana Purchase, the Indian treaties, the treaty of Guadelupe Hidalgo, the Gadsden Purchase, the acquisition of Porto Rico and the Philippines, and the comparatively recent purchase of the Danish West Indies, now the Virgin Islands, are cases in point.

It is very likely that the American people would be content to accept a partial settlement of the European debts in territory. Ceding the territory in question would be a convincing evidence that England is willing to bear part of the burden which it now seems she is trying to place upon our unaided shoulders. If this understanding of her intentions is unfair, this proposed territorial suggestion would be a splendid way to prove it.

The territory is extensive. It comprises some 400 islands and the mainland colonies of British Honduras in Central America and British Guiana in South America. The area involved is some 110,000 square miles and the population about 2,300,000.

The possessions of France in American waters are less extensive than those of England, but are important. They begin on the north with St. Pierre and Miquelon and include Martinique, the Guadeloupe Islands, and French Guiana, the latter a mainland colony with some coastal islands. The total area is 33,000 square miles and the population 529,000.

The people of the United States have already proved their willingness to help England and France; it is time for those countries to demonstrate their willingness to recognize our past helpfulness and to relieve the United States of the presence of foreign naval bases in our home waters. We have no territorial ambitions in Europe.

The transfer of the territory in question at fair valuations would also serve to relieve the burden of payment which now rests on British and French taxpayers.

XV

REPARATION BONDS AND
FOREIGN SECURITIES

RECONSTRUCTION FINANCE CORPORATION

January 13, 1932

Mr. McFADDEN. Mr. Chairman, I think at the outset in the discussion of this particular measure that is now pending before the House, I should refer to that period of time between 1921-22 up until we reached the speculative period of 1929. That is the period of time that stands out as the period of inflation and deflation of the people in the United States. It was a period of inflation by the Federal reserve system whose operations synchronized with the bankers who were building up a situation which has resulted in the chaotic condition we now find ourselves.

That was a period of time when our large bankers, our international bankers, were engaged in the flotation and sale in the United States of foreign securities. It was that period of time when domestic bankers were reorganizing the industries of the United States, the railroads, and of consolidations and new creations. These consummations were brought together in New York and other large cities, devising new securities which were issued, enormous profits were taken out, in sale

276

of stocks and bonds issued and sold to the innocent public.

The innocent public were on the up and up, so far as the investment news were concerned. They were the investors, and there was plenty of whoopee made by the bankers to induce the public to purchase this class of securities.

In that period of time the international bankers unloaded on these investors billions of dollars worth of foreign securities, and billions of dollars of securities almost of the same type that were known as domestic securities.

It was in 1924 or 1925, as chairman of the Committee on Banking and Currency, during hearings that I first discovered what our bankers were doing to this country and I began an intensive study from that time on up to the present time. I frequently called attention of the membership of this House to what was taking place, without much result, I regret to say. I have before me here now a copy of the hearings before the Committee on Banking and Currency of the House of Representatives of the Seventy-first Congress, second session, on House Joint Resolution 364, which I introduced, and on which hearings were held before that committee. The resolution prohibited the purchase of German reparation bonds by national banks, Federal reserve banks, and member banks of the Federal reserve system.

I did all I could to secure the passage of that resolution, and I caused to be called before the committee the Secretary of the Treasury and the Secretary of State. The administration then in power in this House gave no consideration to it. What was the result? The international bankers were then engaged or were about to engage in the sale of $100,000,000 worth of German commercialized reparation bonds in the United States. They were offering those bonds at 91¼ to the innocent American people, and they were subscribed by a syndicate of bankers headed by J. P. Morgan & Co., Kuhn, Loeb & Co., and others of the international banking group, and I suppose most of them are held now by the banks and by the people of the United States, who paid 91¼ for them. Those bonds have recently been down to as low as 22, and they are around 30 or

277

35 to-day. I did all in my power to stop the sale of foreign securities in the United States. I am very happy now that in the other end of the Capitol the Finance Committee of the Senate is looking into this question. They are finding out that some of the things that I have been saying for a long time are true. They are finding out that the American people have been exploited by these bankers and that enormous profits have been made from the distribution and sale in the United States of these billions of dollars worth of securities. They have not done the people in the United States any good. The last sale of this hundred million dollars worth of reparation bonds in the United States I firmly believe did not do the Germans any good. It was an unloading process. It would be interesting to know, if we could know, what became of the proceeds from the sale of those bonds and to know how much of them went to take up other loans, the profits of the distributing houses who sold them. It is interesting to me to know now and see disclosed in these hearings the tremendous profits which are being made and the commissions paid and acknowledged as having been made by these bankers who are responsible to a very great degree for the financial and economic situation that we find ourselves in at this time. These bankers are also responsible in a similar manner for the distribution of worthless securities on the innocent American public through the consolidations and the maneuverings in the past 10 years, in the unloading of the securities which they had in the manner in which it was done. They were purely speculative manipulations filled with greed and desire to make money, with little regard as to security back of the issues, so long as the public would buy.

I call attention also, as I have previously on the floor of this House, to another method of taking the people's money from them in the United States and sending it abroad. It was through the use of acceptance credits, and billions of dollars have gone into foreigners' hands, and the people of the United States have been deprived of the use of that money through this source. There is still another source, and it is about time that Congress or the people who are dealing with these situations began to look for the facts. What we are doing here now is dealing with the effects and not with the causes.

I refer now to another angle of this exploitation of the American public through the sale of investment securities by these same houses, and I refer now to stocks—stocks in foreign banks, stocks in foreign insurance companies, stocks in all kinds of business enterprises abroad. Thousands and hundreds of thousands of shares of stock in the German Reichsbank have been sold by these bankers to American investors, and they are held by American investors to-day. Gentlemen, you have no idea of the quantities of foreign securities that are still held here in the banks, in trust funds, in insurance companies, and all classes of investors pools. The investments trusts are loaded to the hilt with this class of securities, and American people who are buying investment trust securities to-day do not know what is back of those investments. Hundreds of millions of dollars of foreign securities go to back up securities which they are buying. I believe I am not exaggerating it to any extent when I say that we have in excess of $40,000,000,000 worth of this kind of securities in the United States to-day, that we have shipped abroad in this particular class over $40,000,000,000, and how much of it are we going to get back? We see in to-day's papers and in yesterday's papers where word is being sent to us that they do not intend to pay. It is nothing but exploitation. During this period of time or just prior to it we were engaged in the World War. The World War cost us between forty billions and fifty billions of dollars. In addition to that add to it $40,000,000,000 worth of foreign securities held in this country which took that amount of money out of this country, and is it any wonder that we are in the position that we are in to-day, and that we are asked to pass the kind of legislation that is proposed here? Where does the request for this legislation come from? It comes from the very same bankers I am referring to. The first knowledge that I had of the need for this legislation came when Members of Congress were called to the White House and there given a review of the financial condition of Europe and then the financial condition of the United States. A crisis was painted. We were told then that conferences had been held with New York bankers, with clearing-house bankers.

We knew just prior to that that the New York bankers had been here consulting with high officials of the Government. We were told definitely that something had to be done. The New York bankers had agreed to organize the National Credit Corporation, with a capital of $500,000,000. We were told they would subscribe $150,000,000 of the capital that this organization might be able to meet the requirements of the drastic situation that was then presented. The fear at that time was that there might be $1,800,000,000 worth of gold withdrawn from New York. It was a desperate situation. We were told that in case the National Credit Corporation could not cope with the distressing financial situation there might be a possibility that we would have to revive, when Congress convened, an institution similar to the War Finance Corporation. It has arrived here. We have it now before us. It is the Reconstruction Finance Corporation. It proposes to organize, not with bankers' subscriptions—and those bankers have been perfectly willing that Uncle Sam should take the risk—a corporation with a capital of $500,000,000 of taxpayers' money. It provides a vehicle through which there can be issued and sold $1,500,000,000 worth of debentures, bonds, or other securities; a total of $2,000,000,000; and the United States is to guarantee the payment of all of it.

Gentlemen, I have referred, and referred rather mildly, to this exploitation that has been taking place. Millions of people have lost their all by this manipulation, which was deliberate on the part of these bankers. There has been great suffering, there is great suffering to-day, and there is going to be more.

This morning I received a letter from a man in Pittsburgh, and I want to quote from that letter. I am getting letters along this line continually, and I suppose every other Member of Congress is getting them also. I quote:

Heaven knows the higher-ups are already in sufficiently bad odor all over the country, the feeling is widespread and growing daily; no one seems to have the slightest confidence in either the ability or the integrity of the international bankers, and each time one of them goes upon the witness stand that feeling, among the people at large, is intensified. It is a highly unfortunate state of affairs into which this country has been plunged, and it savors not a little of irony, not to suggest the comparison with that famous cake-eating episode of Marie Antoinette, that the very men who brought about our major troubles are to be intrusted with the cure. No provision whatever has been made, so far as I can see, to restore labor to the pay roll, and the wage-cutting program still continues. The bankers will continue to deflate labor until labor deflates the bankers. The people have been lied to and imposd upon, stolen from, and otherwise treated outrageously. Personally I would not care to be numbered among the victims of their righteous wrath.

Mr. Chairman, this particular bill is a scheme for taking $500,000,000 out of the Treasury of the United States. It is a scheme for taking a half billion dollars of the people's money, produced by labor at the cost of toil and suffering, and give it to a supercorporation for the sinister purpose of helping a gang of financial looters to cover up their tracks. It is a scheme for giving those financial looters a chance to dispose of evidence, which, if brought out into the light of day, would cause the doors of our Federal penitentiaries to close upon them for a long term of years. As such, it is unfit for your consideration.

I was very much interested in listening to the distinguished gentleman from Virginia, whom we all love and whom we respect as one of the leading constitutional lawyers of the House. I want to quote from some other good sources. How would General Washington regard such conduct which we now are about to witness? In his Farewell Address in 1796, he advised his country as follows:

All obstructions, * * * all combinations and associations, under whatever plausible character, with the real design to direct, to control, counteract, or awe the regular deliberation and action of the constituted authorities, are destructive of this fundamental (checks in the Constitution) principle, and of fatal tendency. They serve to organize faction * * * to put in the place of the delegated will of the Nation the will of * * * a small but enterprising minority, and * * * to make the public administration the mirror of the ill-concerted and incongruous projects of a faction, rather than the organ of consistent and wholesome plans digested by common counsels and mutual interests. * * * The habits of thinking in a free country should inspire caution in those intrusted with its administration to confine themselves within their respective constitutional spheres, avoiding the exercise of the powers of one department to encroach upon another. The spirit of encroachment tends to consolidate the powers of all departments in one, and thus to create, whatever the form of government, a real despotism. * * * The necessity of reciprocal checks in the exercise of political power * * * is evinced by experience, ancient and modern. To preserve them must be as necessary as to institute them. * * * Let there be no change by usurpation, for * * * this is the customary weapon by which free governments are destroyed.

Mr. STAFFORD. Again the gentleman is making most serious charges. Will the gentleman inform the committee of the basis upon which he makes the statement that this bill is for the relief of looters and the other charges he has made; whether anything like that is in the hearings before the Senate committee or the House committee?

Mr. McFADDEN. No. Unfortunately, there is not.

Mr. STAFFORD. On what does the gentleman base these serious charges?

Mr. McFADDEN. I am basing them on the use which the Federal reserve system has made of the acceptance credits, both domestic and international.

Mr. STAFFORD. Then, the gentleman is indicting the operations of the Federal reserve system?

Mr. McFADDEN. I am making statements in regard to them that are very serious; and I will say to the gentleman that I have a resolution before this House, which should be passed, calling for an investigation and audit of the affairs of that system.

Mr. STAFFORD. As a member of the House Committee on Banking and Currency, did the gentleman at any time in the hearings advise the committee of the charges which the gentleman is now making?

Mr. McFADDEN. I spoke in regard to these acceptance matters; yes.

Mr. STAFFORD. And that instrumentality is largely for the benefit of looters of finance?

Mr. McFADDEN. I did not say it in just those words.

Mr. STAFFORD. But in stronger words.

Mr. McFADDEN. I can not yield further. The matter was discussed in committee. I want to quote from Thomas Jefferson, who advised his followers in this language:

The spirit of the times may alter, will alter—

He says in his Notes on Virginia—

our rules will become corrupt, our people careless [divine prophesy]. A single zealot may become persecutor and better men be his victims. ° ° ° The time for fixing our rights on a legal basis is while our rulers are honest. ° ° ° From the conclusion of this war we will be going down hill. It will then not be necessary to resort every moment to the people for support. They will be forgotten and their rights disregarded. They will forget themselves in the sole faculty of making money, and will never think of uniting to effect a due respect for their rights. The shackles, therefore, which shall be knocked off at the conclusion of this war will be heavier and heavier, until our rights shall revive or expire in a convulsion.

In his Kentucky Resolutions of 1798, in Section IX, this patron saint of Democracy says:

It would be a dangerous delusion were a confidence in men of our choice to silence our fears for the safety of our rights; that confidence is everywhere the parent of despotism; free government is founded in jealousy and not confidence; it is jealousy and not confidence which prescribes limited constitutions to bind down those whom we are obliged to trust with power; that our Constitution has accordingly fixed the limits to which and no further our confidence may go. ° ° ° In questions of power, then, let no more be heard of "confidence in man," but bind him down from mischief by chains of the Constitution.

For the former Judge Advocates now in Congress, who, incongruously enough, claim to admire the wisdom of great jurists like Story and Marshall, yet have never appeared before the Supreme Court to overthrow Webster's supremacy, though they are willing to defend this new race of rulers we have among us, let me quote from Mr. Justice Joseph Story's opinion:

But a new race of men is springing up to govern the Nation; they are the hunters after popularity, men ambitious, not of honor so much as of profits of office, the demagogues whose principles hang laxly upon them, and who follow not so much what is right as what leads to a temporary vulgar applause. There is great, very great danger that these men will usurp so much popular favor that they will rule the Nation; and, if so, we may yet live to see many of our best institutions crumble in the dust.

In his classic work, the Commentaries on the Constitution, Mr. Justice Story continues:

Let the American youth never forget that they possess a noble inheritance, bought by the toils, and sufferings and blood of their ancestors. ° ° ° It may, nevertheless, perish in an hour of folly, or corruption, or negligence of its only keepers.

I want to now quote from another eminent authority, Daniel Webster, who said, when a question similar to that which is now pending was discussed and where the principles were alike:

The people of this country have not established for themselves such a fabric of depotism. They have not purchased at vast expense of their own treasure, and their own blood, a Magna Charta to be slaves. * * * Who will show me any constitutional injunction which makes it the duty of the American people to surrender everything valuable in life, and even life itself, not when the safety of their country may demand the sacrifice, but whenever the purpose of an ambitious and mischievous government may require it? Sir, I almost disdain to go to quotations and references to prove that such an abominable doctrine has no foundation in the Constitution of the country!

To transform our Constitution into the "magna charta of slaves" and cowards has always been the aim of some of our European neighbors, who find it more easy to manipulate the ambitions of a few than to bribe the whole Nation. From its very institution our form of government—a deliberative government—has withstood the torrents of invectives of its enemies that have flown unceasingly from the subsidized press of this country in all periods of our history under the Constitution. And how would the martyred Lincoln advise us to-day were he here to witness this assault on your constitutional privileges and duties? Where would he look for the danger? Let us hear him speak:

If destruction be our lot, we must ourselves be its author. * * * When the vicious portion of our population shall be permitted * * * to silence at their pleasure those opposed to their procedure * * * the best citizens will become alienated from our institutions and it will be left without sufficient friends to defend it effectually. At such times and under such circumstances men of sufficient ambition will not be wanting to seize the opportunity, strike the blow, and overturn that fair fabric which has been the fondest hope of the lovers of freedom throughout the world!

I want to quote from still another eminent authority, John Adams. In that letter to Jack Taylor, which you will find in the Works of Adams, volume 6, page 467, he had this to say about the necessity of sprinkling checks all through the Constitution:

First, the States are balanced against the general government. Second, the House of Representatives is balanced against the Senate and the Senate against the House. Third, the executive authority is in some degree balanced against the Legislature. Fourth, the judiciary is balanced against the Legislature, the Executive, and the State governments. Fifth, the Senate is balanced against the President in all appointments to office and in all treaties. Sixth, the people hold in their own hands the balance against their own representatives with periodic elections. Seventh, the legislatures of the several States are balanced against the Senate by sexennial elections. Eighth, the electors are balanced against the people in their choice of President and Vice President.

Listen to the clarion call of Theodore Roosevelt to the American people to abolish this obnoxious and cowardly concept of nonresisting obedience to boss rule from their councils. In Senate Document 904, Sixty-second Congress, second session, his words thunder:

I deny that the American people have surrendered to any set of men, no matter what their position or their character, the final right to determine those fundamental questions upon which free government ultimately depends. The people themselves must be the ultimate (interpreters of their rights) and, when their agents differ in their interpretations of the Constitution, the people themselves * * * after full and deliberate judgment should settle what interpretation it is that their representatives shall adopt as binding.

"After full and deliberate judgment"! Does this sound like "after getting their orders from the boss"? What is "deliberate judgment"? How can a representative "judge" of anything without going through the mental and logical process of judging the relative merits of many differing views of any question?

Roger Williams in 1644, when founding his Rhode Island Colony, said:

> The sovereign, original power lies in the people. * * * They are distinct from the "government" they set up to do their bidding; the "government" is but the peoples' servant, not their master. * * * Civil magistrates, whether kings or parliaments, states and governors, can do no more in justice than what the people allow, and are, therefore, but the eyes and hands and instruments of the people whose rights they must preserve. * * *

Gentleman of the Congress, this particular bill, in my judgment, encroaches upon the Constitution of the United States to a very great extent. I want to read the solemn oath which each of us takes when we come into the Halls of this Congress to represent our constituency:

> I do solemnly swear (or affirm) that I will support and defend the Constitution of the United States against all enemies, foreign and domestic; that I will bear true faith and allegiance to the same; that I take this obligation freely, without any mental reservation or purpose of evasion, and that I will well and faithfully discharge the duties of the office on which I am about to enter. So help me God.

We are about to pass our judgment on a measure which deals vitally with every man, women, and child in this United States, and it behooves us to carefully remember our obligation and the fact that we are representing the people of the United States.

Mr. SIROVICH. On the Senate side they have allocated the sum of $50,000,000 from this Reconstruction Finance Corporation for the benefit of the farming interests of our Republic.

Would the gentleman be in favor of allocating a certain sum of this money for the benefit of the large cities of the United States which, while solvent in every conceivable way, are denied the privilege of getting money from the local banks of their communities to further the best interests of the public welfare?

Mr. McFADDEN. I would say in answer to that that here is an institution that is being organized by this Government out of the taxpayers' money. To be fair in the administration of this act they should take care of the necessary needs of all of its people. I can see no reason why, if you are going to help one class of people, the bankers of the country, the railroads of the country, and the insurance companies of the country, you should not also help the cities of the country, why you should not help the counties of the country; and why you should not help the municipalities that are in trouble.

This is a bill to establish a reconstruction finance corporation. After wrecking the business fabric of the country, the looters now come forward with a scheme for taking over the remaining property values of the entire United States. They propose to put the United States in pawn for 10 years to pay their losses on worthless foreign paper. As Franklin-Bouillon lately said concerning international bankers and their victims, "Usurers first, victims afterwards."

Instead of paying their own losses as other citizens have to do, these financial magnates ask us to pass a law for their especial benefit. They ask us to establish a supercorporation to shelter them and to conceal the details of their misdeeds from the public. They ask for $500,000,000 to keep themselves out of prison. They have already in the last several years filched from the United States Treasury enough money to pay the entire national debt, but that does not prevent them from staging another raid on it. With this last grand steal they propose to avail themselves of a supercorporation with a detective service de luxe, and by means of this super-corporation controlling all other corporations and spying on every individual in the country they propose to spread their losses over the

288

entire population of the United States.

These are the railroads which, during the war, when it got to the point that they saw they were going to sustain a great loss, rushed to Washington and asked Uncle Sam to take over and administer the railroads and assume the losses. This cost Uncle Sam about $3,000,000,000 that time.

The man who does not owe any money is to be held up under a threat and forced to give up anything he may happen to have left in order to pay them for Germany's new planetariums, her splendid new factories, her newly created residential suburbs, her blue-ribbon ocean liners, and her new war cruisers. What the rest of the world has been excused from paying to us the American workingman must make good.

American labor has paid $500,000,000 in hard-earned taxes and is now invited to watch that $500,000,000 being taken out of the United States Treasury and handed over to a super-corporation to serve a special class. Senator WALCOTT has said that this money is to be used to help "going concerns." If they are "going concerns," why do they come here asking for doles from the United States Government and the overburdened United States Treasury? It is because they have put their signatures on illegal, worthless, and uncollectible paper and they are unwilling to take part in the rehabilitation of this country unless and until the United States Government takes over that paper and relieves them of their responsibilities concerning it. Their scheme is to make the people of the United States furnish a purchase price for their frozen assets, to have the Government put its signature on those assets, to tie them up in a different package, and then to sell them again to the general public. What else? The scheme is dangerous, unsound, and dishonest.

A bank loss is a bank responsibility. The collective losses of United States banks should be borne by the banks and not by the general public. The banks have a recourse in the case of every loss they have sustained. The courts are open to them. The guarantors of the circulating evidences of debt upon which the banks recklessly advanced funds belonging to the American bank depositors are fully liable and there is no reason why the people of this country should shoulder their responsibility. If the accepting banks of this country and the 10 great and powerful discount dealer corporations which sit at the receipt of custom in New York and levy tribute on every item of American business can not honor their signatures, the law should look after their condition and conduct an examination of their business. There is no reason why we should permit them to reimburse themselves at the expense of the general American public.

This thing has been in progress here for 17 years. It became acute in 1920 and then the farmers had to bear the cost of it. The credit rationers recouped their losses in 1920 by deflating American agriculture—a blow from which it has never recovered. The present scheme does not select any one class to pay for the orgies of the credit rationers but it proposes instead to collect tribute from every member of the population. The first tribute is the $500,000,000 which is to be taken out of the people's Treasury. This invention, widely advertised as a cure-all, is not worth half a billion dollars of the taxpayers' money. We have no right to take that money out of the Treasury and to spend it on doubtful expedients. We have no right to take that money and to use it for what you must all agree is nothing more than a cheap promoter's scheme for creating a temporary illusion of prosperity. The establishment of this expensive corporation will leave the underlying evils of the present situation uncorrected; in fact, it will intensify them. It will not alleviate the present distress.

They tried to sell this scheme to the banks and the banks would not take it. They organized a National Credit Corporation in the hope that the banks would subscribe to its capital and the banks would not do it. The banks passed the burden back to the administration. They reminded the Government that the common people are the goat in this country and that whenever there is any wreckage to be cleared up, the American wage earner is the person who is supposed to pay the cost of it. Hence this assessment, this raid on the taxes that have been paid in.

The name of the proposed supercorporation is worth noticing. It was given in advance. It is a high-sounding name—the Reconstruction Finance Corporation. That name to make the people believe that this is a bill devised in their interest, whereas it is one of the boldest raids on the United States Treasury that has ever been perpetrated. The issue might as well be joined now. Sooner or later there will be a struggle here between the people and the overlords of wealth and privilege.

Summer says:

> The next great struggle the human race will have to face is the struggle between plutocracy and democracy.

That struggle is beginning. Read this bill and you will see the predatory interests preparing to move in here with their dictators and subdictators, their secret police files, and their detectives. How long do you think the American people can be held in subjection by the power which conceived this bill and dictated the provisions of it and which is now engaged in disguising the real purpose of it? Last week Father Cox, of Pittsburgh, led an army of men here to the very door of the capitol to warn us that there will be trouble in this country if something is not done by the Federal Government to relieve the sufferings of the unemployed and their dependents. He was told that this so-called relief measure was on its way. Was that a sufficient answer? I think not. If, as Eugene Meyer and Ogden Mills declare, the object of creating this supercorporation is chiefly psychological, we had better discard it and turn immediately to a more common-sense course. Psychology is a poor substitute for reality. It will not feed a starving man or shelter him against the cold. While the emissaries of the international bankers move to and fro behind the scenes, telling you that this country is distressed and that theirs is the only scheme that will cure it, better measures, more honest measures, as for instance the relief bills of Senator LA FOLLETTE and Senator COSTIGAN are neglected. There is no bread for the hungry in this bill, as there is in theirs.

The common man does not want to fight, and he will not fight against his government but he will fight to defend it and to rescue it from those who abuse it. We have an army of the dispossessed—women sleeping in the open and children crying for bread. This is a condition which can not long endure. It would be a reflection on the men of this country if they should allow it to endure much longer. And yet we hear Senator WALCOTT himself saying that the benefit of this bill will be largely psychological; that it will create confidence, and that confidence is what is needed. Half a billion dollars taken from the United States Treasury and used to relieve the richest class in the country is not likely to create a feeling of confidence in the mind and heart of the general public. You must remember that this bill saddles the United States Government with a debt of $2,000,000,000. The only securities the Government is offered for this huge advance of cash and credit are the frozen assets no man will buy and which the National Credit Corporation could not persuade the banks to accept as a common burden. Nor is the liability of the Government limited to $2,000,000,000. The bill provides that—

> In the event that the corporation shall be unable to pay upon demand, when due, the principal of, or interest on notes, debentures, bonds, or other such obligations issued by it, the Secretary of the Treasury shall pay the amount thereof, which is hereby authorized to be appropriated, out of any moneys in the Treasury not otherwise appropriated, and thereupon to the extent of the amounts so paid the Secretary of the Treasury shall succeed to all amounts so paid the Secretary of the Treasury shall succeed to all the rights of the holders of such notes, debentures, bonds, or other obligations.

In other words, the obligations of the corporation are to be the financial risks and obligations of the United States Government and they are to be paid by the Secretary of the Treasury when the responsibility reaches the Government, which, in my opinion, will be soon and often. These obligations of the United States Government may be issued in lieu of cash when the corporation makes a loan. They may be peddled in this country and in foreign countries as well at any price the corporation may determine to place upon them. This bill unlocks the door of the United States Treasury and decrees that it shall be left open for 10 years to come. It offers a sanctuary to the predatory interests. Do you think the people of the United States will permit such a state of things to exist? Do you think they will permit themselves to be taxed to keep this financial monstrosity alive? The obligations of the corporation can be used. That means they can be used as collateral security for Federal reserve notes. In other words, one obligation of the Government is to be used to secure another obligation of the Government.

Mr. SEIBERLING. In order to keep the record straight, does not the bill provide that the indebtedness of the corporation shall never exceed the amount of $2,000,000,000?

Mr. McFADDEN. The gentleman is quite correct, but I am pointing out to the gentleman here the possibilities of a $30,-000,000,000 inflation, where these securities, when held by corporations, can be placed with banks as security for their note, and their note discounted in the Federal reserve, and the Federal reserve can issue Federal reserve notes thereunder.

Mr. BLANTON. It is said that the Treasury lacks about $1,200,000,000 of having anything in it; where are we going to get this money?

Mr. McFADDEN. I have just been telling the gentlemen here that we are going to issue one obligation on another obligation.

Mr. BLANTON. Where is the Government going to get the initial $500,000,000?

Mr. McFADDEN. I think, if it gets it at all, it is going to get it through the Federal reserve system. The gentlemen at the other end of the Capitol, I understand, say that the Federal reserve system shall not furnish any money to this corporation through rediscount in any manner of its obligations.

Mr. BLANTON. But as soon as this corporation is organized and it makes a call on the Treasury for the $500,000,000, where is it coming from? If the Treasury lacks $1,200,000,000 of having anything in it, how is it going to pay it?

Mr. McFADDEN. The Treasury will have to borrow it.

Mr. BLANTON. How?

Mr. McFADDEN. Through bond or note issues.

Mr. BLANTON. When we made an attempt to pay the just debt that our Government owed our soldiers Mr. Mellon and the President said that we did not have any money and that it would disrupt the Government to pay $1,000,000,000 in that matter. I was wondering how they were going to explain this.

Mr. McFADDEN. As the gentleman knows, the Secretary recommends this bill.

Can obligations secure obligations? Can debts secure obligations? Is it so written in the Constitution? Is it so held in any court of law? Do we intend to consecrate such a financial heresy by law? If we do, we shall make ourselves the laughingstock of the world.

Under this bill the obligations of the corporation can be used by member banks as collateral security for their promissory notes to secure advances from Federal reserve banks. You all know that provision of the Federal reserve act. It was intended for emergency use only. Do you know the extent to which it has been abused? I will tell you.

In 1928, in the period of wild speculations, when the Federal reserve was permitting credit to be used in the New York stock market and brokers' loans were on the up and up, they were assisting in making the prices go up and up and getting the public in—in 1928 member banks borrowed $60,-598,690,000 from the Federal reserve banks.

How many of you gentlemen knew that? Think of it. Sixty billion dollars payable upon demand in gold in the course of one single year.

Mr. SIROVICH. Was not that also for accounts receivable besides collateral securities?

Mr. McFADDEN. I am talking of the total amount the Fed-

294

eral reserve banks advanced in credit in 1928.

The actual payment of such obligations calls for six times as much monetary gold as there is in the entire world. Such transactions represents a grant in the course of one single year of about $7,000,000 to every member bank of the Federal reserve system.

Mr. McGuGIN. I take it the gentleman has gone into this matter in great detail, and I would like to ask about three questions.

In the first place, from the gentleman's study of the situation, does the gentleman have any idea that $2,000,000,000 will start to stabilize the banking structure of the country and liquidate the bad paper?

Mr. McFADDEN. My best answer to that is to refer to the figures I have just given of the use in the year 1928 of $60,000,-000,000 worth of Federal-reserve credit, which was largely used in the stock-market orgy which took place at that time.

Mr. McGuGIN. Now I would like to ask the gentleman another question. Does the gentleman have any idea that any reasonable or appreciable amount of this $2,000,000,000 will ever reach down to the country banks and the country institutions, unless we provide in the bill that a certain percentage of it must be confined to smaller loans?

Mr. McFADDEN. I can not answer the gentleman as to what the administration of this organization will do. It is only fair to say, however, that in the administration of the War Finance Corporation there were some loans made in the country.

Mr. McGuGIN. There was an entirely different situation then from the situation now. The War Finance Corporation was not organized with a bunch of vultures outside the door ready to grab it as soon as soon as it was organized.

Mr. McFADDEN. Is it any wonder that there is a depression in this country? Is it any wonder that American labor, which ultimately pays the cost of all the banking operations of this country, has at last proved unequal to the task of supplying this huge total of cash and credit for the benefit of stock-market manipulators and foreign swindlers?

The proposed corporation will furnish fresh obligations which may be used as security for similar loans from the Federal reserve banks and thus again and in a different way these corporation obligations of the United States Government will be used to secure other obligations of the Government.

According to the bill, the obligations of the proposed corporation are to consist of notes, bonds, debentures, and other obligations. Of these the last mentioned are to be short-term obligations rediscountable at Federal reserve banks. Here again you see a proposal to offer these corporation-Government obligations in return for Federal reserve notes. This is akin to the excessively evil short-term Treasury certificate which was introduced into this country in 1929 under the influence of certain experimenters who infest the Treasury and are ever on the alert to try out new schemes on the general public at public expense. The use of this credit instrument—the short-term Treasury certificate—is not allowed in France, and it should be forbidden here. Instead of creating new forms of it we should rid ourselves of the one we have, because the sole purpose of these obligations is to facilitate the manipulation of the money market for the benefit of insiders. About the time Mr. Mills discovered the short-term Treasury certificates as a credit instrument and while he was descanting on its merits and delivering himself of loud cries concerning this "new and prime credit instrument" the ancient dodge was known for what it was worth in Europe—that is, a means of fooling the people, an instrument of destruction and control. The bill under consideration sets up the same instrument, but in this case the Treasury has no actual power to decide when emissions of these instruments shall take place. The proper functions of the Treasury, its power to issue the obligations of the United States Government, are given over to the Reconstruction Finance Corporation. Are we to sanction such an innovation?

This bill attacks the highest prerogatives of the Government. The very fact that it has been introduced here shows the growing audacity of the forces which have destroyed our

our American way of doing business and which are now seeking to destroy the Constitution itself. They will not destroy it, because the people who sent us here will not allow it to be destroyed.

Lord God of Hosts, be with us yet
Lest we forget, lest we forget!

This is 1932, the bicentennial of the birth of George Washington, the Father of our Country. What was his advice to the infant Republic whose greatness he foresaw, whose trials he anticipated? It was brief and to the point. No one connected with the Government has the least excuse for forgetting it. "Avoid entangling alliances." What would he think if he could know that we had permitted designing international bankers to come here and to introduce the outworn banking and financial machinery of European countries in definance of our Constitution and in violation of our rights? What would he think if he could know that our wealth by the billions has been fraudulently transferred to foreign lands, and that in consequence of this grave disaster we are now brought so low that we are actually being urged to take the last fatal plunge to betray America and to let her be sold down the river to the leeches of Wall Street? History is filled with ironies, but there never yet was any irony comparable to this—that we should celebrate the bicentennial of George Washington by passing this bill, this product of un-American minds, here in the House of his friends. [Applause.]

XVI

THE TREACHEROUS AND DISLOYAL CONDUCT OF THE FEDERAL RESERVE BOARD AND THE FEDERAL RESERVE BANKS

Friday, June 10, 1932

Mr. McFADDEN. Mr. Chairman, we have in this country one of the most corrupt institutions the world has ever known. I refer to the Federal Reserve Board and the Federal reserve banks. The Federal Reserve Board, a Government board, has cheated the Government of the United States and the people of the United States out of enough money to pay the national debt. The depredations and the iniquities of the Federal Reserve Board and the Federal reserve banks acting together have cost this country enough money to pay the national debt several times over. This evil institution has impoverished and ruined the people of the United States; has bankrupted itself, and has practically bankrupted our Government. It has done this through the defects of the law under which it operates, through the maladministration of that law by the Federal Reserve Board, and through the corrupt practices of the moneyed vultures who control it.

Some people think the Federal Reserve Banks are United States Government institutions. They are not Government institutions. They are private credit monopolies which prey upon

298

the people of the United States for the benefit of themselves and their foreign customers; foreign and domestic speculators and swindlers; and rich and predatory money lenders. In that dark crew of financial pirates there are those who would cut a man's throat to get a dollar out of his pocket; there are those who send money into States to buy votes to control our legislation; and there are those who maintain an international propaganda for the purpose of deceiving us and of wheedling us into the granting of new concessions which will permit them to cover up their past misdeeds and set again in motion their gigantic train of crime.

Those 12 private credit monopolies were deceitfully and disloyally foisted upon this country by bankers who came here from Europe and who repaid us for our hospitality by undermining our American institutions. Those bankers took money out of this country to finance Japan in a war against Russia. They created a reign of terror in Russia with our money in order to help that war along. They instigated the separate peace between Germany and Russia and thus drove a wedge between the allies in the World War. They financed Trotsky's mass meetings of discontent and rebellion in New York. They paid Trotsky's passage from New York to Russia so that he might assist in the destruction of the Russian Empire. They fomented and instigated the Russian revolution and they placed a large fund of American dollars at Trotsky's disposal in one of their branch banks in Sweden so that through him Russian homes might be thoroughly broken up and Russian children flung far and wide from their natural protectors. They have since begun the breaking up of American homes and the dispersal of American children.

It has been said that President Wilson was deceived by the attentions of these bankers and by the philanthropic poses they assumed. It has been said that when he discovered the manner in which he had been misled by Colonel House, he turned against that busybody, that "holy monk" of the financial empire, and showed him the door. He had the grace to do that, and in my opinion he deserves great credit for it.

President Wilson died a victim of deception. When he came to the Presidency, he had certain qualities of mind and heart which entitled him to a high place in the councils of this Nation; but there was one thing he was not and which he never aspired to be; he was not a banker. He said that he knew very little about banking. It was, therefore, on the advice of others that the iniquitous Federal reserve act, the death warrant of American liberty, became law in his administration.

Mr. Chairman, there should be no partisanship in matters concerning the banking and currency affairs of this country, and I do not speak with any.

In 1912 the National Monetary Association, under the chairmanship of the late Senator Nelson W. Aldrich, made a report and presented a vicious bill called the National Reserve Association bill. This bill is usually spoken of as the Aldrich bill. Senator Aldrich did not write the Aldrich bill. He was the tool, but not the accomplice, of the European-born bankers who for nearly 20 years had been scheming to set up a central bank in this country and who in 1912 had spent and were continuing to spend vast sums of money to accomplish their purpose.

The Aldrich bill was condemned in the platform upon which Theodore Roosevelt was nominated in the year 1912, and in that same year, when Woodrow Wilson was nominated, the Democratic platform, as adopted at the Biltmore convention, expressly stated: "We are opposed to the Aldrich plan or a central bank." This was plain language. The men who ruled the Democratic Party then promised the people that if they were returned to power there would be no central bank established here while they held the reins of government. Thirteen months later that promise was broken, and the Wilson administration, under the tutelage of those sinister Wall Street figures who stood behind Colonel House, established here in our free country the wormeaten monarchical institution of the "king's bank" to control us from the top downward, and to shackle us from the cradle to the grave. The Federal reserve act destroyed our old and characteristic way of doing business;

it discriminated against our 1-name commercial paper, the finest in the world; it set up the antiquated 2-name paper, which is the present curse of this country, and which has wrecked every country which has ever given it scope; it fastened down upon this country the very tyranny from which the framers of the Constitution sought to save us.

One of the greatest battles for the preservation of this Republic was fought out here in Jackson's day, when the Second Bank of the United States, which was founded upon the same false principles as those which are exemplified in the Federal reserve act, was hurled out of existence. After the downfall of the Second Bank of the United States in 1837, the country was warned against the dangers that might ensue if the predatory interests, after being cast out, should come back in disguise and unite themselves to the Executive, and through him acquire control of the Government. That is what the predatory interests did when they came back in the livery of hypocrisy and under false pretenses obtained the passage of the Federal reserve act.

The danger that the country was warned against came upon us and is shown in the long train of horrors attendant upon the affairs of the traitorous and dishonest Federal Reserve Board and the Federal reserve banks. Look around you when you leave this chamber and you will see evidences of it on all sides. This is an era of economic misery and for the conditions that caused that misery, the Federal Reserve Board and the Federal reserve banks are fully liable. This is an era of financed crime and in the financing of crime, the Federal Reserve Board does not play the part of a disinterested spectator.

It has been said that the draughtsman who was employed to write the text of the Federal reserve bill used the text of the Aldrich bill for his purpose. It has been said that the language of the Aldrich bill was used because the Aldrich bill had been drawn up by expert lawyers and seemed to be appropriate. It was indeed drawn up by lawyers. The Aldrich bill was created by acceptance bankers of European origin in New York City. It was a copy and in general a translation of the statutes of the Reichsbank and other European central banks.

Half a million dollars was spent on one part of the propaganda organized by those same European bankers for the purpose of misleading public opinion in regard to it, and for the purpose of giving Congress the impression that there was an overwhelming popular demand for that kind of banking legislation and the kind of currency that goes with it, namely, an asset currency based on human debts and obligations instead of an honest currency based on gold and silver values. Dr. H. Parker Willis had been employed by the Wall Street bankers and propagandists and when the Aldrich measure came to naught and he obtained employment from CARTER GLASS to assist in drawing a banking bill for the Wilson administration, he appropriated the text of the Aldrich bill for his purpose. There is no secret about it. The text of the Federal reserve act was tainted from the beginning.

Not all of the Democratic Members of the Sixty-third Congress voted for this great deception. Some of them remembered the teachings of Jefferson; and, through the years, there have been no criticisms of the Federal Reserve Board and the Federal reserve banks so honest, so outspoken, and so unsparing as those which have been voiced here by Democrats. Again, although a number of Republicans voted for the Federal reserve act, the wisest and most conservative members of the Republican Party would have nothing to do with it and voted against it. A few days before the bill came to a vote, Senator Henry Cabot Lodge, of Massachusetts, wrote to Senator John W. Weeks as follows:

New York City, December 17, 1913.

*My Dear Senator Weeks: * * * Throughout my public life I have supported all measures designed to take the Government out of the banking business * * *. This bill puts the Government into the banking business as never before in our history and makes, as I understand it, all notes Government notes when they should be bank notes.*

The powers vested in the Federal Reserve Board seem to

me highly dangerous, especially where there is political control of the board. I should be sorry to hold stock in a bank subject to such domination. The bill as it stands seems to me to open the way to a vast inflation of the currency. There is no necessity of dwelling upon this point after the remarkable and most powerful argument of the senior Senator from New York. I can be content here to follow the example of the English candidate for Parliament who thought it enough "to say ditto to Mr. Burke." I will merely add that I do not like to think that any law can be passed which will make it possible to submerge the gold standard in a flood of irredeemable paper currency.

I had hoped to support this bill, but I can not vote for it as it stands, because it seems to me to contain features and to rest upon principles in the highest degree menacing to our prosperity, to stability in business, and to the general welfare of the people of the United States.

Very sincerely yours,

HENRY CABOT LODGE.

In the 18 years which have passed since Senator Lodge wrote that letter of warning all of his predictions have come true. The Government is in the banking business as never before. Against its will it has been made the backer of horse-thieves and card sharps, bootleggers, smugglers, speculators, and swindlers in all parts of the world. Through the Federal Reserve Board and the Federal reserve banks the riffraff of every country is operating on the public credit of the United States Government. Meanwhile, and on account of it, we ourselves are in the midst of the greatest depression we have ever known. Thus the menace to our prosperity, so feared by Senator Lodge, has indeed struck home. From the Atlantic to the Pacific our country has been ravaged and laid waste by the evil practices of the Federal Reserve Board and the Federal reserve banks and the interests which control them. At no time in our history has the general welfare of the people of the United States been at a lower level or the mind of the people so filled with despair.

Recently in one of our States 60,000 dwelling houses and farms were brought under the hammer in a single day. According to the Rev. Father Charles E. Coughlin, who has lately testified before a committee of this House, 71,000 houses and farms in Oakland County, Mich., have been sold and their erstwhile owners dispossessed. Similar occurrences have probably taken place in every county in the United States. The people who have thus been driven out are the wastage of the Federal reserve act. They are the victims of the dishonest and unscrupulous Federal Reserve Board and the Federal reserve banks. Their children are the new slaves of the auction block in the revival here of the institution of human slavery.

In 1913, before the Senate Banking and Currency Committee, Mr. Alexander Lassen made the following statement:

> But the whole scheme of a Federal reserve bank with its commercial-paper basis is an impractical, cumbersome machinery, is simply a cover, to find a way to secure the privilege of issuing money and to evade payment of as much tax upon circulation as possible, and then control the issue and maintain, instead of reduce, interest rates. It is a system that, if inaugurated, will prove to the advantage of the few and the deteriment of the people of the United States. It will mean continued shortage of actual money and further extension of credits; for when there is a lack of real money people have to borrow credit to their cost.

A few days before the Federal reserve act was passed Senator Elihu Root denounced the Federal reserve bill as an outrage on our liberties and made the following prediction:

> Long before we wake up from our dreams of prosperity through an inflated currency, our gold, which alone could have kept us from catastrophe, will have vanished and no rate of interest will tempt it to return.

If ever a prohphecy came true, that one did. It was impossible, however, for those luminous and instructed thinkers to control the course of events. On December 23, 1913, the Federal reserve bill became law, and that night Colonel House wrote to his hidden master in Wall Street as follows:

> I want to say a word of appreciation to you for the silent but no doubt effective work you have done in the interest of currency legislation and to congratulate you that the measure has finally been enacted into law. We all know that an entirely perfect bill, satisfactory to everybody, would have been an impossibility, and I feel quite certain fair men will admit that unless the President had stood as firm as he did we should likely have had no legislation at all. The bill is a good one in many respects; anyhow good enough to start with and to let experience teach us in what direction it needs perfection, which in due time we shall then get. In any event you have personally good reason to feel gratified with what has been accomplished.

The words "unless the President had stood as firm as he did we should likely have had no legislation at all," were a gentle reminder that it was Colonel House himself, the "holy monk," who had kept the President firm.

The foregoing letter affords striking evidence of the manner in which the predatory interests then sought to control the Government of the United States by surrounding the Executive with the personality and the influence of a financial Judas. Left to itself and to the conduct of its own legislative functions without pressure from the Executive, the Congress would not have passed the Federal reserve act. According to Colonel House, and since this was his report to his master, we may believe it to be true, the Federal reserve act was passed because Wilson stood firm; in other words because Wilson was under the guidance and control of the most ferocious usurers in New York through their hireling, House. The Federal reserve act became law the day before Christmas Eve in the year 1913, and shortly afterwards the German international bankers, Kuhn, Loeb & Co., sent one of their partners here to run it.

In 1913, when the Federal reserve bill was submitted to the Democratic caucus, there was a discussion in regard to the form the proposed paper currency should take.

The proponents of the Federal reserve act, in their determination to create a new kind of paper money, had not needed to go outside of the Aldrich bill for a model. By the terms of the Aldrich bill, bank notes were to be issued by the National Reserve Association and were to be secured partly by gold or lawful money and partly by circulating evidences of debt. The first draft of the Federal reserve bill presented the same general plan, that is, for bank notes as opposed to Government notes, but with certain differences of regulation.

When the provision for the issuance of Federal reserve notes was placed before President Wilson he approved of it, but other Democrats were more mindful of Democratic principles and a great protest greeted the plan. Foremost amongst those who denounced it was William Jennings Bryan, the Secretary of State. Bryan wished to have the Federal reserve notes issued as Government obligations. President Wilson had an interview with him and found him adamant. At the conclusion of the interview Bryan left with the understanding that he would resign if the notes were made bank notes. The President then sent for his secretary and explained the matter to him. Mr. Tumulty went to see Bryan and Bryan took frm his library shelves a book containing all the Democratic platforms and read extracts from them bearing on the matter of the public currency. Returning to the President, Mr. Tumulty told him what had happened and ventured the opinion that Mr. Bryan was right and that Mr. Wilson was wrong. The President then asked Mr. Tumulty to show him where the Democratic Party in its national platforms had ever taken the view indicated by Bryan. Mr. Tumulty gave him the book, which he had brought from Bryan's house, and the President read very carefully plank after plank on the currency. He then said, "I am convinced there is a great deal in what Mr. Bryan says," and thereupon it was arranged that Mr. Tumulty should see the proponents of the Federal reserve bill in an effort to bring about an adjustment of the matter.

The remainder of this story may be told in the words of Senator GLASS. Concerning Bryan's opposition to the plan of allowing the proposed Federal reserve notes to take the form of bank notes and the matter in which President Wilson and the proponents of the Federal reserve bill yielded to Bryan in return for his support of the measure, Senator GLASS makes the following statement:

> The only other feature of the currency bill around which a conflict raged at this time was the note-issue provision. Long before I knew it, the President was desperately worried over it. His economic good sense told him the notes should be issued by the banks and not by the Government; but some of his advisers told him Mr. Bryan could not be induced to give his support to any bill that did not provide for a "Government note." There was in the Senate and House a large Bryan following which, united with a naturally adversary party vote, could prevent legislation. Certain overconfident gentlemen proferred their services in the task of "managing Bryan." They did not budge him. ° ° ° When a decision could no longer be postponed the President summoned me to the White House to say he wanted Federal reserve notes to "be obligations of the United States." I was for an instant speechless. With all the earnestness of my being I remonstrated, pointing out the unscientific nature of such a thing, as well as the evident inconsistency of it.

> "There is not, in truth, any Government obligation here, Mr. President," I exclaimed. "It would be a pretense on its face. Was there ever a Government note based primarily on the property of banking institutions? Was there ever a Government issue not one dollar of which could be put out except by demand of a bank? The suggested Government obligation is so remote it could never

be discerned," I concluded, out of breath.

"Exactly so, GLASS," earnestly said the President. "Every word you say is true; the Government liability is a mere thought. And so, if we can hold to the substance of the thing and give the other fellow the shadow, why not do it, if thereby we may save our bill?"

Shadow and substance! One can see from this how little President Wilson knew about banking. Unknowingly, he gave the substance to the international banker and the shadow to the common man. Thus was Bryan circumvented in his efforts to uphold the Democratic doctrine of the rights of the people. Thus the "unscientific blur" upon the bill was perpetrated. The "unscientific blur," however, was not the fact that the United States Government, by the terms of Bryan's edict, was obliged to assume as an obligation whatever currency was issued. Mr. Bryan was right when he insisted that the United States should preserve its sovereignty over the public currency. The "unscientific blur" was the nature of the currency itself, a nature which makes it unfit to be assumed as an obligation of the United States Government. It is the worst currency and the most dangerous this country has ever known. When the proponents of the act saw that Democratic doctrine would not permit them to let the proposed banks issue the new currency as bank notes, they should have stopped at that. They should not have foisted that kind of currency, namely, an asset currency, on the United States Government. They should not have made the Government liable on the private debts of individuals and corporations and, least of all, on the private debts of foreigners.

The Federal reserve note is essentially unsound.

As Kemmerer says:

> The Federal reserve notes, therefore, in form have some of the qualities of Government paper money, but in substance, are almost a pure asset currency possessing a Government guaranty against which contingency the Government has made no provision whatever.

Hon. E. J. Hill, a former Member of the House, said, and truly:

* * * They are obligations of the Government for which the United States has received nothing and for the payment of which at any time it assumes the responsibility looking to the Federal reserve bank to recoup itself.

If the United States Government is to redeem the Federal reserve notes when the general public finds out what it costs to deliver this flood of paper money to the 12 Federal reserve banks, and if the Government has made no provision for redeeming them, the first element of their unsoundness is not far to seek.

Before the Senate Banking and Currency Committee, while the Federal reserve bill was under discussion, Mr. Crozier, of Cincinnati, said:

In other words, the imperial power of elasticity of the public currency is wielded exclusively by these central corporations owned by the banks. This is a life and death power over all local banks and all business. It can be used to create or destroy prosperity, to ward off or cause stringencies and panics. By making money artificially scarce interest rates throughout the country can be arbitrarily raised and the bank tax on all business and cost of living increased for the profit of the banks-owning these regional central banks, and without the slightest benefit to the people. These 12 corporations together cover the whole country and monopolize and use for private gain every dollar of the public currency and all public revenues of the United States. Not a dollar can be put into circulation among the people by their Government without the consent of and on terms fixed by these 12 private money trusts.

In defiance of this and all other warnings, the proponents of the Federal reserve act created the 12 private credit corporations and gave them an absolute monopoly of the currency of the United States, not of Federal reserve notes alone, but of all the currency, the Federal reserve act providing ways by means of which the gold and general currency in the hands of the American people could be obtained by the Federal reserve banks in exchange for Federal reserve notes, which are not money but merely promises to pay money. Since the evil day when this was done the initial monopoly has been extended by vicious amendments to the Federal reserve act and by the unlawful and treasonable practices of the Federal Reserve Board and the Federal reserve banks.

Mr. Chairman, when a Chinese merchant sells human hair to a Paris wigmaker and bills him in dollars, the Federal reserve banks can buy his bill against the wigmaker and then use that bill as collateral for Federal reserve notes. The United States Government thus pays the Chinese merchant the debt of the wigmaker and gets nothing in return except a shady title to the Chinese hair.

Mr. Chairman, if a Scotch distiller wishes to send a cargo of Scotch whiskey to the United States, he can draw his bill against the purchasing bootlegger in dollars and after the bootlegger has accepted it by writing his name across the face of it the Scotch distiller can send that bill to the nefarious open discount market in New York City, where the Federal Reserve Board and the Federal reserve banks will buy it and use it as collateral for a new issue of Federal reserve notes. Thus the Government of the United States pays the Scotch distiller for the whiskey before it is shipped, and if it is lost on the way, or if the Coast Guard seizes it and destroys it, the Federal reserve banks simply write off the losses and the Government never recovers the money that was paid to the Scotch distiller. While we are attempting to enforce prohibition here the Federal Reserve Board and the Federal reserve banks are financing the distillery business in Europe and are paying bootleggers' bills with the public credit of the United States Government.

Mr. Chairman, if a German brewer ships beer to this country or anywhere else in the world and draws his bill for it in dollars, the Federal reserve banks will buy that bill and use it as collateral for Federal reserve notes. Thus, they compel our Government to pay the German brewer for his beer. Why should the Federal Reserve Board and the Federal reserve banks be permitted to finance the brewing industry of Germany, either in this way or as they do by compelling small and fearful United States banks to take stock in the Isenbeck brewery and in the German bank for brewing industries?

Mr. Chairman, if Dynamit Nobel of Germany wishes to sell dynamite to Japan to use in Manchuria or elsewhere, it can draw its bill against its Japanese customers in dollars and send that bill to the nefarious open-discount market in New York City, where the Federal Reserve Board and the Federal reserve banks will buy it and use it as collateral for a new issue of Federal reserve notes, while at the same time the Federal Reserve Board will be helping Dynamit Nobel in stuffing its stock into the United States banking system. Why should we send our representatives to the disarmament conference at Geneva while the Federal Reserve Board and the Federal reserve banks are making our Government pay Japanese debts to German munitions makers?

Mr. Chairman, if a bean grower of Chile wishes to raise a crop of beans and sell them to a Japanese customer, he can draw a bill against his prospective Japanese customer in dollars and have it purchased by the Federal Reserve Board and the Federal reserve banks and get the money out of this country at the expense of the American public before he has even planted the beans in the ground.

Mr. Chairman, if a German in Germany wishes to export goods to South America or anywhere else, he can draw his bill against his customer and send it to the United States and get the money out of this country before he ships or even manufactures the goods.

Mr. Chairman, why should the currency of the United States be issued on the strength of Chinese human hair? Why should it be issued on the trade whims of a wigmaker? Why should it be issued on the strength of German beer? Why

311

should it be issued on a crop of unplanted beans to be grown in Chile for Japanese consumption? Why should the Government of the United States be compelled to issue many billions of dollars every year to pay the debts of one foreigner to another foreigner? Was it for this that our national bank depositors had their money taken out of our banks and shipped abroad? Was it for this they had to lose it? Why should the public credit of the United States Government and likewise money belonging to our national bank depositors be used to support foreign brewers, narcotic drug vendors, whiskey distillers, wigmakers, human hair merchants, Chilean bean growers, and the like? Why should our national bank depositors and our Government be forced to finance the munition factories of Germany and Soviet Russia?

Mr. Chairman, if a German, in Germany, wishes to sell wheelbarrows to another German, he can draw a bill in dollars and get the money out of the Federal reserve banks before an American farmer could explain his request for a loan to move his crop to market. In Germany, when credit instruments are being given, the creditors say, "See you, it must be of a kind that I can cash at the reserve." Other foreigners feel the same way. The reserve to which these gentry refer is our reserve, which, as you know, is entirely made up of money belonging to American bank depositors. I think foreigners should cash their own trade paper and not send it over here to bankers who use it to fish cash out of the pockets of the American people.

Mr. Chairman, there is nothing like the Federal reserve pool of confiscated bank deposits in the world. It is a public trough of American wealth in which foreigners claim rights equal to or greater than those of Americans. The Federal reserve banks are the agents of the foreign central banks. They use our bank depositors' money for the benefit of their foreign principals. They barter the public credit of the United States Government and hire it out to foreigners at a profit to themselves.

All this is done at the expense of the United States Government, and at a sickening loss to the American people. Only our great wealth enabled us to stand the drain of it as long as we did.

I believe that the nations of the world would have settled down after the World War more peacefully if we had not had this standing temptation here—this pool of our bank depositors' money given to private interests and used by them in connection with illimitable drafts upon the public credit of the United States Government. The Federal Reserve Board invited the world to come in and to carry away cash, credit, goods, and everything else of value that was movable. Values amounting to many billions of dollars have been taken out of this country by the Federal Reserve Board and the Federal reserve banks for the benefit of their foreign principals. The United States has been ransacked and pillaged. Our structures have been gutted and only the walls are left standing. While this crime was being perpetrated everything the world could rake up to sell us was brought in here at our own expense by the Federal Reserve Board and the Federal reserve banks until our markets were swamped with unneeded and unwanted imported goods priced far above their value and thus made to equal the dollar volume of our honest exports and to kill or reduce our favorable balance of trade. As agents of the foreign central banks, the Federal Reserve Board and the Federal reserve banks try by every means within their power to reduce our favorable balance of trade. They act for their foreign principals and they accept fees from foreigners for acting against the best interests of the United States. Naturally there has been great competition among foreigners for the favors of the Federal Reserve Board.

What we need to do is to send the reserves of our national banks home to the people who earned and produced them and who still own them and to the banks which were compelled to surrender them to predatory interests. We need to destroy the Federal reserve pool, wherein our national-bank reserves are impounded for the benefit of foreigners. We need to make it very difficult for outlanders to draw money away from us. We need to save America for Americans.

Mr. Chairman, when you hold a $10 Federal reserve note in your hand you are holding a piece of paper which sooner or later is going to cost the United States Government $10 in gold, unless the Government is obliged to give up the gold standard. It is protected by a reserve of 40 per cent, or $4 in gold. It is based on Limburger cheese, reputed to be in a foreign warehouse; or on cans purporting to contain peas but which may contain no peas but salt water instead; or on horse meat; illicit drugs; bootleggers' fancies; rags and bones from Soviet Russia of which the United States imported over a million dollars' worth last year; on wine, whiskey, natural gas, on goat or dog fur, garlic on the string, or Bombay ducks. If you like to have paper money which is secured by such commodities, you have it in the Federal reserve note. If you desire to obtain the thing of value upon which this paper currency is based—that is, the Limburger cheese, the whiskey, the illicit drugs, or any of the other staples—you will have a very hard time finding them. Many of these worshipful commodities are in foreign countries. Are you going to Germany to inspect her warehouses to see if the specified things of value are there? I think not. And what is more, I do not think you would find them if you did go.

Immense sums belonging to our national-bank depositors have been given to Germany on no collateral security whatever. The Federal Reserve Board and the Federal reserve banks have issued United States currency on mere finance drafts drawn by Germans. Billions upon billions of our money has been pumped into Germany and money is still being pumped into Germany by the Federal Reserve Board and the Federal reserve banks. Her worthless paper is still being negotiated here and renewed here on the public credit of the United States Government and at the expense of the American people. On April 27, 1932, the Federal reserve outfit sent $750,000, belonging to American bank depositors, in gold to Germany. A week later, another $300,000 in gold was shipped to Germany in the same way. About the middle of May $12,000,000 in gold was shipped to Germany by the Federal Reserve Board and the Federal reserve banks. Almost every week there is a shipment of gold to Germany. These shipments are not made for profit on exchange since German marks are below parity against the dollar.

Mr. Chairman, I believe that the national-bank depositors of the United States are entitled to know what the Federal Reserve Board and the Federal reserve banks are doing with their money. There are millions of national-bank depositors in this country who do not know that a percentage of every dollar they deposit in a member bank of the Federal reserve system goes automatically to the American agents of foreign banks and that all of their deposits can be paid away to foreigners without their knowledge or consent by the crooked machinery of the Federal reserve act and the questionable practices of the Federal Reserve Board and the Federal reserve banks. Mr. Chairman, the American people should be told the truth by their servants in office.

In 1930 we had over half a billion dollars outstanding daily to finance foreign goods stored in or shipped between foreign countries. In its yearly total, this item amounts to several billion dollars. What goods are those upon which the Federal reserve banks yearly pledge several billion dollars of the public credit of the United States? What goods are those which are hidden in European and Asiatic storehouses and which have never been seen by any officer of this Government, but which are being financed on the public credit of the United States Government? What goods are those upon which the United States Government is being obliged by the Federal reserve banks to issue Federal reserve notes to the extent of several billion dollars a year?

The Federal Reserve Board and the Federal reserve banks have been international bankers from the beginning, with the United States Government as their enforced banker and supplier of currency. But it is none the less extraordinary to see those 12 private credit monopolies buying the debts of foreigners against foreigners in all parts of the world and asking the Government of the United States for new issues of Federal

315

reserve notes in exchange for them.

I see no reason why the American taxpayers should be hewers of wood and drawers of water for the European and Asiatic customers of the Federal reserve banks. I see no reason why a worthless acceptance drawn by a foreign swindler as a means of getting gold out of this country should receive the lowest and choicest rate from the Federal Reserve Board and be treated as better security than the note of an American farmer living on American land.

The magnitude of the acceptance racket, as it has been developed by the Federal reserve banks, their foreign correspondents, and the predatory European-born bankers who set up the Federal reserve institution here and taught our own brand of pirates how to loot the people, I say the magnitude of this racket is estimated to be in the neighborhood of $9,000,000,000 a year. In the past 10 years it is said to have amounted to $90,000,000,000. In my opinion, it has amounted to several times as much. Coupled with this you have, to the extent of billions of dollars, the gambling in United States securities, which takes place in the same open discount market — a gamble upon which the Federal Reserve Board is now spending $100,000,000 a week.

Federal reserve notes are taken from the United States Government in unlimited quantities. Is it strange that the burden of supplying these immense sums of money to the gambling fraternity has at last proved too heavy for the American people to endure? Would it not be a national calamity if the Federal Reserve Board and the Federal reserve banks should again bind this burden down on the backs of the American people and, by means of the long rawhide whips of the credit masters, compel them to enter upon another 17 years of slavery? They are trying to do that now. They are taking $100,000,000 of the public credit of the United States Government every week in addition to all their other seizures, and they are spending that money in the nefarious open market in New York City in a desperate gamble to reestablish their graft as a long concern.

They are putting the United States Government in debt to the extent of $100,000,000 a week, and with this money they are buying up our Government securities for themselves and their foreign principals. Our people are disgusted with the experiments of the Federal Reserve Board. The Federal Reserve Board is not producing a loaf of bread, a yard of cloth, a bushel of corn, or a pile of cordwood by its check-kiting operations in the money market.

A fortnight or so ago great aid and comfort was given to Japan by the firm of A. Gerli & Sons, of New York, an importing firm, which bought $16,000,000 worth of raw silk from the Japanese Government. Federal reserve notes will be issued to pay that amount to the Japanese Government, and these notes will be secured by money belonging to our national-bank depositors.

Why should United States currency be issued on this debt? Why should United States currency be issued to pay the debt of Gerli & Sons to the Japanese Government? The Federal Reserve Board and the Federal reserve banks think more of the silkworms of Japan than they do of American citizens. We do not need $16,000,000 worth of silk in this country at the present time, not even to furnish work to dyers and finishers. We need to wear home-grown and American-made clothes and to use our own money for our own goods and staples. We could spend $16,000,000 in the United States of America on American children and that would be a better investment for us than Japanese silk purchased on the public credit of the United States Government.

Mr. Speaker, on the 13th of January of this year I addressed the House on the subject of the Reconstruction Finance Corporation. In the course of my remarks I made the following statement:

> In 1928 the member banks of the Federal reserve system borrowed $60,598,690,000 from the Federal reserve banks on their 15-day promissory notes. Think of it! Sixty billion dollars payable upon demand in gold in the course

of one single year. The actual payment of such obligations calls for six times as much monetary gold as there is in the entire world. Such transactions represent a grant in the course of one single year of about $7,000,000 to every member bank of the Federal reserve system. Is it any wonder that there is a depression in this country? Is it any wonder that American labor, which ultimately pays the cost of all the banking operations of this country, has at last proved unequal to the task of supplying this huge total of cash and credit for the benefit of stock-market manipulators and foreign swindlers?

Mr. Chairman, some of my colleagues have asked for more specific information concerning this stupendous graft, this frightful burden which has been placed on the wage earners and taxpayers of the United States for the benefit of the Federal Reserve Board and the Federal reserve banks. They were surprised to learn that member banks of the Federal reserve system had received the enormous sum of $60,598,-690,000 from the Federal Reserve Board and the Federal reserve banks on their promissory notes in the course of one single year, namely, 1928. Another Member of this House, Mr. BEEDY, the honorable gentleman from Maine, has questioned the accuracy of my statement and has informed me that the Federal Reserve Board denies absolutely that these figures are correct. This Member has said to me that the thing is unthinkable, that it can not be, that it is beyond all reason to think that the Federal Reserve Board and the Federal reserve banks should have so subsidized and endowed their favorite banks of the Federal reserve system. This Member is horrified at the thought of a graft so great, a bounty so deterimental to the public welfare as sixty and a half billion dollars a year and more shoveled out to favored banks of the Federal reserve system.

I sympathize with Mr. BEEDY. I would spare him pain if I could, but the facts remain as I have stated them. In 1928, the Federal Reserve Board and the Federal reserve banks presented the staggering amount of $60,598,690,000 to their member banks at the expense of the wage earners and taxpayers of the United States. In 1929, the year of the stock market crash, the Federal Reserve Board and the Federal reserve banks advanced fifty-eight billions to member banks.

In 1930, while the speculating banks were getting out of the stock market at the expense of the general public, the Federal Reserve Board and the Federal reserve banks advanced them $13,022,782,000. This shows that when the banks were gambling on the public credit of the United States Government as represented by Federal reserve currency, they were subsidized to any amount they required by the Federal Reserve Board and the Federal reserve banks. When the swindle began to fail, the banks knew it in advance and withdrew from the market. They got out with whole skins and left the people of the United States to pay the piper.

On November 2, 1931, I addressed a letter to the Federal Reserve Board asking for the aggregate total of member bank borrowings in the years 1928, 1929, 1930. In due course, I received a reply from the Federal Reserve Board, dated November 9, 1931, the pertinent part of which reads as follows:

My Dear Congressman: In reply to your letter of November 2, you are advised that the aggregate amount of 15-day promissory notes of member banks during each of the past three calendar years has been as follows:

1928	$60,598,690,000
1929	58,046,697,000
1930	13,022,782,000

*   *   *   *   *   *

Very truly yours,

CHESTER MORRILL, SECRETARY.

This will show the gentleman from Maine the accuracy of my statement. As for the denial of these facts made to him by the Federal Reserve Board, I can only say that it must have been prompted by fright, since hanging is too good for a Government board which permitted such a misuse of Government funds and credit.

My friend from Kansas, Mr. McGUGIN, has stated that he thought the Federal Reserve Board and the Federal reserve banks lent money by rediscounting. So they do, but they lend comparatively little that way. The real rediscounting that they do has been called a mere penny in the slot business. It is too slow for genuine high flyers. They discourage it. They prefer to subsidize their favorite banks by making these $60,000,-000,000 advances, and they prefer to acquire acceptances in the notorious open discount market in New York, where they can use them to control the prices of stocks and bonds on the exchanges. For every dollar they advanced on rediscounts in 1928 they lent $33 to their favorite banks for gambling purposes. In other words, their rediscounts in 1928 amounted to $1,814,271,000, while their loans to member banks amounted to $60,598,690,000. As for their open-market operations, these are on a stupendous scale, and no tax is paid on the acceptances they handle; and their foreign principals, for whom they do a business of several billion dollars every year, pay no income tax on their profits to the United States Government.

This is the John Law swindle over again. The theft of Teapot Dome was trifling compared to it. What king ever robbed his subjects to such an extent as the Federal Reserve Board and the Federal reserve banks have robbed us? Is it any wonder that there have lately been 90 cases of starvation in one of the New York hospitals? Is it any wonder that the children of this country are being dispersed and abandoned?

The Government and the people of the United States have been swindled by swindlers de luxe to whom the acquisition of American gold or a parcel of Federal reserve notes presented no more difficulty than the drawing up of a worthless acceptance in a country not subject to the laws of the United States, by sharpers not subject to the jurisdiction of the United States courts, sharpers with a strong banking "fence" on this side of the water—a "fence" acting as a receiver of the worthless paper coming from abroad, indorsing it and getting the currency out of the Federal reserve banks for it as quickly as possible, exchanging that currency for gold, and in turn transmitting the gold to its foreign confederates.

Such were the exploits of Ivar Kreuger, Mr. Hoover's friend, and his hidden Wall Street backers. Every dollar of the billions Kreuger and his gang drew out of this country on acceptances was drawn from the Government and the people of the United States through the Federal Reserve Board and the Federal reserve banks. The credit of the United States Government was peddled to him by the Federal Reserve Board and the Federal reserve banks for their own private gain. That is what the Federal Reserve Board and the Federal reserve banks have been doing for many years. They have been peddling the credit of this Government and the signature of this Government to the swindlers and speculators of all nations. That is what happens when a country forsakes its Constitution and gives its sovereignty over the public currency to private interests. Give them the flag and they will sell it.

The nature of Kreuger's organized swindle and the bankrupt condition of Kreuger's combine was known here last June when Hoover sought to exempt Kreuger's loan to Germany of one hundred twenty-five millions from the operation of the Hoover moratorium. The bankrupt condition of Kreuger's swindle was known here last summer when $30,000,000 was taken from American taxpayers by certain bankers in New York for the ostensible purpose of permitting Kreuger to make a loan to Colombia. Colombia never saw that money. The nature of Kreuger's swindle and the bankrupt condition of Kreuger was known here in January when he visited his friend, Mr. Hoover, at the White House. It was known here in March before he went to Paris and committed suicide there.

Mr. Chairman, I think the people of the United States are entitled to know how many billions of dollars were placed at the disposal of Kreuger and his gigantic combine by the Federal Reserve Board and the Federal reserve banks and to know how much of our Government currency was issued and lost in the financing of that great swindle in the years during which the Federal Reserve Board and the Federal reserve banks took care of Kreuger's requirements.

Mr. Chairman, I believe there should be a congressional investigation of the operations of Kreuger and Toll in the United States and that Swedish Match, International Match, the Swedish-American Investment Corporation, and all related enterprises, including the subsidiary companies of Kreuger and Toll, should be investigated and that the issuance of United States currency in connection with those enterprises and the use of our national bank depositors' money for Kreuger's benefit should be known to the general public. I am referring, not only to the securities which were floated and sold in this country, but also to the commercial loans to Kreuger's enterprises and the mass financing of Kreuger's companies by the Federal Reserve Board and the Federal reserve banks and the predatory institutions which the Federal Reserve Board and the Federal reserve banks shield and harbor.

A few days ago the President of the United States, with a white face and shaking hands, went before the Senate on behalf of the moneyed interests and asked the Senate to levy a tax on the people so that foreigners might know that the United States would pay its debts to them. Most Americans thought that it was the other way around. What does the United States owe to foreigners? When and by whom was the debt incurred? It was incurred by the Federal Reserve Board and the Federal reserve banks when they peddled the signature of this Government to foreigners for a price. It is what the United States Government has to pay to redeem the obligations of the Federal Reserve Board and the Federal reserve banks. Are you going to let those thieves get off scot free? Is there one law for the looter who drives up to the door of the United States Treasury in his limousine and another for the United States veterans who are sleeping on the floor of a dilapidated house on the outskirts of Washington?

The Baltimore & Ohio Railroad is here asking for a large loan from the people and the wage earners and the taxpayers of the United States. It is begging for a hand-out from the Government. It is standing, cap in hand, at the door of the Reconstruction Finance Corporation, where all the other jackals have gathered to the feast. It is asking for money that was raised from the people by taxation, and it wants this money of the poor for the benefit of Kuhn, Loeb & Co., the German international bankers. Is there one law for the Baltimore & Ohio Railroad and another for the needy veterans it threw off its freight cars the other day? Is there one law for sleek and prosperous swindlers who call themselves bankers and another law for the soldiers who defend the United States flag?

Mr. Chairman, some people are horrified because the collateral behind Kreuger and Toll debentures was removed and worthless collateral substituted for it. What is this but what is being done daily by the Federal reserve banks? When the Federal reserve act was passed, the Federal reserve banks were allowed to substitute "other like collateral" for collateral behind Federal reserve notes but by an amendment obtained at the request of the corrupt and dishonest Federal Reserve Board, the act was changed so that the word "like" was stricken out. All that immense trouble was taken here in Congress so that the law would permit the Federal reserve banks to switch collateral. At the present time behind the scenes in the Federal reserve banks there is a night-and-day movement of collateral. A visiting Englishman, leaving the United States a few weeks ago, said that things would look better here after "they cleaned up the mess at Washington." Cleaning up the mess consists in fooling the people and making them pay a second time for the bad foreign investments of the Federal Reserve Board and the Federal reserve banks. It consists in moving that heavy load of dubious and worthless foreign paper—the balls of wigmakers, brewers, distillers, narcotic drug vendors, munition makers, illegal finance drafts, and worthless foreign securities, out of the banks and putting it on the back of American labor. That is what the Reconstruction Finance Corporation is doing now. They talk about loans to banks and railroads but they say very little about that other business of theirs which consists in relieving the swindlers who promoted investment trusts in this country and dumped worthless foreign securities into

323

them and then resold that mess of pottage to American investors under cover of their own corporate titles. The Reconstruction Finance Corporation is taking over those worthless securities from those investment trusts with United States Treasury money at the expense of the American taxpayer and wage earner.

It will take us 20 years to redeem our Government, 20 years of penal servitude to pay off the gambling debts of the traitorous Federal Reserve Board and the Federal reserve banks and to earn again that vast flood of American wages and savings, bank deposits, and United States Government credit which the Federal Reserve Board and the Federal reserve banks exported out of this country to their foreign principals.

The Federal Reserve Board and the Federal reserve banks lately conducted an anti-hoarding campaign here. Then they took that extra money which they had persuaded the trusting American people to put into the banks and they sent it to Europe along with the rest. In the last several months, they have sent $1,300,000,000 in gold to their foreign employers, their foreign masters, and every dollar of that gold belonged to the people of the United States and was unlawfully taken from them.

Is not it high time that we had an audit of the Federal Reserve Board and the Federal reserve banks and an examination of all our Government bonds and securities and public moneys instead of allowing the corrupt and dishonest Federal Reserve Board and the Federal reserve banks to speculate with those securities and this cash in the notorious open discount market of New York City?

Mr. Chairman, within the limits of the time allowed me, I cannot enter into a particularized discussion of the Federal Reserve Board and the Federal reserve banks. I have singled out the Federal reserve currency for a few remarks because there has lately been some talk here of "fiat money." What kind of money is being pumped into the open discount market and through it into foreign channels and stock exchanges? Mr. Mills of the Treasury has spoken here of his horror of the printing presses and his horror of dishonest money. He has no horror of dishonest money. If he had, he would be no party to the present gambling of the Federal Reserve Board and the Federal reserve banks in the nefarious open discount market of New York, a market in which the sellers are represented by 10 great discount dealer corporations owned and organized by the very banks which own and control the Federal Reserve Board and the Federal reserve banks. Fiat money, indeed!

After the several raids on the Treasury Mr. Mills borrows the speech of those who protest against those raids and speaks now with pretended horror of a raid on the Treasury. Where was Mr. Mills last October when the United States Treasury needed $598,000,000 of the tarpayers' money which was supposed to be in the safe-keeping of Andrew W. Mellon in the designated depositories of Treasury funds, and which was not in those depositories when the Treasury needed it? Mr. Mills was the Assistant Secretary of the Treasury then, and he was at Washington throughout October, with the exception of a very significant week he spent at White Sulphur Springs closeted with international bankers, while the Italian minister, Signor Grandi, was being entertained—and bargained with—at Washington.

What Mr. Mills is fighting for is the preservation whole and entire of the bankers' monopoly of all the currency of the United States Government. What Mr. PATMAN proposes is that the Government shall exercise its sovereignty to the extent of issuing some currency for itself. This conflict of opinion between Mr. Mills as the spokesman of the bankers and Mr. PATMAN as the spokesman of the people brings the currency situation here into the open. Mr. PATMAN and the veterans are confronted by a stone wall—the wall that fences in the bankers with their special privilege. Thus the issue is joined between the hosts of democracy, of which the veterans are a part, and the men of the king's bank, the would-be aristocrats, who deflated American agriculture and robbed this country for the benefit of their foreign principals.

Mr. Chairman, last December I introduced a resolution here asking for an examination and an audit of the Federal Reserve Board and the Federal reserve banks and all related matters. If the House sees fit to make such an investigation, the people of the United States will obtain information of great value. This is a Government of the people, by the people, for the people, consequently nothing should be concealed from the people. The man who deceives the people is a traitor to the United States. The man who knows or suspects that a crime has been committed and who conceals or covers up that crime is an accessory to it. Mr. Speaker, it is a monstrous thing for this great Nation of people to have its destinies presided over by a traitorous Government board acting in secret concert with international usurers. Every effort has been made by the Federal Reserve Board to conceal its power but the truth is the Federal Reserve Board has usurped the Government of the United States. It controls everything here and it controls all our foreign relations. It makes and breaks governments at will. No man and no body of men is more entrenched in power than the arrogant credit monopoly which operates the Federal Reserve Board and the Federal reserve banks. These evildoers have robbed this country of more than enough money to pay the national debt. What the National Government has permitted the Federal Reserve Board to steal from the people should now be restored to the people. The people have a valid claim against the Federal Reserve Board and the Federal reserve banks. If that claim is enforced, Americans will not need to stand in breadlines or to suffer and die of starvation in the streets. Homes will be saved, families will be kept together and American children will not be dispersed and abandoned. The Federal Reserve Board and the Federal reserve banks owe the United States Government an immense sum of money. We ought to find out the exact amount of the people's claim. We should know the amount of the indebtedness of the Federal Reserve Board and the Federal reserve banks to the people and we should collect that amount immediately. We certainly should investigate this treacherous and disloyal conduct of the Federal Reserve Board and the Federal reserve banks.

Here is a Federal reserve note. Immense numbers of these notes are now held abroad. I am told they amount to upward of a billion dollars. They constitute a claim against our Government and likewise a claim against the money our people have deposited in the member banks of the Federal reserve system. Our people's money to the extent of $1,300,-000,000 has within the last few months been shipped abroad to redeem Federal reserve notes and to pay other gambling debts of the traitorous Federal Reserve Board and the Federal reserve banks. The greater part of our monetary stock has been shipped to foreigners. Why should we promise to pay the debts of foreigners to foreigners? Why should our Government be put into the position of supplying money to foreigners? Why should American farmers and wage earners add millions of foreigners to the number of their dependents? Why should the Federal Reserve Board and the Federal reserve banks be permitted to finance our competitors in all parts of the world? Do you know why the tariff was raised? It was raised to shut out the flood of Federal reserve goods pouring in here from every quarter of the globe—cheap goods produced by cheaply paid foreign labor on unlimited supplies of money and credit sent out of this country by the dishonest and unscrupulous Federal Reserve Board and the Federal reserve banks. Go out in Washington to buy an electric light bulb and you will probably be offered one that was made in Japan on American money. Go out to buy a pair of fabric gloves and inconspicuously written on the inside of the gloves that will be offered to you will be found the words "made in Germany" and that means "made on the public credit of the United States Government paid to German firms in American gold taken from the confiscated bank deposits of the American people."

The Federal Reserve Board and the Federal reserve banks are spending $100,000,000 a week buying Government securities in the open market and are thus making a great bid for foreign business. They are trying to make rates so attractive that the human-hair merchants and distillers and other business entities in foreign lands will come here and hire more of the public credit of the United States Government and pay the Federal reserve outfit for getting it for them.

Mr. Chairman, when the Federal reserve act was passed the people of the United States did not perceive that a world system was being set up here which would make the savings of an American school-teacher available to a narcotic-drug vendor in Macao. They did not perceive that the United States was to be lowered to the position of a coolie country which has nothing but raw materials and heavy goods for export. That Russia was destined to supply man power and that this country was to supply financial power to an international superstate— a superstate controlled by international bankers and international industrialists acting together to enslave the world for their own pleasure.

The people of the United States are being greatly wronged. If they are not, then I do not know what "wronging the people" means. They have been driven from their employments. They have been dispossessd of their homes. They have been evicted from their rented quarters. They have lost their children. They have been left to suffer and to die for the lack of shelter, food, clothing, and medicine.

The wealth of the United States and the working capital of the United States has been taken away from them and has either been locked in the vaults of certain banks and great corporations or exported to foreign countries for the benefit of the foreign customers of those banks and corporations. So far as the people of the United States are concerned, the cupboard is bare. It is true that the warehouses and coal yards and grain elevators are full, but the warehouses and coal yards and grain elevators are padlocked and the great banks and corporations hold the keys. The sack of the United States by the Federal Reserve Board and the Federal reserve banks and their confederates is the greatest crime in history.

Mr. Chairman, a serious situation confronts the House of Representatives to-day. We are the trustees of the people and the rights of the people are being taken away from them. Through the Federal Reserve Board and the Federal reserve banks, the people are losing the rights guaranteed to them by the Constitution. Their property has been taken from them without due process of law. Mr. Chairman, common decency requires us to examine the public accounts of the Government to see what crimes against the public welfare have been or are being committed.

What is needed here is a return to the Constitution of the United States. We need to have a complete divorce of Bank and State. The old struggle that was fought out here in Jackson's day must be fought over again. The Independent United States Treasury should be reestablished and the Government should keep its own money under lock and key in the building the people provided for that purpose. Asset currency, the device of the swindler, should be done away with. The Government should buy gold and issue United State currency on it. The business of the independent bankers should be restored to them. The State banking systems should be freed from coercion. The Federal reserve districts should be abolished and State boundaries should be respected. Bank reserves should be kept within the borders of the States whose people own them, and this reserve money of the people should be protected so that international bankers and acceptance bankers and discount dealers can not draw it away from them. The exchanges should be closed while we are putting our financial affairs in order. The Federal reserve act should be repealed and the Federal reserve banks, having violated their charters, should be liquidated immediately. Faithless Government officers who have violated their oaths of office should be impeached and brought to trial. Unless this is done by us, I predict that the American people, outraged, robbed, pillaged, insulted, and betrayed as they are in their own land, will rise in their wrath and send a President here who will sweep the money changers out of the temple. [Applause.]

XVII

IMPEACHMENT OF
HERBERT HOOVER,
PRESIDENT OF THE UNITED STATES

Tuesday, December 13, 1932

Mr. McFADDEN. Mr. Speaker, I rise to a question of constitutional privilege.

On my own responsibility as a Member of the House of Representatives, I impeach Herbert Hoover, President of the United States, for high crimes and misdemeanors, and offer the following resolution.

The SPEAKER. The Clerk will report the resolution.

The Clerk read as follows:

Whereas Herbert Hoover, President of the United States, has, in violation of the Constitution and laws of the United States, unlawfully attempted to usurp and has usurped legislative powers and functions of the Congress of the United States, which violations make him guilty of high crimes and misdemeanors and subject to impeachment; and

Whereas the said Herbert Hoover, President of the United States, has, in violation of the Constitution and laws of the United States, publicly shown disrespect for the Congress of the United States, which violation makes him him guilty of high crimes and misdemeanors and subject to impeachment; and

Whereas the said Herbert Hoover, President of the United States, has, in violation of the Constitution and laws of the United States, pursued a policy inimical to the welfare of the United States by employing means to influence the deliberations of the legislative branch of the United States Government and has interfered with freedom of debate in Congress and has forced unsound and unconstitutional legislation upon the people of the United States, which violations make him guilty of high crimes and misdemeanors and subject to impeachment; and

Whereas the said Herbert Hoover, President of the United States, has, in violation of the Constitution and laws of the United States, attempted unlawfully to dissipate and has unlawfully dissipated financial resources and other resources of the United States, which violations make him guilty of high crimes and misdemeanors and subject to impeachment; and

Whereas the said Herbert Hoover, President of the United States, in violation of the Constitution and laws of the United States, has, to the great loss and detriment of the United States and to the benefit of foreign nations, unlawfully attempted to impair the validity of contracts existing between the United States and foreign nations, which violations make him guilty of high crimes and misdemeanors and subject to impeachment; and

Whereas the said Herbert Hoover, President of the United States, has, in violation of the Constitution and laws of the United States, unlawfully interfered with and prevented the receipt by the United States of payments of money lawfully due to the United States from foreign nations and has inflicted great losses, financial and otherwise, upon the Government and the people of the United States and has injured the credit and financial standing of the United States Government and has increased unemployment and suffering from physical want in the United States, and has caused a deficit in the accounts of the United States Treasury which has rendered necessary the imposition of additional taxes upon the people of the United States, which violations make him guilty of high crimes and misdemeanors and subject to impeachment; and

Whereas the said Herbert Hoover, President of the United States, has, in violation of the Constitution and laws of the United States, initiated and carried on secret conversations, ignominious to the United States, with German Government officials and international bankers and others, with intent to deceive and to injure the Government and the people of the United States, and thereby has injured the Government and the people of the United States; and whereas the said Hoover ignominiously caused a prearranged request to be improperly made to himself by General von Hindenburg, President of Germany, for the commission of an unlawful act injurious to the United States and caused such request to be made for the purpose of deceiving and injuring the people of the United States and for the purpose of covering up a conspiracy against the United States which was taking place between himself and others, which conspiracy culminated in the Hoover moratorium proposal and the London conference of July, 1931; and whereas the said Hoover, with intent to injure the United States and to destroy financial assets of the United States, unlawfully declared the so-called Hoover moratorium and unlawfully initiated the international political conference which took place at London in July, 1931, which violations make him guilty of high crimes and misdemeanors and subject to impeachment; and

Whereas the said Herbert Hoover, President of the United States, has publicly stated in the press that his declaration of the moratorium has meant sacrifices by the American people, and that the economic load most seriously oppressing the peoples of Germany and Central Europe will be immensely lightened, and whereas the infliction of suffering upon the American people for the benefit of foreign nations on his part, the part of the said Hoover, is a violation of the Constitution and laws of the United States, the said admission shows him to be guilty of high crimes and misdemeanors and subject to impeachment; and

Whereas the said Herbert Hoover, President of the United States, has failed to obey and to uphold the law passed by the

332

Seventy-second Congress of the United States forbidding cancellation in whole or in part of the war debts due to the United States from foreign nations, and is endeavoring and has endeavored to nullify the contracts existing between the United States and its foreign debtors, and whereas such failure to obey and to uphold the law constitutes a violation of the Constitution and laws of the United States and makes him guilty of high crimes and misdemeanors and subject to impeachment; and

Whereas the said Herbert Hoover, President of the United States, has, in violation of the Constitution and laws of the United States, initiated the German stillholding agreement, and whereas the said stillholding agreement has never become law in the United States, but has unlawfully been put into effect here by the said Hoover in his usurpation of legislative power and by interested private parties trespassing upon the rights and privileges of the United States Government, and whereas the said stillholding agreement violates the terms of the Federal reserve act, the national bank act, and other laws of the United States, and is injurious to the United States, such violations make him, the said Hoover, guilty of high crimes and misdemeanors and subject to impeachment; and

Whereas an international conference composed of ministers of Great Britain, France, Germany, Belgium, Italy, Japan, and the United States took place at London from Monday, July 20, to Thursday, July 23, 1931, at the invitation of the British Government but on the initiative of the said Hoover, and was attended and participated in by Andrew W. Mellon, Secretary of the United States Treasury, and by Henry L. Stimson, United States Secretary of State, acting as representatives of the United States; and whereas the said Stimson presented a certain proposal to it; and whereas the said London conference took action affecting the United States and exercising sway over the United States and action affecting the war debts due to the United States; and whereas the representative of the United States entered into agreements on behalf of the United States with the ministers of Great Britain, France, Germany, Belgium, Italy, and Japan; and whereas such agreements entailed the surrender of rights of the United States; and whereas the said agreements so made have never been disclosed or submitted to the Congress of the United States for ratification and have never become law in the United States; and whereas a second conference, composed of a committee appointed by direction of the aforesaid London conference under stipulation that it should consist of representatives nominated by the governors of the central banks interested and that it was to take place at Basle under the Bank for International Settlements; and whereas Albert H. Wiggin appeared at the said conference at Basle as the representative of the United States on the nomination of George L. Harrison, of the Federal Reserve Bank of New York, an individual who had no power to make the said nomination; and whereas control of all the banking systems of the United States including the fiscal agents of the United States Government with their control of United States Treasury funds was given to this London conference committee, consisting of Albert H. Wiggin, Alberto Beneduce, Dr. R. G. Bindschedler, E. Franqui, P. Hofstede de Groot, Walter T. Layton, C. Melchoir, E. Moreau, O. Bydbeck, T. Tanaka, upon which the so-called United States representative was outnumbered nine to one by the nominees of the heads of foreign central banks; and whereas control of all the banking systems and all the wealth of the United States and control of the United States Treasury was thus given to foreign powers; and whereas actions taken by the said committee made it impossible for the banks of the United States to withdraw the funds of their depositors and other funds from Germany and obliged the banks of the United States continually to maintain the volume of the funds in Germany and made it impossible for the Treasury of the United States to withdraw moneys unlawfully taken from it and placed in Germany; and whereas such actions in regard to the banks and banking systems of the United States were unlawful and were unnecessary for any benefit to Germany, whose economic and budgetary situation according to the report of the London conference did not justify a lack of confidence; and whereas the said actions were taken as measures of deflation against the American people to impound United States funds in Germany under foreign control, to paralyze United States banks, to injure the United States Treasury, and to keep the United States in a condition of depression until misery and fear and starvation would drive the people of the United States into submission and compel them to cancel the war debts due to them; and whereas the said Wiggin had no lawful power to represent the banking systems of the United States at the said conference at Basle; and whereas the nomination of the said Wiggin by an individual at the direction of the ministers of Great Britain, France, Germany, Belgium, Italy, Japan, and the United States was unlawful; and whereas the agreements made and the action taken by the London conference committee at Basle have never been submitted to the Congress of the United States; and whereas billions of dollars in bank deposits have been lost by American citizens on account of the said agreements, and many United States banks have failed by reason of them and the Reconstruction Finance Corporation has made loans of public money to banks and institutions injured by them and the public debt of the United States and the deficit in the United States Treasury have been increased by the actions of the London conference committee at Basle; and whereas the said actions were taken on the initiative and by the direction of the said Hoover; and whereas the stillholding agreement entered into at Basle by the said Wiggin was unlawful and was prepared concurrently with the terms of the Hoover moratorium proposed by the said Hoover and others and was presented to the London conference by Henry L. Stimson as a joint product of British and American participation and was a part of a conspiracy designed to force the United States into submission to foreign nations and international bankers and thus to obtain cancellation of the war debts; and whereas in violation of the Constitution and laws for the United States, Herbert Hoover, President of the United States, initiated the London conference and the prearranged events which flowed from it; and whereas the London conference was deceitfully initiated by the said Hoover for the purpose of securing cancellation of the war debts as shown by facts and circumstances; and whereas the *Herald Tribune* published a report at the close of the London conference, a part of which reads as follows:

"If, as these British leaders expect, the committee recommends a considerable extension of credits to Germany; if it indicates, further, that permanent amelioration of that situation depends upon reconsideration of the war debts and reparations problem, and if the interested powers take action along these lines the British admit that something indeed will have been accomplished."

Which article shows the British expectation that the said London conference would result in a recommendation, by the committee appointed at its direction to meet at Basle, that permanent amelioration of the situation would depend upon reconsideration of the war debts and reparations, and whereas the said committee of individuals nominated by the heads of foreign central banks, which central banks are foreign government institutions, and Albert H. Wiggin, who unlawfully appeared as the representative of the United States and of all the banking systems of the United States, did make the pre-arranged recommendation by means of a report which is nothing less than an argument for a reconsideration of the war debts and reparations, and whereas the said Hoover initiated the London conference for the purpose of defrauding and injuring the United States and signing over majority control of the banking systems of the United States, which represent the wealth and savings of the American people, to foreign nations and for the purpose of bringing about a cancellation of war debts, in violation of the Constitution and laws of the United States, his actions in connection therewith make him guilty of high crimes and misdemeanors and subject to impeachment; and

Whereas the said Herbert Hoover, President of the United

States, did in 1932, after the passage of the law passed by the Seventy-second Congress of the United States forbidding cancellation or reduction of the war debts, appoint one Andrew W. Mellon, then Secretary of the United States Treasury, ambassador to a foreign power while a resolution for the impeachment of the said Mellon for violations of United States law and misconduct in office was being heard by the Judiciary Committee of the House of Representatives, which appointment of the said Mellon was ignominious to the United States and showed disrespect for the House of Representatives, and whereas the said Hoover has permitted without contradiction the publication of statements concerning the said appointment of the said Mellon as having been made by him with a consideration of Mellon's fitness to conduct conversations with the said foreign power for the purpose of cancelling the debt of that foreign power to the United States, thus admitting an effort on his part, the part of the said Hoover, to bring about cancellation in whole or in part of the war debt due from the said foreign nation to the United States, and in violation of the rights of the sovereign people of the United States, which effort on his part, as further evidenced by his actions showing a conspiracy against the United States between himself and the said Mellon and others and by his secret conversations, ignominious to the United States, with Ramsay MacDonald, Montague Norman, and other subjects of the King of England and officials of the British Government, and others, showing a willingness and an intention on his part to defraud the people of the United States, makes him guilty of high crimes and misdemeanors and subject to impeachment; and

Whereas the said Herbert Hoover, President of the United States, has, in violation of the Constitution and laws of the United States, and for the benefit of foreigners, unlawfully attempted to interfere with the operation of international agreements and has thereby furnished an excuse, albeit one of no value, for the ultimatum addressed to the United States by the British Government on December 1, 1932, and has caused the Government of France, under the mistaken assumption that the said Hoover has autocratic power, to declare in its note of December 2, 1932, that the President of the French Council *"agreed with the President of the United States on the terms of a communiqué, stating that in the matter of intergovernmental debts a new arrangement covering the period of the depression might be necessary, provided that the initiative came from the European powers principally concerned. In conformity with this text, which seems to constitute a novation in equity in the régime of international debts, this initiative was taken. Within the sphere where only the European powers were involved the arrangement provided for has been brought about."* And whereas the said communiqué so described by the French Government is legally unknown to the Government of the United States, never having been presented by the said Hoover to the Congress for ratification, and never having been ratified by the Congress of the United States, and whereas such opinions and such envisagements of potentialities, and such readings of the future as the French Government state may be found in it were definitely and irrevocably rejected by the Congress of the United States in the law passed by the said Congress concerning the Hoover moratorium and signed by the said Hoover on Dec. 23, 1931, nevertheless the agreement on the part of the said Hoover with the President of the French Council on the terms of the said abortive communiqué mentioned by the French Government in its note of December 2, 1932, was injurious to the United States and ignominious to the United States and constitutes a violation of the Constitution and laws of the United States; and whereas a movement, which appears to be a concerted one, on the part of the foreign debtors of the United States is taking place under the apparent leadership of the said Hoover, the said Mellon, and others, having for its object the cancellation, for the benefit of foreign nations and individuals, of the war debts due to the United States; and whereas the said Hoover may have offered or may have taken a bribe, the said violations make him, the said Hoover, guilty of high crimes and misdemeanors and subject to impeachment; and

Whereas the said Herbert Hoover, President of the United States, in violation of the Constitution and laws of the United States, has unlawfully conducted conversations ignominious to the United States and has attempted to negotiate treaties and agreements ignominious to the United States for the benefit of foreign nations and individuals, which violations make him guilty of high crimes and misdemeanors and subject to impeachment; and

Whereas the said Herbert Hoover, President of the United States, has, in violation of the Constitution and laws of the United States, unlawfully attempted to enter into secret and ignominious agreements with representatives of foreign powers, the subject matter of which is contrary to the laws of the United States, and has failed to disclose the nature and extent of those agreements and their true import to the Congress and the people of the United States, and has put into effect secret and unratified agreements between himself and foreign powers, which violations make him guilty of high crimes and misdemeanors and subject to impeachment; and

Whereas the said Herbert Hoover, President of the United States, has been accused of having conveyed to foreign governments his promise that if Germany were released by them from the necessity of paying reparations the United States would cancel the war debts due to it from the said foreign government and other governments, and whereas although it is well known to all the governments of the world that the said Hoover is and always has been without power to bind the United States to any promise or agreement whatsoever, his alleged conduct has caused a foreign government to seek to take advantage of the United States on account of it and to state in a sharply worded and threatening diplomatic communication that it entered into provisional but inconclusive negotiations with Germany at Lausanne for devising a settlement of reparations with the "cognizance and approval" of the United States Government, and whereas such negotiations with Germany, if so undertaken, were conceived without due regard to facts if they were based on any promises made by the said Hoover and

339

were not undertaken with the "cognizance and approval" of the United States Government, nevertheless, "approval" of them, if so vouchsafed to any foreign government by Herbert Hoover as a part of a bargain or conspiracy to deprive the United States of all or any part of the amount now due to it from foreign nations, was a violation of the Constitution and laws of the United States and makes him, the said Hoover, guilty of high crimes and misdemeanors and subject to impeachment; and

Whereas the said Herbert Hoover, President of the United States, has in his message to the United States Congress of December 6, 1932, stated that he has promised certain foreign nations that he will recommend to the Congress methods to overcome "temporary exchange difficulties," although he does not state what such exchange difficulties are, in connection with the payments due to the United States on December 15, 1932, and whereas such methods must necessarily be aside from and in violation of the contracts under which the said payments are to be made, and whereas the recommendation of them would be an attempt to deprive the United States of moneys which are due to it, and whereas such recommendation of methods might be used as an excuse for non-payment or as an argument disturbing to the peace of the world for cancellation of the war debts due to the United States, and whereas such a recommendation would be in favor of foreign nations at the expense of the people of the United States; and whereas the said Herbert Hoover has by all his actions endeavored to nullify the contracts concerning war debts existing between the United States and foreign nations, and has endeavored to bring about a revival of the Debt Funding Commission to alter the said contracts in favor of foreign nations at the expense of the Government and the people of the United States, and has endeavored to bring about a cancellation of the said war debts, and has by all his actions encouraged foreign nations to default on their obligations to the United States and is now encouraging them so to default, such promise on his part to foreign nations constitutes a violation of the

Constitution and laws of the United States and makes him guilty of high crimes and misdemeanors and subject to impeachment; and

Whereas the said Herbert Hoover, President of the United States, in violation of the Constitution and laws of the United States, accepted the resignation from the Federal Reserve Board of Edmund Platt in September, 1930, in circumstances which make it appear that a bribe may have been offered to cause the said Platt to resign his position as a member of the Federal Reserve Board and an officer of the United States Government; and

Whereas the said Herbert Hoover, President of the United States, in violation of the Constitution and laws of the United States, unlawfully designated Eugene Meyer governor of the Federal Reserve Board when he appointed the said Meyer a member of the Federal Reserve in September, 1930, to serve the unexpired portion of the term of Edmund Platt, and has permitted the said Meyer to act as governor of the Federal Reserve Board continuously ever since, notwithstanding the fact that the said Meyer is serving the unexpired portion of the term of Edmund Platt and is not eligible to act as governor of the Federal Reserve Board, which violations make him, the said Herbert Hoover, guilty of high crimes and misdemeanors and subject to impeachment; and

Whereas the said Herbert Hoover, President of the United States, in violation of the Constitution and laws of the United States, accepted the resignation from the Federal Reserve Board of Roy A. Young in September, 1930, thus creating a vacancy on the Federal Reserve Board, and has willfully failed and neglected to appoint an individual to fill the vacancy on the Federal Reserve Board occasioned by the absence of Roy A. Young, which violations make him guilty of high crimes and misdemeanors and subject to impeachment; and

Whereas the said Herbert Hoover, President of the United States, has, in violation of the Constitution and laws of the United States, failed to designate as governor a member of the Federal Reserve Board who is lawfully qualified and eligible to act as governor thereof, and has failed to designate a member of the Federal Reserve Board as vice governor thereof, which violations make him guilty of high crimes and misdemeanors and subject to impeachment; and

Whereas the said Herbert Hoover, President of the United States, in violation of the Constitution and laws of the United States, permitted Eugene Meyer to act as a member and as chairman of the board of the Reconstruction Finance Corporation, well knowing that the said Meyer was not lawfully qualified or eligible to act as a member of that board or as chairman thereof and unlawfully permitted the illegally constituted Reconstruction Finance Corporation, under the illegal chairmanship of the said Eugene Meyer, unlawfully to distribute immense sums of money belonging to the people of the United States, which violations make him guilty of high crimes and misdemeanors and subject to impeachment; and

Whereas the said Herbert Hoover, President of the United States, has, in violation of the Constitution and laws of the United States, failed and neglected to take care that the Federal reserve law be faithfully executed and has permitted the said law to be administered unlawfully and by an illegally constituted Federal Reserve Board and has permitted violations of the Federal reserve law which has resulted in grave financial losses to the Government and the people of the United States, which violations make him guilty of high crimes and misdemeanors and subject to impeachment; and

Whereas the said Herbert Hoover, President of the United States, has, in violation of the Constitution and laws of the United States, permitted irregularities in the issuance of Federal reserve currency which have occasioned great losses to the United States and have deprived the United States of legal revenue and has permitted the Federal Reserve Board and the Federal reserve banks unlawfully to take and to use Government credit for private gain and has permitted grave irregularities in the conduct of the United States Treasury, which violations make him guilty of high crimes and misdemeanors and subject to impeachment; and

Whereas the said Herbert Hoover, President of the United States, has treated with contumely the veterans of the World War who came to the District of Columbia in the spring and summer of 1932 in the exercise of their constitutional rights and privileges, and whereas the said Hoover did nothing to relieve, even temporarily, the distress of the said veterans, their wives, and children while they were destitute at Washington, although Congress allows the Executive a large fortune yearly for the purpose of entertaining United States citizens and others from time to time as may be necessary, and whereas the said Hoover has shown a lack of respect for the flag of the United States by denouncing the said veterans as being for the most part criminals and undesirable low-world characters, thus holding those veterans of the World War and defenders of the United States flag up to scorn before their countrymen and their companions in arms across the sea, and whereas the said Hoover sent a military force heavily armed against homeless, hungry, sick, ragged, and defenseless men, women and children, and drove them, by force of fire and sword and chemical warfare, out of the District of Columbia, which act constituted an infringement upon the constitutional rights of the said men, women, and children; and whereas such acts stamp their perpetrator as one who is socially and morally unfit to be President of the United States, and such unfitness for office and such disgrace of office as the said acts denote make him, the said Hoover, guilty of high crimes and disdemeanors and subject to impeachment; and

Whereas the said Herbert Hoover, President of the United States, has publicly stated that there is a Government at Washington which knows how to deal with the mob, meaning himself and his treatment of a group of veterans of the World War, their wives, and children; and whereas the said statement is disrepute, is injurious to the conception of a democratic government, and betrays a purpose in his actions which does not accord with the rights of a free people among whom there are no nobles and no serfs or peasants, no mob and no master, but a government of the people, by the people, for the people; and

343

whereas the making of the aforesaid statement constitutes conduct unbecoming a President of the United States and makes him, the said Herbert Hoover, guilty of high crimes and misdemeanors and subject to impeachment: Therefore be it

Resolved, That the Committee on the Judiciary is authorized to investigate the official conduct of Herbert Hoover, President of the United States, and all matters related thereto, to determine whether in the opinion of the said committee he has been guilty of any high crime or misdemeanor which, in the contemplation of the Constitution, requires the interposition of the constitutional powers of the House. Such committee shall report its findings to the House, together with such resolution of impeachment or other recommendation as it deems proper, in order that the House of Representatives may, if necessary, present its complaint to the Senate, to the end that Herbert Hoover may be tried according to the manner prescribed for the trial of the Executive by the Constitution and the people be given their constitutional remedy and be relieved of their present apprehension that a criminal may be in office.

For the purposes of this resolution, the committee is authorized to sit and act during the present Congress at such times and places in the District of Columbia or elsewhere, whether or not the House is sitting, has recessed, or has adjourned, to hold such hearings, to employ such experts, and such clerical, stenographic, and other assistants, to require the attendance of such witnesses and the production of such books, papers, and documents, to take such testimony, to have such printing and binding done, and to make such expenditures as it deems necessary.

(Congressman McFadden's resolution to impeach President Hoover was tabled by a vote of 361 to 8, with 60 recorded as not voting. —ED.)

344

XVIII

WE WILL FIGHT IT OUT UNTIL EVERY DOLLAR STOLEN FROM THE AMERICAN PEOPLE IS REPAID WITH COMPOUND INTEREST TO THE UNITED STATES TREASURY

Thursday, May 4, 1933

Mr. McFADDEN. Mr. Chairman, the United States is bankrupt. It has been bankrupted by the corrupt and dishonest Federal Reserve Board and the Federal Reserve banks. It has repudiated its debt to its own citizens. Its chief foreign creditor is Great Britain, and a British bailiff has been at the White House and British agents are in the United States Treasury making inventories and arranging terms of liquidation. In close cooperation with the British bailiff a French bailiff has been standing by with a staff of experts and 25 of the leading French journalists. The "united front" has arrived at Washington.

Mr. Chairman, the Federal Reserve Board has offered to collect the British claims in full from the American public by trickery and corruption, if Great Britain will help it to conceal its crimes. The British are shielding their agents, the Federal Reserve System, because they do not wish that system of robbery destroyed here. They wish it to continue for

345

their benefit. By means of it Great Britain has become the financial mistress of the world. She has regained the position she occupied before the World War. For several years she has been a silent partner in the business of the Fderal Reserve Board and the Federal Reserve banks. Under threats of blackmail, or by bribery, or by their native treachery to the people of the United States, the officials in charge of the Federal Reserve banks unwisely gave Great Britain immense gold loans of our national-bank depositors' money. They did this against the law. They gave England gold loans running into hundreds of millions of dollars. Those gold loans were not single transactions. They were revolving loans. They gave Great Britain a borrowing power in the United States of billions. She squeezed billions out of this country by means of her control of the Federal Reserve Board and the Federal Reserve banks. As soon as the Hoover moratorium was announced—and it was Great Britain who instructed Hoover how to declare it—Great Britain moved to consolidate her gains. After the treacherous signing away of American rights at the 7-power conference at London in July 1931 which put the Federal Reserve System under the control of the Bank for International Settlements, Great Britain began to tighten the hangman's noose around the neck of the United States. She abandoned the gold standard and embarked upon a campaign of buying up the claims of foreigners against the Federal Reserve banks in all parts of the world. She has now sent her bailiff, Ramsay MacDonald, here to get her war debt to this country canceled. She has a club in her hand. She has title to the gambling debts which the corrupt and dishonest Federal Reserve Board and the Federal Reserve banks incurred abroad. Ramsay MacDonald, the Labor Party deserter, has come here to compel the President to sign on the dotted line and that is what Roosevelt is about to do. Roosevelt will endeavor to conceal the nature of his action from the American people. But he will obey the international bankers and transfer the war debt that Great Britain should pay to the American people to the shoulders of the American taxpayers.

Mr. Chairman, the bank holidays in the several States were brought about by the corrupt and dishonest Federal Reserve Board and the Federal Reserve banks. Those institutions manipulated money and credit and caused the States to order bank holidays. Those holidays were "frame-ups." They were dress rehearsals for the national-bank holiday which Franklin D. Roosevelt promised Sir Ronald Lindsay that he would declare. There was no national emergency here when Roosevelt took office except the bankruptcy of the Federal Reserve Board and the Federal Reserve banks—a bankruptcy which has been going on under cover for several years and which has been concealed from the people so that the people would continue to permit their bank deposits and their bank reserves and their gold and the funds of the United States Treasury to be impounded in the bankrupt institutions. Under cover, the predatory international bankers have been stealthily transferring the burden of the Federal Reserve debts to the people's Treasury and to the people themselves. They have been using the farms and the homes of the United States to pay for their thievery. That is the only national emergency there has been here since the depression began. Someone asked Mr. Ogden Mills what caused the depression. He answered quite truthfully, "The Federal Reserve lent so much money abroad that it broke down the system." Mr. Chairman, those who have lost everything they possessed through the evil practices of the Federal Reserve Board and the Federal Reserve banks should at least be told the truth about how it happened. The veterans of the World War should know that the Federal Reserve Board and the Federal Reserve banks paid the dole in England, and are still paying it, and that that is the reason why the resident agents of England in this country have cut the pensions of the United States soldiers $400,000,000 a year.

The week before the bank holiday was declared in New York State the deposits in New York savings banks were greater than the withdrawals. There were no runs on New York banks. There was no need of a bank holiday in New York or of a national holiday. Roosevelt did what the international bankers ordered him to do. When Sir Ronald Lindsay was at Warm Springs, Ga., when Franklin D. Roosevelt violated the Logan Act, the obnoxious Lindsay was promised that the United States would be taken off the gold standard "without debate" and "by surprise" and that was what England wanted and was insisting upon. Sir Ronald Lindsay hotfooted it to London to tell the good news to the English Cabinet. They did not trust the mail or their favorite instrument, the transatlantic telephone. Do not deceive yourself, Mr. Chairman, or permit yourself to be deceived by others into the belief that Roosevelt's dictatorship is in any way intended to benefit the people of the United States. He is preparing to sign on the dotted line. He is preparing to cancel the war debts by fraud. He is preparing to internationalize this country and to destroy our Constitution itself in order to keep the Federal Reserve Board and the Federal Reserve banks intact as a money-making institution for foreigners.

Mr. Chairman, I have received an inquiry from one of my constituents in regard to his right to have gold and gold certificates; silver and silver certificates; and all other forms of coin and currency issued by the United States Government in his personal possession or in the possession of his agents. Mr. Chairman, I have informed my constituent that he has a constitutional right to have gold and silver in his possession, either in the form of bullion or of coins, and that he has a right to have United States currency of every description in his possession, and that his right to hold such private property is absolute and that such private property may not be taken away from him without due process of law.

Mr. Chairman, I see no reason why citizens of the United States should be terrorized into surrendering their property to the international bankers who own and control the Federal Reserve Board and the Federal Reserve banks. The statement that gold would be taken from its lawful owners if they did not voluntarily surrender it to private interests shows that there is an anarchist in the Government. The statement that it is necessary for the people to give their gold—the only real money—to the banks in order to protect the currency is a statement of calculated dishonesty.

By his unlawful usurpation of power on the night of March 5, 1933, and by his proclamation, which in my opinion was in violation of the Constitution of the United States, Roosevelt divorced the currency of the United States from gold, and United States currency is no longer protected by gold. It is, therefore, sheer dishonesty to say that the people's gold is needed to protect the currency. Roosevelt ordered the people to give their gold to private interests—that is, to banks—and he took control of the banks, so that all the gold values in them or given into them might be handed over to the predatory international bankers who own and control the Federal Reserve Board and the Federal Reserve banks. Roosevelt cast in his lot with the usurers. He agreed to save the corrupt and dishonest Federal Reserve Board and the Federal Reserve banks at the expense of the people of the United States. He took advantage of the people's confusion and weariness and spread a dragnet over the United States to capture everything of value that was left in it. He made a great haul for the international bankers.

Mr. Chairman, the terms of Roosevelt's surrender were arranged between himself, certain international bankers, and Sir Ronald Lindsay. A British paper has lately said that Roosevelt refrained from accepting responsibility before he acquired authority in all matters except the matter of the war debts. So you see, Mr. Chairman, before entering the Presidency he took up the matter of the war debts. He violated the terms of the Logan Act.

Mr. Chairman, statements in the newspaper to the effect that the conferences now taking place are mere academic and preparatory discussions between officials of the United States Government and representatives of foreign nations are false. The Prime Minister of England came here for money. He came here to collect cash. He came here with Federal Reserve currency and other claims against the Federal Reserve System which England has bought up in all parts of the world and

349

he has presented them for redemption in gold.

Mr. Chairman, I am in favor of compelling the Federal Reserve Board and the Federal Reserve banks to pay their own debts. I see no reason why the general public should be forced to pay the gambling debts of the international bankers.

By his action in closing the banks of the United States, Roosevelt seized the gold value of the forty billions and more of bank deposits in the United States banks. Those deposits were deposits of gold values. By his action he has rendered them payable to the depositors in paper money only, if payable at all, and the paper money he proposes to pay out to bank depositors and to the people generally in lieu of their hard-earned gold values is of no intrinsic value in itself and, being based on nothing into which the people can convert it, the said paper money is of negligible value altogether. It is paper money which is not convertible into gold or silver. It is the money of slaves, not of free men. If the people of the United States permit it to be imposed upon them at the will of the credit masters, the next step in their downward progress will be their acceptance of orders on company stores for what they eat and wear. Their case will be similar to that of starving coal miners. They, too, will be paid with orders on company stores for food and clothing, both of indifferent quality, and be forced to live in company-owned houses, from which they may be evicted at the drop of the hat. More of them will be forced into conscript labor camps under military supervision.

At noon on the 4th of March 1933 Franklin Delano Roosevelt, with his hand on the Bible, took an oath to preserve, protect, and defend the Constitution of the United States. At midnight on the 5th of March 1933 he confiscated the property of American citizens. He took the currency of the United States off the gold standard of value. He repudiated the internal debt of the Government to its own citizens. He destroyed the value of the American dollar. He released, or endeavored to release, the Federal Reserve banks from their contractual liability to redeem Federal Reserve currency in gold or lawful

350

money on a parity with gold. He depreciated the value of the national currency. The people of the United States are now using irredeemable paper slips of money. The Treasury cannot redeem that paper in gold or silver. The gold and silver of the Treasury has unlawfully been given to the corrupt and dishonest Federal Reserve Board and the Federal Reserve banks. And the administration has since had the effrontery to raid the country for more gold for the private interests by telling our patriotic citizens that their gold is needed to protect the currency. It is not being used to protect the currency. It is being used to protect the corrupt and dishonest Federal Reserve Board and the Federal Reserve banks. The directors of those institutions have committed criminal offenses against the United States Government, including the offense of making false entries on their books and the still more serious offense of unlawfully abstracting funds from the United States Treasury. Roosevelt's gold raid is intended to help them out of the pit they dug for themselves when they gambled away the wealth and savings of the American people.

The international bankers set up a dictatorship here because they wanted a dictator who would protect them. They wanted a dictator who would issue a proclamation giving the Federal Reserve Board and the Federal Reserve banks an absolute and unconditional release from their contractual liability to redeem their special currency in gold or lawful money at any Federal Reserve bank. Has Roosevelt released any other class of debtors in this country from the necessity of paying their debts? Has he made a proclamation telling the farmers that they need not pay their mortgages? Has he made a proclamation to the effect that mothers of starving children need not pay their milk bills? Has he made a proclamation relieving householders from the necessity of paying rent? Not he. He has issued one kind of proclamation only, and that is a proclamation to relieve international bankers and the foreign debtors of the United States Government.

Mr. Chairman, the gold in the banks of this country belongs to the American people, who have paper money contracts for it in the form of national currency. If the Federal Reserve banks cannot keep their contracts with United States citizens to redeem their paper money in gold or lawful money, then the Federal Reserve banks must be taken over by the United States Government and their offices must be put on trial. There must be a day of reckoning. If the Federal Reserve banks have looted the Treasury, so that the Treasury cannot redeem the United States currency for which it is liable in gold, then the Federal Reserve banks must be driven out of the Treasury.

Mr. Chairman, a gold certificate is a warehouse receipt for gold in the Treasury, and the man who has a gold certificate is the actual owner of a corresponding amount of gold stored in the Treasury and subject to his order. As Charles N. Fowler, a former Member of this House, said when he was chairman of the House Banking and Currency Committee, "A gold certificate is its own redeemer."

Now comes Roosevelt, who seeks to render the money of the United States worthless by unlawfully proclaiming that it may not be converted into gold at the will of the holder.

When Daniel Webster was in the Senate, he said, with rugged honesty:

I profess to be a bullionist in the usual and accepted sense of that word. I am for a specie basis for our circulation and for specie as a part of the circulation so far as it may be practicable and convenient. I am for giving no value to paper merely as paper. I abhor paper; that is to say, irredeemable paper—paper that may not be converted into gold and silver at the will of the holder.

This House and this Government should stay where God put them. He should maintain our intellectual honesty and our dignity. We should be able at all times to say with Webster:

I am where I have been, and ever mean to be, standing on the platform of the Constitution—a platform broad enough and firm enough to uphold every interest of the whole country.

Roosevelt's next haul for the international bankers was a reduction in the pay of all Federal employees. The poor clerk in a Government office is compelled to give up 15 percent of his salary while the international bankers are presented with all the gold in the country. Next in order are the veterans of all wars, many of whom are aged and infirm and others sick and disabled. Those men had their lives adjusted for them by acts of Congress determining the amount of their pensions, and, while it is meet that every citizen should sacrifice himself for the good of the United States, I see no reason why these poor people, these aged Civil War veterans, and war widows, and half-starved veterans of the World War should be compelled to give up their pensions for the financial benefit of the international vultures who have looted the Treasury, bankrupted the country, and traitorously delivered the United States to a foreign foe. There are many ways of raising revenue that are better than this barbarous act of injustice. Why not collect from the Federal Reserve Board and the Federal Reserve banks the amount they owe to the United States Treasury in interest on all the Federal Reserve currency they have taken from the United States Government? That would put billions of dollars into the United States Treasury. If Franklin D. Roosevelt is as honest as he pretends to be he will have that done immediately. And, in addition, why not compel the Federal Reserve Board and the Federal Reserve banks to disclose their profits and to pay the Government its share? Until that is done, it is rank dishonesty to talk of maintaining the credit of the United States Government.

The Federal Reserve Board and the Federal Reserve banks have stolen the income taxes and other taxes paid into the United States Treasury by Federal employees, and because that money and other public funds have been stolen by them and the United States Treasury is bankrupt, the Government clerk is told, "Yes; we know you paid your income tax, but the Federal Reserve Board and the Federal Reserve banks took your money out of the United States Treasury and treated it as their own and they have it where Uncle Sam cannot get it, so you, poor creature, must let your salary be reduced by 15 percent."

Mr. Chairman, the salaries of Members of Congress may not be changed during the lifetime of the Congress in which the Members participate. Nevertheless the salaries of Members have been reduced. I object to this on constitutional grounds.

Mr. Chairman, my own salary as a Member of Congress has been reduced, and while I am willing to give the part of it that has been taken away from me to the United States Government, I regret that the United States has suffered itself to be brought so low by the vultures and crooks who are operating the roulette wheels and faro tables in the Federal Reserve banks that it is now obliged to throw itself on the mercy of its own legislators and charwomen, its clerks, and its poor old pensioners, and to take money out of our pockets to make good the defalcations of the international bankers who were placed in control of the Treasury and given a monopoly of United States currency by the misbegotten Federal Reserve Act.

Mr. Chairman, I am well aware that the international bankers who drive up to the door of the United States Treasury in their limousines look down with scorn upon Members of Congress because we work for so little, while they draw millions a year. The difference is that we earn or try to earn what we get and they steal the greater part of their takings.

Mr. Chairman, I do not like to see vivisections performed on human beings. I do not like to see the American people used for experimental purposes by the credit masters of the United States. They predicted among themselves that they would be able to produce a condition here in which American citizens would be completely humbled and left starving and penniless in the streets. The fact that they made that assertion while they were fomenting their conspiracy against the United States shows that they like to see a human being, especially

354

an American, stumbling from hunger as he walks. Something should be done about it, they say. Five-cent meals or something! But Franklin Delano Roosevelt will not permit the House of Representatives to investigate the condition of the Federal Reserve Board and the Federal Reserve banks. Franklin D. Roosevelt will not do that. He has certain international bankers to serve. They now look to him as the man higher up who will protect them from the just wrath of an outraged people.

Mr. Chairman, the international bankers have always hated our pensioners. A man with a small pension is a ward of the Government. He is not dependent upon them for a salary or wages. They cannot control him. They do not like him. It gave them great pleasure, therefore, to slash the veterans. The veterans are counted upon to make up $400,000,000 a year to pay for the defalcations of the Federal Reserve Board and the Federal Reserve banks. The plutocrats who own and operate those un-American institutions have their gold safely bestowed, while the American people have a huge deficit in their Treasury. But Franklin D. Roosevelt will never do anything to embarrass his financial supporters. He will cover up the crimes of the Federal Reserve Board and the Federal Reserve banks.

Before he was elected Mr. Roosevelt advocated a return to the earlier practices of the Federal Reserve System, thus admitting its corruptness. The Democratic platform advocated a change in the personnel of the Federal Reserve Board and the Federal Reserve banks. Those remarks were campaign bait. As a prominent Democrat lately remarked to me and he is not very far away from where I am standing at the present moment, "There is no new deal. The same old crowd is in control."

Mr. Chairman, the claims of the foreign creditors of the Federal Reserve Board and the Federal Reserve banks have no validity in law. The foreign creditors were the receivers — and the willing receivers — of stolen goods. They have received through their banking fences immense amounts of currency and that currency was unlawfully taken from the United States Treasury by the Federal Reserve Board and the Federal Reserve banks. England discovered the irregularities of the Federal Reserve System quite early in its operation and through fear, apparently, the Federal Reserve Board and the Federal Reserve banks have, for years, suffered themselves to be blackmailed and dragooned into permitting England to share in the business of the Federal Reserve banks.

The Federal Reserve Board and the Federal Reserve banks have unlawfully taken many billions of dollars of the public credit of the United States and have given it to foreign sellers on the security of the debt paper of foreign buyers in purely foreign transactions, and when the foreign buyers refused to meet their obligations and the Federal Reserve Board and the Federal Reserve banks saw no honest way of getting the stolen funds back into their own possession, they decided by control of the Executive to make the American people pay their losses. They likewise entered into a conspiracy to deprive the people of the United States of their title to the war debts and, not being able to do that in the way they intended, they are now engaged in an effort to debase the American dollar so that foreign governments will have their debts to this country cut in two and then by means of other vicious underhanded arrangements, they propose to remit the remainder.

Mr. Chairman, I am of the opinion that England should be left to secure redress from the original welchers on the gambling debts of the Federal Reserve Board and the Federal Reserve banks. Failing that, let her look to the international bankers who undertook to finance the world—at a price—with the funds they stole from the United States Treasury.

So far as the United States Treasury is concerned, the gambling counters have no legal standing. The United States Treasury cannot be compelled to make good the gambling ventures of the corrupt and dishonest Federal Reserve Board and the Federal Reserve banks. Still less should the bank deposits of the American people be used for that purpose. Still less should the national currency have been made irredeemable in gold so that the gold which was massed and stored to redeem the currency for American citizens may be used to pay the gambling debts of the Federal Reserve Board and the Federal Reserve banks for England's benefit. The American people should have their gold in their own possession, where it cannot be held under secret agreement for any foreign central bank or world bank or foreign nation. Our own citizens have the prior claim to it. The paper money they have in their possession deserves redemption far more than the United States currency and credit which was stolen from the United States Treasury and bootlegged abroad. Why should foreigners be made preferred creditors of the bankrupt United States? Why should the United States be treated as a bankrupt? This Government has assets. This Government has immense sums due to it from the Federal Reserve Board and the Federal Reserve banks. The directors of those institutions are men of great wealth. Why should the guilty escape the consequences of their misdeeds? Why should the people of the United States surrender the gold value of their bank deposits and the gold value of their currency to pay the gambling debts of the bankers? Why should Roosevelt promise foreigners that the United States will play the part of a good neighbor "meeting its obligations"? Let the Federal Reserve Board and the Federal Reserve banks meet their own obligations.

Every member of the Federal Reserve Board and every Federal Reserve bank director should be compelled to disgorge, and every acceptance banker and every discount corporation which has made illegal profits by means of public credit unlawfully bootlegged out of the United States Treasury and hired out by the crooks and vultures of the Federal Reserve Board and the Federal Reserve banks should be compelled to disgorge. After the disgorgement, if the amount of the contributions is not sufficient to pay the gambling debts of the Federal Reserve Board and the Federal Reserve banks, then let there be a capital levy to pay them. Yes, Mr. Chairman, if those gambling debts must be paid, let them be paid by a capital levy so that the corporations which profited by the international bankers' exploits shall be the ones who pay the international bankers' gambling debts. Gambling debts due to foreign receivers of stolen goods should not be paid by sacrificing our title to the war debts, the assets of the United States Treasury, which belong to all the people of the United States and which it is our duty to preserve inviolate in the people's Treasury. The United States Treasury cannot be made liable for them. Federal Reserve currency must be redeemed by the Federal Reserve banks or else the Federal Reserve banks must be liquidated.

Mr. Chairman, we know from assertions made here by the Honorable John N. Garner, the present Vice President of the United States, that there is a condition in the United States Treasury which would cause American citizens, if they knew what it was, to lose all confidence in their Government. That is a condition which Roosevelt will not have investigated. He has brought with him from Wall Street, James Warburg, the son of Paul M. Warburg. Mr. Warburg is the head of the Bank of Manhattan Co. Mr. Warburg, alien born and the son of an alien who did not become naturalized here until seven years after this Warburg's birth, is a son of a former partner of Kuhn, Loeb & Co., a grandson of another partner, a nephew of a former partner, and a nephew of a present partner. He holds no office in our Government, but I am told that he is in daily attendance at the Treasury, and that he has private quarters there. In other words, Mr. Chairman, Kuhn, Loeb & Co. now control and occupy the United States Treasury.

Mr. Chairman, the text of the Executive order which seems to place an embargo on shipments of gold permits the Secretary of the Treasury, a former director of the Federal Reserve Bank of New York, the practices of which have been corrupt, to issue licenses in his discretion for the export of gold coin, or bullion, earmarked or held in trust for a recognized foreign government or foreign central bank, or for the Bank for International Settlements. Now, Mr. Chairman, if gold held in trust for those foreign institutions may be sent to them, I see no reason why gold held in trust for American citizens as evidenced by their gold certificates and other currency issued by the United States Government should not be paid to them. I think an American citizen is entitled to treatment at least as good as that which the present administration is extending to foreign governments, foreign central banks, and the Bank for International Settlements. I think a veteran of the World War, with a $20 gold certificate is at least as much entitled to receive his own gold for it as any international banker in the city of New York or London.

Mr. Chairman, by the terms of the same Executive order, which seems to place an embargo on shipments of gold, the Secretary of the Treasury, in his discretion, may issue licenses authorizing the export of gold coin or bullion imported for re-export or gold in reasonable amounts for usual trade requirements of refiners importing gold-bearing materials under agreement to export gold. This, Mr. Chairman, would permit foreign nations who hold our gold coins to send them here and have them melted down for reshipment back to Europe.

Again, Mr. Chairman, by the terms of the Executive order, gold may be exported if it is actually required for the fulfillment of any contract entered into prior to the date of this order by an applicant who, in obedience to the Executive order of April 5, 1933, has delivered gold coin, gold bullion, or gold certificates. This means that gold may be exported to pay the obligations abroad of the Federal Reserve Board and the Federal Reserve banks which were incurred prior to the date of the order, namely, April 20, 1933.

If a European central bank should send $100,000,000 in Federal Reserve currency to a bank in this country for redemption, that bank could easily ship gold to Europe in exchange for that currency. Such Federal Reserve currency would represent "contracts entered into prior to the date of the order." If the Bank for International Settlements or any other foreign bank holding any of the present gambling debt paper of the Federal Reserve Board and the Federal Reserve banks should draw a draft for the settlement of such an obligation, gold would be shipped to them because the debt contract would have been entered into prior to the date of the order. So you see, Mr. Chairman, every provision seems to have been made for the export of gold to pay the gambling debts of the Federal Reserve Board and the Federal Reserve banks.

Mr. Chairman, the Federal Reserve Act requires the Federal Reserve banks to redeem their Federal Reserve notes in gold, or lawful money. Federal Reserve currency constitutes a first and paramount lien on all the assets of the Federal Reserve banks. That is the law of the United States. They have to give up everything they possess and go through liquidation and have their books examined before they can run out on the public and refuse to redeem their currency. Roosevelt, however, by his action has said to them, "You need not pay American citizens gold in exchange for the paper money you took from the United States Treasury. You need not pay them anything of value."

Mr. Chairman, I demand that all the gold in the custody of the Federal Reserve Board and the Federal Reserve banks be placed in the Treasury of the United States. The Federal Reserve banks cannot be relieved of their contractual liabilities and at the same time keep the gold belonging to the Treasury and to the people in their private possession. That gold must be placed in the people's Treasury in the custody of the United States Government.

Mr. Chairman, we will fight it out on this line if it takes all summer. We fill fight it out until every dollar stolen from the American people by the international bankers of New York is repaid with compound interest to the United States Treasury. [Applause.]

XIX

IMPEACHMENT OF FEDERAL RESERVE BOARD SPEECH MADE IN THE HOUSE

May 23, 1933

IMPEACHMENT CHARGES

Mr. McFADDEN. Mr. Speaker, I rise to a question of constitutional privilege. On my own responsibility as a Member of the House of Representatives, I impeach Eugene Meyer, former member of the Federal Reserve Board; Roy A. Young, former member of the Federal Reserve Board; Edmund Platt, former member of the Federal Reserve Board; Eugene R. Black, member of the Federal Reserve Board and officer of the Federal Reserve Bank of Atlanta; Adolph Caspar Miller, member of the Federal Reserve Board; Charles S. Hamlin, member of the Federal Reserve Board; George R. James, member of the Federal Reserve Board; Andrew W. Mellon, former Secretary of the United States Treasury and former ex-officio member of the Federal Reserve Board; Ogden L. Mills, former Secretary of the United States Treasury and former ex-officio member of the Federal Reserve Board; William H. Woodin, Secretary of the United States Treasury and ex-officio member of the Federal Reserve Board; John W. Pole, former Comptroller of the Currency and former ex-officio member of the

Federal Reserve Board; J. F. T. O'Connor, Comptroller of the
Currency and ex-officio member of the Federal Reserve Board;
F. H. Curtis, Federal Reserve agent of the Federal Reserve
Bank of Boston; J. H. Case, Federal Reserve agent of the
Federal Reserve Bank of New York; R. L. Austin, Federal
Reserve agent of the Federal Reserve Bank of Philadelphia;
George De Camp, former Federal Reserve agent of the Federal
Rererve Bank of Cleveland; L. B. Williams, Federal Reserve
agent of the Federal Reserve Bank of Cleveland; W. W. Hox-
ton, Federal Reserve agent of the Federal Reserve Bank of
Richmond; Oscar Newton, Federal Reserve agent of the Fed-
eral Reserve Bank of Atlanta; E. M. Stevens, Federal Reserve
agent of the Federal Reserve Bank of Chicago; J. S. Wood,
Federal Reserve agent of the Federal Reserve Bank of St.
Louis; J. N. Peyton, Federal Reserve agent of the Federal
Reserve Bank of Minneapolis; M. L. McClure, Federal Reserve
agent of the Federal Reserve Bank of Kansas City; C. C. Walsh,
Federal Reserve agent of the Federal Reserve Bank of Dallas;
Isaac B. Newton, Federal Reserve agent of the Federal Reserve
Bank of San Francisco, jointly and severally, of high crimes
and misdemeanors, and offer the following resolution:

*Whereas I charge the aforesaid Eugene Meyer, Roy A.
Young, Edmund Platt, Eugene R. Black, Adolph Caspar Miller,
Charles S. Hamlin, George R. James, Andrew W. Mellon,
Ogden L. Mills, William H. Woodin, John W. Pole, J. F. T.
O'Connor, members of the Federal Reserve Board; F. H. Cur-
tiss, J. H. Case, R. L. Austin, George De Camp, L. B. Williams,
W. W. Hoxton, Oscar Newton, E. M. Stevens, J. S. Wood,
J. N. Peyton, M. L. McClure, C. C. Walsh, Isaac B. Newton,
Federal Reserve agents, jointly and severally, with violations
of the Constitution and laws of the United States, and whereas
I charge them with having taken funds from the United States
Treasury which were not appropriated by the Congress of the
United States, and I charge them with having unlawfully taken
over $80,000,000,000 from the United States Government in
the year 1928, the said unlawful taking consisting of the un-
lawful creation of claims against the United States Treasury*

to the extent of over $80,000,000,000 in the year 1928, and I charge them with similar thefts committed in 1929, 1930, 1931, 1932, and 1933, and in years previous to 1928, amounting to billions of dollars; and

Whereas I charge them, jointly and severally, with having unlawfully created claims against the United States Treasury by unlawfully placing United States Government credit in specific amounts to the credit of foreign governments and foreign central banks of issue; private interests and commercial and private banks of the United States and foreign countries, and branches of foreign banks doing business in the United States, to the extent of billions of dollars; and with having made unlawful contracts in the name of the United States Government and the United States Treasury; and with having made false entries on books of account; and

Whereas I charge them, jointly and severally, with having taken Federal Reserve notes from the United States Treasury and with having issued Federal Reserve notes and with having put Federal Reserve notes into circulation without obeying the mandatory provision of the Federal Reserve Act which requires the Federal Reserve Board to fix an interest rate on all issues of Federal Reserve notes supplied to Federal Reserve banks, the interest resulting therefrom to be paid by the Federal Reserve banks to the Government of the United States for the use of the said Federal Reserve notes, and I charge them with having defrauded the United States Government and the people of the United States of billions of dollars by the commission of this crime; and

Whereas I charge them, jointly and severally, with having purchased United States Government securities with United States Government credit unlawfully taken and with having sold the said United States Government securities back to the people of the United States for gold or gold values and with having again purchased United States Government securities with United States Government credit unlawfully taken and with having again sold the said United States Government securities back to the people of the United States for gold or gold values, and I charge them with having defrauded the United States Government and the people of the United States by this rotary process; and

Whereas I charge them, jointly and severally, with having unlawfully negotiated United States Government securities, upon which the Government's liability was extinguished, as collateral security for Federal Reserve notes and with having substituted such securities for gold which was being held as collateral security for Federal Reserve notes, and with having by this process defrauded the United States Government and the people of the United States, and I charge them with the theft of all the gold and Federal Reserve currency they obtained by this process; and

Whereas I charge them, jointly and severally, with having unlawfully issued Federal Reserve currency on false, worthless, and fictitious acceptances and other circulating evidences of debt, and with having made unlawful advancements of Federal Reserve currency, and with having unlawfully permitted renewals of acceptances and renewals of other circulating evidences of debt, and with having permitted acceptance bankers and discount dealer corporations and other private bankers to violate the banking laws of the United States; and

Whereas I charge them, jointly and severally, with having conspired to have evidences of debt to the extent of over $1,000,000,000 artifically created at the end of February 1933 and early in March 1933, and with having made unlawful issues and advancements of Federal Reserve currency on the security of the said artifically created evidences of debt for a sinister purpose, and with having assisted in the execution of the said sinister purpose; and

Whereas I charge them, jointly and severally, with having brought about a repudiation of the currency obligations of the Federal Reserve banks to the people of the United States, and with having conspired to obtain a release for the Federal Reserve Board and the Federal Reserve banks from their contractual liability to redeem all Federal Reserve currency in gold or lawful money at any Federal Reserve bank, and with having defrauded the holders of Federal Reserve currency, and with having conspired to have the debts and losses of the Federal Reserve Board and the Federal Reserve banks unlawfully transferred to the Government and the people of the United States; and

Whereas I charge them, jointly and severally, with having unlawfully substituted Federal Reserve currency and other irredeemable paper currency for gold in the hands of the people after the decision to repudiate the Federal Reserve currency and the national currency was made known to them, and with having thus obtained money under false pretenses; and

Whereas I charge them, jointly and severally, with having brought about a repudiation of the national currency of the United States in order that the gold value of the said currency might be given to private interests, foreign governments, foreign central banks of issue, and the Bank for International Settlements, and the people of the United States be left without gold or lawful money and with no currency other than a paper currency irredeemable in gold, and I charge them with having done this for the benefit of private interests, foreign governments, foreign central banks of issue, and the Bank for International Settlements; and

Whereas I charge them, jointly and severally, with conniving with the Edge law banks and other Edge law institutions, accepting banks, and discount corporations, unlawfully to finance foreign governments, foreign central banks of issue, foreign commercial banks, foreign corporations, and foreign individuals with funds unlawfully taken from the United States Treasury; and I charge them with having unlawfully permitted and made possible "mass financing" of foreigners at the expense of the United States Treasury to the extent of billions of dollars and with having unlawfully permitted and made possible the bringing into the United States of immense quantities of foreign securities, created in foreign countries for export

365

to the United States, and with having unlawfully permitted the said foreign securities to be imported into the United States instead of gold, which was lawfully due to the United States on trade balances and otherwise, and with having unlawfully permitted and facilitated the sale of the said foreign securities in the United States in a manner prejudicial to the public welfare and inimical to the Government of the United States; and

Whereas I charge them, jointly and severally, with having unlawfully made loans of gold and of gold values belonging to the bank depositors and the general public of the United States to foreign governments, foreign central banks of issue, foreign commercial banks, foreign corporations, and individuals, and the Bank for International Settlements, to the loss and detriment of the Government and the people of the United States; and

Whereas I charge them, jointly and severally, with having unlawfully exported gold reserves belonging to the national bank depositors and gold belonging to the general public of the United States to foreign countries, and with having converted the said gold into foreign currencies, and with having used it for the benefit of foreigners, and for speculative purposes abroad, and with having unlawfully converted to their own use and the use of others gold belonging to the United States stored or held in foreign countries, and with having unlawfully prevented the shipment to the United States of the said gold which was due to the United States, and with having permitted the importation under their supervision of false, worthless, and fictitious trade paper and foreign securities of doubtful value in lieu of it, and with having caused the United States to lose the said gold; and

Whereas I charge them, jointly and severally, with having unlawfully exported United States coins and currency for a sinister purpose, and with having deprived the people of the United States of their lawful circulating medium of exchange, and I charge them with having arbitrarily and unlawfully reduced the amount of money and currency in circulation in the United States to the lowest rate per capita in the history of the

Government, so that the great mass of the people have been left without a sufficient medium of exchange, and I charge them with concealment and evasion in refusing to make known the amount of United States money in coins and paper currency exported abroad and the amount remaining in the United States, as a result of which refusal the Congress of the United States is unable to ascertain where the United States coins and issues of currency are at the present time and what amount of United States currency is now held abroad; and

Whereas I charge them, jointly and severally, with having arbitrarily and unlawfully raised and lowered the rates on money and with having arbitrarily increased and diminished the volume of currency in circulation for the benefit of private interests and foreign speculators at the expense of the Government and the people of the United States and with having unlawfully manipulated money rates, wages, salaries, and property values, both real and personal, in the United States, by unlawful operations in the open discount market and by resale and repurchase agreements unsanctioned by law; and

Whereas I charge them, jointly and severally, with having brought about the decline in prices on the New York Stock Exchange and other exchanges in October 1929 by unlawful manipulation of money rates and volume of United States money and currency in circulation; by thefts of funds from the United States Treasury; by gambling in acceptances and United States Government securities; by services rendered to foreign and domestic speculators and politicians, and by the unlawful sale of United States gold reserves, and whereas I charge that the unconstitutional inflation law imbedded in the so-called "Farm Relief Act" by which the Federal Reserve Board and the Federal Reserve banks are given permission to buy United States Government securities to the extent of $3,000,000,000 and to draw forth currency from the people's Treasury to the extent of $3,000,000,000 is likely to result by connivance on the part of the said accused with others in the purchase by the Federal Reserve banks of United States Government securities to the extent of $3,000,000,000 with the

367

United States Government's own credit unlawfully taken, it being obvious that the Federal Reserve Board and the Federal Reserve banks do not intend to pay anything of value to the United States Government for the said United States Government securities—no provision for payment in gold or lawful money appearing in the so-called "Farm Relief Act"—and that the United States Government will thus be placed in the position of conferring a gift of $3,000,000,000 in United States Government securities on the Federal Reserve Board and the Federal Reserve banks to enable them to pay more of their bad debts to foreign governments, foreign central banks of issue, private interests, and private and commercial banks, both foreign and domestic, and the Bank for International Settlements, and whereas the United States Government will thus go into debt to the extent of $3,000,000,000 and will then have an additional claim for $3,000,000,000 in currency unlawfully created against it and whereas no private interests should be permitted to buy United States Government securities with the Government's own credit unlawfully taken and whereas currency should not be issued for the benefit of the said private interests or any interests on United States Government securities so acquired, and whereas it has been publicly stated and not denied that the inflation amendment to the Farm Relief Act is the matter of benefit which was secured by Ramsay MacDonald, the Prime Minister of Great Britain, upon the occasion of his latest visit to the White House and the United States Treasury, and whereas there is grave danger that the accused will employ the provision creating United States Government securities to the extent of $3,000,000,000 and $3,000,000,000 in currency to be issuable thereupon for the benefit of themselves and their foreign principals, and that they will convert the currency so obtained to the uses of Great Britain by secret arrangements with the Bank of England of which they are the agents, and for which they maintain an account and perform services at the expense of the United States Treasury, and that they will likewise confer benefits upon the Bank for International Settlements for which they maintain an account and perform services at the expenses of the United States Treasury; and

Whereas I charge them, jointly and severally, with having unlawfully concealed the insolvency of the Federal Reserve Board and the Federal Reserve banks and with having failed to report the insolvency of the Federal Reserve banks to the Congress and with having conspired to have the said insolvent institutions continue in operation, and with having permitted the said insolvent institutions to receive United States Government funds and other deposits, and with having permitted them to exercise control over the gold reserves of the United States and with having permitted them to transfer upward of $100,000,000,000 of their debts and losses to the general public and the Government of the United States, and with having permitted foreign debts of the Federal Reserve banks to be paid with the property, the savings, the wages, and the salaries of the people of the United States and with the farms and homes of the American people, and whereas I charge them with forcing the bad debts of the Federal Reserve banks upon the general public covertly and dishonestly and with taking the general wealth and savings of the people of the United States under false pretenses, to pay the debts of the Federal Reserve banks to foreigners, and

Whereas I charge them, jointly and severally, with violations of the Federal Reserve Act and other laws; with maladministration of the Federal Reserve Act; and with evasions of Federal Reserve law and other laws, and with having unlawfully failed to report violations of law on the part of Federal Reserve banks which, if known, would have caused the said Federal Reserve banks to lose their charters, and

Whereas I charge them, jointly and severally, with failure to protect and maintain the gold reserves and the gold stock and gold coinage of the United States and with having sold the gold reserves of the United States to foreign governments, foreign central banks of issue, foreign commercial and private banks, and other foreign institutions and individuals at a profit to themselves, and I charge them with having sold gold reserves of the United States so that between 1924 and 1928 the United States gained no gold on net account, but suffered a decline in its percentage of central gold reserves from 45.9 percent in 1924 to 37.5 percent in 1928 notwithstanding the fact that the United States had a favorable balance of trade throughout that period; and

Whereas the United States was the only country which lost a considerable quantity of gold during that period, to wit, 1924 to 1928, inclusive, I charge them with the theft and sale of the said gold to their foreign principals, and I charge them with the theft and sale of 10 percent of the entire gold stock of the United States during the last 4 months of 1927 and during 1928 after crediting all importations of gold received by the United States during that period, this theft and sale of 10 percent of the gold stock of the United States occasioning the largest gold outflow from the United States that had ever theretofore occurred, and I charge them with the theft and sale of all the gold reserves exported from the United States from the year 1928 to the present time, a period during which the United States has lost gold continuously and has gained no gold on net account, nothwithstanding the fact that the balance of trade and accounts throughout the entire period has been in favor of the United States; and

Whereas the United States has received no gold on net account since 1923, a period of 10 years during which the United States has had a favorable balance of trade and has had large sums due to it and payable in gold from foreign nations and has not received such sums in gold, I charge them, the said accused, with the theft of gold which was lawfully due to the United States, with the theft of gold belonging to the United States, and with the unlawful diversion of United States gold to the treasuries and central banks of foreign countries, and I charge them with concealment of the true condition and amount of the gold reserves of the United States at the present time; and

Whereas I charge them, jointly and severally, with having conspired to concentrate United States Government securities *and thus the national debt of the United States in the hands of foreigners and international money lenders and with having conspired to transfer to foreigners and international money lenders title to and control of the financial resources of the United States; and*

Whereas I charge them, jointly and severally, with having fictitiously paid installments on the national debt with Government credit unlawfully taken; and

Whereas I charge them, jointly and severally, with the loss of United States Government funds intrusted to their care; and

Whereas I charge them, jointly and severally, with having destroyed independent banks in the United States and with having thereby caused losses amounting to billions of dollars to the depositors of the said banks and to the general public of the United States; and

Whereas I charge them, jointly and severally, with failure to furnish true reports of the business operations and the condition of the Federal Rtserve banks to the Congress and the people, and with having furnished false and misleading reports to the Congress of the United States; and

Whereas I charge them, jointly and severally, with having published false and misleading propaganda intended to deceive the American people and to cause the United States to lose its independence; and

Whereas I charge them, jointly and severally, with unlawfully allowing Great Britain to share in the profits of the Federal Reserve System at the expense of the Government and the people of the United States; and

Whereas I charge them, jointly and severally, with having entered into secret agreements and illegal transactions with Montagu Norman, governor of the Bank of England; and

Whereas I charge them, jointly and severally, with swindling the United States Treasury and the people of the United States in pretending to have received payment from Great Britain of the amount due on the British war debt to the United States in December 1932; and

Whereas I charge them, jointly and severally, with having

conspired with their foreign principals and others to defraud the United States Government and to prevent the people of the United States from receiving payment of the war debts due to the United States from foreign nations; and

Whereas I charge them, jointly and severally, with having robbed the United States Government and the people of the United States by their theft and sale of the gold reserve of the United States and other unlawful transactions, and with having created a deficit in the United States Treasury which has necessitated to a large extent the destruction of our national defense and the reduction of the United States Army and the United States Navy and other branches of the national defense; and

Whereas I charge them, jointly and severally, with having reduced the United States from a first-class power to one that is dependent, and with having reduced the United States from a rich and powerful Nation to one that is internationally poor; and

Whereas I charge them, jointly and severally, with the crime of having treasonably conspired and acted against the peace and security of the United States, and with having treasonably conspired to destroy constitutional government in the United States: Therefore be it

RESOLVED, *That the Committee on the Judiciary is authorized and directed, as a whole or by subcommittee, to investigate the official conduct of Eugene Meyer, Roy A. Young, Edmund Platt, Eugene R. Black, Adolph Caspar Miller, Charles S. Hamlin, George R. James, Andrew W. Mellon, Ogden L. Mills, William H. Woodin, John W. Pole, J. F. T. O'Connor, members of the Federal Reserve Board; and F. H. Curtis, J. H. Case, R. L. Austin, George De Camp, L. B. Williams, W. W. Hoxton, Oscar Newton, E. M. Stevens, J. S. Wood, J. N. Payton, M. L. McGlure, C. C. Walsh, Isaac B. Newton, Federal Reserve agents, to determine whether, in the opinion of the said committee, they have been guilty of any high crime or misdemeanor which, in the contemplation of the Constitution, requires the interposition of the constitutional powers of the House. Such committee shall report its findings to the House, together with such resolution or resolutions of impeachment or other recommendations as it deems proper.*

For the purposes of this resolution the committee is auth-ized to sit and act during the present Congress at such times and places in the District of Columbia or elsewhere, whether or not the House is sitting, has recessed, or has adjourned, to hold such clerical, stenographic, and other assistants, to require the attendance of such witnesses and the production of such books, papers, and documents, to take such testimony, to have such printing and binding done, and to make such expenditures as its deems necessary.

(Congressman McFadden's charge and resolution to impeach both present and former members of the Board of Governors of the Federal Reserve Board were moved to the Committee on the Judiciary. The committee never reported the resolution to the floor. —ED.)

XX

TAXES

May 26, 1933

Mr. TREADWAY. Mr. Chairman, I yield 4 minutes to the gentleman from Pennsylvania [Mr. McFADDEN].

Mr. McFADDEN. Mr. Chairman, I ask unanimous consent to revise and extend my remarks.

The CHAIRMAN. Without objection, it is so ordered.

Mr. McFADDEN. Mr. Chairman, I am concerned about the power Congress is proposing to give to a centralized group who will control the operation of this particular legislation. I have particularly in mind that class of industry in the United States which has been built up by careful planning, independently owned and controlled, where the lives of men have been devoted to that industry. These industries have been built up, scattered all over the country, and are the backbone of American industry in the United States. I am not referring to the big trusts. The financial groups that we hear so much about these days have time and again tried to get control, to worm themselves into these industries and take them away from the owners, the people who have built them up.

You are creating an organization here now that is going to be able to control these industries. Under the operation of the provisions of this law, they may be forced to consolidate with competitors that are owned and controlled by the very group of people who have been trying to break into privately

374

owned industries. Big business wants to swallow independent business that remains in the United States. Big private banking houses in New York want these small independent profit-making industries.

I am wondering what these industries that have been built up by the owners with their own money, with genius and brains, who have treated the employees properly and are the very lifeblood of many small communities, are going to say or do when they are called before this board and are told that they no longer can control their own business, and that, unless they obey the dictates of big bankers and big business, their main competitors, they will have to consolidate their business with other groups of business people—these other groups of people may be the very persons who have been trying for years to take the business away from them.

That is one of the dangers that I see in the bill. Further than that, I want to say to you and the administration that this department of Government which you are setting up here today must not be managed by the type of men we are hearing about who are controlled by the financial group appearing and other similar groups of New York bankers who will later appear for examination before the Senate Banking Committee at the other end of the Capitol. [Applause.] This administration has got to purge itself of that J. P. Morgan & Co., Kuhn, Loeb & Co., Speyer & Co., Warburg group of private bankers' control or you are going to have revolution in the United States. It cannot continue any longer.

This is to be an institution for the control of industry, all industry, privately owned industry. You have already given control of the railroads, you have already given control of the farming industry, you have given control of the finances of the country to the banker groups.

I simply want to warn the administration that this cannot continue. The people have rights in these United States, and when they awake they will take their rights.

Now, in the few brief moments that still remain I want to refer to the tax features provided in the bill.

I need not tell you that I have been seeking for a long time to get the Income Tax Division of the Treasury Department to collect taxes due the United States. If you would, if this Congress would report out a resolution of investigation which will result in unearthing the reasons why the Income Tax Division does not function we might collect hundreds of millions of dollars that are actually due at this time.

Who is holding up my resolution to do this? What must be done to get action in this House to make the Income Tax Bureau of the United States Treasury to do its duty, and collect taxes that are being fraudulently withheld? Is it that these tax-racketeering lawyers and certified public accountants, are so strongly intrenched, or are the Mellons, Morgans, and Dohertys so strong politically, that they can even reach the leadership in this House?

Of course, I had every evidence in the Hoover Administration that Morgan, Mills, Ballantine, and Burnet had no intention of interfering with this ring of income-tax racketeers. We were all led to understand that when the Administration changed the money changers would be thrown out of the temple, but they are still permitted to operate and apparently are being protected, and the regime is to be perpetuated. The definite proof of this is the appointment of Dean G. Acheson, formerly of the law firm of Covington, Burling and Rublee, Union Trust Building, Washington, D.C. This firm of lawyers, with whom Mr. Acheson was connected, are the attorneys for Price, Waterhouse and Co., a British accounting house and one of the largest practitioners in income-tax matters before the Treasury Department. They represent hundreds of the leading taxpayers.

On November 21, 1931, I asked Andrew W. Mellon, Secretary of the Treasury, to disbar this company from practicing before the Treasury Department in connection with any income tax or other matters on evidence that I was submitting to the Department. I pointed out to Mr. Mellon that over a period of years this accounting firm, in collusion with large taxpayers, had been defrauding the United States Government

376

in the receipt of taxes due the Government and suggested that each one of this firm's clients' tax accounts be completely audited and prosecuted. Did Mr. Mellon do this? He did not. On the contrary, in a letter to me under date of November 24, 1931, he defended the activities of this concern, and on December 1, 1931, I sent him additional definite information as to the fraudulent practices of Price, Waterhouse & Co., and submitted definite cases of tax violations running into tens of millions of dollars and called attention for immediate action on account of possible running of the statute of limitations. On December 9, 1931, I again called his attention to these violations and referred him to a conspiracy action that had been entered into between the representatives of these taxpayers, the acting Attorney General of the United States, and himself. Mr. Mellon refused to take any action looking toward the prosecution of these tax violations.

On March 26, 1932, I directed a letter to Ogden L. Mills asking for a report inasmuch as 6 months had elapsed since I had notified the Department of this irregularity, and on April 1, Mr. Ogden L. Mills, the then Secretary of the Treasury, replied that the Department had the matter under consideration.

On June 4, 1932, I introduced a resolution which was referred to the Rules Committee. Extensive hearings were held but Speaker Garner and the Rules Committee failed to carry out their agreement to report favorably on this rule at the last session of Congress.

On May 5, 1933, I sent the following letter to Hon. William H. Woodin, Secretary of the Treasury:

MAY 5, 1933.

HON. WILLIAM H. WOODIN,
SECRETARY OF THE TREASURY, WASHINGTON, D.C.

My Dear Mr. Secretary: Mn March 26, 1932, I addressed the enclosed letter to Hon. Ogden L. Mills, then Secretary of the Treasury. His answer is also enclosed. This matter concerns substantial amounts due to the Treasury of the United States.

Mr. David A. Olson had filed several cases of tax evasion with the Bureau of Internal Revenue. These cases have been in the hands of the Bureau for more than a year. There has been much correspondence and conversation about these cases, but to date no one has been able to secure from the Bureau or the Treasury any definite statement as to the disposition of these matters.

Officials of all parties are working earnestly to evolve means to meet the Government's pressing need of funds, and it seems to me that definite steps should be taken to determine what sum in evaded taxes can be collected in the Olson cases and even more important that those sums be collected and made available for the Treasury.

It is with the hope that you will agree with this statement of the Nation's financial condition that I am addressing you with this request for information.

Has the Bureau of Internal Revenue completed its investigation of these cases or of any of them? What sum has been collected?

What sum of money has been discovered to be due to the Government and from whom?

I shall appreciate your early reply.

Sincerely yours,

L. T. McFADDEN.

Up to this time I have not had the courtesy of a reply. But during this period of time one of the attorneys for Price, Waterhouse & Co., as heretofore stated, has been made an Assistant Secretary of the Treasury, succeeding A. A. Ballantine. His particular duties are the Income Tax Division of the Treasury Department.

Mr. Acheson apparently has had, or may still have, very interesting clients, as is indicated by a letter from a resident of California that has just come to me. In referring to his appointment as Assistant Secretary of the Treasury, this correspondent says: *"He is the man who appeared recently on the*

Pacific coast representing a syndicate of New York bankers in connection with the purchase of Russian bonds at a discount." It was said that this New York syndicate was in possession of special information in regard to the recognition of Russia by the United States, and it was indicated that on the basis of this inside information this New York syndicate was attempting to buy up from the present unfortunate holders of Russian securities in the United States these bonds.

The House of Representatives should know who Mr. Acheson is and whom he represents. The hearings before the Senate Banking Committee have disclosed the fact that he is on the preferred list of friends of J. P. Morgan & Co. I am sure that the membership of this House will understand how impossible it is to expect that these fraudulent tax cases, which I am insisting be investigated, can be investigated and the taxes collected and the taxpayers dealt with in the same manner that the tax-evasion case of Charles E. Mitchell, president of the National City Bank, is being dealt with. I am definitely calling this serious matter to the attention of the administration; and their action in regard to the retention of Mr. Acheson in the Treasury will disclose whether or not the administration intends to deal with these fraudulent tax cases or whether they are going to respond to the demands of political and financial pressure that can be brought to bear by the Mellons, the Morgans, the Kuhn Loebs, and the H. L. Dohertys.

These influences are now trying to control the appointment and confirmation of Guy T. Helvering, of Kansas, to be Commissioner of Internal Revenue. This appointment should not be confirmed by the United States Senate.

The public-utility interests of the type of H. L. Doherty, are doing everything that they possibly can to secure the appointment of Mr. Helvering for this position. I have already shown the Members here that the tax returns of H. L. Doherty, of Cities Service, one of the largest public utilities, should be investigated. It is significant, too, when we understand that Mr. Helvering's appointment is satisfactory to the attorneys

379

practicing before the Income Tax Division of the Treasury Department.

I am reliably informed that Mr. A. W. Mellon has been in Washington the past few days in consultation with Mr. Acheson and the attorneys for Price, Waterhouse & Co. It is not surprising that Mr. Mellon would be here in Washington at this time during the questioning of the members of the firm of J. P. Morgan & Co.

One of the interesting developments of this investigation discloses the fact that the firm of J. P. Morgan & Co. is a copartnership, each partner having an interest in the assets of the copartnership. Therefore it becomes necessary upon a partner leaving the firm or a new partner coming in to estimate the value of the partnership assets as the basis upon which such incoming or outgoing partner may be protected in his investment.

Under Mr. Morgan's statement when Mr. S. Parker Gilbert came into the J. P. Morgan firm, he assumed a sale of the assets of the Morgan firm and thereby reached a valuation predicted upon the sale of the Morgan firm assets. This assumption is not an actual sale but is an assumed price on the assets of the Morgan firm that is fixed by the Morgan firm and whether the property is purchased or sold, the completed transaction is based upon what may be termed the value fixed by Morgan himself, and is not established by an actual sale of the property as contemplated under the income tax law. The whole procedure is one of fiction, the whole price fixed on sale and purchase is fiction, the assumption as a result of the sale is fiction, the estimated losses of $21,000,000 deducted from the income of the firm for the year involved is nothing but a fictitious transaction, which if tested in the courts by the Treasury, would be decided in favor of the Government. If Mr. Morgan is permitted to thus evade the law, which requires the actual sale of the property, then every farmer in the United States has a right to assume a purchase and sale of his own farm, when the farm prices are less than his cost, and make his own showing of the loss.

On the other hand, the merchant in the small town may estimate a sale of his merchandise for the same reason. He may make the sale of the merchandise at a price in his own mind, purely theoretical and imaginary, doing the same as Morgan does, and estimating the price at less than the wholesale price at which he purchased the goods, and can thereby deduct the estimated loss from the income tax return on the basis of a sale having transpired.

It was mentioned by the Morgan partners that they had taken advantage of a loophole in the income tax law. I am reliably informed that there is no such loophole, and if the Treasury Department would only take action against the Morgan partners to collect the tax which was due for that calendar year, their action would be sustained by the courts.

In the case of Lazard-Freres, a New York partnership, the partners of that firm did the same thing in 1929, and I am reliably informed by a man who was present during this transfer, that the attorneys in the case feared that if the Government took action to collect the tax, as legally due, they would be unable to successfully sustain their position in the courts.

Thus it is known to the Bureau of Internal Revenue and the Secretary of the Treasury that the question is a debatable one, and yet there has never been an attempt of the Treasury Department to settle the rule. [Applause.]

[Here the gavel fell.]

XXI

IN THE UNITED STATES TODAY, THE GENTILES HAVE SLIPS OF PAPER WHILE THE JEWS HAVE THE GOLD AND LAWFUL MONEY

Monday, May 29, 1933

Mr. McFADDEN. Mr. Chairman, this repudiation bill is in direct opposition to the Democratic Party platform of 1932 upon which Franklin D. Roosevelt was elected President of the United States. It constitutes a violation of every campaign pledge he made before the people while he was barnstorming the country asking for votes. It is a repudiation of the faith of Jefferson. In a particular sense, I represent the members of the Democratic Party in my district since I was nominated by them as their candidate at the last Congressional election. I was also nominated by the Prohibition Party in my district. And I was nominated by the Republicans. I represent all the people of my district by virtue of my office and I represent all of the political parties of my district by reason of the fact that I was nominated by every one of them in turn. This gives me the right to protest in the name of the Democratic Party in my district against this repudiation bill. Mr. Chairman, the Democrats in my distrist are not welchers. They do not profess one thing and do another. They do not go to the country on one platform and in office act upon another and an entirely different one. They do not set up a party platform and, after winning a popular vote on the strength of it, cynically cast it aside and laugh the people and the people's government to scorn. So far as the people of my district are concerned, the Democratic Members of the House do not need to haul down the Stars and Stripes from the roof of the Capitol today. They do not need to vote under the Union Jack at the dictation of Franklin D. Roosevelt. His political credit is gone. His star has begun to wane. No Democrat needs to follow him into political oblivion.

Mr. Chairman, a law was passed here on May 12, 1933. On May 26, 1933, this bill was introduced asking us to amend the law passed 13 days earlier. Mr. Chairman, this is making a mock of government. The stuff that has been sent to this House during this special session to be obediently and subserviently passed into law, and the manner in which it has been sent and the nonsense that has accompanied it, has been enough to sicken the strongest stomach. It has been said in connection with this repudiation bill, this latest outburst of delirium, that President Roosevelt wishes to have it as a legal record of what has already been done. Mr. Chairman, what has been done was done illegally, and I do not doubt that those who have broken their oaths of office are anxious now to have Congress furnish them with a clean bill of health, but I think it would have been better if Congress had been permitted to function properly from the beginning. It is the custom, I believe, among certain malefactors to break the law and pay the fine afterward; to break the law and then say, "What are you going to do about it?" The crime of kidnapping proceeds that way. The kidnaper says, "Punish me or try to take me and I'll kill the child." So with these wreckers and violators of law and order in office. Mr. Chairman, I think it would be more orderly and less expensive and that it would tax the patience of the country less if Roosevelt sent his backers home to their chosen lairs in Wall Street and himself attended to his own executive business. If he has a yearning to be a legislator, let him resign his Executive office and get himself elected to Congress. He will be welcome here if the people send him to Congress, but he has no business to interfere with the deliberations of this House while he is acting as President of the United States.

Mr. Chairman, this repudiation bill was framed and brought here in the interest of the foreign debtors of the United States. Its aim is a cancellation of war debts by fraud and treachery toward the American people. It gives the foreign nations a way of making entirely fictitious payments on the war debts. It permits them to use the Federal Reserve currency and the United States Government credit which was unlawfully taken by the Federal Reserve Board and its agents and exported abroad. The United States Treasury has been drawn upon by the Federal Reserve Board for paper money and for credit exchangeable for money and these, unlawfully taken, have been sent to the debtor nations. Now comes Roosevelt asking us to pass a law so that the debtor nations may pay their debts to us in that stolen Federal Reserve currency and credit. This repudiation bill also gives them the right to pay us in debased coinage. It repeals the Gold Standard Act of 1900—the sheet anchor of this country's national currency—and it decrees that hereafter the United States shall issue no more national currency for itself at all but shall have nothing more than a debased subsidiary coinage and Federal Reserve currency in the form of Federal Reserve notes and Federal Reserve bank notes, issued at the will of the Roosevelt money changers who now control the Nation.

Mr. Chairman, the people of the United States are not coolies. They will not transact their business and make their interchanges of goods and services with the debased tokens of a subsidiary coinage and slips of paper. The Democratic administration, in violation of its campaign pledges and its party platform, is now endeavoring to foist upon this country currency of no value. It has given the gold and lawful money of the country to the international money Jews of whom Franklin D. Roosevelt is the familiar, and it has sent this bold and dishonest bill here so that it may have the pleasure of seeing Congress jump through another paper hoop and turn another somersault under the whip of the ringmaster.

384

Mr. Chairman, there is not a man within the sound of my voice who does not know that this country has fallen into the hands of the international money changers, and there are few Members here who do not regret it. Why should the fact be hidden? Is it not because those who have betrayed the United States are afraid to face the consequences of their misdeeds? Is it not because every man who hears me knows that there are few things more terrible than citizens armed in a righteous cause defending themselves and their children, their homes and their firesides from the invader? Do you not think at times, Mr. Chairman, of that old wooden bridge built by the Colonists at Concord? Do you not think at times, Mr. Chairman, of what happened there?

> "By the rude bridge that spanned the flood
> Their flag to April breeze unfurled;
> Here once the embattled farmers stood
> And fired the shot heard round the world."

Mr. Chairman, we are on Concord Bridge today. Our enemy—the same treacherous enemy—is advancing upon us. Mr. Chairman, I will die in my tracks before I yield him a square inch of American soil or so much as a one dollar rebate on his war debt to us.

Mr. Chairman, the Constitution of the United States has served us well. I am in favor of defending it against all comers. In the Constitution of the United States, it is written that the United States shall guarantee a republican form of Government to every State in the Union. This guaranty has been broken by Franklin D. Roosevelt in his unlawful assumption of dictatorial powers. It is also written that no State shall make anything but gold or silver coin a tender in payment of debts. This repudiation bill and its predecessors nullify this provision of the Constitution. It is also written in an amendment to the Constitution, "The validity of the public debt of the United States, authorized by law, including debts incurred for payment of pensions and bounties in suppressing insurrection or rebellion, shall not be questioned." Mr. Chairman, this repudi-

385

ation bill questions the validity of the public debt and repudiates it. It repudiates the Liberty bonds; it repudiates the veterans' adjusted-service certificates; it cancels the war debts due to the United States from foreign governments.

Now, Mr. Chairman, we have come to the place where we must decide whether we shall serve God or Mammon. Shall we nullify the Constitution at the behest of the money changers who have unlawfully taken all our gold and lawful money into their own possession or shall we take a stand here in defense of the faith of our fathers? Mr. Chairman, my mind is made up. I will stand by the Constitution. If I should fail to do so, I should expect to be met at the train when I go home to my district by a delegation of honest Pennsylvania citizens with 50 or 100 feet of rope. I should expect to be escorted to the nearest tree to be taught what it means to vote for a nullification of the Constitution in the House of Representatives.

Mr. Chairman, the provisions of this repudiation bill were foretold by a writer in the *Dearborn Independent* some years ago. There is, therefore, nothing novel or original about them. The writer of the article in the *Dearborn Independent* made the following quotation prophesying some of the measures which have been introduced here by the President of the United States:

(2) Confiscation of money in order to regulate its circulation.

(3) We must introduce a unit of exchange based on the value of labor units, regardless of whether paper or wood are used as the medium. We will issue money to meet the normal demands of every subject, adding a total sum for every birth and decreasing the total amount for every death.

(4) Commercial paper will be bought by the Government, which ° ° ° will grant loans on a business basis. A measure of this character will prevent the stagnation of money, parasitism, and laziness, qualities which were

useful to us as long as the gentiles maintained their independence, but which are not desirable to us when our kingdom comes.

(5) We will replace stock exchanges by great Government credit institutions, whose functions will be to tax paper according to Government regulations. These institutions will be in such a position that they may market or buy as many as half a billion industrial shares a day. Thus all industrial undertakings will become dependent on us. You may well imagine what power that will give us.

"Remember that when next you hear the Jewish plan that 'Gentiles' shall do business with their own bits of paper, while Jews keep the gold reserve safely in their own hands. If crash comes, 'Gentiles' have the paper and the Jews have the gold." Says Protocol XXII: "We hold in our hands the greatest modern power—gold; in 2 days we could free it from our treasuries in any desired quantities."

The Jews are economists, esoteric and exoteric: They have one system to tangle up the "Gentile," another which they hope to install when "Gentile" stupidity has bankrupted the world. The Jews are economists. Note the number of them who teach economics in the State universities. Says Protocol VIII:

"We will surround our Government with a whole world of economists. It is for this reason that the science of economics is the chief subject of instruction taught by the Jews."

Mr. Chairman, have not most of these predictions come to pass? Is it not true that, in the United States today, the "gentiles" have the slips of paper while the Jews have the gold and lawful money? And is not this repudiation bill a bill specifically designed and written by the Jewish international money changers themselves in order to perpetuate their power? What else do you make of it, Mr. Chairman? Does it not cancel the war debts? Does it not defraud the holders of Liberty bonds and every other obligation calling for the payment of money? Does it not defraud the veterans of the World War and take the value out of their adjusted-compensation certificates?

Mr. Chairman, I demand that the gold stock of the United States be taken from the Federal Reserve banks and placed in the United States Treasury. I demand an audit of United States Government financial affairs from the top to the bottom. I demand a resumption of specie payment based on full gold and silver values. I demand the currency of the Constitution. I demand the rights of the people guaranteed to them by the Constitution, and that means that I demand a vote which will defeat this repudiation bill.

No man can serve two masters. A vote for this bill is a vote for the money changers. A vote for an audit and an investigation of the Government's financial affairs is a vote for the people.

Mr. Chairman, all I ask of this House, and I ask it in the name of all the people, Jews and Gentiles, citizens and resident aliens alike, is that it, the people's own representative legislative assembly, shall stay close to the people and vote in their interest. Do not cancel the war debts and bind down upon our suffering veterans and our men of toil and our broken-hearted mothers and our starving children, the endless slavery of paying tribute to the "united front" of the war debtors. Do not force Americans to pay tribute to foreign rulers and potentates. Take back this country or perish in the attempt. Let this be our own country again. Let us rebuild it for our own. Let us keep the Stars and Stripes floating over the roof of the Capitol. Let us cling to the Constitution of the United States. This is the way to freedom and prosperity. The way of repudiation is madness. Remember, Mr. Chairman, that the Ship of State has women and children aboard. Do not, therefore, guide it into uncharted waters. Do not allow the great Democratic Party to steer it onto the rocks while the world waits for it to founder and go down so that the international salvage crews may set to work on the wreck of it. [Applause.]

388

XXII

FINANCIAL INTERESTS SHOULD NOT DICTATE FOREIGN POLICY OF UNITED STATES GOVERNMENT

Thursday, June 15, 1933
(legislative day of Wednesday, June 14)

Mr. McFADDEN. Mr. Speaker, I doubt if the history of the relations between this country and Russia is known to every American citizen. It may not be considered amiss, therefore, if I dwell for a few moments on our past relations with that strange and interesting country. To do so it will be necessary for me to go back to the late eighties and the early nineties of the last century, when the United States was turning the corner and becoming rich and powerful. At that time a man named Jacob Schiff came to this country as the agent of certain foreign money lenders. His mission was to get control of American railroads. This man was a Jew. He was the son of a rabbi. He was born in one of the Rothschilds' houses in Frankfort, Germany. He was a small fellow with a pleasant face and, if I remember correctly, his eyes were blue. At an early age he set out from Frankfort to seek his fortune and went to Hamburg, Germany. At Hamburg he entered the Warburg banking establishment. The Warburgs of Hamburg are bankers of long standing, with branches in Amsterdam and

389

Sweden. After Schiff had served his time with them he went to London and worked with their London correspondents. He was also connected with the firm of Samuel Montagu & Co., the London gold merchants. When he came to this country he was well equipped to do business as an international money changer. He knew how to be polite, he could write a smooth letter, and he always pretended to be a man of holiness and a philanthropoist.

Sometime before Schiff's arrival there was a firm of Jewish peddlers or merchants in Lafayette, Ind., by the name of Kuhn & Loeb. I think they were there about 1850. Probably they made money out of the new settlers who passed through Indiana on their way to the Northwest. This firm of Jews had finally moved to New York and had set themselves up as private bankers and had grown rich. Jacob Schiff married Teresa Loeb and became the head of Kuhn, Loeb & Co. Schiff made a great deal of money here for himself and for the Jewish money lenders of London. He began to give orders to Presidents almost as a matter of course. He appears to have been a man who would stop at nothing to gain his own ends. I do not blame him for being a Jew. I blame him for being a trouble maker.

Russia had a powerful enemy in this man, Jacob Schiff. The people of the United States were taught to believe that this enmity of his was caused by wrongs done to Russian Jews. I look elsewhere for the motives which animated him.

In the 1890's Schiff was the agent in this country of Ernest Cassell and other London money lenders. These money lenders were looking forward to a war between England and Russia and were making preparations for propaganda designed to support England in the United States. This country was then a debtor nation, paying a high yearly tribute to Schiff and his principals. Schiff accordingly took it upon himself to create a prejudice in the United States against Russia. He did this by presenting the supposed wrongs of the Russian Jews to the American public. Unpleasant tales began to appear in print. School children in this country were told that Jewish children

390

were crippled for life by Russian soldiers wielding the knout. By unfair means a wedge was driven between Russia and the United States.

One of Schiff's schemes was a sort of wholesale importation of Russian Jews into the United States. He drew up divers and sundry regulations for the temporary transplantation of these Jewish emigrants. He would not, he said, have them enter this country through the port of New York, because they might like New York too well to leave it for the outposts he had selected for them. He said it would be best to have them come in at New Orleans and to have them stay there 2 weeks, "so that they could pick up a few words of English and get a little money" before setting off for what he called the "American hinterland." How they were to get the money he did not say.

Aided by Schiff and his associates, many Russian Jews came to this country about that time and were naturalized here. A number of these naturalized Jews then returned to Russia. Upon their return to that country, they immediately claimed exemption there from the regulations of domicile imposed on Jews; that is, they claimed the right to live on purely Russian soil because they were American citizens, or "Yankee" Jews. Disorders occurred and were exploited in the American press. Riots and bombings and assassinations, for which somebody furnished money, took place. The perpetrators of these outrages appear to have been shielded by powerful financial interests. While this was going on in Russia, a shameless campaign of lying was conducted here, and large sums of money were spent to make the general American public believe that the Jews in Russia were a simple and guileless folk ground down by the Russians and needing the protection of the great benefactor of all the world—Uncle Sam. In other words, we were deceived. We were so deceived that we allowed them to come in here and take the bread out of the mouths of our own American citizens.

I come now to the time when war was declared between Russia and Japan. This was brought about by a skillful use of

391

Japan, so that England would not have to fight Russia in India. It was cheaper and more convenient for England to have Japan fight Russia than to do it herself. As was to be expected, Schiff and his London associates financed Japan. They drew immense quantities of money out of the United States for that purpose. The background for the loans they floated in this country had been skillfully prepared. The "sob stuff", of which Schiff was a master, had sunk into the hearts of sympathetic Americans. The loans were a great success. Millions of American dollars were sent to Japan by Schiff and his London associates. England's stranglehold on India was made secure. Russia was prevented from entering the Khyber Pass and falling on India from the northwest. Japan at the same time was built up and became a great world power, and as such is now facing us in the Pacific. All this was accomplished by control of the organs of American publicity, releases to the effect that Russian Jews and "Yankee" Jews were being persecuted in Russia, and by the selling of Japanese war bonds to American citizens.

While the Russian-Japanese War was in progress President Theodore Roosevelt offered to act as peacemaker, and a conference between representatives of the belligerents was arranged to take place at Portsmouth, N.H.

While the Portsmouth Conference took place, Jacob Schiff attended it and used such influence as he had with Theodore Roosevelt to win favors for Japan at the expense of Russia. His main object, then as always, was humiliation of Russians, whose only crime was that they were Russians and not Jews. He endeavored to humiliate the Russians, but Count Witte, the Russian plenipotentiary, did not allow him to succeed in this attempt. Schiff's power and the power of his organized propaganda were well understood by Count Witte, however. Consequently he was not surprised when President Roosevelt, who was often deceived, twice asked him to have Russia treat Russian Jews who had become naturalized in the United States and who had thereafter returned to live in Russia with special consideration; that is, not as Jews but as Americans. Witte carried home a letter from Roosevelt embodying this plea.

Mr. Speaker, the restrictions upon Jews in Russia at that time may or may not have been onerous. But onerous or not, before the Russians had time to change them, Schiff had the 80-year-old treaty of friendship and good will between Russia and the United States denounced. Speaking of this matter, County Witte says in his autobiography:

The Russians lost the friendship of the American people.

Mr. Speaker, I cannot believe that those people—the real Russians—ever lost the true friendship of the American people. They were done away with to suit the ambitions of those who intend to be the financial masters of the world, and some of us were deceived into thinking that in some mysterious way they themselves were to blame. The chasm that suddenly opened between ourselves and our old friends and well-wishers in Russia was a chasm created by Schiff the vindictive in his inhuman greed, and he created it in the name of the Jewish religion.

Mr. Speaker, it was a mistake for the United States to permit the integrity of its foreign policy to be jeopardized or affected adversely by such religious, racial, and financial meddling as that practiced upon us by Schiff and his London associates. The United States should manage its foreign affairs with more distinction than that which is implied in the picture of Jacob Schiff shaking his fist at the White House and muttering threats against William Howard Taft, then President of the United States, a man who was excessively distinguished in his chosen field and who represented the integrity and the patriotic Americanism of every generation of New Englanders from the first of Massachusetts Bay Colony to his own, and represented them well.

Mr. Speaker, the people of the United States should not permit financial interests or any other special interests to dictate the foreign policy of the United States Government. But in this connection history is now repeating itself. You have heard, no doubt, of the so-called persecution of Jews in Germany.

393

Mr. Speaker, there is no real persecution of Jews in Germany. Hitler and the Warburgs, the Mendelsohns and the Rothschilds, appear to be on the best of terms. There is no real persecution of the Jews in Germany, but there has been a pretended persecution of them because there are 200,000 unwanted Communistic Jews in Germany, largely Galician Jews who entered Germany after the World War, and Germany is very anxious to get rid of those particular Communistic Jews. The Germans wish to preserve the purity of their own blond racial stock. They are willing to keep rich Jews like Max Warburg and Franz Mendelsohn whose families have lived in Germany so long that they have acquired some German national characteristics. But the Germans are not willing to keep the Galician Jews, the upstarts. So a great show is put on, largely by German Jews themselves, in the hope that Uncle Sam will prove himself to be as foolish as he was before and that we will allow those Galician and Communistic Jews to come in here. That is why Miss Perkins has been placed in charge of the Department of Labor. She is there to lower the immigration bars. It is thought that, being a woman, she may disarm criticism. She is an old hand with the international Jewish bankers. If she were not, she would not be here in a Jewish-controlled administration.

When the so-called "anti-Semitic campaign" designed for American consumption was launched in Germany, France was alarmed because she feared the Galician Jews might be dumped on French soil. French newspapers published articles concerning the menace, but now that France has been shown that the purpose of the anti-Semitic campaign is to dump the 200,000 communistic Jews on the United States she is worried no longer. "Ah", she says, "l'Oncle Sam, he is to be the goat. Very good."

Mr. Speaker, I regard it as a pity that there are Americans who love to fawn upon the money Jews and to flatter them. Some of these unfortunates are under obligations to Jewish money changers and dare not cross them. On June 6, 1933, there was a meeting in the city of Washington at which the following resolution was adopted:

> America has been greatly enriched through genera-
> tions past by men and women of high quality who have
> come to our shores as a result of persecution in their own
> lands. Our country is known throughout the world as the
> haven of those who suffer from wrong and injustices, and
> who seek an opportunity for freedom not afforded in their
> own land. The present is another critical time, and there
> are many victims of religious and racial persecution in
> Germany who, because of superior attainments and quali-
> ties of fine citizenship, would make valuable additions to
> our Commonwealth. We, therefore, ask the Government
> temporarily to relax the immigration barriers in favor of
> such persons and urge the passage of such measures as
> will effect this result.

Mr. Speaker, the time for such tactics has gone by. We
would be very foolish to allow Germany to dump her unwanted
Jewish population on the United States. If the money Jews are
as noble as they advertise themselves to be, let them advocate
the payment of the veterans' adjusted-compensation certificates. Let them ease the burdens of the consumptive Jewish
boys who are hauling heavy carts of fur and other material
around the garment center of New York. Let them see that the
long-suffering Jewish school teachers receive the salaries which
are due to them but which are now in arrears. That would be
better than to bring 200,000 Jewish Communists in here for
political purposes.

Mr. Speaker, Jacob Schiff flourished like the green bay
tree during the World War, but there are passages in his life
which show his hysterical despair when the Allies sent their
representatives here to obtain a loan. He endeavored to have
Lord Reading, formerly Rufus Isaacs, prevent any part of it
from going to Russia, although at the time Russia had a very
large army of soldiers in the marshes, including thousands
of Jewish soldiers, fighting the battle of the Allies on short
rations and with insufficient supplies. He was willing to join

in the loan, but he wished to have Russia and Russian Jews excluded from the benefits of it. Upon that occasion he was torn between a desire for profit and his professional hatred of Russia, and he cried out to his fellow directors in Kuhn, Loeb & Co. that he ought not to be placed in such a position. And then I believe he said they could do as they liked about it.

In the end it was one of the European Warburgs, a relative of Schiff's, who went to Brest-Litovsk to negotiate the separate peace—a peace which was deeply resented by a large number of loyal Russian Jews—a peace which was followed shortly afterward by the Third Internationale, one of the purposes of which is the destruction of constitutional government in the United States and the establishment here of the same form of government as that which now prevails in Russia. The rights of the sovereign States in the United States are being steadily undermined for that sinister purpose. How far down into the bottomless pit of communism the United States has been dragged by the Roosevelt administration under the smoke screen of an emergency is shown by a comparison of the program of the Third Internationale and the Roosevelt communistic measures forced into law here during this special session of Congress under threats to deprive Democratic Congressmen of patronage and influence, or, as the President is said to have expressed it to a London correspondent, a determination on his part to keep every Republican officeholder in office until he got what he wanted from the Democratic Congress. Among the tasks set before the communistic party in the United States, as shown in Russia/U.S.S.R.; A Complete Handbook, edited by the scholar, P. Malevsky-Malevitch, and published by Payson in New York this year, I find the following:

Transfer to the State of all gold reserves, valuables securities, deposits, etc., the centralization of all banking operations and the subordination of all the nationalized banks to a central State bank, etc.

You have witnessed the unlawful seizure by Franklin D. Roosevelt of gold reserves and other values belonging to the people of the United States, the destruction of banks, the attempted whitewashing of the Federal Reserve Board and Federal Reserve banks, the corruption of which he admitted in his campaign harangues; and you may have noticed that what was confiscated is not in the hands of the present constitutional Government but in the hands of the international bankers who are the nucleus of the new government Roosevelt is seeking to establish here. Roosevelt's actions are not in accordance with the Constitution of the United States. They are in accordance with the plans of the Third Internationale.

At one time Trotzky was a favorite with Jacob Schiff. During the war Trotzky edited Novy Mir and conducted mass meetings in New York. When he left the United States to return to Russia he is said upon good authority to have traveled on Schiff's money and under Schiff's protection. He was captured by the British at Halifax and immediately, on advice from a highly placed personage, set free. Shortly after his arrival in Russia he was informed that he had a credit in Sweden at the Swedish branch of the bank owned by Max Warburg, of Hamburg. This credit helped to finance the seizure of the Russian revolution by the international Jewish bankers. It assisted them in subverting it to their own ends. At the present time the Soviet Union is in debt.

From the date of Trotzky's return to Russia the course of Russian history has, indeed, been greatly affected by the operations of international bankers. They have acted through German and English institutions and have kept Russia in bondage to Germany and both Germany and Russia in bondage to themselves. Their relatives in Germany have drawn immense sums of money from the United States and have in turn financed their agents in Russia at a handsome profit.

The Soviet Government has been given United States Treasury funds by the Federal Reserve Board and the Federal Reserve banks acting through the Chase Bank and the Guaranty Trust Co. and other banks in New York City. England, no less than Germany, has drawn money from us through the Federal Reserve banks and has re-lent it at high

397

rates of interest to the Soviet Government or has used it to finance her sales to Soviet Russia and her engineering works within the Russian boundaries. The Dnieperstroy Dam was built with funds unlawfully taken from the United States Treasury by the corrupt and dishonest Federal Reserve Board and the Federal Reserve banks.

Mr. Speaker, our workingmen have been told that Russia is the best country in the world to-day for a workingman to live in. They have been made to regret that they cannot go to Russia to work on one of the great enterprises being carried on by the Soviet Government from which American workingmen are excluded. Mr. Speaker, in my opinion the Russians have a right to set up any form of government that pleases them and suits their needs. But for some reason, whether due to some defect in the Soviet form of government or to some other cause, Russia has not been able to maintain its present form of government otherwise than at the expense of countries in which there is greater freedom from individuals and in which the property rights of citizens have been respected and preserved. Open up the books of Amtorg, the trading organization of the Soviet Government in New York, and of Gostorg, the general office of the Soviet trade organization, and of the State Bank of the Union of Socialistic Soviet Republics, and you will be staggered to see how much American money has been taken from the United States Treasury for the benefit of Russia. Find out what business has been transacted for the State bank of Soviet Russia by its correspondent, the Chase Bank of New York; by Lloyd's Bank of London; by Kleinwort Sons & Co. of London, whose correspondents are the principal New York banks; by Glyn Mills & Co. of London and their American agents—that is, the International Acceptance Banks of New York, the Guaranty Trust of New York, the Central Hanover Bank of New York, the Chemical Bank & Trust Co., H. Clews & Co., Kidder Peabody & Co., Winslow Lanier & Co., and Lee, Higginson & Co., the promoters of Swedish Match. Find out how much United States money has passed through the Bank for Russian Trade of London and through the Midland Bank, Ltd.

If the extent of these transactions were known to the American workingman and if he could see that the raw material, the United States dollars, in those transactions came out of his own pocket and the pockets of his fellow citizens, he would understand that Russia is not a good place for a workingman unless other workingmen in other countries are forced to pay tribute to its needs. Russia owes the United States a large sum of money. If we had what Russia owes us today, the veterans of the United States would not need to fear the first of July 1933 when they are to be despoiled of their pension rights and privileges. Mr. Speaker, I am unalterably opposed to a reduction in the pensions that were lawfully conferred upon the United States veterans of all wars, their widows and dependents. I am in favor of the immediate payment of the veterans' adjusted-compensation certificates. If the United States can carry Germany and Soviet Russia and John Bull on its back, it can pay its veterans. If it can lend $50,000,000 to sovietized China and furnish material for the manufacture of high explosives, it can pay its veterans.

Mr. Speaker, an immense amount of United States money has been used abroad in preparations for war and in the acquisition and the manufacture of war supplies. Germany is said to be part owner of a large poison gas factory at Trotsk on Russian soil. China is almost completely sovietized and in the Asiatic interior huge stocks of munitions are said to be stored awaiting the day when the war lords of the United States will ship United States troops to Asia. Mr. Speaker, the United States should look before it leaps into another war, especially a war in Asia. It should decide whether it is worth while to join hands with Russia and China in a war against Japan. For myself, I say and I have said it often that the United States should remember George Washington's advice. It should mind its own business and stay at home. It should not permit the Jewish international bankers to drive it into another war so that they and their Gentile fronts and sycophants by way of Louis McHenry Howe, the graftmaster, may reap rich profits on everything an army needs from toilet kits to airplanes, submarines, tanks, gas masks, poison gas, ammunition, bayonets, guns, and other paraphernalia and instruments of destruction.

XXIII

FRANKLIN D. ROOSEVELT, THE APOSTLE OF IRREDEEMABLE PAPER MONEY

Wednesday, January 24, 1934

Mr. McFADDEN. Mr. Chairman, a citizen of the United States has asked me to explain for his benefit and for the benefit of other United States citizens the real meaning of the Roosevelt gold bill, the bill which the House passed last Saturday by 360 votes to 40, with 32 Members not voting.

Mr. Chairman, a law against the Constitution is void. The gold bill creates a nullity. Old John Marshall said that the words of the Constitution are not to be twisted out of their plain, everyday meaning. The Constitution says Congress shall have power to coin money and to regulate the value thereof. This, Mr. Chairman, means that Congress has power to make coins of metal and to stamp the true value upon each one of them. It does not mean that Congress shall refuse to furnish the people of the United States with an adequate coinage, and it does not mean that a theoretical amount of uncoined metal shall be called a coin. A coin is an object which may be seen and felt and even heard if one tests the ring of it.

Mr. Chairman, the gold bill attempts to cut out, delete,

and destroy that part of our great written Constitution pertaining to the power of Congress to coin money and to regulate; that is, to stamp on the metal coin the value thereof. The bill is unconstitutional on its face because it seeks to nullify the Constitution. Moreover, it is a bill which is contrary to the common law and to the law of custom upon which the common law rests. It attempts to legalize robbery. It attempts by force to deprive the people of the United States of their right to the currency of the Constitution. It gives the international bankers power to send the gold belonging to the people of the United States to a place of deposit reserved to themselves in Europe. Mr. Chairman, the gold bill cannot become a valid law by any constitutional means.

Now, Mr. Chairman, let us look at the bill to see if the legal hirelings of the Bank of England and their agents, the Federal Reserve Board and the Federal Reserve banks, have been able to disguise its purpose. Let us see if they were able to clothe the grisly skeleton of their greed with echoes of glib religiosity, moral precepts, economic jargon, and shop-worn tags of speech, according to the fashion set by the present administration. The first thing that meets my eye is the title. We read:

A bill to protect the currency system of the United States, to provide for a better use of the monetary gold stock of the United States, and for other purposes.

It is indeed a bill to protect the present currency system of the United States, but it is a bill to protect it from the just wrath of United States citizens. It is a bill to save for the Federal Reserve Board and the Federal Reserve banks their gigantic monopoly of a special paper currency which they steal from the Treasury and upon which they charge the people of the United States a heavy toll of interest. It is indeed a bill to provide for a better use of the monetary gold stock of the United States if better use means the issuance of two sets of obligations against one piece of security. It is indeed a bill for "other purposes", and those are purposes which the proponents dare not mention.

Among the purposes of the gold bill not mentioned in the title is that of pretending to take into the Treasury the gold now held by the Federal Reserve Board and the Federal Reserve banks and a great effort has been made to have it appear that the Federal Reserve banks are unwilling to surrender the gold they now hold to the United States Treasury. This effort is dishonest for two reasons. First, the Federal Reserve Board and the Federal Reserve banks have already made a profit of some billions of dollars out of the President's gold seizures and those billions were stolen from the people of the United States; and, second, the transfer is fictitious. The President sought to convince Members of Congress that the Federal Reserve banks were resisting his efforts to have the Treasury take possession of the gold, but one of the members of the Federal Reserve Board spoiled that argument by declaring that the Federal Reserve Board has asked the President to have the Treasury take the gold.

You see, Mr. Chairman, under this bill the United States Treasury has to pay for the gold. Although the gold belongs to the people and was taken away from their bank deposits and their cash registers and their pocketbooks in the first place and put into the Federal Reserve banks, and although the Federal Reserve banks tricked and fooled the people into giving it to them for Federal Reserve currency, which they now refuse to redeem, and although that gold does not belong to the Federal Reserve Board and the Federal Reserve banks, the United States Treasury has to pay the Federal Reserve Board and the Federal Reserve banks for it. Well, how does this bill propose to pay the Federal Reserve outfit, how does this bill provide that the Government shall take over the stolen goods? It provides that the United States Government shall give the Federal Reserve Board and the Federal Reserve banks new gold certificates to the full value of the loot. The gold certificates will give the Federal Reserve Board and the Federal Reserve banks legal title to the gold, and the United States Treasury will be nothing more than its physical custodian. The Secretary of the Treasury will give the Federal Reserve banks gold for their

403

new gold certificates whenever they ask for it. It is a fraudulent transfer.

When the individual citizens of the United States were required to surrender their gold they were required to surrender their gold certificates as well as their gold coin and bullion. The Federal Reserve Board and the Federal Reserve banks are private corporations, but they did not obey the gold orders. They did not surrender any gold coin, gold certificates, or gold bullion. On the contrary, the gold which was commandeered from the people was given to them as a free gift, and now, after they have taken into their possession all the gold belonging to the people they are ready to make a pretended transfer of that gold to the Government. Evidently there is law for the common man and no law for the Federal Reserve Board and the Federal Reserve banks. The common man must toe the mark, but the Federal Reserve Board and the Federal Reserve banks are the agents of the Bank of England, and the law, it seems, does not apply to them. Many of the officials of the Federal Reserve outfit have had charges of impeachment brought against them, but those charges have not been investigated.

The Federal Reserve outfit now has in its possession gold coin, gold certificates, and gold bullion. But this bill does not require them to surrender their present holdings of gold certificates. After this bill becomes law, if such a catastrophe should occur, the Federal Reserve Board and the Federal Reserve banks will still hold their present gold certificates. They may exchange those gold certificates for gold between the time this bill becomes law and the day the President makes his proposed devaluation proclamation. Is not this gift of over $1,000,000,000 in gold a great treasure to bestow upon the Federal Reserve Board and the Federal Reserve banks—the corrupt and sinister organization which has bankrupted the country? Does this not make favorites of the financial crooks who control it?

Mr. Chairman, all the gold in the possession of the Federal Reserve Board and the Federal Reserve banks belongs to the people of the United States. During the last 20 years, under the vicious Federal Reserve Act, they have taken it from the people in exchange for Federal Reserve currency and it has not cost them one penny. Now they come forward to make a pretended transfer of the people's gold coin and bullion to the United States Treasury. Not one penny of the gold they pretend to transfer to the United States Treasury is owned by them; every dollar of it belongs to the individual citizens of the United States. The United States Treasury is to buy it on credit and to pay for it with new gold certificates. How does this transfer title to the United States Treasury? Can the Congress lend itself to such a transaction? Last May I stated that, in my opinion, the people's gold, unjustly impounded in the Federal Reserve banks, should be placed in the people's Treasury, but I did not state that it should be placed there as the property of the Federal Reserve Board and the Federal Reserve banks, to be withdrawn by them with gold certificates and to be made exportable from the United States Treasury to the Bank for International Settlements in Europe. What this bill proposes to do in connection with the President's message suggesting that this United States gold may be sent to Europe to be kept in the Bank for International Settlements with the loot of the central banks of other countries is one of the greatest fiscal frauds in history. It is one of the biggest swindles of all time.

Again, Mr. Chairman, as you very well know, the Federal Reserve Board and the Federal Reserve banks had paper currency outstanding to the extent of about $5,000,000,000 when the present administration came into power. That currency was redeemable in gold. It constituted the people's title to all the gold held by the Federal Reserve outfit. It constituted a first and paramount lien on all the assets of the Federal Reserve Board and the Federal Reserve banks. Instead of taking over the gold and the assets of the Federal Reserve Board and the Federal Reserve banks, including the great hoard of United States wealth which they have hidden in foreign countries, and honestly administering those assets for the benefit of the people

405

who had been defrauded by the Federal Reserve Board and the Federal Reserve banks, the President of the United States unlawfully relieved the Federal Reserve Board and the Federal Reserve banks from their legal liability to redeem their Federal Reserve currency in gold, or in lawful money convertible into gold, and from the surrender of all their assets. Every dollar that was unlawfully taken from the people of the United States by Roosevelt's gold order was given to the Federal Reserve Board and the Federal Reserve banks in preparation for this great steal, this wholesale robbery of the masses for the benefit of the privileged few. And now that American citizens have lost their gold, an entirely fictitious transfer has been arranged to deceive the people. Mr. Chairman, the President may underrate the mental capacity of the American people as much as he likes, but I venture to say there is no man in the United States so dumb that he cannot understand how this bill tricks and deceives him.

The Federal Reserve Board and the Federal Reserve banks have profited to the extent of $5,000,000,000 or more by being released from their obligation to redeem their outstanding $5,000,000,000 of paper Federal Reserve currency in gold. They have profited by having had over a billion dollars in gold certificates saved to them. They have profited during the last 20 years by the criminality of the Federal Reserve Board, which never charged them one penny in interest on the great mass of Federal Reserve currency they have taken from the Government. They have profited from their own wrongdoing by the unlawful creation of fictitious claims against the United States Government and the giving of those claims to foreigners, and they have profited by their control of all the public revenues. And now they come forward with a scheme to sell the gold they have taken from the American people to the Treasury for new gold certificates which will give them a legal title to that gold and permit them to do as they please with it. An era of corruption is culminating in one of the greatest crimes that has ever been perpetrated against the people. Mark my words, Mr. Chairman, there will be trouble

406

here if this bill becomes law.

Why, Mr. Chairman, this fiscal fraud, this crime is so stupendous that the instigators and manipulators of it did not dare to have all the transactions performed by one man. Each man did his part and then got out of Washington pretending that he disagreed with the President's money policy or pretending that he was ill. William H. Woodin, who sat beside Albert H. Wiggin on the board of the Federal Reserve Bank of New York and who acquiesced in and helped to perpetrate the financial misdeeds which bankrupted the country, is now hiding in a western sanitarium. Dr. Sprague, the tool of the international bankers and an employee of the Bank of England, was, in my opinion, put into the Treasury to resign at a certain time and to create uncertainty in the minds of the people by the manner of his going and his subsequent articles pleading for sound money. Mr. Chairman, all the bickering and the resignations and the artful propaganda that has been thrown around the monetary policy of Franklin D. Roosevelt cannt disguise the fact that he was selected by the international bankers to carry on the work they started with the great depression; that is, the pauperization of the masses and the seizure of American property for their own use and benefit, and that he has lent himself to their schemes by unconstitutionally demanding and assuming the dictatorial powers which will enable him to carry them out.

Another purpose of this bill not mentioned in the title is the transference of a very large quantity of United States gold to the Bank for International Settlements. One of the chief objects of the gold policy of the present administration is the sending of gold taken by force from its lawful American owners to the Bank for International Settlements in Europe, where it will be kept with the property of the central banks of the world. According to the Hague convention, under which the Bank for International Settlements was formed, gold deposited in the vaults of the Bank for International Settlements is safe from seizure. Our gold, when it goes there, wlil certainly be safe from seizure by the United States. The Bank for International Settlements is dominated by the Bank of England. It is not on American soil. It is in Europe. American gold, therefore, will be kept in Europe. It will be placed where none of the wage slaves of the United States will ever be able to acquire any of it. It will be the capital and means of oppression of that international superstate, that financial superstate, which has been after Uncle Sam's gold money ever since the wealth of this country attracted the attention of greedy European bankers and brought them flocking over here to set up the suction pumps of the Federal Reserve Board and the Federal Reserve banks.

The Bank for International Settlements is an international bankers' bank. It is a central bank of central banks. The international bankers, who brought about the depression, have been drawing gold to themselves from the common people of every land. It is their intention to use that gold for their own purposes. They propose two kinds of money. Gold—the real money— is what they intend to have for themselves, and paper money, which has no intrinsic value in itself, and which is made out of nothing and is worth nothing unless it can be redeemed by the holder in gold—that is for the common people, or, as they call us, the peasants.

George Washington said:

I never have heard, and I hope I never shall hear, any serious mention of a paper emission in this State; yet such a thing may be in agitation. Ignorance and design are productive of much mischief. The former is the tool of the latter, and is often set at work suddenly and unexpectedly.

While he was here in Congress, Daniel Webster, in 1932, made the following statement:

Of all the contrivances for cheating the laboring classes of mankind, none have been more effectual than that which deludes them with paper money. This is the most effectual of inventions to fertilize the rich man's field by the sweat of the poor man's brow. Ordinary tryranny, oppression, excessive tax-

408

ation—these bear lightly on the happiness of the mass of the community compared with fraudulent currencies and the robberies committed by depreciated paper. Our own history has recorded for our instruction enough, and more than enough, of the demoralizing tendency, the injustice, and the intolerable oppression, on the virtuous and well disposed, of a degraded paper currency, authorized by law, or in any way countenanced by government.

Franklin D. Roosevelt, the high priest of repudiation, the apostle of irredeemable paper money, and the man who intends to send United States gold out of the United States to a place where no American citizen can claim it, this Franklin D. Roosevelt characterizes all those who do not agree with his monetary policy as mules. If that is true, what an awful mule President Wilson must have been. Concerning Andrew Jackson, Wilson said:

He had no idea of allowing the country to undertake the fatal experiment of an irredeemable paper currency.

This is the fatal experiment Franklin D. Roosevelt has undertaken. This is a part of his policy of "bold experimentation." Not long ago he told the people at Savannah that George Washington, like himself, was an experimenter. Mr. Chairman, there are no points of rememblance between George Washington and Franklin D. Roosevelt, experimental or otherwise. George Washington did not take orders from money changers. He did not rob the people of their gold. George Washington abhorred dishonor in all its forms. He would have died before he would have violated his oath of office or tampered with the Constitution of the United States in the manner of Franklin D. Roosevelt.

In 1837 the *New York Herald* described the crime of suspending payments in specie, that is, in gold or silver, on demand, as follows:

The general suspension of specie payments is a terrible fraud upon the community that will end in destruction to all concerned. This fraud is heightened into crime of the deepest dye, from the fact that it is done to send gold and silver to England by the actual plunder, at the point of the bayonet, of the great mass of the people here * * *. Such an act is a phenomenon in the annals of crime, without a parallel in the history of tyranny, violence, or bad government, from the remotest ages of the world down to the present day.

Now, Mr. Chairman, let us hear the true purpose of the $2,000,000,000 fund which this bill proposes to set up. I quote from the prophecies of Henry Morgenthau, Mr. Barauch's Secretary of the United States Treasury, as shown by the following article which appeared in the *Washington Times* of January 16, 1934:

TREASURY SEES UUITED STATES NEED OF BLUE CHIPS

When you play poker you want just as many blue chips as the other fellow.

That, in a man's language, was the gist of Secretary Morgenthau's summing up of the Roosevelt proposal for a $2,000,000,000 stabilization fund to protect the currency of the United States.

In other words, the American Government is engaged in probably the greatest gamble of all time. The stake is the credit of the United States.

TO EQUAL BRITISH

When asked why a figure of $2,000 millions for the stabilization fund had been asked, Morgenthau said:

"*We figured we might need an amount substantially equal to the British stabilization fund.*

"*We want every piece of machinery the other countries have. We want to be in a position to buy gold and to sell gold.*"

The 2,000-million stabilization fund will be derived from the Government's profit on the debasing of the value of the dollar to from 50 to 60 percent of the normal valuation.

FUND FROM PROFITS

If the debasement is 50 percent, the profit to the Government will be $4,000,000,000 in round numbers. A 60-cent dollar will mean about 2,666 millions in profits.

Out of these profits will come the stabilization fund to be administered by the Secretary of the Treasury, the remainder being available for any Government expenditure. Morgenthau said:

It is possible that the mere existence of the fund will be sufficient to carry out the law which requires that the Secretary of the Treasury maintain all lawful money of the Government on parity with gold."

The Secretary of the Treasury is charged with the responsibility of administration of the fund to carry out that purpose. If any particular type of currency issued— United States notes, for instance—should become depreciated in value, the Treasury would go into the market and buy a sufficient quantity of that currency to maintain its parity. Operations in the foreign markets to protect possible depreciation of the dollar would be similar.

Let this quotation from Morgenthau go down into history. Long from now some curious investigator of the present age of witchcraft and magic in the White House may unearth it and reconstruct the financial history of the "new deal" from it, as science from a single part reconstructs the entire animal.

Mr. Chairman, it is not the gambler's voice in Mr. Morgenthau's confession which most deserves political attention. We are becoming accustomed here to gambling terms as they are employed by the executive branch of the Government, and we can well understand that the Executive and his favorites must of necessity speak the lingo of their kind. This is a gambler's administration, and all the "big shot" gamblers are here to revel in it. Mr. Roosevelt does not deny his gambling propensities. He is a "new dealer." He is "on his way", but he "doesn't know where he is going." He is for a policy of "bold

411

experimentation", just as Samuel Insull was for a policy of bold experimentation. He has not been Ben Smith's patron all these years for nothing. But, Mr. Chairman, there is something apart from the vice of gambling to be observed in Mr. Morgenthau's utterance, and that is its entire untruthfulness. He would have us believe that the United States is on one side of the fence and Great Britain on the other. That, of course, is not the case. The United States has been placed in a position of financial servitude to Great Britain, and Mr. Morgenthau's loud-sounding propaganda is designed to conceal that fact from the people. Great pains have been taken to conceal it. It would be very damaging to this administration if certain people in the United States should find out about the great sums of United States money which have been sent to England during the past summer. Those funds were appropriated by Congress for the people of the United States.

Mr. Chairman, why should tax money paid by American citizens be sent to London? When England makes her periodical gesture of insult toward the United States by paying a small installment on the war debt she owes us, she pays us in debased coins, in "token" coins, to be exact. But when Mr. Roosevelt sends American money to England he sends it in gold or its equivalent. When Mr. Morgenthau obtains his "kitty", for this, I have been told, is what he called the proposed stabilization fund at the White House a week ago last Sunday evening, American funds will be fed to Europe more expeditiously and with less secrecy than such operations now require. If Congress puts the people's property into a "kitty", someone, if he cannot be the knight of the bedchamber, can at least pose before royalty as the knight of the "kitty."

Mr. Chairman, understanding that Henry Morgenthau is related by marriage to Herbert Lehman, Jewish Governor of the State of New York, and is related by marriage or otherwise to the Seligmans, of the international Jewish firm of J. & W. Seligman, who were publicly shown before a Senate committee of investigation to have offered a bribe to a foreign government; and to the Lewissohns, a firm of Jewish inter-

412

nation bankers; and to the Warburgs, whose operations through Kuhn, Loeb & Co., the International Acceptance Bank, and the Bank of Manhattan Co. and other foreign and domestic institutions under their control, have drained billions of dollars out of the United States Treasury and the bank deposits belonging to United States citizens; and to the Strauses, proprietors of R. H. Macy & Co., of New York, which is an outlet for foreign goods dumped upon this country at the expense of the United States Government, which is compelled to issue paper money on the said foreign goods of the Strauses; and that Mr. Morgenthau is likewise related or otherwise connected with various other members of the Jewish banking community of New York and London, Amsterdam, and other foreign financial centers, and that he has as his assistant, presiding over public funds, Earle Bailie, a member of the firm of J. & W. Seligman, bribe givers as aforesaid, it seems to me that Henry Morgenthau's presence in the United States Treasury and the request that Congress now give him a $2,000,-000,000 "kitty" of the people's money for gambling purposes is a striking confirmation of the statement made by me on the floor of the House on May 29, 1933. *(See pages 385 thru 388)*

Mr. Chairman, do you not see in this "kitty" bill the identical features outlined in the Protocols of Zion? Do you not see the Protocols of Zion manifested in the appointment of Henry Morgenthau as Secretary of the Treasury? It is not by accident, is it, that a representative and a relative of the money Jews of Wall Street and foreign parts has been so elevated?

Why, Mr. Chairman, this "kitty" bill takes the hitherto obscure young Henry Morgenthau and makes of him a central bank of the United States. It makes of him a central bank, an institution which Jefferson declared is one of deadly hostility to the free institutions of the United States. It exalts him above all other men. Under the powers to be granted him, his conduct is not subject to review or control by any other officer of the United States Government, not even the President.

What this "kitty" bill really does is to slide into the hands of Henry Morgenthau the emergency powers which Congress granted to the President. Those powers will not lapse. Instead, they are being slyly and dishonestly transferred to the bankers and after the bankers, in the person of Henry Morgenthau, have exercised them long enough to get the gold of the United States into their exclusive possession and to transfer it to their den of thieves, the Bank for International Settlements, Congress may take back its constitutional power over the currency, but it will have nothing left to exercise it on. The monetary gold of the people of the United States will, like the sons of the people, be buried in a foreign field.

Mr. Chairman, if you, as one of the party in power, are thinking of remaking the world so that the old America we knew and loved is to be no more; if you are one of those who is countenancing the placing of this country under the British Crown and the pooling of all American resources with those of England and Soviet Russia; if you are one of those to whom a title of nobility appears to be more desirable than plain citizenship in the Republic founded by George Washington, I trust that you will some day descend from the Speaker's chair and let us know the reasons for your preference. If, on the other hand, you are not what these words depict, I trust that you will come down to the floor, and tell us how constitutional government is to be maintained in this country if the plutocratic managers of the Democratic Party continue their efforts to destroy it. You, if anyone, should be able to give the people of the United States an answer to this question.

Under this administration the result of the American Revolution has been reversed. The United States has become an economic vassal of Great Britain. The once proud Republic of the United States with its great charter of human freedom, the Declaration of Independence, and its written Constitution, which had kept it free and independent for over 140 years, and its flag first made by the hands of Betsy Ross in Philadelphia, and its national anthem, born within earshot of the British guns that shelled Fort McHenry—all these, like the American dollar, were brought down from their high estate.

Oh, say, can you see by the dawn's early light
What so proudly we hailed at the twilight's last gleaming?

Mr. Chairman, you know very well that you cannot see that flag there as it used to be. Others started very cautiously to pull it down. But it was Franklin D. Roosevelt, in his unlawful and unconstitutional assumption of dictatorial powers, who finally lowered it and tore it from its standard.

XXIV

PUBLIC INTEREST MUST NOT BE
SUPPRESSED BY PARTISANSHIP
AND AN
ABANDONED CONSTITUTION

Wednesday, January 31, 1934

Mr. McFADDEN. Mr. Chairman, this session of Congress has been in being less than 30 days, a very short time, and yet long enough to make painfully clear that Congress has ceased to exist as the legislative branch of the Government.

Free speech has been suppressed in this House by gag rules, the taskmaster's whip has been cracked over our backs by limitation of debate, we have been threatened with the displeasure and discipline of the Executive if we do not spend in 4 weeks more money than this Government can collect by legitimate taxation in 4 years.

We are told by leaders that the President demands these things and that the country stands back of the President unanimously. Not yet in words, but in inference, we are threatened with lynching at the hands of an outraged public if we so much as stop to ask where we are going.

There are two things which a man must have if he is to be called a leader. He must be going some place and somebody must be following him. The gentlemen who appear as leaders on this floor are not leaders in any sense of the word.

416

They do not lead. They follow. They do not hold the status of generals or colonels or majors or captains or even second lieutenants. They are corporals and file closers, whose only permitted function is to shout "Hep! Hep!" and pass the orders to this awkward squad which is not yet trained to the technique of the goosestep.

I am not making a partisan Republican speech. I was thrown out of the Republican Party by the alleged leadership of that organization 2 years ago. I have had my own experiences with leadership. When I was cast into the outer darkness by the leaders of the party of which I have been a member all my life, the Republican voters of my district went out into the shadows with me. After looking over their surroundings, the Democratic voters of my district followed their Republican neighbors and joined us in the wilderness of Presidential disapproval, I was reelected on both Democratic and Republican tickets, and I hold my warrant as a Member of this House from the people and not from the parties of my district.

If I am partisan—and I may as well admit that I am—that partisanship is for the people whom I represent. I received their orders in November 1932. Those orders have never been countermanded, and I will follow them until they are countermanded by the people from whom I accepted them. I will take orders from no one else.

Franklin Delano Roosevelt received his orders on the same day that I received mine. The orders he is following today are not the orders he accepted then—and the orders he accepted then were drafted by himself in his campaign pledges and sealed with his inaugural oath. I do not know the source of the orders he is following today. I do not know that he is following either order or orders. He admits himself that he is trying first one course of procedure and then another in the hope of finding a good one. He has not presented to this body, to the Senate, or to the public any plan nor any program of what he proposes to do with us.

He has shown but one of the qualifications of leadership. People are following him, but he does not know where he is going. I cannot follow him until I know his destination—not and keep my self-respect as a man and an American. Neither can the people of the United States. Neither will the people of the United States.

His friends will say, "But he should be given his chance." Right. But so should the rest of the country. I do not question the sincerity or the courage of Mr. Roosevelt. I question his ability and his judgment, and shall continue to question them until I have seen more proof of his infallibility than I have seen to date.

Any man who asked for such unprecedented power as he seeks should be willing to show that he has the capacity to use that power properly, effectively, and without danger to the country. No such proof has been forthcoming. All that we have had is a hallelujah chorus of adulation delivered through a controlled radio and such part of the press as could be bullied or frightened into complaisance. This Roosevelt opera is all overture so far. It is time for the curtain to go up.

What we may wish to say upon this floor as Representatives of the people of the United States may be wrong, but it is our inalienable duty and our inalienable right to say it. What truth we may wish to disclose in the public interest must not be suppressed for any reason—least of all to delude the people or to establish or maintain in this country any form of government other than that provided in our Constitution.

Partisanship! Gentlemen of the majority, you are creating partisanship. There is no longer a Republican Party. It choked itself to death trying to swallow the candidacy of Herbert Hoover for reelection to the Presidency. There is no longer a Democratic Party. There is only Franklin Delano Roosevelt.

The partisanship that you are creating is a partisanship that will aline two opposing forces in this country—the people versus the Government. The American people are thoughtful and deliberate, but they always achieve decision in the end. When this extravaganza of experiment and expenditure, this

418

blind stumbling in the face of disaster, shall have reached its inevitable climax, when all our alphabetical overlords shall have unified themselves into one mighty final set of initials and those initials the fateful I.O.U., then gentlemen of the majority, you will have partisanship. It will be partisanship based on bitterness and disillusionment.

Why is it that you fear debate? Why is it that your leader answers no questions, gives no information, offers no chart or road map, but demands only unthinking obedience to orders which he himself cannot put into words? Gentlemen of the majority, why do you sit silent and refuse to defend your course? Is it because that course has no defense—or is it because you do not know what the course is nor whether there is any defense for it?

This is a two-party system of government. Today there is only one party. That party seeks to rule with an absolute hand. It seeks to suppress opposition. So far as the Republican opposition is concerned, you have succeeded, but not through your own efforts. The Republican Party destroyed itself by the course which you yourselves condemned before election and embraced after inauguration.

This is still a two-party system of government. There will be another party forced into existence by your attempt to establish a dictatorship. Every man and woman within sound of my voice knows that such a party is being born in the womb of the public mind. Most of you are thinking very seriously about the effect upon your own political futures of that foreshadowed event.

In these remarks I am defending the people and institutions of the United States. In saying that there will inevitably be born a new political party to oppose the present control of our national affairs I am not speaking alone. Many competent and reputable agencies of public opinion have already reflected popular opposition to the present attempt to strangle free speech and a free press in the United States.

Only a few weeks ago the *Saturday Evening Post*, our most outstanding weekly publication, editorially expressed the rising demand for a new political party that should be free of the unfortunate alliances and obligations of the present organizations. Mr. William Randolph Hearst has used the columns of his newspapers to protest against improper alien influence in our National Government and against any limitation in the traditional freedom of the press. Col. Robert R. McCormick, publisher of the *Chicago Tribune*, has made many eloquent pleas against any infringement upon the constitutional right of free expression in public matters.

Gentlemen of the majority, these and many other moving fingers have penned the handwriting on this wall you have tried to build around the rights and privileges which you ask that we surrender to your leader.

For many years the affairs of this country were mishandled by self-styled financial experts who seized upon political power in the name of business. Their dishonesty of thought and method were the fabric of our disaster. The land rose and cried out against these men. You seized the public resentment as your opportunity and by promising to it satisfaction for its wrongs, you won your way into power. You had a great opportunity. What did you do with it?

You turned over the processes of government to the very same individuals who had wrecked us as financial experts, giving them barely time to change their clothes and rechristen themselves economic experts. You asked and secured unlimited executive power in the name of emergency and then turned that power over to the men you had denounced as criminals, giving them legal protection and unlimited use of the public funds to bring their personal ambitions to a profitable conclusion.

No single evil of the Hoover administration has been corrected. Many of them have been perpetuated. Men who acquired fortune and dishonor by swindling the pubilc as individuals are now placed in official positions where they can swindle us collectively through control of our Federal Treasury.

We are asked to believe that virture and wisdom are conferred upon men by appointment to Federal office. The great

420

effort to make all men virtuous by legislation having failed, it is now sought to do the same thing by proclamation.

The Civil Works Administration is an example of the unholy result. Petty extortions from hungry men, graft squeezed from their few weekly dollars, became so uncontrollable a scandal that the C.W.A. had to put itself under martial law by calling upon the Army to direct its activities. Is this a foretaste of military dictatorship, to be made necessary by the failure of civil government?

Free government can rest upon no foundation but that of truth. Censorship, propaganda, suppression—all these are the enemies of truth. All three are practiced by this administration in the name of emergency.

Particularly is this true of the newest avenue to public attention—radio. Some time ago the Columbia Broadcasting Co. announced its intention to furnish to its listeners a daily news service. The company employed several Washington newspapermen and established a news bureau which has paid particular attention to proceedings in both Houses of Congress. It has been their custom to broadcast this news at a certain hour each evening. Last Saturday evening, January 27, Mr. Farley, who in his one person combines the functions of the Warwick and the Sancho Panza of this administration, appeared at a political rally in Boston, Mass. He desired that his remarks on that occasion be put upon the air. The Columbia Broadcasting Co. canceled its news service for the evening, gave its local news-gathering employees a holiday, and gave the news period to Mr. Farley for his remarks. Either they valued their news service too little or the words of Mr. Farley too much. A news service that has to make way for propaganda is not an independent news service, nor can its professed "news" be given any serious consideration.

Let me offer two quotations. The first is from the *Washington Post* of November 5, 1933. It reads:

Herbert L. Pettey, Secretary of the Radio Commission, has been directed to coordinate radio speeches of officials, obtain free time on the air for them from the radio stations licensed by his agency, and with the aid of R. Fred Roper, executive secretary of the Democratic National Committee, revise or censor such speeches with the view of making every word count for the administration.

Pettey was assigned to the job by Postmaster General Farley.

The next quotation is from the *New York Herald Tribune* of November 2, 1933. It reads:

ROCHESTER, November 1.—Assemblyman Richard L. Saunders today charged in a statement that he had been given a "raw deal" and had been ruled off the air by the management of station WHAM because of criticism of Postmaster General Farley in a speech prepared for delivery last night in answer to an address Monday night by the Democratic leader.

Assemblyman Saunders said he had presented his speech for approval, and had been asked if it could not be "toned down." On his reply that it could not, said Saunders, he was told that he could not make the speech.

Newspapers justify their existence by their willingness to print the news, whether or not that news agrees with the political opinions of their publishers. Radio must learn the same lesson before it presumes to put itself forward as a medium for the dissemination of news. News is a record of events. It is not a medium for propaganda. The newspaper which prints a statement puts itself upon record; forever afterwards the printed words themselves commit such newspapers to full legal responsibility for what they have said. Copies of their own pages are evidence of what they have said and in the event that charges of libel are made, those same pages may be introduced in court as competent evidence.

The newspaper is bound by what it says and makes no effort to avoid that responsibility.

Radio, on the other hand, is limited to the spoken word, heard but once and nowhere upon record. Many times I have sought to obtain from radio stations transcripts of statements that have been made to their listeners through their facilities. Sometimes I have been successful in securing such transcripts. More often I have not been so successful—and the latter instances often occurred in cases where the reported accounts of what had been said implied a legal responsibility on the part of the radio station.

Radio is a sort of mechanical back-fence gossip, utilizing the poisoned word, the slighting accent, the sarcastic tone and all those shades of meaning which are so much more available in appealing to the ear than in appealing to the eye. Added to its greater versatility of expression, it has the additional advantage of being able to avoid responsibility for what it says. It now seeks to have itself accepted on a par with newspapers as a medium for the dissemination of public information.

Withal it takes its news responsibilities so lightly that it is willing to discard them to win the pleasure of anyone who holds a position of political power. I do not believe that radio should be admitted to any parity with newspapers so far as having access to the press gallery or any other restricted source of news is concerned.

There are newspapers which I do not like. There are newspapers which do not like me. When either of us is moved to utter an opinion about the other, that opinion becomes a matter of printed record. Neither of us can or will try to hide behind a denial.

Free criticism is an inalienable right under free government. Full responsibility for that criticism is a moral responsibility which should be as inalienable as the right to make it.

There is now before the proper committee of this body a resolution calling for a full investigation into the conduct of the radio business in the United States. I introduced that resolution in the last Congress and it is still alive. No action has been taken upon it. Like many other matters pending before this Congress, no attention will be paid to it unless it has Presidential approval. Will the administration get Presidential approval of this?

Will the Rules Committee put that resolution upon its passage, and will the majority pass it and conduct a full and impartial investigation? No Member of this House who reads his mail can say that there is no public demand for such an investigation. You all know that there is, and you all know that the radio situation should be dealt with by Congress and that without further delay.

I sometimes feel that all that this House is, now that we have abandoned the Constitution, and resolved ourselves into a rubber stamp, is a sounding board and, even at that, we are restricted lest that sounding board produce something which, in the judgment of the administration of this House, should not be heard.

I know now that nothing I say upon this floor will receive the compliment of attention from the majority. I am listed as a "trouble maker", as a critic of all administrations, as one whose outlook upon life and affairs is through blue glasses.

That is not the truth. I am not against anyone, except as that person or group is against the interest of the public. I am a defender, not an assailant. I present my complaint against conditions to the House, fully and fairly in the RECORD, not by whispered innuendo or implied suggestion. I present my complaint, knowing that it will receive no attention from a majority which is blind because it will not see, which is deaf because it is forbidden to hear. I present my complaint so that it will be a matter of record. I fear that I am right in surmising that your decision will be against me and against the people for whom I speak. I know that I must appeal from your decision and that I am prepared to do. My appeal will be to the highest court in this land, one above any party or any official. That is the court of public opinion, whose next session will be held on the first Tuesday after the first Monday of next November.

When I speak of a new party, I do not mean any of the strange assortments of odd people who proclaim themselves to be political parties and who propound strange panaceas and programs of public conduct as the reason for their being. Those we have always with us. What I do mean is a great gathering of those men and women to whom America is more than a word, the Constitution more than an antique—that great middle class who are the sinew and backbone of this United States, that class of people who are being strangled at this moment by the policies under which you are being led.

The Republican Party itself was born out of the failure of Whigs and Democrats to meet the moral issues of 1856. The moral needs of 1934 will bring forth the answer to our political problem of today.

Gentlemen of the majority, I might be one of you if I chose. I was elected to this House upon the Democratic as well as upon the Republican ticket. I cannot join you. You do not carry your power gracefully. You have yet to learn moderation. Power is like alcohol. A little raises one's spirit to the heights. Too much puts body and soul in the gutter.

Ambition, too, is a thing that calls for moderation. Lucifer was ambitious to be the dictator of heaven. Hell was created for his punishment.

XXV

BANKHEAD COTTON
CONTROL BILL

March 13, 1934

Mr. McFADDEN. Will the gentleman yield for a question?

Mr. JONES. I yield to the gentleman from Pennsylvania.

Mr. McFADDEN. Will the gentleman tell the House something of the authorship of this bill? I would like to know where it originated.

Mr. JONES. I will endeavor to do that, but I do not think it makes very much difference. The real question is not its authorship, but its merits. I hope the gentleman will not divert me from the substance to the shadow.

Mr. McFADDEN. Will not the gentleman answer my question?

Mr. JONES. I am coming to that directly.

Mr. McFADDEN. I hope the gentleman will answer my question.

Mr. JONES. I decline to yield further. * * *

May I further say, for the information of the gentleman who is anxious to find out something about the authorship of this bill, that the BANKHEAD brothers first introduced it. My attention was first called to it last year by Senator BANK-

426

HEAD, who made an effort to get consideration at that time. The administration did not seem to favor it last year. He introduced it again this year and it has been thoroughly gone over. The committee has added a great many amendments.

Mr. MILLARD. The gentleman from Pennsylvania wants to know who prepared the bill, not who presented it to the Senate and House.

Mr. JONES. I am stating that, if the gentleman will listen. Senator BANKHEAD introduced the bill again this year.

It came before the House Committee and the House Committee practically rewrote the bill in many respects. We put in about 50 or 60 amendments and changed the bill from a permanent to a temporary bill. If the gentleman is interested, he may go back and get a copy of the original bill and compare it with the one we have before us today. He will find the bill has been worked on in collaboration with the BANKHEAD brothers and with various Members of the committee who are interested.

Mr. McFADDEN. Will the gentleman yield?

Mr. JONES. I am sorry, I cannot yield further.

Mr. McFADDEN. I am trying to get some information.

Mr. JONES. Is the gentleman for the bill?

Mr. McFADDEN. I do not know. I want some information that will decide the matter. I want to know the origin of the first bill, and my reason, if the gentleman will let me state——

Mr. JONES. I do not care about the reason. Sitting back there is the man who introduced the first bill, and I know he has been working on it a long time.

Mr. McFADDEN. It is not a question of the introduction of the bill. It is the principle involved in the original legislation. I would like to know whether it came from Mr. Tugwell and Mr. Ezekiel.

Mr. JONES. I have never discussed the terms of this measure with either of those gentlemen. So far as I know it is Mr. BANKHEAD's idea. Of course the question of taxing excess production as a means of control has been long discussed. I have heard it for years. There are not many new ideas in the world.

I think that this has been discussed for years, but usually there is an enterprising man who has industry enough to take an idea that has been floating around, capture it, and reduce it to terms. So far as I know, Senator Bankhead has the honor of having done just that very thing.

He introduced a very similar measure at the last session. He did not press it at that time and introduced a much more elaborate bill at the present session. I would rather he would furnish the information, if the gentleman is interested. He is sitting in the Chamber and I know he will be happy to tell the gentleman. Personally I do not care whose brain child it is, I only want to know whether it is worthy.

* * * * * * * *

Mr. McFadden. Will the gentleman yield?

Mr. Jones. I am sorry I cannot yield. I am taking time that I have promised to other people and I must go on now without yielding further.

Mr. Busby. The gentleman does not care to yield at this time?

* * * * * * * *

Mr. McFadden. Mr. Chairman, I make the point of no quorum. The gentleman is refusing to answer pertinent questions in regard to this bill and I think we should have a quorum present.

The Chairman (Mr. Busby in the chair). The gentleman from Pennsylvania makes the point of no quorum. The Chair will count. [After counting.] One hundred and three Members present, a quorum.

* * * * * * * *

Mr. McFadden. Mr. Chairman, will the gentleman yield?

Mr. Hope. I yield.

Mr. McFadden. I tried to elucidate from the chairman of the committee, of which the gentleman is the ranking member, the origin of this idea. He was reluctant to answer definitely, although I am of the opinion that he knows. Since asking the gentleman for this information I have learned the authorship. The authors of the plan are Mordecai Ezekiel, Mr. Tugwell, and others of those gentlemen who have been preparing the socialistic plan.

This is part of the whole plan of setting up a corporate state in the United States.

Mr. Hope. I thank the gentleman for his contribution.

Mr. Focht. It is molded after the Soviet Government.

 *   *   *   *   *   *   *   *

Mr. McFadden. Will the gentleman yield?

Mr. Chase. I gladly yield to the gentleman from Pennsylvania.

Mr. McFadden. I want to ask the gentleman whether he is familiar with the bill which is in the offing and will be presented to Congress in the near future, to amend the A.A.A. Act. I saw a typewritten copy of that bill, and it provided for a licensing system, limitation of acreage, limitation of farm production, and fixed a penalty.

Mr. Chase. I am somewhat acquainted with some features of the bill, and desired to discuss some prospective legislation in connection with the pending legislation but decided that the bill immediately before the House is sufficient for me to bring to your attention the problem, even speaking exclusively on this one point.

Mr. McFadden. Let me say that there is a great similarity between this bill and that bill, and I am informed and believe that the two bills originated under the direction of Mordecai Ezekiel and Mr. Tugwell.

Mr. Bankhead. Will the gentleman yield?

Mr. Chase. I yield with pleasure to the gentleman from Alabama.

Mr. Bankhead. I want to tell the gentleman from Pennsylvania that there is not a scintilla of basis for the suggestion he has just made. Neither gentleman he referred to, as far as I know, and I think I know something about this bill, have been consulted or had any hand in the preparation of this bill.

The gentleman from Pennsylvania is drawing vividly on his imagination.

Mr. Jones. Will the gentleman from Minnesota yield to me?

Mr. Chase. With pleasure, to my chairman.

Mr. Jones. I want to say that neither one of the gentlemen referred to by the gentleman from Pennsylvania appeared before the committee, and no member of the committee had anything to do with them, as far as I know.

Mr. McFadden. My authority is as responsible as any thing that has been said on this floor. I want to call the attention of the gentleman to this significant fact. And that is that this bill fits into the form of government that is being advocated by Mr. Tugwell and those associated with him.

* * * * * * * *

Mr. McFadden. Mr. Chairman, will the gentleman yield?

Mr. Chase. With pleasure.

Mr. McFadden. In view of what the gentleman has just said, I recall that Theodore Roosevelt, the year that he passed on, made a statement to the effect that Felix Frankfurter is the most dangerous man in the United States to our form of government.

* * * * * * * *

Mr. McFadden. Will the gentleman yield?

Mr. Pierce. I yield to the gentleman from Pennsylvania.

Mr. McFadden. May I call the gentleman's attention to the fact that the article of Secretary Wallace, to which the gentleman refers, is a copyrighted article by the "Foreign Policy Association", one of our leading international associations that is working to internationalize the United States?

* * * * * * * *

March 15, 1934

Mr. McFadden. Mr. Chairman, I rise in opposition to the amendment.

Mr. Chairman, I am opposed in principle to this class of legislation, for the reason that it is unconstitutional and that there is no emergency which demands legislation of this kind at this time.

I repeat that in the enactment of this particular legislation the Constitution of the United States is being violated, and because of this fact I direct the attention of the membership of this House to the oath which each and every Member has taken. It is as follows:

I do solemnly swear that I will support and defend the Constitution of the United States against all enemies, foreign and domestic; that I will bear true faith and allegiance to the same; that I take this obligation freely, without any mental reservation or purpose of evasion, and that I will well and faithfully discharge the duties of the office on which I am about to enter. So help me God.

In support of what I have just said, I wish to call your attention to the last paragraph of the minority views in the report on this bill, as follows:

This measure constitutes a definite step down a strange, unfamiliar, and dangerous road leading to regimentation of agriculture and industry. It initiates for the first time in America compulsory control of production in place of the freedom of action which has always been considered an inherent right of our American citizenship. While earnest attempts have been made in this bill to meet constitutional objections which may be made to a measure of this kind, yet we are convinced that in view of the decisions of the courts this measure is unconstitutional. Although in form a taxing measure, the entire purpose and effect of the bill negates the fact that it is expected to produce revenue. Rather it is a regulatory measure, going beyond any authority which Congress possesses in that regard, and using the taxing power as a subterfuge.

The particular section of the bill that is now being discussed should be considered in connection with section 23 of the bill which gives the President authority to enter into agreements with foreign countries in relation to the sale of cotton.

This particular piece of legislation is a part of the program to establish in this country a new form of government, and it is my understanding that this bill is to be followed by other legislation of a simliar nature which will endeavor to control the entire acreage on the farms in the United States, and will attempt to control the products from these farms, and will make violation an offense punishable by a fine of $1,000, and will make every district attorney in every county in the United States a Federal officer to enforce this law.

It is right in line with the plan which is now being worked out in England. I want to point out to the House that there is a concerted movement not only in England but in the United States. In the United States this movement is in charge of certain men now engaged in writing legislation in the Department of Agriculture. I refer to Mr. Tugwell, Mr. Mordecai Ezekiel, and Mr. Frank, and their immediate associates, some of whom are in other departments and some of whom are outside; and I may even go so far as to say that they are aided and abetted in this matter apparently by the Secretary of Agriculture. Their action in this matter is also assisted and aided through the agency of the Foreign Policy Association of the United States, which is directly connected with the Fabian Society, or a branch of it, in England, which at the present time is attempting to take over the control of agriculture and its operation in England, as well as the industries therein located. I call your especial attention to the recent article, America Must Choose, by Secretary of Agriculture Wallace, a syndicated article put out under the auspices of the Foreign Policy Association of New York and copyrighted by them. This article is quite in keeping with the plan of the British offspring of the Fabian group.

One of the stalwarts against the move in England is Stanley Baldwin. Mr. Baldwin issued a statement which was printed in the United States recently. It was a statement made over the radio, and, if I have time, I will read it to you, because he is standing today against the movement in England that I am speaking against now, and that movement is evidenced by this legislation and any other kind of legislation following, which have for their purpose the regimenting of all production in the United States, leading up to an absolute dictatorship.

The quotation I refer to from Mr. Baldwin is as follows:

Our freedom did not drop down like manna from heaven. It has been fought for from the beginning of our history and the blood of men has been shed to obtain it. It is the result of centuries of resistance to the power of the executive and it has brought as equal justice, trial by jury, freedom of worship, and freedom of religious and political opinion.

Democracy is far the most difficult form of government because it requires for perfect functioning the participation of everybody. Democracy wants constant guarding, and for us to turn to a dictatorship would be an act of consummate cowardice, of surrender, of confession that our strength and courage alike had gone.

It is quite true the wheels of our stage coach may be creaking in heavy ground, but are you sure the wheels of the coach are not creaking in Moscow, Berlin, and Vienna, and even in the United States?

The whole tendency of a dictatorship is to squeeze out the competent and independent man and create a hierarchy accustomed to obeying. Chaos often results when the original dictator goes.

The rise of communism or fascism—both alike believe in force as a means of establishing their dictatorship— would kill everything that had been grown by our people for the last 800 or 1,000 years.

The plan in England to which I am referring is the "political economic plan", drawn up by Israel Moses Sieff, the director of a chain-store enterprise in England called Marks

& Spencer. This enterprise declared a dividend of 40 percent for 1933, and was enabled to do so by the fact that it has until now handled almost exclusively all imports from Soviet Russia, which has enabled this house to undersell competitors.

Some of this plan was set forth in a newspaper called *The Week End Review*, at which time Lord Beaverbrook was cooperating. It is fair to say that Lord Beaverbrook disapproved of their plans. Such persons as the following are members of the "political economic plan": Ramsay MacDonald, Premier of England; Mrs. Leonard Elmhurst, formerly Mrs. Dorothy Willard Straight; Sir Basil P. Blackett, of the Bank of England; Sir Henry Bunbury: Graeme Haldane; I. Hodges; Lady Reading; Daniel Neal; H. V. Hodson; Sir Arthur Salter; Sir Oswald Moseley; Lord Eustis Percy; Lord Melchett; Sir Christopher Turnor; Malcolm MacDonald, son of the Premier.

This "political economic plan" organization is divided into many separate and well-organized and well-financed departments; for instance, town and country planning, industry, international relations, transport, banking, social services, civic division, and an agricultural department. The head of the agricultural department is Leonard Elmhurst, whose wife was formerly Mrs. Willard Straight, who manages a school for agriculture on "political economic plan" at Dartington Hall, Totnes, Devonshire.

May I point out to you that this is a secret organization with tremendous power? The definition of their organization is as follows:

A group of people who are actively engaged in production and distribution in the social services in town and country plan, in finance, in education, in research, in persuasion, and in various other key functions within the United Kingdom.

The "political economic plan" is in operation in the British Government by means of a tariff advisory board. This organization has gathered all data and statistics obtained by governmental and private organization in administrative, industrial, trade, social, educational, agricultural, and other circles. Air-force statistics are in their hands, as well as those of the law and medical professions. This organization or group have had access to all archives of the British Government, just as the "brain trust" here in the United States have had access to the archives of our Government departments.

Through the Tariff Advisory Board, which was created in February of 1933, and headed by Sir George May, the control of industry and trade is being firmly established in the British Empire. The Tariff Advisory Board works in direct connection with the Treasury, and together with it devises the tariff policy.

In this bill and the tariff bill which follows it is proposed to set up just such a board, under the direction of the President, as the tariff advisory board in England.

The tariff board in England has been granted the powers of a law court and can exact under oath that all information concerning industry and trade be given it. Iron and steel, as also cotton and industrials, in England have been ordered by the tariff advisory board to prepare and submit plans for the reorganization of their industries and warned that should they fail to do so, a plan for complete reconstruction would be imposed upon them. May I suggest to you the similarity of this plan with the N.R.A., and also suggest to you that the tariff advisory board in England has been granted default powers and can, therefore, impose its plan.

The tariff board is composed, in addition to Sir George May, of Sir Sidney Chapman, professor of economics and statistics, and Sir George Allen Powell, of the British Food Board and Food Council. And it is a well-known fact that this particular "political economic group" has close connection with the Foreign Policy Association in New York.

I wish to quote from a letter from a correspondent of mine abroad, as follows:

It appears that the alleged "brain trust" is supposed to greatly influence the present United States policy.

Neither you nor I are particularly interested in what takes place in England, but what should interest us both, it seems to me, is that there is a strong possibility that certain members of the "brain trust" around our President are undoubtedly in touch with this British organization and possibly are working to introduce a similar plan in the United States.

I understand the "brain trust" is largely composed of Professor Frankfurter, Professor Moley, Professor Tugwell, Adolph Berle, William C. Bullitt, and the mysterious Mordecai Ezekiel. I think there is no doubt that these men all belong to this particular organization with distinct Bolshevik tendencies. So it is quite possible that should this "political economic plan" be developed in the United States, if this alleged "brain trust" has really a serious influence over the judgment of our President, this plan may be attempted in our country.

Need I point out to you, who have been observing the activities of the so-called "brain trust" in the writing and sending to the Congress of legislation, that this legislation has for its purpose the virtual setting up in the United States of a plan similar to that which is being worked out in England?

I am assured by serious people, who are in a position to know, that this organization practically controls the British Government, and it is the opinion of those who do know that this highly organized and well-financed movement is intended to practically sovietize the English-speaking race.

I wish to quote again from my correspondent, as follows:

> Some 2 months ago when Israel Moses Sieff, the present head of this organization, was urged to show more activity by the members of his committee, he said, "Let us go slowly for a while and wait until we see how our plan carries out in America."

I shall also quote a paragraph from Freedom and Planning, which is issued by the Inner Council of the members of the "Political Economic Plan" as affecting the producer:

The position of the farmer and the manufacturer under a system of planned production can only be sketched in broad outlines. He may be conceived of as remaining in full control of all the operations of his farm or factory, but receiving from the duly constituted authority instructions as to the quantity and quality of his production, and as to the markets in which he will sell. He will himself have had a voice in setting up his constituted authority and will have regular means of communicating with it and influence its policy. He will be less exposed than at present to interference from above. He will be less free to make arbitrary decisions as to his own business outside the region of day-to-day operation of plant or farm.

It is further suggested that these plans are not very different from that which already occurs in particular organized industries, but must be conceived of as applying generally to most, if not all, of the major fields of production and as a part of a consciously and systematically planned agricultural and industrial organization.

There is to be a national council for agriculture, a national council for industry, a national council for coal mining, a national council for transport, and so on; a series of statutory or chartered corporations; for example, a cotton industry corporation, a steel industry corporation, a milk producers' corporation, organized on the lines of public-utility companies, serving at least to federate in suitable cases to own the plants, factories, and so forth, engaged in production.

There is an interesting paragraph—Compulsion and Private Ownership of Land—in which it is stated:

From the standpoint of encroachments upon freedom, apart from the denial of the tenets of individualism, the most obvious targets for attack are perhaps the proposed grant of powers to compel minorities and the probable necessity for drastic changes in the ownership of land.

Another paragraph says:

What is required, with only a view to equitable treatment of individuals, is transfer of ownership of large blocks of land, not necessarily of all the land in the country, but certainly of a large proportion of it, into the hands of the proposed statutory corporations and public-utility bodies and of land trusts.

This proposal is quite in keeping with the recently announced plan of Mr. Tugwell in dealing with the farm-land situation in the United States.

It is not possible for me to quote the full text of this plan, but I have touched upon enough of it to indicate to any fair-minded person that what is proposed in this bill and in the other various steps that have been taken and that are now immediately in contemplation is a plan to be set up here by the "brain trust" quite similar to the one I have outlined that is in operation in England today and is the one to which I have heretofore referred as being opposed by Stanley Baldwin. It is unconstitutional. It is un-American. And as one Member of this House who reveres his oath of office and believes in the Constitution of the United States, I shall not be a party to this scheme.

March 17, 1934

Mr. McFADDEN. Mr. Chairman, I move to strike out the last word.

Supplementing what I have said, Mr. Chairman, in opposition to this bill, I want to add that this is sectional legislation. It is class legislation, dealing with a commodity which is the principal commodity, that is raised on the farms in this country, which enters into international trade; and it gives the President of the United States authority to enter into trade agreements with other nations of the world on this special commodity, cotton. It takes from the Congress of the United States the right to handle the question of international trade through tariffs, a right which is fundamental to our form of government. I want to reiterate that this legislation is unconstitutional, and any Member of this House who votes for this bill violates his oath of office, because the oath of office of a Member of this House requires that he will protect the Constitution of the United States from both foreign and domestic attacks.

This bill violates the Constitution of the United States, and I want to make that as plain as I possibly can in regard to legislation of this kind. This is not the initial act which violates the Constitution. There have been several other acts. This is simply one of the stones in the arch. There will be other pieces of legislation which will follow this which will also violate the Constitution, all tending to set up a new form of government. In referring to what the gentleman from Mississippi [Mr. BUSBY] said in the controversy he had with the Chairman of the Committee on Agriculture, in which the gentleman from Texas [Mr. JONES] said he was tearing up the bill, if I have a choice between tearing up this bill and the Constitution of the United States, I will do everything within my power to tear up this bill rather than the Constitution. I want to make that as clear and decisive as possible.

I want to say also that the difficulty in selling cotton abroad is entirely different than that which has been discussed today. The reason more cotton cannot be sold abroad is because of the fact that the foreigner has not the means with which to buy cotton or other products.

An added reason why the foreigner does not buy more cotton and more wheat is the fact that our financial system, under international control which dominates it, forbids transactions and sale of American commodities in foreign ports. The three-cornered arrangement which has been in operation for several years between Great Britain, South America, and the United States compels the United States to pay hundreds of millions of dollars to Great Britain, which is in its operation a strangle hold upon America's right to do business not only with Great Britain but with the other countries of the world. I say we are still dealing with the effects and not the causes of our economic and financial ills. What should be done is to so regulate the control of our finances in this country that the free flow of the surplus production in this country can go into world markets; and they will not go, no matter what legislation you enact, until you correct the control of your financial system.

XXVI

PRESENT-DAY GOVERNMENT

RADIO ADDRESS

Wednesday Evening, May 2, 1934

(Printed in the Congressional Record of May 3, 1934)

Mr. McFadden. Mr. Speaker, under leave to extend my remarks in the Record I include the following address made by me yesterday evening over Station WOL in Washington, D.C.:

Just prior to and since the election of President Franklin D. Roosevelt in 1932 this country has been educated to a new phase in government, "brain trust advisers", and through them the "new deal" has introduced a national political economic planning scheme which seems to have permeated all branches of Government.

The original "brain trust" was composed of Prof. Raymond Moley, Prof. Rexford Tugwell, and Justice Brandeis' contribution, A. A. Berle, Jr., and Bernard M. Baruch's contribution, Gen. Hugh S. Johnson. To these must be added Prof. George F. Warren and Prof. James Rogers, the gold specialist twins, and another Justice Louis D. Brandeis confrere, Prof. Felix Frankfurter, James M. Landis, Jerome Frank, and another Bernard M. Baruch contribution, Donald Richberg, Frederic C. Howe, Harry L. Hopkins, Clarence Darrow, Mordecal Ezekial, Harold Ickes, and one must not omit Secretary of Agriculture

441

Henry A. Wallace, nor the other Cabinet member, Henry Morgenthau, Jr., nor should we omit Henry Morgenthau, Sr., who is a sort of super-adviser for his illustrious son.

These men are now or have been actively engaged in the various phases of the political economic plan called the "new deal."

The country has recently been treated to the spectacle of the present administration's attempt to ridicule the idea that there is a definite new plan of government in process. Without attempting to comment in any manner whatever on the attempt to disarm the public, I desire now to refer briefly to a plan that was advocated as far back as 1918 when A. A. Berle had some very definite ideas regarding the establishing of a new State. Indeed, he wrote a little book on "The Significance of a Jewish State", dedicated to his friend, Louis D. Brandeis. In it he regarded the Jew as "the barometer of civilization at all times." He recognized the inability of Christianity to avert war or "to do a single thing towards mitigating its worst effects", and seemed to think the Jews were the only power that could do anything about it.

He believed "A Jewish state would be a 'Hague' which could, and which would, command the attention and govern the thought of the world."

He did not wait for the public recognition of the "brain trust" to start a campaign for social regeneration. In 1918 he said: "There have been many of us who for many years have seen in the Hebrew laws the elements of the social regeneration of the world. * * * It would have commanded interest to the entire world to see a State, albeit a small one, work these problems through, and especially a State which could, and which would, call to its aid the finest body, collectively, of intellectual force and discrimination which the world knows. * * * A rationalized Hebrew State, founded on Hebrew fundamental laws—ethical, social, sanitary, dietary, and all the rest— would be a working laboratory of social regeneration which would excite breathless attention. * * *"

In this State he advocated: "Concessions to intending

builders could be made on the national plan and automatically agreeing with the national interest and the public welfare. The industrial expansion, therefore, could be without those weary steps toward freedom, which all other industrial civilizations have to undergo. Almost from the beginning land and industries, public resources, mineral and otherwise, could be nationally administered, and all this would make a most novel and striking page in statecraft. ° ° °"

An attempt to establish a political economic plan is now in operation under the leadership of a group, formerly connected with the Fabian Society in England. This, until the present, secret political economic plan was drawn up by Israel Moses Sieff, an Israelite, the director of a chain-store enterprise in England, called "Marks & Spencer", which house handles almost exclusively imports from Soviet Russia, which enables them to undersell its competitors. Prominent members of this organization in England, besides Sieff, are Ramsay Macdonald; his son, Malcolm Macdonald; Sir George May; Kenneth Lindsey; Gerald Barry; I. Nicholson; Sir Henry Bunbary; Graeme Haldane; I. Hodges; Lady Reading; Daniel Neal; Sir Basil P. Blackett; Sir Arthur Salter; Sir Oswald Moseley; Sir George Allan Powell; Sir Sydney Chapman; Lord Eustace Percy; Ronald Davison; Lord Melchett; Sir Christopher Turnor; Mrs. Leonard Elmhirst, formerly Dorothy Willard Straight nee Whitney, of New York.

This political economic plan organization, now secretly operating in England, is designated "Freedom and Planning", and is divided into many well-organized and well-financed departments, such as Town and Country Planning, Industry, International Relations, Transportation, Banking, Social Services, Civil Division. It is already in operation in the British Government by means of the Tariff Advisory Board. It has gathered all data and statistics obtainable by governmental and private organizations in administrative, industrial, trade, social, educational, agricultural, and other circles. Through its Tariff Advisory Board it has control over industry and trade and works in direct connection with the British Treasury, and together they devise the British tariff policy. It has also been granted the power of a law court and can exact, under oath, that all information concerning industry and trade be given it. Iron and steel and cotton industrials have been ordered by the Tariff Advisory Board to prepare and submit plans for the reorganization of their industries, and have been warned that should they fail to do so a plan for complete reconstruction will be imposed upon them. This board has been granted default powers, and can, therefore, enforce its plans.

May I pause here to suggest the similarity of the "Freedom and Planning" scheme of the political economic group in England with the N.R.A., the Bankhead cotton bill, the control of farm acreage, and the other planned developments of the "new deal" under the direction of the "brain trust" and their cohorts?

Neither you nor I are particularly interested in what takes place in England, but what should interest us Americans, it seems to me, are the strong indications that point to the putting into operation definitely of this plan in the United States, with the necessary changes to adapt it to our conditions. This is made pertinent by the well-known fact that this particular English group have very close connections with the Foreign Policy Association of New York. This association was largely organized and fostered by Felix Frankfurter and the late Paul N. Warburg. In this group we must also place Henry A. Wallace, the present Secretary of Agriculture, for the reason that he has recently caused to be published under the auspices of the Foreign Policy Association a copyrighted article entitled "America Must Choose." This article is quite in keeping with the "Freedom and Planning" group in England.

There is no doubt, I think, that Professors Frankfurter, Moley, Tugwell, Berle, Jr., and the mysterious Mordecai Ezekiel are all members of this particular group who are carrying out a world plan.

That this political economic group practically control the British Government is indicated by the fact that Prime Minister

444

MacDonald and his son and J. H. Thomas and other influential Britishers are officers of the group.

An interesting sidelight is that some 6 months ago when the father of this plan, Israel Moses Sieff, was urged to show more activity by the members of his committee, his answer was "Let us go slowly for awhile and wait until we see how our plan carries out in America." That statement indicates that a plan similar to theirs is being tried in America.

When we consider Professor Tugwell's announced plans for control of all land in the United States and the production therefrom, and when we consider the plans of Professor Berle, Jr., for the railroads and finances of this country, and when we consider the Mordecai Ezekiel-Tugwell-Bankhead cotton control bill and the Wallace hog, corn, and wheat control plans, and the Ickes control of mineral and petroleum industries, and General Johnson's N.R.A. control of industry, we must know that something is being tried out here. And, again, when we hear President Roosevelt say, as he did on April 25, 1934, that this is "evolution not revolution", in his address at the opening of a subsistence homestead exhibit, at which time, according to press reports, he made an appeal for the recognition of the importance of long-range national planning as a step toward permanent improvement of the economic and social structure of the Nation, and he stated that the administration was going ahead with its experiments, can we say that this is mere experimentation? Further the President said, "If we look at this thing from the broad national viewpoint, we are going to make it a national policy if it takes 50 years." Again he said, "The time is now ripe, overripe, for planning to prevent in the future the errors of the past and to carry out social and economic views new to the Nation." Also, yesterday, President Roosevelt announced the formation of a "plan committee on national land problems", with the apparent purpose of coordinating and stimulating the Federal program for retiring submarginal land—the Tugwell plan—which he designated as one of the main divisions of national "long-range planning." The avowed purpose of the committee, according to the White House announcement, will be to improve "practices of land utilization" and achieve "better balancing of agricultural production, aiding in the solution of human problems in land use and developing of a national land program."

In view of all these things, can we say that this is mere experimentation? Or shall we say that which it is? It is assuredly "Freedom and Planning", adapted to the United States. Stripped of all its camouflage, it is the guild form of government, and is the kind of government that has recently been established in Italy and Austria and which will be established in England if this particular group under the leadership of Israel Moses Sieff succeed in their plans. The guild form of government is directly the opposite of the constitutional form of government. It is the Jewish plan of a World State.

XXVII

FREEDOM AND PLANNING

Document by Israel Moses Sieff, London, England, entitled
"Freedom and Planning"

Friday, June 8, 1934

Mr. McFADDEN. Mr. Speaker, under the leave to extend my remarks in the RECORD, I include the following secret document entitled "Freedom and Planning" issued from the inner council of the members of the Political Economic Plan, otherwise termed "P.E.P." The chairman of the organization and author of the document is Israel Moses Sieff, London, England. At a later date an analysis of this plan will follow.

FREEDOM AND PLANNING
COLLAPSING CIVILIZATION

This generation is faced with the threat of a world collapse of modern civilization and the advent of a period comparable with the dark ages which followed on the collapse of the Roman Empire in the fifth century A.D.

We are apt to regard such statements as pleasantly scarifying, pardonable exaggerations in the mouths of those who are trying to spur us to action against the very real ills of the times, but not meant quite seriously.

The threat is serious.

Chaos will overtake us if we cannot show intelligence enough to extricate ourselves.

447

For more than a year now nothing has enabled civilization to keep some sort of course and to ride out the storm except the immense momentum of ordinary economic processes and the inertia of habit and custom. It is the resisting powers of these forces and human intelligence which has thus far staved off the collapse.

They cannot bring us back prosperity, but they may suffice to carry the world through the immediate crises. If so, we shall for a time be able to live on our capital, the material capital stored up from past generations, the intellectual and moral capital of men and women trained for civilization and citizenship. But what chance will the next generation have, if half of them find no employment for their youthful energies, and all of them are living under the oppression of hopelessness and decay?

What forms collapse will assume no one can foresee. It may not come suddenly. More probably there will be a gradual decline with fleeting periods of revival.

SHRINKING CREDIT AND SHRINKING TRADE

Modern life depends on world-wide interchanges of goods and services. These in turn depend on confidence and credit. Confidence and credit are being progressively impaired. Without them it is impossible to maintain for long not merely existing standards of life but even life itself for a large proportion of the world's population.

Imagine the plight of Great Britain if the complex economic and financial machinery which supplies the vast bulk of our population with its food were to cease to function. Such a catastrophe is not, it is true, as yet in sight, but this machinery depends wholly on confidence and credit, and with dwindling world trade and social and political trouble growing in other countries the moment is not far off when we shall be unable in these islands to support either present standards or our present aggregate population.

Applied science puts at man's disposal foodstuffs, raw materials, services of all kinds, in ever growing abundance, enough not alone to maintain existing standards of life but to raise these standards for all far above the highest now enjoyed by any of us.

Only our intelligence and powers of organization and our moral and spiritual capacity to work in mutual cooperation with each other are proving insufficient to meet the growing complexity of the machinery for regulating production, distribution, and consumption.

First one then another vital part of the machine is being thrown out of gear. Increasing friction is being generated in the effort to distribute to the consumer that which man is producing. The quantity of things produced and things consumed declines. The volume of world trade, both of internal trade within each country and still more of international exchanges of goods and services, is progressively lessened.

WORLD-WIDE ECONOMIC DISTRESS

Cracks are appearing everywhere. In China and in India economic distress is both aggravated and concealed by the social and political unrest of which it is the main root.

In South America revolution has become endemic and all but one or two of the most solid countries are financially in default.

In central and southeastern Europe financial default is imminent, but that is by itself of little moment in comparison with the consequent social and political upheaval which will follow. It is open to question whether the populations of Germany and central Europe can be fed and kept alive next winter and how long any organized government can control the situation in these countries.

In the United States of America loss of confidence is absolute. The strain of material suffering in a population none too homogenous, accustomed for generations to rapidly increasing prosperity, may lead to a break-down of existing institutions and forms of government. The outcome is unpredictable, but the consequences throughout the globe may be catastrophic.

449

World disorganization, famine, pestilence, and the submergence of our civilization are visible on the horizon.

WHY?

Not because nature has been niggardly. Not because individual human achievement or capacity have grown less. They have won ever greater and greater triumphs over nature and throughout the material field in the last two generations.

These triumphs have been won by an ever-wider and even bolder application of the principle of division of labor, till man's powers of large-scale organization have been overstrained. He can control and adapt the forces of nature, but the task which he has now set himself requires more than that. He has still to learn so to control and adapt his own human nature and so to work together with the human nature of his fellows as to fit them and himself into their proper places in the organization without losing for himself and for them all that makes life worth living.

"Mankind is not clever enough to control the machine which he has created."

There is no lack of human good will and desire to serve our generation. Yet all of us are acutely conscious of the exasperating frustration of our best efforts. We see the evil plight to which we and the world are being reduced, and we confess that for the moment human intelligence seems bankrupt.

A RESPITE?

This essay cannot concern itself with remedies for the immediate crisis or with the means we may hope to restore for a time some semblance of order in the world's economy. It is necessary to assume that, whether with or without the help of intelligent human leadership, the economic structure will find within itself enough powers of resistance to secure for us a temporary respite.

The respite will be a short one. We must use it to make a new start or our doom is sealed.

Britain's Plight

Great Britain and some parts of the British Empire have in some degree improved their own position since last autumn. Absolutely the improvement in Great Britain has been small, though relatively to other countries it is striking.

This achievement is of real value to the world, even though some part of it has been made at the expense of added difficulties for others.

It has been attained thanks to a remarkable demonstration of the self-discipline and well-disposed spirit of public service and the sober imperturability and reasonableness of the British citizen in face of a crisis.

Britain's Need of a Prosperous World

It is in this evidence of British character that the best hope for the future rests.

Britain cannot, however, prosper in a distressed world. Entirely dependent on external trade for her food and raw materials, Britain cannot escape world catastrophe by isolating herself.

Moreover, that world-wide loss of control of the machinery of civilization is all too visible in Britain and in British institutions.

If Britain is to save herself and give the world that leadership which is urgently demanded, the first need is for complete reconstruction of our national life on lines fitted for the new needs of the twentieth century.

Here a fundamental difficulty must be faced. Economic nationalism is no solution. On the contrary, it is among the main causes of the world's troubles. Recovery depends on building up afresh and extending even more widely than before world-wide exchanges of goods and services which everywhere cross national and political boundaries.

The United Kingdom is far too small in area to form today an economic unit commensurate with the vast scale of modern commercial and industrial operations.

451

The aim must always be the widest possible international cooperation.

To assume, however, that for this reason the first steps must be international would under present conditions result in mere futility. Action, if it is to be both practicable and advantageous, must be taken within the sphere now open to us. Economic reconstruction within that sphere will, moreover, at least in the earlier stages, tend to draw other countries within the orbit of returning prosperity.

Our attention must first be directed to the United Kingdom and to those regions, whether within the British Empire or in countries of complementary trade, where political and economic associations offer promising opportunities of effective cooperation.

Every care must, however, be taken to secure that in focusing our gaze on our own sphere of action we do nothing to exclude the wider division, and that we work gradually for the extention of complementary planned relations over the widest possible area.

THE NEED FOR PLANNING

"Almost all British constitutional safeguards are safeguards against being governed."

"Communism is a tremendous extension of government and consequently a great encroachment on liberty."

"Mussolini understood that what was keeping the people slaves was their determination to be what they called free."

"No real business that had to do positive work could achieve anything on the British parliamentary system."

None of these aphorisms of Mr. Bernard Shaw can be rejected as untrue, even though they offer no proof that communism or fascism are either necessary or desirable.

Their truth can be illustrated in every branch of our present-day life.

We have allowed the numbers of our feeble-minded to double themselves in the last 20 years.

We have watched the purchasing power of our country

fluctuate widely and play havoc with our economic life, and have been powerless to help ourselves.

The Road Act of 1910 gave powers both to build motor roads and to prevent ribband-building, but we still permit it and spoil our countryside and our motor roads .

Notoriously unsuitable candidates "got themselves elected" (this is our habitual way of speaking of what happens) to parliament and local councils.

Prime ministers got nervously worn out in the mere effort to grapple with the everyday business which faces them.

In the imperial sphere there is practical unanimity as to the need for organizing the Empire as an economic family, and yet we have the spectacle of the imperial conference of 1930.

In the sphere of foreign affairs the nations sign the Kellogg Peace Pact and arm themselves to the teeth.

Or, again, we keep alive the pretense that reparations and inter-governmental debts will continue to be paid, and because we dare not settle these obligations on terms which seem to involve inequitable distribution of the sacrifices involved, we wait with folded hands for the enforced default which will involve even greater iniquity and will strike a further blow at the foundations of the world's economic life. A year ago a broadminded settlement would have restored economic activity and staved off the financial crisis. Today, though an essential step on the road to recovery, cancelation of these obligations will by itself be of little avail. Its chief value now would be the evidence it would give to our capacity to reach international agreement.

THE FAILURE OF OUR POLITICAL AND ECONOMIC MACHINERY

Our political and economic machinery is breaking down. The great fund of individual and corporate good will, greater probably than at any previous period of our history, goes to waste and all our wills are frustrated for want of a large-scale plan of national reorganization.

Neither in politics nor in economics have we grasped that the first and urgent necessity is planning ahead.

Particular projects often of great potential value are put forward in Parliament or elsewhere without any effort being made to relate them to each other or to a national plan, and they either break down or function imperfectly through needless friction engendered by absence of ordered planning.

Frequently where public opinion has become exasperated at its failure to get something done to remedy a defect which everyone recognizes as intolerable, our distracted legislators with desperate unanimity unite to pass into law a compromise which is wanted by no one and merely aggravates the evil.

It is a common occurrence for a government to be pursuing two or more mutually inconsistent policies at one and the same time.

CAN WE SAVE OUR FREEDOM?

Mr. Bernard Shaw's mordant words pose directly the poignant question—Is national reconstruction possible without sacrifice of the essentials of personal and political freedom?

For all their difference, bolshevism and fascism have two outstanding features in common. Both stress the primary need for conscious forward planning on a national scale. Both repudiate the claims of personal and individual freedom.

In this country we hold fast to the concept of freedom as one of absolute validity.

We know in our hearts that we are in imminent danger of losing both our freedom and our material well-being if we go on drifting.

But, if, indeed, national reorganization has to be bought at the price of losing our freedom, many of us feel that it would be better for humanity to descend once again into the the abyss of barbarism and struggle back painfully at some later epoch to a civilization capable of satisfying both its material desires and its spiritual aspirations.

Is the dilemma absolute? Can conscious forward planning of our economic life be reconciled with the essential and over-riding claim of freedom?

Is it true that what we need is more government and a

great encroachment on liberty?

Observe that it is in the sphere of our economic life, in the sphere of material things only, that conscious forward planning is demanded.

May it not be that an unprejudiced reexamination of what we call freedom may reveal unexpected possibilities?

Our ideal is a nation of free men and women self-disciplined by an active social conscience.

FREEDOM AND THE MOTORIST

The growth of a code of law and of custom for motorists shows what can be done by free cooperation. The law and the custom are dynamic; not static. They are continually developing. At the moment, indeed, the toll of life and limb on the public roads is evidence of the urgent need for further improvements both in law and in custom. As a rule the law steps in only to interpret the collective will already expressed in a code of behavior, and to put compulsion not on the motorist in general, but only on the road hog.

Self-discipline and collective action enable the motorist to enjoy a large measure of freedom. Without the help of the code and without the intervention of authority to help him to enforce it, the will of the motorist in general would be everywhere frustrated and he would enjoy far less freedom than is now secured for him.

Is this "more government and a great encroachment on liberty"?

Can we not do for ourselves as a nation what we as motorists have done for ourselves as motorists?

"The law came in because of sin," but insofar as we are self-disciplined and our social consciences are active, we have won true freedom for ourselves in the particular field of motoring.

We do not rely solely on the enlightened self-interest and unregulated competitiveness of motorists to serve providentially the greatest good of the greatest number, and sternly forbid legislative intervention.

455

Yet so long as we worship at the altar of laissez faire as the guiding principle of our economic life, we are trying to conduct our industry and commerce in exactly that spirit which we have wisely rejected in the field of motoring.

Laissez faire represented a reaction against the doctrine of mercantilism and in its day has served this country and the world admirably, but our free institutions were won long before the principle of laissez faire was enunciated.

There is not a priori reason for regarding freedom of thought, freedom of speech, freedom of conscience, free institutions, as incompatible with conscious forward planning of our economic life.

A SUBSTITUTE FOR LAISSEZ FAIRE

The problem, then, is to find a new economic philosophy to replace the doctrine of laissez faire. The great virtue of laissez faire was that it seemed to provide a miraculous self-adjusting system of regulating the flow of production in accordance with demand in a freely competitive individualistic world. Even today there are unrepentant individualists whose cry is for a return to unrestricted laissez faire. Sweep away, they urge, all governmental and bureaucratic interference, abolish unemployment insurance and health insurance and all these new-fangled social services. Reduce taxation correspondingly, and industry will look after itself.

It is not always realized how fortuitous and temporary were many of the conditions on which the successes of laissez faire depended in the nineteenth century.

In many cases the economic life of the world has become too complex, the scale too large, the marvelous stream of new scientific invention too bewildering, the annihilation of distance, and the speed of transport and communication have drawn the Nation too closely together to allow of any return to nineteenth century methods. The mere size of the modern industrial unit is alone enough to destroy the effectiveness of the old methods.

And the social conscience of mankind has rightly revolted

against the brutality of the economic adjustments on which in the last analysis depended the self-regulating machinery of the system of laissez faire.

Moreover, however firm their faith in the doctrine, statesmen and governments always tempered its rigors with pragmatic justice by intervening at this point and at that to enforce factory acts, acts restricting hours of labor, and the like. And the rigidity of trade-union regulations today is part of our evil inheritance from the intolerance of laissez faire doctrinaires.

With the advent of the twentieth century and particularly after the war, Government intervention began rapidly to operate in increasingly wider spheres. And by this date the nature, form, and extent of Government intervention tended to be more and more uneconomic and antieconomic in their results precisely because they were conceived and applied by local authorities, Government departments, and parliaments and cabinets which still did lip service without conscious hypocrisy to the principles of laissez faire.

It was in principle permissible for the State to levy taxation on industry according to the needs of the public purse. It was in principle permissible for the State to make laws and regulations restricting the freedom of business activities in the interests of health, sanitation, safety of life and limb, conditions of labor. It was not permissible in principle for the State to recognize responsibility for the efficiency or remunerativeness of business. That was intolerable State interference in a region which it had no right to enter.

The rigidity of the doctrine has indeed been relaxed in many directions, and with the advent of a protective tariff we have entered on an entirely new era in the relations between State and business. Yet it remains true that taxation and regulation of industry have been excessively and needlessly hampering in their effects just because our political and economic philosophy forbade the State to "interfere with the free-play of natural economic forces."

It must be left for separate essays to deal in greater detail with suggestions for building up a plan of national reconstruc-

457

tion in the special fields of agricultural and industrial production, finance, marketing, transport, housing, town and country planning, and the like.

The purpose of this essay is rather to examine how far it is true that conscious forward planning involves encroachment on freedom.

THE FREEDOM OF THE CONSUMER

The basic principle of human economic activities, except in Soviet Russia, is, and has been ever since, the first steps in the direction of the division of labor were taken, that the would-be consumer determines for himself which of his competing wants he will satisfy within the range of choice which his available purchasing power (even when he was living under a system of barter before money was invented) and the available supply of goods and services offered.

It is the consumer's choice which settles the relative prices of the various goods and services which the producer (or middleman) offers for sale.

The Communist system attempts to fix relative prices and to deny to the consumer the right to exercise this fundamental freedom of choice. The reason for this is that the Communist ideal is a mechanized state which will produce according to plan the maximum output of consumable goods and distribute them with maximum efficiency. The state accordingly fixes by decree the quantity and quality of production of all kinds and cannot afford to leave it in the power of the human consumer to cause variations in demand by exercising a free choice among his competing wants.

The consumer, in fact, is treated not at all as a consumer but as a part of the mechanism of production requiring a given quantity of fuel, etc., to keep him going as a producer. There is no reason whatever to regard this ultimate denial of freedom to humanity as necessary to conscious forward planning.

Reasonable standarization of some articles of ordinary consumption and some limits to excessive stimulation of the

458

demand for the satisfaction of more whims which arises from unbridled competition among those who cater to them may indeed be welcomed. But the economic aim of a free community must always be to give the consumer the widest opportunities for satisfying as many of his wants as possible.

If there is to be a planning authority, its functions must be to attempt to forecast demand and to regulate production and distribution accordingly, not to control or dictate consumption.

Control of consumption on special cases, e. g., of alcoholic liquor, may be necessary for reasons arising out of human weakness, but the limits of such control are narrow, and its existence does not invalidate the general argument.

Again rates and taxes levied for such purpose as the provision of free education or for display of flowers in a public park involve the enforcement of a form of collective consumption, but the individual is not compelled to use the public park or the free education if he has the desire and the means to choose alternatives.

This last example is, however, a significant illustration of our ready acceptance of collective restraints in our own or the general interests without feeling that our freedom is being filched from us.

A PLANNING AUTHORITY

Conscious planning leaves the consumer free but involves the substitution of some organized control over overproduction and distribution on behalf of the community to take the place of that free play of supposedly automatic economic forces on which laissez faire relied.

Control implies a controlling authority. To the average man and woman among us there jumps to the mind at once the picture of a large number of new Government departments and hordes of new officials attempting to take the place and to do the work of the business man, the manufacturer, the farmer, the banker, the shopkeeper, or at least to tie them all up hand and foot and dictate to them in the management of their daily affairs, and we see further a glimpse of Parliament and local bodies overwhelmed by the task of fulfilling their new functions.

Few people today would deny that the old social idea of putting the whole business of the Nation into the hands of bureaucratic Government departments would prove a hopeless failure in practice and would be no improvement on present conditions.

Is there not a middle way, or better still a new way, of meeting the need for organization and coordination of those economic tasks which the break-down of laissez faire is leaving unaccomplished?

THE PUBLIC-UTILITY CONCERN

Without much distinction of party successive governments have tended in recent years to try, in various fields, to find a new way forward through the setting up of public-utility bodies, of which the B. B. C., the central electricity board, and the projected London passenger-transport board are outstanding examples. These bodies are not government departments, and their methods of management and direction and control are modeled rather on those of commercial concerns. Their purpose is to perform collectively for the community certain functions and to provide collectively certain services, in which monopoly rather than competition is, in the general belief, likely to give the best results. For this reason it is felt to be necessary to put the emphasis on the rendering of public service and not on the securing of profits while insisting that the work ought to be done on a self-supporting basis and not dependent on a subsidy from the rates or taxes.

In all the instances cited the earning of surplus profits for private shareholders is excluded, and this must no doubt be the usual argument where monopoly is involved. It need not, however, be an invariable rule.

One special merit of this form of organization is that it claims to give flexibility of management and avoid the major risks of red tape, and while maintaining the ultimate control of Parliament and the nation provides for a large degree of

460

self-government, and so reduce rather than increase the amount of governmental interference.

It is possible to envisage a considerable extension of this form of organization of the nation's business. A new picture begins to emerge in outline of industry, agriculture, transport, etc., enjoying if not Dominion status, at any rate wide powers of local self-government, with the Cabinet, Parliament, and the local authorities liberated from duties to which they are not ideally suited and free to perform their essential functions on behalf of the community.

THE ANALOGY OF THE ELECTRICITY GRID SYSTEM

The analogy of the grid system of the central electricity board, not itself undertaking the production of power nor the final distribution of electricity services to the consumer but providing a coordinated system of carrying the electricity produced from the big generating stations to local distributing centers all over the country, can be suggestively applied to other services.

Imagine the dairy farmers of the country or of various regional divisions of the country as the milk-generating stations, and the retailers of milk as the local distributing centers, with a central milk board conducting the business of bulk marketing of milk as the providers of the milk grid of Britain. Already under the agricultural marketing act there are signs of the coming of such a milk grid as a natural development to meet the needs of the day. An extension of the system with suitable adaptions to other agricultural products easily suggests itself, and even more directly as a method of dealing with the needs of modern transport by rail, road, water, and air.

ORGANIZED PRODUCTION

When we come to the organization of producers, agricultural, industrial, and extractive, the central electricity model becomes more difficult to follow. Generally speaking, organization on public-utility lines seems to be adapted rather to the rendering of services in the sphere of distribution than to the business of production. It may be significant that the central electricity board was excluded from the ownership of generating stations. For reasons which have their roots deep in our human nature, we seem to be much readier to admit the principles of controlled monopoly and the domination of the motive of public service over the motive of private profit in the sphere of distribution than in the two spheres of original production and final retailing between which distribution services are intermediate.

Methods of retailing cannot indeed be left entirely unchanged in the face of twentieth-century needs. The multiple shop and the chain store are already bringing about notable modifications. The waste involved in the 500,000 or more retail shops—1 shop for every 20 households—cannot be allowed to continue to block the flow of goods from producer to consumer. And reorganization of retail methods is necessary to achieve adequate organization of production. In general, however, it will probably be found that there is a large place in the business of retailing for the continued play of individualism and personal enterprise. The individualist consumer and his free choice call for some corresponding individuality of outlook in the retailer who caters to him.

Not so in the sphere of production. The business of production must be planned, if it is to possess adequate means of keeping the volume and quality of the goods produced in reasonable relation to demand.

The development of an organized grid system for the distribution of milk must, it is certain, lead to a profound modification of the traditional individualism of outlook of the dairy farmer. And so it will be in other producing industries; cooperative organization of the business of distribution cannot fail to bring about conditions in which both the need and the will to organize themselves on a cooperative basis will arise amongst the producers, whether they be agriculturalists, or producers of coal or iron from the mines, or manufacturers of steel or of cotton or of wool.

Whether we like it or not—and many will dislike it in-

462

tensely—the individualist manufacturer and farmer will be forced by events to submit to far-reaching changes in outlook and methods. The danger is that in resisting them because he regards them as encroachments on what he calls his "freedom", he will make things worse for himself and for the community. Resistance is likely to play into the hands of those who say that tinkering is useless and that full-flooded socialism and communism are the only cure. Or he may be tempted to flirt with Fascist ideas. In either case he loses his cherished freedom, and it is only too probable that Fascism and communism alike would be but short stages on the road to barbarism.

THE CONDITIONS OF ECONOMIC FREEDOM

It is idle to deny that some, at least, of the changes required when conscious forward planning extends into the field of production are of a revolutionary character.

It is all important, therefore, that we should appraise them soberly and without prejudice and distinguish clearly between unavoidable alterations of methods of economic organization and fundamental attacks on our personal and political freedom.

Our economic freedom must be and always has been tempered by the conditions of our environment and by our relations with our fellows, without whose mutual aid we could not enjoy the advantages which material well-being brings. Spiritual freedom in a highly organized and complex society of civilized men and women is attainable only by ready cooperation in so arranging our economic life as to provide the best attainable material surroundings.

PLANNING AND THE PRODUCER

Without entering more deeply into details than space here allows, the position of the farmer and manufacturer under a system of planned production can only be sketched in broad outlines.

He may be conceived of as remaining in full control of all the operations of his farm or factory, but receiving from the duly constituted authority instructions as to the quantity and

463

quality of his production, and as to the markets in which he will sell. He will himself have had a voice in setting up his constituted authority and will have regular means of communicating with it and of influencing its policy. He will be less exposed than at present to interference from above; that is, from Government departments and local bodies and their inspectors. He will be less free to make arbitrary decisions as to his own business outside the region of day-to-day operation of plant or farm.

It must be presumed that the constituted authority will be armed by enabling act of Parliament and by a majority decision of its own members, presumably elected by the votes of those with whose affairs they deal, to exercise powers of compulsion over minorities in clearly specified cases.

All this is not very different from that what already occurs in particular organized industries, but must be conceived of as applying generally to most if not all of the major fields of production, and as part of a consciously and systematically planned agricultural and industrial organization.

A NATIONAL PLAN IN OUTLINE

An outline of the organization contemplated would be somewhat as follows:

A national planning commission, with advisory, not executive, functions, subordinate to the cabinet and to Parliament, but with clearly defined powers of initiative and clearly defined responsibilities, its personnel representative of the nation's economic life.

A national council for agriculture, a national council for industry, a national council for coal mining, a national council for transport, and so on, all statutory bodies with considerable powers of self-government, including powers of compulsion within the province with which they are concerned.

A series of statutory or chartered corporations, e. g., a cotton-industry corporation, a steel-industry corporation, a milk-producers' corporation, organized on the lines of public-utility concerns, serving at least to federate, and in suitable cases to own, the plants, factories, etc., engaged in production.

A series of public-utility corporations dealing with distributive services, e. g., the central electricity board, the national transport board (or a number of regional transport boards), and the national milk marketing board.

In the constitution of these bodies provision would naturally be made for suitable representation of interest, including organized labor, and for their due coordination by means, for example, of the election by the various corporations of some of their members to serve on the national councils. To all of them Parliament would delegate considerable powers to regulate the affairs of their particular industries.

COMPULSION AND PRIVATE OWNERSHIP OF LAND

From the standpoint of encroachments upon freedom, apart from the denial of the tenets of individualism, the most obvious targets for attack are perhaps the proposed grant of powers to compel minorities and (point not yet mentioned) the probable necessity for drastic changes in the ownership of land.

Powers of compulsion of minorities are not unknown even under present conditions and will probably not arouse very violent antagonism on grounds of high principle.

The question of private ownership of land is one which never fails to encounter deep-rooted passions. It is also one which arises immediately in almost every aspect of conscious-planned reconstruction.

The conclusion seems unescapable that whether in the field of town-and-country planning or in that of agriculture (or rural) planning or in the organization of industry it is not possible to make reasonable progress without drastic powers to buy out individual owners of land.

This is not to say that land nationalization, in the ordinary sense of the term, is either necessary or desirable. Far from it. Nothing would be gained by substituting the State as landlord. What is required, if only a view to equitable treatment of individuals, is transfer of ownership of large blocks of land—not necessarily of all the land in the country, but certainly of a large proportion of it—into the hands of the proposed statutory corporations and public-utility bodies and of land trusts.

In many cases all that would be needed would be the conversion of rights of ownership of land into rights of participation as shareholders or stockholders in the new corporations or in land trusts. It would be possible further in a large number of cases to leave management undisturbed, together with the enjoyment of many of the amenities which at present go with ownership, subject to the transfer of title to the corporations or trusts.

Here again limits of space preclude fuller treatments of the subject. All that is here relevant is the inevitable conclusion that the planned economy which the Nation needs to meet the demands of the twentieth century must clearly involve drastic inroads upon the rights of individual ownership of land as at present understood.

FINANCE

Thus far in this essay finance has been purposely left aside.

The assumption is that consciously planned reconstruction of the economic life of the Nation will increase, and indeed is necessary to maintain, the present national dividend. There is no reason to believe that overhead charges for government and administration will be increased. On the contrary, they should be diminished by the elimination of the fraction and waste arising from present unplanning and disorder.

It should be possible also with industry and production re-planned and coordinated so as to rearrange taxation as to take from the national dividend that part of it which is required for collective expenditure by the community at an economic cost less burdensome to the Nation than is involved by our existing rates and taxes.

From the standpoint of the national and local budgets, therefore, there is no cause for anticipating financial difficulties.

The question remains what changes are required in the financial machinery of the country. It is in the sphere of distribution, and especially in that important part in the mechanism of distribution which belongs to finance, that the worst disorders of the present economic system have shown themselves.

In no sphere is the evidence of our loss of control of the machine of civilization more evident than in that of finance.

The catastrophic fall of prices has resulted in complete disequilibrium between the cost of production and the price which the consumer can pay, and in particular, between the relative prices of agricultural and manufactured products.

Mismanagement of the standard of value is apparent throughout the world.

It is by no means so clear how recovery is to be brought about. Cheap money is obviously essential, but it is only if and when it leads to a revival of activity, to increased demand for goods and services, and an increase in the volume of trade, followed by a recovery of prices to a remunerative level, and it serves any useful purpose.

Mere manufacture of paper purchasing power is of little avail, more especially if with waning political confidence the basis of credit shrinks faster than the manufactured paper money increases.

This is not the place to examine the problem of escape from the immediate financial crisis.

The same assumption must be made as was made earlier in this essay that the inertia and momentum of the economic structure and of habit and custom will carry us somehow through for the moment and that we shall be given a respite.

STABLE MONEY

One basic need of the new economic organization is the stabilization of the purchasing power of money. Stable money and conscious forward planning are mutually dependent.

The elimination of violent fluctuations of the general price level will immensely facilitate improved organization of production and distribution.

No question arises of fixing the prices of individual commodities.

Once equilibrium between costs of production and prices to the consumer has been established, our first efforts must be directed to securing stability of the purchasing power of our money.

This question is dealt with at length in a separate essay and the conclusion must perforce be taken for granted here.

Stable money cannot be secured without considerable extension of control on behalf of the community over the flow of investment and the uses which the individual makes of his capital.

While as consumer he can retain full freedom of choice as to which of his competing wants he will satisfy, there are real difficulties in leaving him entirely free to invest his savings in any way he chooses.

It is probable that many of these difficulties can be solved on the one hand by extension of the system of insurance, on lines to which recent developments of the motoring law again supply suggestive analogies, and on the other hand by means which, while leaving the small capitalist untrammelled, will so canalize the flow of both long-term and short-term investment of the large sums which are at the disposal of banks and financial institutions as well as funds in the hands of large insurance companies as to insure that adequate capital is available for the big industrial, agricultural, and distributive corporations already envisaged.

It is necessary to insist that finance shall take its proper place as the servant and not the master of industry and commerce. The stabilization of the purchasing power of money will by itself go far to secure this subordination.

THE BANKS AND PLANNING

The Bank of England has in the course of its history lost practically all of its original profit-making characteristics and become in fact, if not in form, a leading example of a public-utility corporation devoted to rendering public service. It has also many of the features of a self-governing institution, its relations to the Government delicately adjusted so as to combine both due subordination and administrative independence, so as to offer a significant parallel to the new institutions suggested earlier in the sphere of industry and distribution. It would appear to be sufficiently flexible to enable it to adapt itself to filling its place in the new order without requiring any radical changes in its constitution.

The logical completion of the process of amalgamation which has reduced the number of the major joint-stock banks to five would clearly be to merge them all in one and to give them some monopolistic privileges in return for converting themselves into a real public-utility corporation.

This is a delicate process, and it may be unwise to force the pace, seeing that natural developments are tending to bring about much the same results without outside intervention.

Careful study is needed of the relations between planned industry and the stock exchange, the acceptance houses, the issuing houses, and other parts of our financial machinery. It may well be that with industry, agriculture, transport, etc., organized on the lines suggested, and with the adoption of the steps necessary to stabilize the purchasing power of money, the problems which are in prospect somewhat terrifying of bringing about a suitable reorganization of our financial institutions will be found largely to have solved themselves. For finance, as the servant of industry, can have no motive to do otherwise than adjust itself to the new needs.

LABOR

Little has been said hitherto on the subject of organized labor.

Clearly, labor must have effective representation and play an adequate part in the new statutory councils and public-utility corporations and in all the activities of the replanned nation.

The most difficult task will perhaps be to reconcile the trade unions to the remodeling of many of their existing regulations and to the change in outlook which conscious planning requires.

469

Stable money and the discarding of the doctrines of individualism and laissez faire will between them make obsolete many of the objectives and many of the issues which at present bulk largely in the minds of trade-unionists. In planned industry the employee takes his true place more clearly than before as a partner in production.

The changes required in the organization of labor are obviously not such as can rightly be described as encroachment on freedom.

Difficult, therefore, as the right solution of the knotty problems which arise may prove, they need not detain us further in this examination of the relations of planning to freedom.

THE SOCIAL SERVICES

Nor need we pause here to examine what planning may mean in other parts of the structure of our economic life, education, health service, housing, provision for leisure.

Each of these subjects and others will need detailed investigation, and the methods of organization adopted must be fitted into and form part of a complete whole with the new model for industry. It is high time that man should make effective use of biological knowledge to improve the human race and make himself more fit for his twentieth century responsibilities. In the health services and the province of medicine it is urgently necessary to shift the emphasis from cure to prevention, from negative to positive health, and this may well call for a big change in the organization of the medical profession, which has at present too often a vested interest in disease. But there is no reason for supposing that in order to deal with these various questions any new invasions of freedom will be called for which in degree or kind go further than what has already been contemplated in the industrial field.

IMPERIAL PLANNING

Many of the problems of national reconstruction extend into the imperial and international field. The United Kingdom by itself is far too small to provide an adequate economic unit for planning.

A planned economy for Britain implies as the next step a planned imperial economic family. Considerable interrelations or imperial cooperation from the outset is essential, as a minimum, for success in certain directions.

The stabilization of the purchasing power of money calls for action not only in the Empire but also in such countries as Argentina and Scandinavia, which belongs to "terlingaria", the area where British sterling is indisputably the international medium of exchange. Tariffs and agreements for industrial cooperation with other parts of the British Empire will have to be fittled into the framework of our national industrial system in order to make reasonably possible the successful functioning of such projected bodies as the Steel Industry Council or the Statutory Cotton Corporation. The subject matter with which there bodies will deal includes large questions of export trade, and is not, as in the case of the Central Electricity Board, confined to the provision of services within our national boundaries.

INTERNATIONAL PLANNING

The interrelations of national planning and international problems are peculiarly difficult. An ideal national plan cannot be framed and brought into operation without complete international cooperation. Yet to wait till conditions are propitious for an intelligent international reorganization of our own and the world's economic life will not help us.

And with Russia and Italy embarked on plans which definitely override the claims of freedom, complete world-wide agreement is not within reach.

The better is the enemy of the good. Within the boundaries of the United Kingdom we have ample opportunities, if we set ourselves whole-heartedly to the task, to achieve that national reconstruction which is so sorely needed. Within the British Empire and even beyond it in countries whose economic ties with Britain are historically close and whose trade is complementary, we have reasonable prospects of securing fruitful results by political and economic cooperation.

We dissipate our strength and overstrain our resources if we attempt more before first putting our own house in order. It is not selfishness or aggressive nationalism or imperialism which puts a limit on our immediate sphere of action, but a sober estimate of our political and economic powers.

The goal of world-wide international cooperation must never be lost from sight, and advantage must be taken of every opportunity for bringing it nearer. The very fact that it extends planning across existing political boundaries is of special value. Nevertheless our first task is to replan Britain, with an economic organization that will fit harmoniously into the planned imperial economic family, and in so doing to give leadership and new hope to a distressed world.

Men's powers of large-scale organization and of harmonious cooperation will be further tested by the need for economic planning which transcends national boundaries and in due course demands world-wide cooperation. National and imperial and ulitmately international political and economic practices and institutions will doubtless undergo profound modifications in adapting themselves to the twentieth century.

The constitutional development of the British Empire may indeed provide a model more suitable for adaptation to the needs of world cooperation than any at present in existence. The harmonious and free cooperation within a single system of a number of states enjoying sovereignty and independence as equal partners in a commonwealth of nations would appear to offer possibilities of extending itself indefinitely till it covers the whole world. Proof of the ability of the British commonwealth to provide its citizens with an economic organization that ministers effectually to their well-being will be the surest way of winning world-wide approval.

The only rival world political and economic system which puts forward a comparable claim is that of the Union of Soviet Republics.

If planning and freedom are to be reconciled, the solution

must be found along the lines of the British approach.

PLANNING AND POLITICS

Effective planning on the economic side and even the introduction of desirable reforms in detail has become impossible without a drastic overhauling both of Parliament and the central government and of the machinery of local government. Political and economic planning are complementary and supplementary to each other and must be carefully interrelated. We need new economic and political institutions to match the new social adjustments which applied science has created and a new technique both in politics and in industry to enable us to find intelligent methods of surmounting new difficulties and complexities.

It has been suggested more than once in the course of this essay that devolution of powers to statutory bodies will be an important feature of the new order, and that in the result Parliament and the Cabinet will be relieved of some part of their present duties and set free to the great advantage of themselves and of the nation for their proper tasks of directing and guiding public policy.

Big consequent changes will follow in the machinery of government. The British constitution is, however, accustomed to changes of this sort. It is continually developing and adapting itself to new conditions. The further development now contemplated will be a natural evolution along lines consistent with British traditions.

Here, as elsewhere, vested interests will doubtless feel themselves challenged, and be inclined to resist. That is inevitable, but the essentials of constitutional freedom will remain unshaken. In some of its aspects the Tariff Advisory Committee already suggests the nucleus of a national planning commission. In due course we shall perhaps be astonished not at the magnitude of the changes but at their relative smallness.

473

PLANNING AND ECONOMIC FREEDOM

One further question remains to be touched upon before the summing up is reached.

Let it be granted, a well-disposed critic may say, that what you propose involves no fundamental attack on freedom; granted that your plan of reconstruction is not open to the charge of encroaching upon spiritual freedom, and, if successful, would provide a better material environment for the realization of humanity's higher aspirations; do you not run the risk of so trammeling and shackling man's economic freedom that the result will be less production not more, less enterprise and initiative, a drying up of the incentives to progress, and final loss not gain in material well-being?

One possible answer is, of course, to refer our critic to what was said at the outset as to the imminence of catastrophe if we continue to drift. We must regain control of the machinery of civilization if we and it are to survive.

Reluctance to embark on a doubtful adventure deserves a less negative treatment.

The dangers which our critic fears are real dangers. Red tape is not confined to Government departments. Our statutory corporations and public-utility boards may all too easily become unadventurous obstacles to progress, determined enemies to all new ideas.

It may be indeed that one of the lessons we have to learn from our present distresses is that scientific invention itself requires some planning in its application to the economic structure of the Nation.

The problem of progress is no longer the problem of getting enough change to prevent routine from deadening effort, but the problem of preventing change from destroying both routine and all social stability.

This, however, is no justification of institutions which deaden effort.

Our proposals must rather be defended by the claim they will liberate the spirit of initiative and not deaden it, in that they will provide means by which the energetic man of business may escape from the disheartening frustrations and failures which are caused by the complexity of the machine, and will give him scope for serving his generation in a larger kingdom than the narrow field of competition with rivals in paricular industrial or commercial pursuits.

Though organized on public-utility lines with monopolistic privileges, the great chartered industrial corporations will find ample room for energy and initiative in performing their primary task of combining maximum output with minimum costs of production. The executive heads of particular factories will not lack the spur of competition.

THE PROFIT-MAKING MOTIVE

It is no part of our plan to enshrine equalitarian doctrines or to eliminate from business life the desire to better oneself and the motive of personal reward. Subordination of the motive of profit to the motive of service does not imply that the motive of profit has no useful part to play even within a public-utility concern not working for profit. It is not absent in the B. B. C. nor in the central electricity board.

Nor is it suggested that public-utility concerns or bodies analogous in character should be set up to deal with any but the major "key" business activities of the Nation.

For example, the specialized steel industries of Sheffield would not, unless by their special desire, find a place within the organization of the chartered steel corporation. They would be ancillary to it and would not doubt cooperate with it in suitable ways, but would remain independent.

In general, specialized production and skilled craftsmanship would continue to be the field of individualistic effort. So also would retail business.

Experience alone can prove the justice of our claim that economic freedom will not be fatally shackled by the effects of conscious forward planning. Experience, too, will be needed to make clear the boundaries of the province within which individualistic effort can best be relied upon to secure the highest national dividend.

But we do make the claim that national reconstruction along the lines indicated is not only urgent and essential to salvation, but is also rightly calculated to improve the economic environment of our national life.

A CONSERVATIVE EVOLUTION

Indeed, the Socialist or the Communist will condemn our planning as mere tinkering with the outworn machine of capitalism. To him it will appear as a hopelessly conservative and anemic attempt to stave off the red-blooded revolution which alone would satisfy him.

Our plan is, we claim, conservative in the truest and best sense. It is conservative, not destructive, and builds solidly upon the present and the past. It faces the issues boldly and is not afraid to challenge vested interests and deeply cherished habits of thought and action. It does not, however, propose to expropriate anyone, and, in requiring the application of compulsion in a limited sphere, it is not doing more than extend and make explicit and give systematic application to tendencies and practices already at work.

The purpose of this essay is not to put before the reader any complete or fully worked-out plan of national reconstruction. That can be done only in a series of separate essays, and even then much of the necessary details would have to be left out.

Such sketch in the broadest outline of the lines which reconstruction might take as has been given here must inevitably raise more questions in the mind of the attentive reader than it answers.

PLANNING FREEDOM

Our purpose has been to vindicate by reasoned presentation our faith that national reconstruction on the basis of conscious forward planning, besides being urgent and necessary, is compatible with the preservation of our freedom.

Vested interests, ingrained prejudices, traditions, customs, and points of view which have proved their value in the past are challenged by us to give way to the needs of the present. This generation is called upon to accept modifications in the structure of its economic life, which are profound enough to require an altogether new outlook on the content and meaning of economic freedom. The old spiritual values which belong to personal and political freedom are not challenged. They are accepted as absolute and in full. It is because they are accepted as absolute and because there is urgent need to safeguard them in the changed world of the twentieth century, that new methods of economic organization have to be devised.

Economic freedom must always be relative to its environment. Economic freedom demands that form of economic organization of civilized society which will provide men and women with the highest standards of material well-being attainable by the use of their powers of scientific production and cooperative endeavor in order that the environment thus afforded may present the widest possible opportunities for the exercise of the human nature.

In the haphazard and disorganized economic structure of today men and women are balked alike of economic and spiritual freedom.

If by conscious forward planning they can escape present frustrations, they will rightly be judged to be more truly free.

XXVIII

ANALYSIS OF FREEDOM
AND PLANNING

Friday, June 8, 1934

Mr. McFADDEN. Mr. Speaker, this analysis is divided into two parts, and represents only a portion of the data I possess showing a well-organized plan for world control. It is given with a view of furnishing a synopsis or outline of a hellish conspiracy to enslave and dominate the free peoples of the earth. There are sufficient facts herein to give the key to the thoughtful student of our national affairs so that he may be on guard against the sinister and ambitious Caesars in our midst.

I

FREEDOM AND PLANNING AS APPLIED TO THE BRITISH GOVERNMENT

This "political economic plan", as it is also called, was prepared under the direction of Israel Moses Sieff, an English Jew, the director of a chain-store enterprise in England called "Marks & Spencer." This enterprise declared a 40-percent dividend during 1933 and was enabled to do so by the fact that it had handled almost exclusively all imports from Soviet Russia, thus being able to undersell established British competitors.

The political economic plan group are a branch of the Fabian Society.

In this connection I wish to quote from a Paris publication, Revue Internationale des Sociétés Secrètes, under date of January 25, 1931:

On the 1st of November 1930, the Evening Standard, an English daily paper, contained the following lines:

"GOVERNMENT BY FABIANS

"Many Labor members are talking about the dominance in the Government of that very academic body, the Fabian Society. I find that many people believed that this organization, through which many intellectuals entered the socialist movement, had ceased to exist. But it goes on with membership, small but influential—some 5,000.

"Yet practically every recent appointment, either to high or low office, in the Labor administration has been made from the membership of the society, the latest examples of which are the new Air Minister, Lord Amulree, and the new Solicitor General, Sir Stafford Cripps. I am told that at least 90 percent of the members of the Government are in the rolls of the society, and that, contrary to regulations, so are a good many highly placed civil servants.

"The civil servants would probably defend themselves by saying the society is more intellectual than political.

"This ascendancy is, of course, due to the all-powerful influence of Lord Passfield and his wife, Mrs. Sidney Webb, with whom the Fabian Society has been the passion of their lives."

What, therefore, is the Fabian Society, the members of which, according to the Evening Standard, govern England? The answer is given us by the society itself in the Basis of the Fabian Society, which is appended to every book and tract it issues, and it runs thus:

"BASIS OF THE FABIAN SOCIETY

"The Fabian Society consists of Socialists.

"It therefore aims at the reorganization of society by the emancipation of land and industrial capital from individual ownership and the vesting of them in the community for the general benefit. In this way only can the natural and acquired advantages of the country be equitably shared by the whole people.

"The society accordingly works for the extinction of private property in land, with equitable consideration of established expectations, and due provision as to the tenure of the home and homestead; for the transfer to the community, by constitutional methods, of all such industries as can be conducted socially; and for the establishment, as the governing consideration in the regulation of production, distribution, and service of the common good instead of private profit.

"The society is a constituent of the Labor Party and of the International Socialist Congress, but it takes part freely in all constitutional movements, social, economic, and political, which can be guided toward its own objects. Its direct business is (a) the propaganda of socialism in its application to current problems; (b) investigation and discovery in social, industrial, political, and economic relations; (c) the working out of Socialist principles in legislation and administative reconstruction; (d) the publication of the results of its investigations and their practical lesson.

"The society, believing in equal citizenship of men and women in the fullest sense, is open to persons irrespective of sex, race, or creed, who commit themselves to its aims and purposes as stated above and undertake to promote its work."

One cannot refrain from noticing the irony of the words, "by constitutional methods", contained in the above basis. Everyone knows that the Socialist-Bolshevists of Russia claim to have confiscated and expropriated "by constitutional means" which are in reality legalized theft.

The society took the name of Fabian from the policy of temporizing it adopted, claiming to imitate that of the Roman prodictator, Fabius Cunctator, during his fight against Hannibal, whom he eventually defeated at Tarentum, 209 B.C.

Frank Podmore, well-known spiritualist and occultist, one of the founders of the Fabian Society, is quoted as saying to the earliest members: "For the right moment you must wait, as Fabius did most patiently, when warring against Hannibal, though many censured his delays; but when the time comes, you must strike hard, as Fabius did, or your waiting will be in vain and fruitless."

The Fabian Society waited 40 years, striking a continual series of covert blows at the political, economic, social, and religious structure of England, and in 1924 it came to power with the advent of the first labor government, which can be called the offspring of the Fabian Society.

The period of waiting had been fruitful, if long.

There is no gainsaying that the Fabian Society has been first and foremost a gathering of intellectuals; it might be said of a rebellious intelligentsia, whose accomplishments seem the realization of Weishaupt's dream of masonic illuminism, cleverly combined with Moses Mendelssohn's dream of Jewish illuminism (Haskalah).

Historically, it was founded in 1883 at the time when, in the realm of philosophy and metaphysics, the political economy of John Stuart Mill, in England, and the positivism of Auguste Comte in France had thrown perturbation in the minds of numerous thinkers and given abundant food to the free thinkers of the epoch. Henry George's book on socialism, *Progress and Poverty*, was in great vogue. The direct influence leading to the formation of the Fabian Society was, according to E. R. Pease, its historian, exercised by Thomas Davidson, the founder of the Fellowship of the New Life, which society culmniated in the Ethical Society of Culture in New York. Considerable impulse was also given to the budding association by its assimilation of Robert Dale Owen's socialistic principles.

It may be of interest to the readers of the R. I. S. S. to remember the fact that among the earliest members of the Fabian Society who had participated in the Fellowship of New Life were freemasons and spiritualists, some becoming later affiliated with Madame Blavatsky's Theosophy. The activities of Frank Podmore in both Masonry, occult and spiritual, and Fabian socialism are a study of themselves.

Among the intellectuals who joined the Fabian Society soon after its inception in 1884 was the Irishman, Bernard Shaw, who was elected a member that year.

481

At that time the Fabian Society had completely seceded from the Fellowship of the New Life and formulated its own socialistic program. The following year Sidney Webb, now Lord Passfield, Minister of the Colonies, and Sydney Oliver, now Lord Oliver, who has held several government appointments, were elected members of the Fabian Society. Soon afterward, Mrs. Annie Besant, the present head of the theosophical movement, also was elected a member.

Fabian socialism at the outset groped its way along all the beaten paths of the social revolutionists who had preceded them. It also made incursions into Babouvism, Marxism, Bakounist anarchism, and the then existing various social democratic group. Being, however, mainly composed of intellectuals, bureaucrats, civil servants, journalists, etc., the Fabians, whose fundamental slogan was the righting of the wrongs of the working class had no keen desire for riotous street manifestations, and confined their earliest activities to drawing-room meetings.

It does not enter within the limits of the present sketch to retrace the history of the Fabian Society, but the point which should be regarded as of great importance is that out of the drawing-room meetings alluded to above, there emerged the tactic truly Fabian of temporizing and the decision taken and followed of penetrating into or, as Bernard Shaw himself expressed it, "permeating" numerous existing societies with Fabian socialistic ideas and principles.

This method of penetrating into organizations, political and economic, and boring from within, gave in time remarkable results. Fabians, mainly civil servants, easily found their affinities into liberal circles, and, moreover, owing to their loudly proclaimed socialistic profession of faith, obtained the confidence of the working classes. They were indeed sitting on both sides of the fence and recruiting the good will of both liberal and labor organizations.

The study of Fabianism is one of almost unparelleled opportunism. Fabians seemed to have formulated no original creed of their own, but were only animated by an unswerving resolve to get to the top and govern England. Consequently, they adjusted themselves to whatever was the creed or tenets of any camp they penetrated into, and by degrees converted its adherents to a turn of mind designed to procure the advancement of Fabian members in political, industrial, or educational lines, with the final result that they secured "key positions." To suit even anarchism, they formed a special Fabian branch which bore the name of Fabian Parliamentary League.

No field of exploitation seems to have been overlooked by these Socialist intellectual illuminati:

1. Politics: In politics, their range of activities has been well defined by one of its leaders, Bernard Shaw, in a paper he read at a conference in 1892, at Essex Hall. The policy of "permeation" of the Fabian Society was clearly outlined and much stress laid upon the enumeration of results already achieved. Within a year of this conference, in January 1893, the Independent Labor Party was formed by the grouping of the local Fabian societies then in existence. These groups under the leadership of Keir Hardie, Friedrich Engels (co-worker of Karl Marx) and Marx's daughter, E. Eveling, had accepted as their code Marxism thus summarized: "To establish a Socialist state where land and capital will be held by the community." On such principles was Russia transformed into Soviet Russia in 1917.

The author of the *History of the Fabian Society* does not fail to point it out as the parent society emphasizing the fact that the Marxist Independent Labor Party was but its offspring. Thus, leading on the one hand Marxist Socialism, and having, on the other, so permeated the Liberal Party that they also practically ruled it, the Fabians were soon able to set about taking part in local elections, and proposing their own candidates for appointments on school boards, vestry, county councils, women's liberal federation, liberal and radical unions, etc. They spared no pains in pushing forward the autonomy of municipalities as well as the various schemes for national insurance, old-age pensions, tariff reform, employer's liabilities, workmen's compensation.

Politically also, through their offspring, the Independent Labor Party, they asserted their defeatist and antipatriotic tenets during the Boer War 1899-1902, when they expressed their wish "to see the Boers successful and the British Army driven into the sea."

By 1903 the Independent Labor Party, after 10 years of indefatigable efforts among the trade unionists, gave its parent, the Fabian Society, the opportunity and satisfaction of presenting England with a full-fledged labor party. Up to that time, Fabian candidates had contested and won seats in Parliament as Liberals. The practice of the policy of interlocking directorates had never been better evidenced than by the tactics of Fabianism.

The outbreak of the war in 1914 furnished the illuminati of socialism with the opportunity of manifesting their antipatriotic feelings much more openly than they had done during the Boer War. It was then that their policy of interlocking directorates bore abundant fruit. What one might call the "melting" property of the Fabian Society became more evident, for as such it did not create a record of antipatriotism. That particular task was intrusted to its members of the Labor Party and the Independent Labor Party, who took a prominent part in the formation of the "Union of Democratic Control", which counted the Zionist Jew, Israel Zangwill, among its leading bandmasters.

The shameful defeatist, pro-German activities of the present Prime Minister of England, Ramsay MacDonald, Fabian and Laborite during the World War, and the open support given to bolshevism by his Labor Party have forever sullied the political honor of England and are a matter of history.

Yet another aspect of Fabianism is the great part it took in the formation and, later, direction of the League of Nations, which Bernard Shaw calls "an incipient international government." Fabians have even been known to revendicate it as one of their creations, but there, at any rate, they are guilty of overrating their powers, for to all readers of the protocols of the Wise Men of Zion it is known beyond the shadow of a doubt that the superstate is a Jewish creation. So far as we know, the Fabians have not laid any claims to the authorship of the famous protocols written even before the Fabian Society came into existence. Still it is comparatively easy to conjecture that, owing to their close connections with such a Sage of Zion as Israel Zangwill, they may have been led to adopt this deep-rooted idea of his coreligionists. In other words, the permeating Fabian Society became in its turn permeated by Jews. However, so far it has consciously or unconsciously failed to acknowledge that it is nothing more nor less than a tool in the hands of Judeo-Masonry.

2. Economics: In the realm of the economic, industrial, and financial life of England the Fabian Society played no lesser a part than in politics. With its slogan of "progressive policy" it invaded agriculture, preaching the nationalization of land; in other words, the confiscation of landed property. (Note: At a lecture given before the Comité National d'Etudes in Paris by a Fabian, Mr. Noel Buxton, in May 1928, a member of the audience put it clearly to the orator that the agrarian program of the Labor Party spelled nothing other than expropriation.) It took on, though subsequently dropped guild socialism, but carried much weight with trade-unionism and a kind of syndicalism.

The first blow to industry was struck in Lancashire in 1890, the stronghold of English industry, with the help of Mrs. A. Besant, as chief spokesman and agitator. Later the co-operative movement was captured and Fabianized and subsequently delivered over to the Independent Labor Party and Labor Party. It is due to the Socialists having been so successful in conquering industry that during the World War sabotage assumed such appalling proportions in the munition factories in England.

As to the financial "ideals" of the Fabians, whose basic principle is the ruin of capitalism, they became realties when taxation of the people took undue proportions in the shape of income tax, supertax, death duties, which are to be capped by capital levy. The promised benefits to the working class to be derived from such schemes as the national health insurance and workmen's compensation and dole, old-age and widow's pensions, have proved a myth. Yet they have gone a long way toward furthering the plans exposed in the "protocols" which aim at reducing to bondage the "Goyim" rich and poor alike.

3. Education: In the matter of education the Fabian Illuminati have followed a theory which is none other than that suggested by one of the souls of Bavarian illuminism, Nicolai, in the eighteenth century. Having secured posts in the school boards of the country, it became very easy for Fabian Socialists to instill their educational de-Christianized principles in the school curriculum. Their attack on religious teaching was subtle but deadly, as seen in the education bill of 1902. They boast openly of having in their ranks several Anglican bishops and divines, the list being headed by Bishop Headlam, one of the earliest Fabians. Eventually they won, having, as has always been their wont, resorted to intensive propaganda, generously distributing their tracts and leaflets.

Under Fabian educational schemes come the formation of the educational groups and of the "nursery", the later designed as a kind of training school for very young prospective Socialists. Women's groups were also formed, the members of which participated in all movements tending to a fuller feminist emancipation. But by far one of the most important steps taken by the Fabians along educational lines has been their inauguration in existing universities of "University Socialist Societies", which in 1912 were finally grouped by Clifford Allen into the "Universities Socialist Federation." Fertile seeds of Fabian socialism are also sown at the summer school organized annually by the society, which E. R. Pease rightly terms a "propagandist society." The culminating triumph of the Fabians in the realm of education was the creation of the London School of Economics and Political Science at the London University, where today one of the chief lectures is the Jew Socialist, Harold Laski, member of the executive committee of the Fabian Society and chairman of its publishing committee.

As was suggested already, and as can be seen from the succinct exposé here given, Fabianism left no field unexplored and unexploited. For 50 years it has treated England to doses of both pure and diluted Marxism, mostly diluted, as the English, by the very nature of their steady and conservative characteristics are not easily aroused to excesses as those perpetrated by the Paris Communards of 1871. But, on the other hand, they have been thoroughly permeated and their poisoning has been one of long process. It is true also to add that the war paved an easy way for the onward progress of socialism.

The young generations who had still been nurtured in the spirit of Christian tradition and family conservatism perished on the battlefields of France. Their virility would no doubt have constituted the barrier of opposition to this pernicious Fabianism. ° ° ° As to the older generation that preceded that of the young martyrs falling in the name of patriotism and honor, they knew little and wanted to know still less, keen on believing that nothing could ever shake the security of England. How few among them wanted to understand the Protocols of the Wise Men of Zion, published in 1920, and fight the Christian fight to prevent the full accomplishment of the fateful Judeo-Masonic program therein contained. A limited effort was made by a group of Britons which in no time permeated by emissaries of the powerful enemy and became sick unto death. ° ° ° A noble and steadier effort made by a group publishing the *Patriot*, and spasmodic outbursts of righteousness made by the *Morning Post*, is all the resistance that England has been able to oppose to the devastating forces of Judeo-Masonic illuminism; that is, Fabian socialism.

The results are, to the naked eye, the history of England since the war, politically and economically.

Lloyd George's coalition government had been kind to socialism, but the real harvest time came when the Labor Party won the election in 1924 and its members governed or rather misgoverned England. It needed nothing short of the Bolshevist alliance which MacDonald wished to force upon the country to provoke the remaining sound reaction of the

English people and prompt them to overthrow the Labor government. But this show of resistance was ephemeral.

How pitiful it is to know that the return of the Labor Party to power in May 1929 is entirely due to the incompetence of a conservative government, in which the people trusted for the sane administration of the affairs of state. Yet the Prime Minister, leader of the Conservative Party, Mr. Baldwin, could not claim ignorance of the Judeo-masonic plans contained in the protocols of the Wise Men of Zion. He found it easier to deliberately disregard them. Be it as it may, England is once more in the hands of the Labor Party, with the inevitable and ubiquitous Ramsay MacDonald, and according to the latest report issued by the society, "8 Fabians are members of the Cabinet and 14 others hold offices in the Government without seats in the Cabinet."

Outside of England the Fabians are affiliated with strong Socialist groups professing the same ideas—in Copenhagen, in Canada and Australia, Japan, the United States of America, Spain, and Germany. It is our opinion that the Fabian Society is in close connection with the French Comite d'Etudes Nationales, which has already been mentioned to the readers of the R. I. S. S. and also with the Club du Faubourg, as well as with the Socialist Party headed by the Jew Leon Blum.

Less than 50 years of combined efforts, made by some intellectual and determined Jews and Masons, has cast over the world a dragnet in which all the nations of the world have been ensnared, and they are to be the prey of triumphant Jews.

Surely neither the fanatic illuminatus Nicolai nor his friend and master, the Jew Mendelssohn, ever conceived a better accomplishment of their ideals.

Yet, judging by the financial and economic situation of England at the close of 1930, the practical experiments of the Fabian-Socialist-Marxist theories of the illuminati governing the country have doomed it to irreparable ruin.

According to the *Clarion*, a Fabian weekly organ, still more disturbances are in store for the unhappy English nation. Its Parliament is to be "democratized" and one, or possibly two,

488

"national assemblies"—one for England, another for Scotland—will be created.

But, and here comes the anomaly which is nothing short of ludicrous, for Mrs. Sidney Webb, the author of the proposed Fabian plan, announces that the sovereign power will remain vested in the King, Lords, and Commons! * * *

Propaganda will once again come into play to sow disorder in the already much troubled minds and empty stomachs of a large number of English people. England as a whole refuses to believe that she is in the grip of bolshevism because she still sees the image of a throne, not realizing that this symbol of fallen royal power is kept by the Socialist for commercial purposes. It cannot be denied that without a court which panders to the futile snobism of American women, American dollars would not annually pour into England. Thus does the English throne which alone is left undisturbed and unshaken serve several purposes.

It hypnotizes the people into a false feeling of security, it is also an excellent commercial proposition, and, last but not least, let us remember that it is at the hands of a sovereign that titles are bestowed, and Jews and Fabians alike are eagerly seeking such dignities. Lord Melchett, Marquess of Reading, Lord Passfield, Lord Oliver * * * such is the ruling aristocracy of England. Without a king they would have remained Mond, Isaacs, Webb, Oliver, which emphasizes the need of at least one Socialist kingdom to serve the various ends of Judeo-Masonry which, outside of the lodges where titles are granted, wants to have its own aristrocracy with sonorous titles.

As a last consideration, one fails to see why English economist and financiers express a too naive atstonishment at France's policy of recalling from England all her gold resources. It needs no violent stretch of imagination to foresee that at any time such men as MacDonald, Snowden, Henderson, Webb-Passfield, and so forth, all of them Fabians, might decree the nationalization, confiscation, and expropriation by bolshevist constitutional methods of all public and private property.

Let us not forget that in conjunction with this eventuality, the insurance companies have already insured themselves against meeting any claims arising from the loss of insured property in cases of "confiscation by the state."

During 1931 this group of Fabians—among them Gerald Barry, I. Nicholson, and Kenneth Lindsay—used a newspaper at that time owned by Lord Beaverbrook and called "*The Week End Review*" as a vehicle for their ideas. It is understood that Beaverbrook, upon becoming familiar with their plans, disapproved; whereupon they left his paper and continued to publish their ideas in another on means furnished, according to my informant, by Mrs. Leonard Elmhirst, formerly Dorothy Willard Straight, nee Whitney, Sir Basil P. Blackett, governor of the Bank of England, became chairman of the group in 1931. From this time the organization was called the "political economic plan." Among other members were Israel Moses Sieff, Sir Henry Bunbury, Graeme Haldane, I. Hodges, Lady Reading, Daniel Neal, and H. V. Hodson. Monthly meetings were held, at which Mrs. Elmhirst was present. Finally the group split on international policy, and Sir Basil P. Blackett resigned and Israel Moses Sieff became chairman in July 1932. It is said that since becoming head of the group Sieff has spent £60,000 on the movement. In the fall of 1932 the following people joined the political economic plan: Sir Arthur Salter; Sir Oswald Moseley, the head of the new British Union of Fascists; Lord Eustace Percy; Lord Melchett, the son of the late Alfred Mond; and Sir Christopher Turnor.

The "political economic plan" organization is divided into many separate, well-organized, and well-financed departments. For instance, town and country planning; industry; international relations; transport, controlled by Lord Ashfield; banking; social services, civic division, chairman, Ronald Davison; and an agricultural department, the head of which is Leonard Elmhirst, husband of the former Dorothy Willard Straight. Mrs. Elmhirst manages a school for agriculture on "political economic plan" lines at Dartington Hall Totnes, Devonshire.

490

The document Freedom and Planning, heretofore inserted in the RECORD, is entirely secret and, to the best of my belief, has never before been published. However, the "political economic plan" has published broadsheets which in a rather veiled manner treat of some of the subjects dealt with in the secret document. These broadsheets are intended only for members and are almost impossible to procure. In a broadsheet dated April 25, 1933, they define their organization as follows:

A group of people who are actively engaged in production and distribution, in the social services, in town and country planning, in finance, in education, in research, in persuasion, and in various other key functions within the United Kingdom.

Emphasizing the secrecy of the organization on the last page of this broadsheet occurs the following paragraph:

You may use without acknowledgment anything which appears in this broadsheet on the understanding that the broadsheet and the group are not publicly mentioned, either in writing or otherwise. This strict condition of anonimity, upon which the broadsheet goes to you, is essential in order that the group may prove effective as a nonpartisan organization making its contributions outside the field of personal or party polemics.

Perhaps the first and only publicity the organization has had was in the *Daily Herald* April 28, 1933, which published an article referring to a private dinner given at the Savoy by the "political economic plan" on March 29 at which the chairman, Israel Moses Sieff, and the secretary, Kenneth Lindsay, made speeches. The caption in the *Daily Herald* was "Mystery Group Out to Re-Plan British Industry; P. E. P. at Work on New 'Control.' "

The "political economic plan" group members hold the meetings in a private room of the House of Commons. One of the first meetings was held on October 31, 1932, with the cognizance of Prime Minister MacDonald. Among those present were Malcolm MacDonald, son of the Prime Minister, J. H. Thomas, Sir Ernest Bennet, Lord Delawarr, Israel Moses Sieff, and Kenneth Lindsay, the secretary of the "Political Economic Plan."

The plan is already in operation in the British Government by means of the Tariff Advisory Board which in many of its powers is somewhat comparable to the National Recovery Administration in the United States.

This group organization has gathered all data and statistics obtained by governmental and private organization in administrative, industrial, social, educational, agricultural, and other circles; and Army, Navy, and airport statistics are in their hands as well as those of the law and medical professions. This has been made possible from the fact that the Prime Minister, Ramsay MacDonald, being a Fabian, the "political economic plan" Fabian group has had all archives at its disposal.

Through the Tariff Advisory Board created in February 1933 and headed by Sir George May, the control over industry and trade is being firmly established. This board works in direct connection with the treasury and with its devises the tariff policy. It has also been granted the powers of a law court and can exact under oath that all information concerning industry and trade be given it.

Iron and steel, as also cotton industrials in England, have been ordered by the Tariff Advisory Board to prepare and submit plans for the reorganization of their industries and warned that should they fail to do so a plan for complete reconstruction would be imposed upon them. The Tariff Advisory Board has been granted default powers and can, therefore, impose its plan.

The committee of the Tariff Advisory Board is composed of Sir George May, Sydney Chapman, professor of economics and statistician, and Sir George Allan Powell, of the food board and food council.

An interesting bit of information has come to me in this connection to the effect that this Fabian group has close connections with the foreign-policy association in New York City. This foreign-policy association was largely sponsored by the late Paul M. Warburg and has received the close attention and support of Bernard M. Baruch and Felix M. Frankfurter.

Many serious people in England feel that this Fabian organization practically controls the British Government and that this Government will soon be known as "His Majesty's Soviet Government." It is asserted that both Prime Mniister MacDonald and his son belong to the organization and that the movement is well organized and well financed and intends to practically sovietize the English-speaking race.

About 3 months after the passage of the National Recovery Act of the United States, when Israel Moses Sieff was urged by members of his committee to show more activity, he said:

Let us go slowly for a while and wait until we see how our plan carries out in America.

II

THE PLAN IN THE UNITED STATES

During the past several months Bernard M. Baruch, Felix Frankfurter, and the New York Jewish lawyer, Samuel T. Untermyer, have made several visits to Europe and spent considerable time there. There is justification for the belief that they have contacted with members of the British Fabian group and are familiar with their plans. The same system, in a somewhat adapted form, has been placed upon the statute books in the United States, and the iron hand of world control is fast being closed upon American agriculture, labor, and industry. The people in the United States have been propagandized into the belief that the National Industrial Recovery Act is a product of the political genius of Franklin Delano Roosevelt. There is no greater popular fallacy. The National Industrial Recovery Act was formulated before Franklin Delano Roosevelt had any well-defined ideas as to its existence, and it is doubtful that even now he appreciates its significance. It required 15 years of hard effort on the part of Mr. Baruch and his associates to foist this act upon the American people, and it was only through the sufferings over a period of great stress that he was enabled to do it. Baruch himself stated before the War Policies Commission in reference to the genesis of this act, "For 13 years I have been coming down and working with my associates in the War Department * * *." It might be stated that practically every year since the war Baruch has been going to the Army War College and giving our future generals lectures along these lines. However, these addresses are clothed in secrecy and we do not know just what he says. During the spring of 1931, in appearing before the War Policies Commission, Mr. Baruch stated, in part:

* * * *Our industry must, at last analysis, mobilize itself. What is required is leadership of a type that will persuade cooperation in every branch. This leadership must be backed by sanctions of far greater force than can or ought to be used in peace. It is a spontaneous sort of function, utterly inappropriate to any imaginable form of bureaucratic organization.*

As I have said, I do not favor an involved statute attempting to anticipate the requirements of another war.

I think plans should be made and revised yearly. I think some steps should be taken to keep selected industrial leaders informed of these plans so that when the principal actors in the 1918 mobilization pass from the scene there will be a nucleus of personnel to take their places. I do not believe that we can go further.

But, for a very special reason, I do believe that there should be one statute on the books the very existence of which would be a constant warning to everybody that never again in America will any man make as much profit in war as he can make in peace. There need be nothing complex nor involved about it. Purely for purposes of discussion I have prepared a rough draft, eliminating enacting clauses and formalities. It follows:

"That whenever Congress shall declare war or the existence of an emergency due to the imminence of war, then from and after a date prior to such declaration, which date the President is hereby authorized and directed to determine and announce, it shall be unlawful for any person to buy, sell, or otherwise contract for any service, right, or thing at a higher rate, rent, price, wage, commission, or reward than was in effect at the date so determined.

"Whenever, in the sole discretion of the President, he shall determine that any maximum price, wage, rent, rate, commission, or reward should be adjusted either upward or downward, he is hereby authorized to make and proclaim such adjustment; and such adjustment shall have the full force and effect under this statute of such price, wage, rent, rate, commission, or reward before such adjustment.

"During the period of any war or emergency declared by Congress thereunder the President is authorized to determine, and by proclamation announce, what classes of public service, or of dealers or manufacturers of any article or commodity shall be required to operate under licenses, to fix a condition of such licenses, and to grant licenses under such conditions. After such determination by the President it shall be unlawful for any public service, dealer, or manufacturer in such determined classes to engage in business without such license.

"During the period of any war or emergency declared by Congress hereunder the President is authorized to determine the order of priority in which any manufacturer, dealer, or public service in the United States shall fill customers' or other orders and after such determination it shall be unlawful for any such manufacturer, dealer, or public service to fill such order in any other order of priority."

So much for the bill he proposed, but bear in mind he was emphatic that it should be used only in the event of war or an emergency caused by the imminence of war. He further stated:

Nobody with any familiarity with industry could seriously

495

urge a wholesale assumption by any Federal bureau of the responsibility for management of any or all of the vast conjuries of manufacturing establishments upon which we must rely for extraordinary effort in event of war. Even if such bureau management could prove adequate to the task (which it could never do), the mere process of change would destroy efficiency at the outset.

The industrial pattern of the United States is a delicate mesh of interrelated strands. It has been evolved in response to the needs of the Nation and under natural economic law but dimly understood. It is a sensitive living organism, and the injection of arbitrary and artifical interference could be attempted only at the risk of starting a sequence of upheavals, the ends of which no man can see. * * *

Baruch also presented to the War Policies Commission a draft of a proposed act regarding price fixing, and stated:

General Johnson, who was instrumental in drawing up the selective-service legislation, as it was submitted to Congress during the war, and who wrote the selective-service regulations, assisted in preparing this draft. * * *

Johnson, as well as Herbert Bayard Swope, was present with Baruch during these hearings, and they appeared to be his lieutenants, Johnson especially acting in the capacity of an assistant.

General Johnson in the last few months has become well known to the American public, and there can be little doubt that his first allegiance is to Bernard M. Baruch, with whom he has been associated so long.

We find in the activities of General Johnson, in the promulgation of codes upon the industry of the United States and in the activities of that other "brain truster", Prof Rexford Tugwell, in promoting agriculture codes and controlled agricultural industry of the Nation, the very same machinery in operation as was proposed in Freedom and Planning.

However, Baruch, Johnson, Tugwell, Frankfurter, et al.

seem to be more brazen in their efforts in this country. Frankfurter has been furnishing most of the legal brains for the outfit, and it is said that no legal position of any consequence can be secured by any lawyer in the present administration without it has first had the approval of Frankfurter. And it is a startling fact, in connection with this, that most of the legal advisers, especially in key positions, are Jews. Felix Frankfurter's adept student and protégé, Jerome N. Frank, general counsel of the Agricultural Adjustment Administration, delivered an address before the Association of American Law Schools, thirty-first annual meeting, at Chicago, December 30, 1933, on Experimental Jurisprudence and the New Deal. A reading of this address shows the contempt of the Frankfurter lawyers for the Constitution of the land and an expressed determination to obviate and avoid constitutional barriers in their administration of the Nation's affairs. Those in charge of the plan and its administration in the United States have for years considered methods for accomplishing their ends without regard to the Constitution of the United States. They recognize the fact that the National Industrial Recovery Act did not give them all of the power they desired in order to break down the barriers enacted in our Constitution, preserving certain rights to the various States of the Union, as well as other features. Therefore, in the promulgation of the various codes affecting industry and agriculture throughout the country they have sought to compel, browbeat, and bulldoze the business interests of this country to engage in private contract so that they would have the power to require the business interests of the Nation to do their wishes regardless of the Constitution. The "new-deal" lawyers now have no hesitancy in appearing in court and asserting that private citizens can contract away their constitutional rights. It has been through this method that they have broken down State lines and invaded the most private affairs of our citizens. It will be through this method, for instance, that the little retailer of the country will be driven out of business and chain-store-system control by them put into operation, just as they are attempting in England.

There is no better illustration of this group of international would-be Caesars to control the industry and agricultural interests of this Nation than that demonstrated in the methods they have employed to try to coerce and compel the Ford Motor Co. to sign the automobile manufacturers' code. It should be borne in mind that even General Johnson himself has had to admit to the Comptroller General of the United States that he has no evidence of code or law violation on the part of the Ford Motor Co. It should also be borne in mind that the little Jewish Assistant Attorney General, Cahffetz, who appeared in the Supreme Court of the District of Columbia for the Government in recent cases brought therein by a Ford dealer, admitted to the court that he had no evidence of law violation. Therefore a question of whether or not the Ford Motor Co. has violated the law or the codes is not raised. It is admitted by the Government that they have not. Then why all this stir to prevent the purchase by the Government of Ford products? There are two outstanding reasons: One is that the Ford Motor Co. represents the last stronghold of independent industry in this Nation, hence it must be destroyed. It interferes with their plans. Next, so long as the Ford Motor Co. refuses to sign any code and thus engage in private contract which would give the administration power over and beyond the law it is still free at any time it chooses to attack the constitutionality of these extraordinary measures. Frankfurter lawyers contend that one who has signed the code has waived his rights to make any such attack. Therefore the power of Government will be used to bludgeon and compel, if it can, this last stronghold of independent industry to come within the fold so that it will be safe from attack in this quarter.

The American people may feel exceedingly grateful that someone has shown some degree of patriotic sanity in this respect, and the Ford Motor Co. has a great many of the smaller business enterprises of the Nation with them in their stand.

We not only see the hurried and frenzied regimentation

of industry and agriculture in this Nation by means of codes, but we are also witnessing a most spectacular engagement by government in the private loan field. Billions of dollars are being used to take over debts and pledge the property of industry, farmers, and home owners. This paves the way for the day near at hand when Government corporations will begin to take over and operate industrial enterprises and land and home organizations. We are on the threshold of a modern and Machiavellian feudal system devised and controlled by a group of international usurpers.

It might be well to observe that those who for 15 years have planned this specific legislation which is now operating to take over and control the most intimate affairs of our national life must have foreseen the conditions under which they could make such a plan possible. Therefore, it is reasonable to assume that they had some direct part in bringing about the conditions which make it possible to place the "plan" in operation. There has not been an administration since our advent into the great World War in which Bernard M. Baruch has not been a chief political, economic, and financial adviser, and every administration that has listened to him has carried us deeper and deeper into financial chaos, and today we are operating on his greatest experiment—a planned economy and industrial and agricultural control. The Juggernaut has been built and it is being moved on its cumbersome wheels. It is only a matter of time until it will give its lurch and roll upon and crush those who have built it.

Immediately following the World War, Bernard M. Baruch appeared before a select congressional committee and there testified to the fact that he virtually had complete control of the resources of the American Nation during the war. The colloquy with Congressman Jeffries is in part as follows:

Mr. JEFFRIES. In other words you determined what anybody could have?

Mr. BARUCH. Exactly; there is no question about that. I assumed that responsibility, sir, and that final determination rested with me.

499

Mr. JEFFRIES. What?

Mr. BARUCH. That final determination, as the President said, rested with me; the determination of whether the Railroad Administration could have it, or the Allies, or whether General Allenby should have locomotives, or whether they should be used in Russia, or used in France.

Mr. JEFFRIES. You had considerable power?

Mr. BARUCH. Indeed I did sir.

Mr. JEFFRIES. And all those different lines, really, ultimately centered in you, so far as power was concerned?

Mr. BARUCH. Yes, sir; it did. I probably had more power than perhaps any other man did in the war; doubtless that it true.

It is quite safe to assume today that now in coalition with Frankfurter, Brandeis, Moley, Tugwell, Johnson, Berle, and others of the American group, Mr. Baruch exercises more power than any man in the United States, if not in the world. It is a nice little camouflage for him to talk about getting out of Wall Street and writing the story of his struggling youth. We might as well look for the stream to run up the mountain.

XXIX

COMMUNISTIC PROPAGANDA
IN THE UNITED STATES

Friday, June 15, 1934

Mr. McFADDEN. Mr. Speaker, the recognition of Russia by the United States was consummated by President Roosevelt and M. Litvinoff, alias Finkelstein, representing Russia, at the White House in Washington last November when a joint statement was signed, and Mr. Litvinoff gave President Roosevelt solemn assurance that there would be no further propaganda carried on in this country. This was understood to mean communistic progaganda in the praise of the present Russian government experiment. With hardly any discussion of the merits or demerits of recognition the United States Senate confirmed the treaty. Only a few days had elapsed when Litvinoff made certain statements in Italy that he made no concessions here.

Russia came to us with a treaty in one hand and what in the other? Russia posed as a pacifist nation, although she has a military force that by comparison makes France and Germany look like nations of Boy Scouts.

November 21 last when the present new Russian Ambassador to the United States was interviewed he said that no communistic progaganda will emanate from the Soviet Embassy in Washington. He said further:

Communism is not a thing that can be imported to one country by another. It is not a question of foreign relationship, but a domestic problem. In any event, I can assure you, gentlemen, there will be no communistic activity on the part of any of our officials in America.

The *New York Herald Tribune*, under a Moscow, June 9, 1934, date line, states:

The announcement that the Seventh Congress of the Third Communistic International will convene here next month calls for the reconstruction of the whole question of world revolution and the relation to it of the comintern, on the one hand, and the Union of Soviet Socialist Republics, on the other, established in Moscow in 1919, with the avowed purpose of overthrowing the existing order in all countries and of organizing a world Federation of Socialist Soviet Republics. * * * Trotsky has established a Four Communistic International, which, we are told by its proponents, boasts an increasing number of adherents in France, the United States, Holland, and Spain. Stalin, like Molotov, continues as a member of the comintern's executive committee. * * * In any treatment of the future of the Union of Soviet Socialist Republics and the comintern in their relation to the world revolution careful consideration must be given to the increasing diplomatic activity of the Soviet Government throughout the world.

Diplomatic activity, of course, means the new recognition of Russia on the part of the United States.

Russia now is considering entering the League of Nations. In the light of this, what is to be the future of the comintern and what part is the Union of Soviet Socialist Republics to take in the world revolution?

The Russians say that a revolution—

Can develop only as a result of an unstable domestic situation. They say that while the economic situation in the Soviet Union will improve gradually the situation of the workers in the capitalist countries like the United States will become worse gradually and that eventually the stage for communistic revolutions abroad will be advanced—

And that—

The communistic revolution will come after capitalistic countries have gone through a period of fascism; and they mention Italy as an example.

The corporate state is fascism, and in the United States today a correct interpretation of the "new deal", with all of its alphabetical departments, is the introduction of the corporate state, or Fascist, form of government.

Russia is quite content because she has worked out these things in her own way. The Soviet authorities are now prepared to watch and wait and to continue their diplomatic activities.

On December 2, 1933, Matthew Woll, vice president of the American Federation of Labor, said:

I am not optimistic as to our relations with the Communist government of Russia. Pleasantries in Washington (having reference to the M. Litvinoff treaty negotiations with President Roosevelt) have not changed the character of the Soviet Government. The pledge given by Maxim Litvinoff (alias Finkelstein) has not divorced the Third Internationale from the Russian Soviet Government. These two and the Communist Party of Russia continue as the three joint elements of a unified Communist control in which each of the three parties is incapable of independent action not in accord with the program and desires of the others.

Speaking of the treaty agreement, Mr. Woll continued:

This agreement frankly does not assure harmonious relations with revolutionary communism. * * * Communism is communism * * * as long as its philosophy

503

remains, the conflict between communism and democracy must go on. To think of it as stopped by an agreement signed by two men in Washington is to forget all of the lessons we have learned and to overlook all of the facts available.

There is in the Litvinoff agreement no promise to repudiate the Communist philosophy, no promise to repudiate the doctrine that it is a Communist obligation to deceive the rest of the world, no promise to repudiate the Third Internationale, no promise to cease doing any of the things that have made communism the enemy of all the rest of the civilized world. * * * There is even no repudiation of the Moscow order published in America while Litvinoff conferred in Washington (at the White House with President Roosevelt) and which order was published in Moscow on October 23, 1933, by the central office of the Communist Party of the U. S. S. R., 2 days after the publication of the correspondence between President Roosevelt and President Kalinin. Omission of any reference to this Moscow order is all the more remarkable because of the bitter attack made in it upon President Roosevelt and the N. R. A. program. The fact that the American Federation of Labor was likewise attacked may perhaps be of little importance to some. This document was headed "Roosevelt Starvation Program." It was addressed to communistic and revolutionary groups in the United States and was officially approved by the soviet censorship bureau. It contained detailed orders and instructions to oppose President Roosevelt's program, to exploit the wave of discontent, to convert this discontent into a gigantic proletariat struggle, to formulate the plans of a counterrevolutionary organization without delay, and immediately to instigate open revolts, fights, and strikes against the administration's measures.

Do I need to call your attention to the strikes, the labor disputes, fights, and revolts, that are now taking place in the United States?

And I quote further from Mr. Woll's statement:

It is clearly evident that, regardless of recognition, regardless of promises given and pledges made, Soviet Russia is as determined as ever to create internal strife within our Nation and to foment world revolution. * * * Do I believe Communist propaganda will cease? Most assuredly I do not. I am confident there will be plenty of communistic progananda, ordered in accord with the Moscow pattern. * * * We have opened the door, and something is bound to enter.

Russian propaganda is freely circulating in the United States. There is no governmental interference. Influences quite in sympathy with the overthrow of constitutional government in the United States have seen to it that the Department of Justice is not placed in a position to counteract the activities of the Communists, the world revolutionaries, and those hundreds of organizations in the United States who are working to involve the United States in foreign entanglements which will eventually lead this country into communism and world revolution.

As one specific proof of the activities of the Russian Government, I now desire to call your attention to a booklet entitled *"Why Cmmunism?"* by M. J. Olgin, published by Workers Library, publishers, box 148, station D, 50 East Thirteenth Street, New York City; first printing December 1933, second printing February 1934; first revised edition March 1934. I call your attention to the fact that the first edition of this publication followed within 30 days after the treaty between President Roosevelt and Maxim Litvinoff was entered into, and that the second printing and the first revised edition followed almost immediately thereafter.

I quote from this book, page 44:

We Communists say that there is one way to abolish the capitalist state, and that is to smash it by force. To make communism possible, the workers must take hold of the state machinery of capitalism and destroy it.

505

COLLECTIVE SPEECHES OF HON. LOUIS T. MCFADDEN

On page 45, chapter 5, a program of action and economic struggle is outlined, after referring to the capitalist form of government. I quote:

> This leads us to the road along which the working class can arrive at the destruction of the capitalist state—revolutionary struggle. The working class is placed in this capitalist society in a position where to live it must fight. This fight, to be effective, must be aimed not only at the capitalists but also at the state. And once the fight is effective enough, it must inevitably lead to the smashing up of the state. * * * The fight begins in factory, mine, and mill. It is first of all a fight for higher wages, for shorter labor hours, for better working conditions. It is a fight for unemployment insurance, for social insurance generally, by which is understood that the state pays a minimum wage to those out of work, to the sick, the injured, and the aged.

The similarity of this with the present-day happenings in the United States is very marked. Are we in the midst of just such a situation as is set forth on pages 45 and 46 of this booklet?

On page 57 the following statement appears:

> We live in an atmosphere of imminent war. All national policies are now directed toward the preparation of war. What are these so-called "conservation camps" if not training grounds for the future army to be used in the war? What is this militarization of the schools and colleges if not preparation for war? What are these numerous "war games" on the water and in the air, on the land and in the sea, if not preparations of war? What is this mobilization of the industries of the United States, with administrators ready in every section, with the machinery so timed as to make it possible to put the whole country on a war basis within a few hours? What are these repeated declarations by Cabinet members that the Navy was needed for the purpose of "expanding American commerce"?

What is this modernization of the Army, modernization of battleships, and the huge increase in the aerial forces of the United States if not in preparation for war?

Roosevelt's government is a war government. And it is in order to screen these war preparations from the public view for a while that pacifist phrases are used. Roosevelt talking of world peace! Socialists applauding, trying to make the people believe that Roosevelt is an angel of peace. Reformist union leaders singing in unison with Roosevelt's apostles of peace. A mutual admiration society for laying a smoke screen. Gabriel over the White House. * * * A militarist progaganda under the slogan, "Stand behind the President", * * * reminds one of war time under Wilson. * * * The administration of the N. R. A. is backed by the war industries and administered by leading war mongers.

Here as elsewhere we Communists remain political realists. We say to the workers: "Words are chaff; they mean nothing; they mean less than nothing; deeds count. The deeds of the Roosevelt government are war deeds."

On page 60 we find the following directions to American employees from the Communist Party:

Workers in ammunition plants, go on strike! Shut down your plants! Prevent governmental strike breakers from resuming work! Railroad men, refuse to handle war materials or to transport troops! Keep guard over your railroad yards and depots lest transportation facilities be used by governmental agents! Marine workers, do not load either men or ammunition! Truck drivers, refuse to assist in war work! Workers of other industries, help the strikers. Farmers, refuse to give your foodstuffs and raw materials to be used for the slaughter!

* * * * * * * *

We Communists do not close our eyes to the fact that this means civil war.

Victory in the civil war spells the doom of the capitalist state.

Is it not about time our Government takes action to stop this kind of propaganda?

From page 61 I quote:

Congress has ceded its prerogatives of lawmakers to one man, Roosevelt, who is a virtual dictator, acting through a number of boards appointed by him. All this vast economic legislation that has been introduced now is not of congressional origin and has not received congressional approval. In foreign policies Congress has long become nothing but a rubber stamp, while the treaty power is in the hands of the President and his advisers. There was once prevalent in America the theory of the balance of power between the legislative, judicial, and executive branches of the Government. It is no accident that the executive branch has gained ascendancy over the rest. This is in keeping with the interests of Wall Street. It assures quick action. It makes for quiet "deals" away from the glaring light of publicity. It makes it unnecessary to dicker with numerous legislators who may have to reckon with moods of their electors, although by and large it has not been difficult for Wall Street to keep Congress in line. It clears the ground for further developments along the road of an open dictatorship.

Here we have the communistic interpretation of the present development under the "new deal"; a severe arraignment, and no action is taken by the administration.

I quote further from this analysis appearing on page 62:

Wherever capitalist democracy is displaced by open capitalist dictatorship for the primary purpose of crushing the revolutionary labor movement that threatens capitalist rule and for the purpose of fusing the state with big business in order to overcome the crisis of capitalism, there we have fascism. Fascism is brute force against a rising working class which begins to challenge the capitalist power. Fascism at the same time attempts to organize industry and commerce on behalf of the owners of wealth.

It is interesting, in connection with the consideration of this paragraph, to compare the present scope and operation of the N. R. A. and its codes in an attempt to organize industry and commerce on behalf of the owners of wealth in the United States. I again quote from page 62 of this booklet:

The iron hand that is used against the workers and poor farmers is aimed to force them to accept lower wages and worsened working conditions in order thus to secure greater profits for the employers. Government regulation of industry and commerce, Government subsidies and aid from the Treasury, i.e., from the taxes squeezed out of the masses of the population, also have the purpose of increasing the profits of the great industrialists and bankers. Fascism is a form of government which reduces the overwhelming majority of the population to abject poverty and degradation so that a few heads of large corporations may prosper.

And from page 63 I quote:

Fascism, however, may assume different forms and may appear in varying degrees. We in the United States witness the growing fascization of the State. Those attempts to prevent workers from striking; those N. R. A. codes supposed to organize industry and commerce by State regulation; that "partnership" between government and industry and government and labor that has been proclaimed as the policy of the Roosevelt administration; that reign of terror that is sweeping the strike areas of the country—what is it if not the manifestation of Fascist tendencies? That dictatorship of one man so eagerly acquiesced in by everybody. ° ° ° We certainly have a fascization of the governmental apparatus.

To say the least, these are interesting observations by Communists on the "new deal."

From page 77 I quote:

Armed workers and soldiers and marines seize the principal governmental offices, invade the residences of the President and his Cabinet members, arrest them, declare the old regime abolished, establish their own power, the power of the workers and farmers.

And still our present Government permits this kind of propaganda to freely circulate, clearly advocating overthrow of our Government.

In this textbook you have an example of a direct action issued as propaganda by the "Communist Workers, publishers", who, I understand, publish the Communist, the monthly organ of the Communist Party in the United States of America.

I now quote from page 95 of this Communist booklet:

Hand in hand with the Communist Party and under its guidance functions the Young Communist League, the revolutionary organization of the Young Workers, and many other organizations.

There is a Communist Party in every country of the world. All of them work for the same end, and all of them adapt their activities to conditions existing in their country.

And from the last page I quote:

The seat of the comintern is Moscow, because this is the capital of the only workers' and peasants' government in the world, and the comintern can meet there freely. As the workers become the rulers of the other countries the comintern will not have to confine its meetings to Moscow alone.

The Communist Party of the United States of America is thus part of a world-wide organization which gives it guidance and enhances its fighting power. Under the leadership of the Communist Party, the workers of the United States of America will proceed from struggle to struggle, from victory to victory, until, rising in a revolution, they will crush the capitalist state, establish a Soviet state, abolish the cruel and bloody system of capitalism, and proceed to the upbuilding of socialism.

That is why every worker must join the Communist Party.

Here is a document, only one of many now being freely circulated in the United States, which violates the agreement entered into by the Russian Ambassador, Maxim Litvinoff, and President Franklin D. Roosevelt as evidenced by the treaty which was used as the basis to secure ratification by the United States of the Soviet Russian Government. The author of this book, which is Russian Communist propaganda, is Dr. M. J. Olgin, a Russian-born Jew, who has a long history of revolutionary activities in the United States. He has been in the United States since 1915, took a Ph. D. degree at Columbia University. He has been editor of many radical publications in the Soviet Russia and in all Russia before coming here, and in 1924 was a candidate for the New York State Assembly on the Communist Party ticket.

Students of radicalism know that the present Soviet Government in Russia was organized by aliens and usurpers and not representative of the thoughts and ideals of the 150,000,-000 citizens of Russia, and that the controlling body G. P. U. in 1930 in Russia was as follows:

Stalin (Georgian), head of the Soviet political bureau; Micojan (Georgian), agriculture; Monjinsky (Polish), head of the G. P. U.; Ricoff (Russian), head of committees; Litvinoff (Russian Jew), foreign affairs; Tomsky (Polish Jew), trade union control; Kamenev (Russian Jew), concessions department.

The Soviet Government of Russia, in 1917, was composed of 565 persons, as follows:

Russians 32
Poles 2
Czechs 1
Letts 34

511

Finns	3
Armenians	10
Georgians	3
Hungarians	1
Germans	10
Jews	469
	——
Total	565

Note the preponderance of Jews in the Russian Government.

It is significant to note that the recent overthrow of the German Government by the Hitler movement was caused by the preponderance of Jews in the German Government, in the universities, as lawyers, as physicians, as bankers, complete domination of all exchanges, in commerce, in the theater, moving-picture industry, in politics. And now in the present United States Government it is noticed that an increasing number of Jews occupy high key positions in all departments. In this connection I quote from an article appearing in the *Washington Herald* under date of June 2, 1934, as follows:

COMMUNIST STATE FORECAST FOR UNITED STATES

New York, June 2.—Ten thousand persons in Madison Square Garden heard Earl Browder, general secretary of the Communist Party, declare tonight that the forces that created the Soviet Union "are going to create a Soviet power in Germany and the United States." Browder spoke at a meeting under the auspices of 100 Jewish organizations to celebrate the conferring of autonomy upon Biro-Bidjan, in eastern Siberia.

I want to remind loyal Americans that it is well to remember the "boring-from-within" tactics pursued by these aliens and usurpers who pursued tactics in Soviet Russia which caused the downfall of their Government and set up the present Communist-Jewish control government which is now in operation in Russia, and to point out that the same kind of aliens and usurpers are now at work in the United States to establish a form of government other than constitutional government, and in order to do this they are seeking to paralyze industry, to destroy patriotism, and, finally, to secure the overthrow of government itself in the United States.

The publishers of this communistic book by Olgin, the Workers' Library, is the official propaganda medium in the United States of the Communist Party of the United States and is unquestionably subsidized by Moscow along with the International Book Publishing House, as is indicated in the financial report of the executive committee of the Communist International Plenum meeting, September 1932, by an item of $756,900 under the heading of "Expenditures" as subsidies to party newspapers, publishing houses, and cultural educational work.

There have been many Members of both the House and Senate of the United States who have frequently declared that communism in our country was not dangerous to our form of government and the putting over of it was never intended through a program of force and violence. This pamphlet by Olgin refutes this idea in bold form, because on page 44 of this booklet we find the following language:

> We, Communists, say that there is one way to abolish the capitalist state, and that is to smash it by force.

The last paragraph in this book which I have quoted is a positive declaration at variance with Litvinoff's—Finkelstein's—statement made to the press of the country and supposedly to the President of the United States of America and the All Union Bolshevik Party of the Union of Soviet Socialistic Republics.

Proper Government agencies should immediately investigate this particular piece of propaganda, which is one of the most dangerous that has ever been put out in the United States. The circulation of this propaganda is proof that recognition of Russia was obtained under false pretenses.

XXX

THE CONSTITUTION OR
ITS DISAPPROVAL—WHICH?

Friday, June 15, 1934

Mr. McFADDEN. Mr. Speaker, let us suppose that one of the Presidential candidates ni 1932 had promulgated as a platform the following:

First. I propose to undermine confidence in the business leadership of the country generally by parading before the American public, through Congress and commission investigations, outstanding examples of mistakes and malfeasance in all lines of business. I propose that these exposés shall be staged in such a way as to give them utmost publicity possible, with a view to creating the impression that these cases of wrongdoing, whether intentional or not, are typical of all business. I shall in my inaugural address charge the depression and the ills of the public generally to the business leadership of the country and shall state in that inaugural address that the business leaders have been not only incompetent and stubborn but also dishonest in many activities.

Second. I propose to encourage and extend Government competition with many lines of private business and to institute governmental control and regulation of business activities through at least 50 new bureaus and commissions which I will set up in Washington.

514

Third. I shall oust the more experienced Government employees and supplant them with new appointees, exempted so far as possible from civil-service examinations and chosen by my political campaign manager, and I will add at least 50,000 additional Government employees to the Federal pay roll in the first year of my administration.

Fourth. I propose not only to abandon the gold standard but to debase our currency, repudiate the promises of the Government to pay in gold, make it a crime for private citizens to have gold in their possession. I shall call upon some college professors to establish by experiments a new monetary system with no definite and fixed value for the monetary unit.

Fifth. To assist agriculture I shall pay a bounty for the killing of many million pigs and sows and the plowing up of one-fourth of our cotton acreage; and I shall furthermore distribute to farmers from the Federal Treasury sums aggregating several hundred million dollars, in such a fashion that the farmer will receive greater revenue for nonproduction than he will for production. Cotton being one of our principal export commodities, I shall take steps to artifically raise its price so that American cotton will be at a disadvantage in world markets and thus stimulate the expansion of cotton production in foreign countries. In other farm commodities I shall fix the prices regardless of the supply and demand.

Sixth. I propose to demonstrate my faith in the Russian experiment in Communism by recognizing Russia, by reducing the Russian debt to the United States, and by lending the Russian Communist Government a few hundred million dollars from our Treasury.

Seventh. In order that I may not be hampered by the prejudiced viewpoint of adherence to the old system, I shall dispense with and ignore the advice of experienced business and political leaders and surround myself with brilliant and clever young men who have nothing to lose by abandoning the old system but who are bitterly opposed to that system and zealously devoted to the creation of a new order. To these young men I shall entrust the drafting of the important

515

new legislation for carrying out my policies, and this legislation I will drive through Congress, urging the necessity for this new legislation as a part of my program to meet the emergency. I can thus destroy the old order under the guise of trying to save it in an emergency.

Eighth. I propose to tell our people that this being the age of plenty they should work less, and produce less, and demand more for what they do, and to emphasize my belief in this program I shall employ millions of idle people to do unnecessary work and pay them therefor higher wages than are paid by private employers for useful work.

Ninth. I shall advocate the redistribution of wealth, arouse the workers against their employers, the producers against the distributors, and while urging the producers and distributors to increase wages and maintain prices, the consumers will be told that they are being robbed.

Tenth. I shall prevent the criticism of my policies: First, by continual emphasis upon the terrible condition from which I am trying to save the country; second, by controlling the radio through the Federal Radio Commission; third, by establishing such intimate relations with the Washington newspaper correspondents as will cause them to interpret my actions and policies as I desire them interpreted, and by threatening their publishers with loss of advertising and circulation through popular revolt if they criticize. To the more obstreperous I shall throw down the challenge that it is unpatriotic to criticize the President in times of such emergency.

Eleventh. To avoid the constitutional barriers I shall cause attacks to be made upon the strict interpretation of the Constitution as being out of date and no longer adequate to protect the people, and where the judiciary seems unwilling to approve my legislation I shall cause them to be attacked in the press and threaten them with investigations and popular disapproval.

Twelfth. I shall seek to control over all the affairs of the Nation and shall strip the States of all their rights of local self-government. This shall be accompanied by the regimentation—persuasively, if possible, if not, then by coercion, threats, and intimidation—of industry under codes, compelling the business interests of the Nation to engage in private contract to grant my bureaus and administrative authorities complete control of their affairs, constituting them legislators, judges, and juries whose actions and decisions shall be conclusive; and if any recalcitrant member of any industry dares challenge the constitutionality of the act of Congress under which I proceed, my young lawyers will meet them in court and assert my right to do this, and deny their right to challenge it because they have agreed by private contract to my terms and cannot attack the constitutionality of an act under which they have sought to do business.

Finally, I will stultify States, counties, cities, industrial establishments, and individuals by establishing Federal loan agencies that will extend credit to them and mortgage their assets, so that I will have their property in my hands as security for their debts, so that they dare not challenge my actions. This power of debt I will use to the utmost. Thus the Constitution shall be subject to my will, because there will be none left to oppose my interpretation.

XXXI

IMMIGRATION

June 15, 1934

Mr. McFadden. Mr. Speaker, this bill, if enacted into law, would in effect repeal the mandatory provisions of all laws regulating the deportation of aliens in the Immigration Acts of 1917 and of 1924 and make deportation optional with the Secretary of Labor, and although section 6 of the bill provides that it is an addition to and not in substitution for the provisions of the immigration laws, including section 19 of the Immigration Act of February 5, 1917, it is misleading, to say the least, in view of the language of section 3 of the bill. Section 19 of the act of 1917 provides that aliens entering who at the time of entry belonged to the excluded class, aliens entering illegally, aliens advocating the overthrow of the Government of the United States by force, aliens becoming a public charge, within 5 years after entry their cases not affirmatively shown to have arisen subsequent to landing, and certain specified classes of criminals, as well as other classes of aliens, shall, upon warrant of the Secretary of Labor, be taken into custody and deported.

Section 3 of the bill, however, clearly nullifies this mandatory language with respect to six enumerated classes of aliens, otherwise deportable, and permits the Secretary of Labor in her discretion to allow them to remain in the United States, provided only that she finds them to be of good moral character and not convicted of moral turpitude or crimes and not to have engaged in subversive political agitation. It is to be noted that this last qualification would still permit the Secretary to allow an alien to remain who was known to be a member of an organization whose avowed purpose is to overthrow the Government by force, which is clearly not permissible under the present laws making such persons mandatorily deportable.

A careful examination of the six subdivisions of section 3 (p. 3 of the bill) will show that they cover a vast majority of all deportable aliens. From the wording of clauses (1), (5) it is quite clear that illegal entrants are not regarded as those whom the Secretary may not allow to remain as not being of "good moral character", for they obviously relate in several instances to persons who have "entered the United States" in any kind of way; this notwithstanding that under present law illegal entry is a prison offense.

Generally speaking, and excepting persons convicted of crimes involving moral turpitude, clause (1) makes it discretionary with the Secretary to keep in the country all those classes now mandatorily deportable, although legally admitted; and clause (5) allows him to retain here the great majority of the illegal entrants, since it covers every alien who has a near relative who was legally admitted to the country or who is a citizen. This means about four-fifths of all aliens in the country, since the annual reports on immigration for years back show that this proportion of all legally admitted immigrants come "to join relatives." Thus, it clearly appears that the aliens whose deportation would remain mandatory under the misleading language of the bill would be a negligible number.

Clause 3 of section 3 would make a new statute of limitations for the deportation of aliens. Under present law no immigrant who entered legally since the first quota law was passed in 1921 is rendered immune from deportation by mere lapse of time. The clause in question would change this radically and would make an alien entering at any time nondeportable in the discretion of the Secretary of Labor, provided he has succeeded in hiding out for 10 years or has not been attended to by the authorities whose duty it was to deport him within that time.

The amendment of 1929 drawing the line at entrants before 1921 for those who could gain immunity from illegal entry was professedly passed to take care of a considerably large number of immigrants who in fact had entered legally but whom our officials failed to register. Therefore, theoretically, at least, there is no general statute of limitations as to legal entry at present. This is as it should be for the continued residence in this country of an alien who entered in violation of our laws is a continued defiance of those laws, and there can be no greater encouragement to illegal entry—the Achilles' heel of all immigration restriction—than condoning the act itself.

Clause 6 of section 3 would permit an illegal entrant to gain Executive clemency and escape deportation by giving evidence against another illegal entrant.

Clauses 4 and 5, although less important than those already referred to, would have the effect of actually separating families by allowing the alien children under 16 smuggled into the country by their parents to remain here while the parents (who presumably had entered illegally at the same time) might be deported.

Section 3 alone—the heart of the bill—is so destructive of our whole system of immigration restriction as to make it incumbent upon all Members of Congress who are sincere restrictionists to vote as one man against it.

I submit to the membership that we should not repeal these mandatory provisions of the acts of 1917 and 1924 and permit decision on such important matters to lie with the Secretary of Labor.

Mr. DICKSTEIN. Mr. Speaker, will the gentleman yield?

Mr. McFADDEN. I cannot yield.

Mr. DICKSTEIN. I will give the gentleman a minute to answer the question.

Mr. McFADDEN. Very well; I yield.

Mr. DICKSTEIN. I want to assure the gentleman that we

do not repeal one single section of the deportation law. We are adding four additional sections for deportation, and I challenge the gentleman to deny that fact.

Mr. McFADDEN. I deny that fact and with the gentleman's own language. The law is being deliberately weakened to permit easy entry of one class of foreigner. I shall prove that his one purpose in the passage of this bill is to permit Jews from Germany to come in great numbers into the United States.

The SPEAKER. The time of the gentleman from Pennsylvania has expired.

Mr. McFADDEN. I ask the gentleman to yield me that minute now.

Mr. DICKSTEIN. I yield the gentleman 1 minute.

Mr. McFADDEN. Mr. Speaker, I want to say to the gentleman from New York [Mr. DICKSTEIN] that on March 18, 1934, in Chicago, in a broadcast before the Jewish Immigration Relief Society over radio station WENR, he is said to have stated that he deplored the fact of the bars against aliens coming into his country, as it was a fundamental of American doctrine to welcome the oppressed peoples of the world and give succor to their needs. He said further that as drastic as the quota law was before Hoover came into office it became much worse under his orders, and he said that every Jew in Germany who wanted to come here would come under the law of exclusion as it is now read, because no matter how wealthy they had been over there Hitler would not let them take out one cent of their money, and that Hitler was confiscating their property. He stated that Hitler would not grant passports to these refugees nor would he allow them to stay on German soil. He said, "Therefore we Americans must change our law to make it possible for them to come here at once, as there was no other country where they could go." He said further that Hitler's persecution of the Jew was growing rather than diminishing and soon these brothers, sisters, fathers, and mothers of ours will be murdered unless we immediately make it possible for them to leave. He said, "You Jews know that money for these poor oppressed Jews isn't keeping them out

521

of America. Our people here are generous and will take care of that, but it is the law which we must change."

He said further that there had developed a lot of opposition to the plan of having guaranty bonds put up to assure the Government that these people would not become public charges, and that this opposition must be overcome. He said that Germany owes all her culture and her great progress to the Jews; that Germany could not exist as a nation without the Jews, nor could America. He said that most of those coming here would be men like Einstein, men of outstanding achievement, and so forth. He said that no time was to be lost in getting action on this matter, and that he pledged himself to work untiringly for the passage of a law that would allow these brethren a quick relief and welcome to our shores.

I submit that the gentleman from New York [Mr. DICKSTEIN], in this radio talk to the Jewish Immigration Relief Society, had reference to this bill, H. R. 9725, which is now under consideration, and I further point out that his expressions are clearly indicative of the sole purpose of this bill—namely, to permit Jews from Germany to have an unhindered entry into the United States. And I submit that the new four additional sections for deportation are placed in this bill for the sole purpose of giving the Secretary of Labor the right of determination without review as to what deportation should be made, and weaken the provisions of the immigration laws of 1917 and 1924. These laws should not be modified by giving this great discretionary power into the hands of any one person, particularly one that we now know to be a nonrestrictionist and one who is responsive to the fullest degree to those of the type of the gentleman from New York [Mr. DICKSTEIN], who want to make easy entry for German Jews to come into the United States.

Mr. SABATH. Is the gentleman reading from his speech?

Mr. McFADDEN. I am reading from the gentleman's [Mr. DICKSTEIN's] radio speech delivered at Chicago, March 18 last. I will put the rest of it in the RECORD. It was delivered in the gentleman's own city of Chicago before the Jewish Immigration Relief Society at the Stevens Hotel.

The SPEAKER. The time of the gentleman from Pennsylvania [Mr. McFADDEN] has again expired.

Mr. McFADDEN. Mr. Speaker, I ask unanimous consent to extend my remarks in the RECORD and to complete the answer to the question asked.

The SPEAKER. Without objection, it is so ordered.

There was no objection.

Mr. McFADDEN. Mr. Speaker, I desire to call your attention to the fact that the gentleman from New York [Mr. DICKSTEIN] in his desire to amend the immigration laws, as this bill provides, to permit Jews from Germany to freely enter the United States, is supported by a national, if not an international, movement which is participated in by practically all of the Jewish organizations in the United States, which organizations are tied in with a world-wide organization to move Jews out of Germany, not only into the United States but to Palestine and to other countries. This organization was created under the auspices of the League of Nations, and its head is James G. McDonald, formerly president of the Foreign Policy Association of New York, who is now actively engaged in finding a domicile for German Jews. These efforts are tied in with the organization known as the "International Boycott on German Goods", the head of which is Mr. Samuel Untermyer, of New York—a retaliatory method of protest aimed at the present German Government, which boycott, if it fulfilled its purpose, would destroy the present German Government.

Another movement closely associated in this enterprise is that of the National Conference of Jews and Christians of 289 Fourth Avenue, New York, cochairmen of which are Hon. Newton D. Baker, Prof. Carlton J. H. Hayes, and Mr. Roger W. Straus. This is a national organization instigated by the international Jews in the United States having for its purpose the uniting of Gentiles, Catholics, and Jews in protection of the movements which are now being organized throughout the United States in support of the Jewish plan; whatever they may be.

In furtherance of the promotion of the activities along these lines, and as a further protest against the present German Government, the Chairman of the Committee on Immigration last year began an unauthorized investigation of what he termed "Nazi activities" in the United States. I would call your attention also to the fact that the activities of the various Jewish organizations supplementing these activities have resulted in the creation of a special committee of the House of Representatives appointed by the Speaker, and this committee are now engaged in the investigation of these activities and communistic and any other organizations that may have for their purpose the overthrow of our present form of government.

I mention this for the purpose of showing the far-reaching importance of this proposed amendment to the immigration laws of the United States. It is an integral part of a whole scheme.

BIBLIOGRAPHY

ADAMS, Silas W., *Comments on The Federal Reserve System, It's Purposes and Functions*, Omni Publications, 1965.

ADAMS, Silas W., *The Legalized Crime of Banking*, Omni Publications, 1970.

BAKER, Ray Stannard, *Life and Letters of Woodrow Wilson*, Doubleday, Page & Co., 1927-1931.

BATES, Ernest Sutherland, *The Story of Congress*, Harper and Brothers, 1936.

BEARD, Charles A., *The Devil Theory of War*, The Vanguard Press, 1936.
The Economic Basis of Politics, Alfred A. Knoff, 1922.

BISHOP, Joseph B., *Theodore Roosevelt and His Time*, Charles Scribner, 1920.

BOWERS, Claude G., *Beveridge and The Progressive Era*, Houghton Mifflin Co., 1932.

BRANDEIS, Louis D., *Other People's Money*, National Home Library, 1933.

COREY, Lewis, *The House of Morgan*, G. Howard Watt, 1930.

COOGAN, Gertrude M., *Money Creators*, Omni Publications, 1965.

DAWES, Charles G., *Notes as Vice-President*, Little, Brown and Company, 1921.

DENNY, Ludwell, *We Fight for Oil*, Alfred Knopf, 1928.

DENNY, Ludwell, *America Conquers Britain*, 1930.

DUMOND, Dwight L., *Roosevelt to Roosevelt*, Henry Holt and Co., 1937.

BIBLIOGRAPHY

DUFFY, Herbert Smith, *William Howard Taft*, Minton Balch and Company, 1930.

EMERSON, Edwin, *Hoover and His Times*, Garden City Publishing Co., 1932.

FIELD, A. N., *The Truth About The Slump*, Omni Publications, 1963.

FIELD, A. N., *All These Things*, Omni Publications, 1963.

FLYNN, John T., *God's Gold*, Harcourt, Brace and Company, 1932.

HAMILL, J., *The Strange Career of Herbert Hoover Under Two Flags*, William Faro, 1931.

HANSL, Protor W., *Years of Plunder: A Financial Chronicle of Our Times*, Smith and Haas, 1935.

HENDRICK, Burton, *The Life and Letters of Walter Hines Page*, Doubleday, Page and Company, 1922-1925.

HITLER, Adolph, *Mein Kampf*, Reynal and Hitchcock, 1940.

JOHNSON, Hugh, *Blue Eagle From Egg to Earth*, Doran and Company, 1935.

JOHNSTON, Thomas, *The Financiers and the Nation*, Methuen and Co., Ltd., 1934.

JOSEPHINE, Matthew, *The Robber Barons*, Harcourt, Brace and Company, 1934.

KEMMERER, Edwin W., *The ABC of the Federal Reserve System*, Princeton University Press, 1938.

KEYNES, John Maynard, *Economic Consequences of the Peace*, Harcourt, Brace and Company, 1920.

KLEIN, Henry H., *Dynastic America and Those Who Own It*, Isaac Goldman Company, 1935.

LAWSON, Thomas W., *Frenzied Finance*, Ridway-Thayer Company, 1904.

LINDBERGH, Charles A., Sr., *Your Country At War*, 1917.
The Banking and Currency and The Money Trust, 1913, Reprinted 1968.
The Economic Pinch, 1923, Omni Publications, 1968.

BIBLIOGRAPHY

LINDLEY, Ernest K., *Halfway with Roosevelt*, Viking Press, 1936.
The Roosevelt Revolution, 1933.

LODGE, Henry Cabot, *Letters of Theodore Roosevelt to Henry Cabot Lodge*, Charles Scribner's Sons, 1926.

LUNDBERG, Ferdinand, *Imperial Hearst*, Equinox Cooperative Press, 1936.
America's 60 Families, 1937.

MOND, Alfred Sir, *Industry and Politics*, Macmillan & Co., 1927.

MOODY, John, *The Masters of Capital*, The Moody Publishing Co., 1919.

MORGENTHAU, Henry, and STROTHER, FRENCH, *All in a Life Time*, Doubleday, Page and Company, 1922.

MYERS, Gustavus, *History of the Great American Fortunes*, Charles H. Kerr and Company, 1909-1911.

NEARING, Scott and Freeman, JOSEPH, *Dollar Diplomacy: A Study in American Imperialism*, The Viking Press, 1925.

O'CONNOR, Harvey, *Mellon's Millions*, The John Day Company, 1933.

OVERACKER, Louise, *Money in Elections*, The Macmillan Company, 1932.

PERRY, Bliss, *Henry Lee Higginson*, Atlantic Monthly Press, 1921.

PETTIGREW, R. F., *Imperial Washington*, Charles H. Kerr and Company, 1922.

RAUP, Bruce, *Education and Organized Interests in America*, G. P. Putnam's Sons, 1936.

ROCHESTER, Anna, *Rulers of America*, International Publishers, 1936.

ROGERS, Cameron, *The Legend of Calvin Coolidge*, Doubleday, Doran and Company, 1928.

SEYMOUR, Charles, *The Intimate Papers of Colonel House*, Houghton, Mifflin Co., 1926-1928.
Woodrow Wilson and The World War, 1921.

BIBLIOGRAPHY

SMITH, Arthur D. Howden, *Men Who Run America*, Dobbs-Merrill Company, 1936.

STEED, Henry Wickham, *Through Thirty Years 1892-1922*, William Heinemauer, 1924.

STONEMAN, W. H., *Life and Death of Ivar Krueger*, The Dobbs-Merrill Company, 1932.

STRASSER, Otto, *Hitler and I*, Houghton Mifflin Co., 1940.

THOMPSON, C. D., *Confessions of the Power Trust*, E. P. Dutton and Company, 1932.

THYSSEN, Fritz, *I Paid Hitler*, Hodder and Stroughton, 1941.

TYRKOVA, Williams, Ariadna, *From Liberty To Brest Litovsk*, Macmillan and Co., 1919.

VIERECK, George Sylvester, *The Strangest Friendship in History*, Liveright, Inc., 1932.

WINKLER, John K., *Morgan The Magnificent*, The Vanguard Press, 1934.

WARBURG, Paul M., *The Federal Reserve System*, The Macmillan Company, 1932.

WILLIS, Henry P., *The Federal Reserve System*, The Ronald Press Co., 1932.

INDEX

529

INDEX

530

INDEX

INDEX

INDEX

INDEX

INDEX

535

INDEX

INDEX

INDEX

INDEX

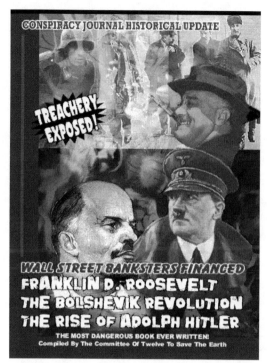

Since the early 1920s, numerous pamphlets and articles, even a few books, have sought to forge a link between "international bankers" and "Bolshevik revolutionaries."

Rarely have these attempts been supported by hard evidence, and never have such attempts been argued within the framework of a scientific methodology. Indeed, some of the "evidence " used in these efforts has been fraudulent, some has been irrelevant, much cannot be checked. Examination of the topic by academic writers has been studiously avoided; probably because the hypothesis offends the neat dichotomy of capitalists versus Communists (and everyone knows, of course, that these are bitter enemies). Moreover, because a great deal that has been written borders on the absurd, a sound academic reputation could easily be wrecked on the shoals of ridicule. Reason enough to avoid the topic.

Fortunately, the State Department Decimal File, particularly the 861.00 section, contains extensive documentation on the hypothesized link. When the evidence in these official papers is merged with nonofficial evidence from biographies, personal papers, and conventional histories, a truly fascinating story emerges.

We find there was a link between some New York international bankers and many revolutionaries, including Bolsheviks. These banking gentlemen -- who are here identified -- had a financial stake in, and were rooting for, the success of the Bolshevik Revolution. Who, why -- and for how much -- is the story in this book.